W9-BGH-871

The Last Segregated Hour

The Last Segregated Hour

The Memphis Kneel-Ins and the Campaign for
Southern Church Desegregation

STEPHEN R. HAYNES

OXFORD
UNIVERSITY PRESS

OXFORD
UNIVERSITY PRESS

Oxford University Press is a department of the University of Oxford.
It furthers the University's objective of excellence in research,
scholarship, and education by publishing worldwide.

Oxford   New York
Auckland   Cape Town   Dar es Salaam   Hong Kong   Karachi
Kuala Lumpur   Madrid   Melbourne   Mexico City   Nairobi
New Delhi   Shanghai   Taipei   Toronto

With offices in
Argentina   Austria   Brazil   Chile   Czech Republic   France   Greece
Guatemala   Hungary   Italy   Japan   Poland   Portugal   Singapore
South Korea   Switzerland   Thailand   Turkey   Ukraine   Vietnam

Oxford is a registered trade mark of Oxford University Press in the UK and certain other countries.

Published in the United States of America by Oxford University Press
198 Madison Avenue, New York, NY 10016

© Oxford University Press 2012

Library of Congress Cataloging-in-Publication Data
Haynes, Stephen R.
The last segregated hour : the Memphis kneel-ins and the campaign
for Southern church desegregation / Stephen R. Haynes.
p.   cm.
Includes bibliographical references (p.   )and index.
ISBN 978-0-19-539505-1
1. Memphis (Tenn.)—Church history—20th century. 2. Southern States—Church history—20th century.
3. United States—Church history—20th century. 4. Segregation—Religious aspects—Christianity—History—20th century.
5. Blacks—Segregation—United States. I. Title.
BR535.H39   2013 *2012*
277.68'190826—dc23   2012003851

3 5 7 9 8 6 4

Printed in the United States of America
on acid-free paper

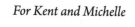

For Kent and Michelle

CONTENTS

PREFACE

The origins of this book are to be found in a class I taught at Rhodes College in 1997 titled "Religion and Racism." Two ambitious students—Amy Riddle and David McCollum—collaborated on a research project dealing with students at Rhodes (then Southwestern) who had engaged in efforts to integrate Memphis's Second Presbyterian Church in 1964. Two years later, student Kelly Gill made the Memphis "kneel-ins" (as attempts to integrate churches were called at the time) the topic of her Senior Paper in Rhodes's History Department, for which I was privileged to serve as a reader. Amy and David married, attended medical school together, joined Baylor College of Medicine's Pediatrics AIDS Corps, and went off to Swaziland to care for HIV-infected children. Kelly worked as a missionary in Berlin for several years before returning home to attend law school. Before they left Memphis, however, these remarkable young people laid the groundwork for a project that would occupy their professor in one way or another for the next fifteen years.

My own study of the Memphis kneel-ins began in 2003 when, with assistance from a Rhodes Faculty Development Endowment Grant, I began tracking down and interviewing those who had been involved in the church desegregation campaign that commenced in Memphis in the spring of 1964. I was assisted in this effort by Megan Murphy, a Georgetown University student from Memphis who proved to be extremely adept at locating potential interviewees and convincing them to tell their stories. In 2004, I hosted a symposium at which several of the protesting students returned to the Rhodes campus to discuss their experiences. I was so intrigued by these former Southwestern students (then in their sixties) and the ways the events of 1964 had shaped their lives that I began to look more deeply into the Memphis kneel-ins and their impact on local people and institutions.

Between 2003 and 2012 I conducted nearly 150 interviews with church members, pastors, protestors, reporters, denominational representatives, and curious onlookers—anyone, in fact, who claimed to have memories of the kneel-in controversy at Second Presbyterian Church in 1964–65. In 2007 I was fortunate to work with students Catherine Lawson and Daniel Vanaman, who conducted their own research related to church desegregation in Memphis as part of the Rhodes Institute for Regional Studies. In 2009–10 I was granted a sabbatical leave from Rhodes College, during which I devoted myself full time to telling the story of the Memphis kneel-ins. A full year of leave was made possible by a generous grant from the Louisville Institute for the Study of American Protestantism.

Because work on this project has covered a large swath of my professional life I am indebted to more people than I can mention. In addition to Megan Murphy, Lauren Marks, and Matthew Haynes, who transcribed taped interviews, I have been assisted by many colleagues and friends, including Tim Huebner, Gail Murray, Charles McKinney, Suzanne Bonefas, Oscar Carr, and Steve Nash. The staff at Rhodes's Barret Library—particularly Bill Short, Elizabeth Gates, and Kenan Padgett—have tirelessly supported my research. Director of Alumni Relations Warren "Bud" Richey helped me locate college alums whom I believed might have stories to tell about activism among Southwestern students in the 1960s.

I received crucial assistance from reference librarians at the Richard B. Russell Library for Political Research and Studies at the University of Georgia Libraries (Abby Griner), the Presbyterian Heritage Center in Montreat, North Carolina (Bill Bynum), the Salmon Library at the University of Alabama Huntsville (Anne Coleman), the Presbyterian Historical Society in Philadelphia (Margery Sly), the Auburn Avenue Research Library on African American Culture and History in Atlanta (Carolyn Clark), and Emory University's Pitts Theological Library (Robert Presutti).

I owe great thanks to the many persons who agreed to be interviewed for this project and spoke honestly about their experiences during a painful period of local history. I am particularly indebted to the ministers, elders, and members of Second Presbyterian Church and Independent Presbyterian Church. If you are part of a congregation with a complicated racial history that you learn is going to be the subject of a book, there are several possible reactions. You can make the gathering of information and interviews as difficult as possible; you can decline to participate and hope for the best; or you can actively cooperate in the project. This book has greatly benefited from the fact that in both cases church leaders have adopted the latter course. Rev. Sanders "Sandy" Willson of Second was generous with his time and insights, and made many of the church's staff and members available for interviews. Revs. Richie Sessions and Richard Pratt and Elder Sam Graham of Independent not only have been helpful and supportive, but have become partners in exploring the church's past and how it might move into a redemptive future.

I must also mention my own church family, which has been a deep source of encouragement throughout the research and writing of this book. Over the past decade the pastors and members of Idlewild Presbyterian Church have supported my family in more ways than I can count. Members of the Pathfinders Sunday School class deserve particular thanks. They invited me to share my research on numerous occasions and always responded with insightful questions and comments. I am also appreciative of the men in my Christ Care Group at Idlewild. Over the past three years they have shared my triumphs and disappointments and taught me much about what it means for Christians to care for one another.

As always, I am indebted to my family—my parents, Jean and Ron Haynes; my siblings, Carter Haynes, Cheryl Silvers, and Susan Mahoney; my wife, Alyce; and my children, Christi, Matthew, and Braden—without whose support and encouragement I could not do the work I love. Finally, I am grateful to the recovery community in Memphis and the experience, strength, and hope its members so generously share. Two people in particular—Kent Fisher and Michelle Rappaport—have helped sustain me through difficult times. This book is dedicated to them, in appreciation of their wisdom and healing gifts.

The Last Segregated Hour

Introduction

Segregation's Last Stronghold

In a 1967 article in *Atlantic Monthly*, Marshall Frady described the spectacle of church integration that had become a Sunday-morning ritual in the South. Frequently, Frady wrote, one would open the Monday paper to find

> a picture of a dozen or so funereal-faced deacons standing shoulder to shoulder on the steps of some small brick church, all of them bare-headed, squinting a little in the Sunday morning sunshine, mouths clamped tightly shut, arms unanimously folded (usually hiding their hands), their black gazes fixed just an inch or two over the heads of a small delegation of Negroes clustered on the sidewalk below them. It was one of the more curious spectacles produced by the most profound domestic moral crisis of our time.[1]

Frady was referring to what were known at the time as "kneel-ins"—that is, attempts by blacks or integrated groups to occupy segregated ecclesiastical space. Yet even though the "curious spectacles" Frady describes are well documented and are estimated to have taken place at hundreds of locations across the South, church desegregation campaigns have received very short shrift in the historiography of the American civil rights movement. These Sunday-morning protests occurred at churches affiliated with every major Christian denomination, involved representatives of key civil rights organizations, and occupied a vital place in the minds of movement spokespersons and strategists. Nonetheless, they have been all but ignored by scholars.

How are we to understand this apparent disinterest in church-based nonviolent protest? Does it reflect a failure to appreciate (or discomfort with exploring) the part religion played in the civil rights movement? Have kneel-ins been disregarded because they rarely turned violent, produced few arrests, and had no discernible economic consequences? Perhaps, given the broad and momentous story of the American civil rights movement, church protests have simply fallen through the sifting bowl of history.[2]

Whatever the explanation, there is a striking discrepancy between the centrality of church-based protest in the theory and practice of nonviolent direct action during the first half of the 1960s and the peripheral role it occupies in scholarly analyses of the period. The problem is evident in historical overviews and specialized studies alike. For instance, the index to Taylor Branch's nearly 3,000-page study of America during the "King years" includes just a single reference to "kneel-ins." Discussions of church protest are absent even from scholarly studies of the Southern Christian Leadership Conference (SCLC) and the Student Non-Violent Coordinating Committee (SNCC), organizations that planned and supported kneel-in campaigns.[3]

Recently, the situation has begun to improve. Monographs exploring how Protestant denominations responded to the civil rights movement have shed light on the reactions of church people when congregations became sites of protest. And kneel-in campaigns in Birmingham and Jackson have been examined in well-received books on the civil rights movements in Alabama and Mississippi, respectively. To date, however, there has been no in-depth study of the kneel-in phenomenon. This book attempts to fill the gap with an overview and analysis of church desegregation campaigns in the South between 1960 and 1965, with the Memphis kneel-ins of 1964–65 serving as an in-depth case study.[4]

The attempt by local college students to desegregate Memphis's Second Presbyterian Church (SPC) in 1964 has fascinated me since it came to my attention fifteen years ago. As my understanding of the kneel-in phenomenon has grown, it has become clear that the Memphis campaign was both typical and distinctive.[5] Unusual features of the SPC kneel-ins were its duration (fourteen Sundays over a ten-month period), the prominent role played by white students, the low profile maintained by the church's ministers during the crisis, and the church schism that resulted. Two other aspects of the SPC protests are particularly intriguing. One is the way they reflect white Southern Christians' differing perceptions of the movement for civil rights, and the lengths they were willing to go to exert pressure on each other when these views came into conflict. Another is the degree to which the Memphis kneel-ins' effects continue to be felt many years afterward.

I was alerted to the long-term impact of church desegregation efforts in Memphis when one of the persons I approached for an interview responded that, while he would be happy to speak with me about the SPC controversy of 1964–65, I had to understand that he "was still not over it." In 1964 this man had been a high school student whose family was very active at SPC; thus I could understand how the kneel-ins there might have left an impression on him. But was it really possible that college, seminary, marriage, a successful career, children, grandchildren, and a new church had not been enough to close the emotional wound suffered forty-five years earlier? As we talked, I realized that at the root of his religious trauma was the sobering recognition that men whom he had regarded as spiritual mentors were driven by racist convictions.

I have come to understand that kneel-in campaigns could traumatize not only individuals, but institutions as well. One of the wounds inflicted by the controversy at SPC was the isolation and shame suffered by the congregation when various constituencies within the Presbyterian Church in the United States (PCUS) urged it to admit racially mixed groups and, when it refused to do so, pressed the denomination to void SPC's contract to host the upcoming annual meeting of the PCUS General Assembly.

The dishonor of being called to task in this way gave rise, understandably, to a narrative of self-justification. The determination to exclude what local papers were calling "biracial groups," church spokesmen said, had nothing to do with race. Rather, it was based solely on the visitors' intention to "demonstrate." Such obfuscations were not uncommon in the heated rhetorical atmosphere of the civil rights era. But when church members and former members continue nearly half a century later to claim that visitors who sought entry to the church in mixed groups were not "true worshippers," they provide a glimpse of how institutional memory can function to soothe decades-old institutional trauma.

A similar obfuscation has long been advanced by representatives of Memphis's Independent Presbyterian Church (IPC), which was formed in 1965 by departing members of SPC. Their dubious claim is that IPC came into being not because the outcome of the kneel-in crisis at SPC made it impossible for segregationists to remain in good standing with the PCUS, but because the congregation's founders dissented from the denomination's growing "liberalism." This assertion, though accurate in the broadest sense, veils the church's racist origins in the myth of a noble quest to defend Christian orthodoxy. As official memory, the myth salves the wounds of institutional dishonor by suppressing the uncomfortable fact that IPC was founded by dedicated segregationists.

These official memories persist because they conceal wounds inflicted on institutions that claim a moral identity. Since most modern organizations do not claim such identities, they are rarely compelled to deny or justify their racist histories. Let me demonstrate this point with a tour through the moral landscape of my own neighborhood.

I live with my family a few hundred yards from Overton Park, an urban green space that is home to the Memphis Zoo, the Brooks Museum of Art, and a public golf course, among other amenities. The zoo and museum were among the first targets of protestors when the Memphis sit-in movement was launched in March 1960. In twenty-plus years of living in Memphis I have encountered very few people who are aware that, less than a generation ago, these prominent institutions excluded the city's African American majority during most of their operating hours. Neither have I met anyone who refuses on principle to play golf on Overton Park's once-segregated public course. A few blocks south of the park is my neighborhood Walgreen's. I sincerely doubt whether any of the local residents who shop there have ever paused to remember the demonstrators who were arrested at the city's only Walgreen's in 1960, or the fact that the drugstore's management chose to remove its lunch counter rather than integrate it. As far as I know, the same collective amnesia applies to the local restaurants, banks, and libraries that were prominent targets of the Memphis Freedom Movement.

On the other hand, I know many Memphians who to this day cannot think of SPC without remembering the biracial groups who stood outside the sanctuary in 1964 and 1965 to protest the church's segregation policy. And I have talked with some who cannot drive past IPC without the moniker "First Segregationist" popping into their heads (even though the church removed references to segregation from its constitution over twenty-five years ago). Clearly, the moral standing of churches in this and other communities makes it difficult for people to forget, let alone excuse, what they perceive as immoral behavior on the part of church representatives. Parks, swimming pools, libraries, department stores, and restaurants, it seems, are judged by a different standard, no matter how hatefully their agents may have conducted themselves in the recent past.

It would be unfair to leave the impression that the Memphis churches at the heart of this story have been frozen in time since 1965; thus I have adopted a longitudinal perspective that takes into account not only the kneel-ins' long-term impact on these congregations, but the ways they have changed and are changing in response to them. As a result I have been forced to reexamine some of my perceptions of contemporary evangelicalism. I had assumed that the evangelical churches I was studying would closely resemble the churches in which I had grown up during the 1970s. That version of evangelicalism was suburban, self-focused, and wedded to reactionary politics (in 1972, my church youth group attended a Re-elect Nixon rally). But this study has introduced me to a new sort of evangelical church where urban problems, including economic injustice and racial alienation, are missional emphases.

For this and other reasons, my respect for evangelical Christians in Memphis has deepened; I have even made some new friends. But I have also been reminded of the ways that cultural and theological barriers alienate members of Christ's body. This alienation was evident in the suspicion I encountered from church members who were asked to collaborate in the work of a scholar they identified with mainline (i.e., "liberal") Protestantism. Many interviewees asked me, quite bluntly, why I was "doing this"—obviously curious why a white man would want to dredge up memories of white racism. Some also wanted to know where I was "from," as if to gauge whether I could understand white, Southern, evangelical culture and judge it fairly—and whether I intended to embarrass the people or churches involved.

Oddly, the facts that I am a Southerner, a life-long Presbyterian, and an ordained minister did little if anything to allay these fears. In part this is because I represent the denomination both churches in this story eventually left for being too "liberal." In part it is because I teach religion at the college that produced many of the student protestors, a college that over the years has steadily relinquished its Presbyterian identity in pursuit of "academic excellence." If colleges like mine are perceived as having sold their souls in exchange for a place of honor at the table of secular higher education, then religion professors like myself are the most egregious personifications of this Faustian bargain.

I attempted to reassure uneasy interviewees that my interest was not in embarrassing individuals or airing the Church's dirty linen, but in accurately describing the Memphis kneel-ins and fairly presenting the perspectives of all who were involved. Nevertheless my prejudices place me squarely on the side of those who sought to break the color line at Christian churches. In that respect, I am myself a product of what Jane Dailey calls "the victory of the theology of the beloved community." For me and for many Christians of my generation, "true" Christianity has become synonymous with "the vision of Martin Luther King and other Christian integrationists." Socialized in the post-civil rights South, I am instinctively opposed to racial discrimination, even if I continue to harbor prejudice myself. Furthermore, I find it nearly impossible to imagine how my white Southern forebears defended segregation with straight faces.[6]

It is also true, however, that studying Christian resistance to integration has enlarged my compassion for white Southerners who grew up in a world whose foundations crumbled in the historical equivalent of the blink of an eye. Without doubt, the South's path toward acceptance of racial integration was a long and circuitous one; but for Southern whites who had come of age before World War II, that path must have seemed like an expressway on which the nation was hurtling toward cultural oblivion.

Among the white Southerners for whom my empathy has grown are the elders of Memphis's SPC, who in 1957 adopted a segregation policy about which they were thoroughly unembarrassed. Their only moral concern at the time was to avoid hypocrisy; so they alerted the press to the "clear, honest Christian statement" they had voted to adopt. In 1964, just seven years later, the same men who had written the policy and announced it to the media found it necessary to defend it among members of their own congregation. Perceiving that it had become indefensible, they were obliged to change the subject and assert that their resistance to black visitors was motivated not by a desire to preserve segregation but by their zeal to protect the sanctity of the church from "demonstrators."

Like other white Southerners, these men were reacting to a social revolution they could not resist. The students from all-white Southwestern College who opposed them were reacting in their own way. By standing outside SPC alongside excluded African Americans, these privileged young people were taking a faltering step onto the stage of civil rights activism. Their black colleagues were all too familiar with the suspicion and ridicule they would meet as they entered social space where they were unwelcome. But for whites who had grown up in a world of black mammies and day laborers, crossing the racial divide was a novel and heady experience, and one they would never forget. Their lives during and after the Memphis kneel-in campaign confirm Jason Sokol's observation that the black freedom struggle "reshaped the lives of white southerners, and worked its way into whites' practices and habits—even into some minds and hearts."[7]

American Christians have long been disturbed by the tragic observation that 11 o'clock on Sunday morning is "the most segregated hour of the week." Today, however, the comment does not induce the guilty consternation it did when it first circulated in the 1950s. In many cities, in fact, the segregation of Sunday morning is rivaled every hour that schools are in session. Furthermore, the racial homogeneity one finds in most churches today is a function of choice rather than necessity. Christians who attend Sunday worship tend to do so in the places they find most comfortable or convenient. It is probably fair to say of most churches that while they have not become models of interracial harmony, they are no more complicit in American self-segregation than a host of other institutions.[8]

But this does not relieve American Christianity of responsibility for its stunning moral failure half a century ago, when many Christians responded to the gradual integration of society by drawing a line in the sand around their churches. As it became clear that segregation could not be sustained in the institutions that shaped their lives Monday through Saturday, they were determined to make Sunday worship in the South the *last* segregated hour. Southern Presbyterian scholar Ben Lacy Rose drew attention to this sad fact in 1957 when he predicted that, given the pace of integration in the wider society, the church was rapidly becoming "the last stronghold of segregation on earth." Lacy could not have imagined the struggle that would be required to infiltrate that stronghold in some churches of his own denomination.[9]

Defending segregation's last stronghold was the intention of the racial hardliners who guided SPC during the Memphis kneel-in campaign. By the time the campaign had run its course and most of these men had departed to form their own congregation, those who remained reiterated the observation Rose had made eight years earlier. "It is ironic," wrote the Women of the Church's historian at SPC, "that white Christians think the church the last stronghold of segregation." This book is about those who were determined to assail segregation's last stronghold, the resistance they encountered, and the still-unfolding legacy of their efforts.[10]

PART ONE

THE FORGOTTEN PROTESTS

"The Start of a New Movement Across the South"

The First Kneel-ins, 1960

During the late 1950s, white churches in the South began to experience growing tensions reflective of the burgeoning civil rights movement. Some congregations declared their intent to preserve segregation regardless of the changes being urged by denominational bodies. Others announced they would no longer honor the practice. There were even isolated incidents of African Americans and racially mixed groups attending white churches. Sometimes these visits created a stir; sometimes the story was how little stir was created.

But in the wake of the 1960 lunch counter sit-ins that began in Greensboro, North Carolina, visits to white churches became an integral part of the larger campaign of nonviolent direct action that was sweeping the South. Beginning in August 1960 and recurring periodically through 1965, there were dozens of attempts to integrate worship at white churches in towns and cities across the South and beyond. Despite early resistance on the part of some black leaders, eventually the major civil rights organizations, including SCLC, SNCC, NAACP (The National Association for the Advancement of Colored People), and CORE (The Congress on Racial Equality), would adopt "kneel-ins" at white churches as a strategy of nonviolent resistance.[1]

Given the six-month lag between the commencement of the student protest movement and the first kneel-ins, it is not clear just how white churches came to be regarded as potential protest sites. At the time some credited Martin Luther King, Jr. with the idea, as he was widely quoted in support of kneel-ins after they had begun. A lawsuit filed in Georgia, in fact, claimed that the kneel-ins were taking place at King's "direction and orders." As we shall see, however, the idea of staging visits to segregated white churches had percolated for some time in

SNCC and NAACP circles, as well as among progressive white Christians, before it was put into action by a group of students in Atlanta.[2]

The first widely publicized attempt to break the ecclesiastical color line took place on August 7, 1960, when racially mixed student groups visited several white Atlanta churches. According to SNCC records, these visits were planned the previous afternoon in a meeting of organization leaders and students from the Atlanta Committee on the Appeal for Human Rights. The Committee, representing Atlanta's six historically black institutions of higher learning, had published "An Appeal for Human Rights" that became the manifesto of the Atlanta sit-in movement. The "Appeal" observed that "our churches which are ordained by God and claim to be the houses of all people, foster segregation of the races to the point of making Sunday the most segregated day of the week." Five months later, the Atlanta students were joining forces with SNCC representatives to address that contradiction.[3]

In the bright light of media attention that followed the initial church visits, SNCC secretary Jane Stembridge predicted that the Atlanta kneel-ins were "the start of a new movement across the South." Martin Luther King, Jr., advisor to the organization, opined that the visitors' generally favorable reception indicated that Southerners wanted an opportunity to rescue the church from what he called its "moral dilemma," adding "we hope college students all over the south will give them the chance this fall." For the rest of August, at least, that is just what they did. The kneel-ins spread quickly from Atlanta to other cities in the Deep South, and then to dozens of towns and cities across the region.[4]

Initial news reports characterized efforts to integrate Atlanta's white churches as "sit-ins," but on August 9 a UPI story introduced the term "kneel-in" and it stuck. Even though very few incidents of church protest in Atlanta or elsewhere would involve kneeling, the neologism indicated that in the minds of participants and onlookers alike, targeted church visits were a form of direct action analogous to sit-ins at restaurants and lunch counters, stand-ins at voter registration sites, ride-ins on public busses, sleep-ins at motels and apartments, read-ins at public libraries, stand-ins at theaters, play-ins at parks, pray-ins at city halls, lie-ins at construction sites, and wade-ins at segregated pools and beaches.[5]

Kneel-ins came to be regarded by civil rights leaders, progressive seminarians and clergymen, and members of independent student groups as a unique strategy for casting segregation in religious perspective. The moral power of the kneel-in was recognized almost immediately in national religious publications like *The Christian Century*, and in the months and years following the initial wave of church protests, kneel-ins would receive mention in news sources as diverse as *The New York Times*, *Life*, and *The National Review*.[6]

Church protests not only caught the public's imagination; they occupied a central place in the minds of civil rights strategists. In fact, as the student protest movement swept the South, kneel-ins were consistently mentioned alongside sit-ins as a chief form of nonviolent direct action. This is exemplified in Martin Luther King, Jr.'s shorthand description of the protest movement as consisting of "sit-ins, kneel-ins, and wade-ins." In addition to becoming part of movement leaders' rhetorical boilerplate, kneel-ins stirred the hopes of foot soldiers as well. An editorialist writing in the August 1960 issue of *The Student Voice* (SNCC's official newsletter) predicted that kneel-ins would be "one of the next important phases of the movement":[7]

> Throughout the years, the white Southerner has failed to realize the moral wrongness of segregation because the problem of segregation has not been presented to him as a moral problem. Today, however, students feel that the time has come to awaken the dozing consciences of white Southerners by carrying the problem of segregation to the church, which they think is the best place for reconciling moral problems. Not only are they appealing to the church because segregation is morally wrong, but because the church is the house of God, to be attended by all, regardless of race, who wish to worship there.[8]

In the same issue of *The Student Voice*, James Laue, later a noted sociologist and theorist of conflict resolution, added his own reflections on the role kneel-ins would play in the struggle ahead. Laue related that since his return to graduate school after a summer spent in the South, many people had asked where the protest movement was headed. "My answer invariably," he wrote, "is 'kneel ins.'"[9]

Spelman College student Ruby Doris Smith, a participant in the Atlanta church visits, agreed that segregation was "essentially a moral problem" and that the Church was the one institution where it could be "thrashed out." In her view, the kneel-in movement was

> an appeal to the consciences of Christians, who are primarily "good" people. Even if we were not admitted to worship, as was true in my case, I think that the attempt in itself was a success, because the minds and hearts of the people who turned us away were undoubtedly stirred. I'm quite sure that they had to do quite a bit of "soul searching" when they realized that they had turned Christians away from the House of God.[10]

As the kneel-in movement spread out from Atlanta in the fall of 1960, commentators expressed their own hopes for church-based nonviolent protest. Harry Brooks, a staff writer for *The Pittsburgh Courier*, even wondered if kneel-ins might have been the place to begin the nonviolent campaign. Violence and arrests would have been less prevalent, Brooks reasoned, had kneel-ins preceded sit-ins and the nonviolent movement had "been initiated on God's level." Brooks's confidence that the church desegregation movement would not provoke violence seems naïve in retrospect; but it reflects the enthusiasm for kneel-ins that was widespread in the fall of 1960.[11]

Moral Spectacles of Exclusion and Embrace

In terms of frequency, number of participants, and degree of social disruption, kneel-ins made a relatively small contribution to the protest movement of the 1960s. Of the perhaps 50,000 children, students, and adults who engaged in nonviolent direct action during this period, only a few hundred chose to break the color line at white churches. Yet as James Laue noted in 1960, these visits possessed a unique ability to "awaken the dozing consciences of white Southerners." Laue's explanation was that while lunch counter sit-ins appealed to the individual conscience, the church was the ideal path into the collective conscience, which "holds an overflowing reservoir of guilt about racial and ethnic injustice, a reservoir long ready for draining."[12]

Many observers shared Laue's view that churches were the ideal venue for highlighting the race issue's moral dimensions. A *Christian Century* editorial opined that "bread served at a lunch counter is one thing; bread shared in church is another." Similarly, the minister of a targeted Georgia church asserted that kneel-ins illumined the battle within each churchgoer between "the white Southerner" and "the Christian," a battle, he declared, that held "much more ultimate importance than any of the pushings and shovings at Woolworth's lunch counter." A Memphis student wrote that "any permanent change in the attitudes of people must . . . come through the church, for the question of justice or injustice of segregation is a moral question that must be answered first on a moral level." And an activist in Alabama determined that if there was "one point on which white people in [Tuskegee] would not relent, it would be the church."[13]

Thus, although startled white Christians invariably viewed them as a form of "political agitation," kneel-ins were designed to move the desegregation debate from civic spaces shaped by concerns for property rights and freedom of association into sacred spaces that were morally and theologically charged. Kneel-ins were staged not to protest unjust statutes, claim rights that had been denied, or expose oppressive law-enforcement practices, but to dramatize a moral query: Would African Americans and their white accomplices be permitted to enter space in which white Christians worshiped a God they claimed loved all persons without distinction? The kneel-in, then, was "a trial in which Christ and racial custom engage[d] in moral struggle for the souls of men." A congregation's response proved whether it was "a church or merely a club."[14]

If the civil rights movement thrived on "moral spectacles" that "held racist violence 'imprisoned in a luminous glare'" (as Martin Luther King, Jr. put it), then kneel-ins were moral spectacles *par excellence*. Depending on a church's reaction, these visits could dramatize unity and reconciliation, or division and exclusion. The more prominent and centrally located the congregation, the more powerful the spectacle. This is undoubtedly why churches in the town square or city center, or churches that were "first" in their respective denominations, were the most common targets.[15]

If black visitors and their fellow-travelers were admitted to one of these leading white churches, they participated in a *spectacle of embrace* that publicly dramatized Christ's reconciling love. Conversely, the barring of blacks or racially mixed groups from worship created a *spectacle of exclusion* that symbolized the valuing of "time-honored tradition" over proclamation of the gospel. Guidance in interpreting these spectacles was sometimes offered by the visitors themselves.[16]

Participants in the 1962 Albany church visits, for instance, distributed a statement claiming that "members of Christ's church are called to a ministry of reconciliation, breaking down the walls of hostility that separate man from his brother and from God." In Memphis in 1964, a student spokesman spelled out the message intended by those participating in kneel-ins there. "Our presence . . . is itself an act of worship," he wrote in a newspaper article, "the presentation of our bodies a symbol of the church's tragic rejection of the gospel message of brotherhood and love. Our remaining outside the church, apart from it, symbolizes the separateness of our people, Negro from white, man from man, the separateness of the 'church' from love."[17]

In most cases, though, the spectacles that took form when unwanted visitors presented themselves for worship at white churches spoke for themselves. Black and white Christians praying, singing, and breaking bread together within "God's house" was a self-explanatory symbol, as was the sight of well-dressed young people keeping vigil outside a church whose members huddled behind locked doors.

Nowhere were the spectacular aspects of the kneel-in more prominently on display than in Jackson, Mississippi. As Charles March explains, the Jackson church "testings" orchestrated by Rev. Ed King were carefully designed "exercises in civil disobedience informed by a radical theological vision." Part of King's strategy for church visits in Jackson, a strategy that would also be employed in Memphis was to reenact spectacles of exclusion until unwelcoming churches were forced to acknowledge the theological bankruptcy of their racial isolation. As King put it,

> if we can't worship the same God together inside the same church buildings, then we will still knock on your door and so irritate you that

you cannot worship your white God in peace, that you cannot escape thinking about the problems of segregation even on Sunday morning, that we are just letting you know that every single aspect of your Southern Way of Life is under attack.[18]

Ecclesiastical spectacles of exclusion and embrace were portrayed in news stories, editorials, and, of course, photographs. An iconic image of embrace was broadcast in April 1963 when *The New York Times* printed a photograph of Rev. Earl Stallings, pastor of Birmingham's First Baptist Church, shaking hands with a black visitor. Spectacles of embrace inside churches were depicted less frequently. On occasion, however, reporters found their way into churches where black visitors had been received. When Florida A&M students staged kneel-ins at two churches in Tallahassee, Florida, in March 1961, they were joined by the managing editor of *The Chicago Defender*, who was in town for a conference. In a *Defender* article, the journalist described how he and a black student "were ushered to front seats [of Trinity Methodist Church] and took communion with several hundred worshippers." After the service, he said, "they were greeted by the pastor . . . and several members of the congregation and were invited to return."[19]

Another attempt to document a spectacle of embrace in North Florida ended in dramatic failure. In September 1960, members of the Jacksonville NAACP Youth Council decided to traverse the ecclesiastical color line at Snyder Memorial Methodist Church. The black students were graciously received by white Methodists at Snyder. But as they knelt at the church's prayer railing they noticed a photojournalist from the *Jacksonville Star* enter the sanctuary and begin taking pictures. At that point, recalls one of the students, "all hell broke loose." Church members may have been willing to kneel alongside black visitors, but they did not wish to have the fact publicized. After the photographer's camera and film were confiscated, he was escorted from the premises.[20]

Since they were often visible from outside targeted churches, spectacles of exclusion were more likely to be broadcast. A quintessential image of church exclusion appeared on the front page of *The New York Times* on August 2, 1965. Over the caption "turned away" was a photograph of three young couples—two black and one white—kneeling in a prayer huddle in front of the First Methodist Church of Americus, Georgia. Standing on the church steps, hovering above the would-be worshippers, were a cluster of middle-aged white men with stern faces and crossed arms. In a tableau that resembled the pause between plays in a football game, the phalanx of ushers appeared ready to "defend" the church from the huddling intruders.[21]

The dramatic quality of church spectacles was enhanced, of course, when they were staged around Easter or other celebrations of Christian unity, such as

World Communion Sunday. On Easter Sunday 1963, Birmingham was the site of several dramatic church visits. As a spectacle of embrace took shape at First Baptist when a group of black visitors stood alongside whites singing "Christ the Lord Is Risen Today," at Sixth Avenue Presbyterian a spectacle of exclusion was revealed when a group of visitors "was met halfway up [the church's] impressive wide tier of stairs by the rector [sic] advancing with palm upraised like a traffic cop, who denied the sanctuary and told them to: 'Go to the colored church.'" At Birmingham's First Christian, meanwhile, two black women who had been denied entrance to the church created their own spectacle by refusing to leave the premises. Engaging in discussion with a group of church officers, the women left "two of the elders in tears, after the six of them prayed together."[22]

Inside Looking Out

From the perspective of those within targeted churches, of course, kneel-ins were not dramatic moral gestures but political stunts organized and perhaps even paid for by civil rights organizations. The decision to exclude visitors was understood not as a theological statement but as a simple reflection of congregational policy or social custom. Yet regardless of how it was justified, the repeated exclusion of black worshippers inevitably created unfavorable publicity, locally and beyond. Reports of neatly dressed African Americans being turned away from prominent white churches were routinely picked up by national media outlets and could even come to the attention of American Christians living abroad. These included missionaries who warned that the circulation of such stories inhibited the gospel's spread overseas.[23]

Beyond the prospect of bad publicity, kneel-ins threatened to illuminate a church's internal fractures. A majority of church members might favor welcoming black visitors, but find themselves opposed by a minority of hard-line segregationists who were determined to keep them out. Kneel-ins could also expose the differing racial attitudes of pastors and their congregants, conflicts that often reflected broader tensions between denominational policies and local traditions. Some moderate clergymen reminded parishioners that closed worship had no basis in Scripture or denominational policy, and a few drove home the point by warmly greeting black visitors. The distance between local practice and Church policy was further dramatized when denominational representatives traveled long distances to break the color line at recalcitrant churches or stand in solidarity with the excluded.[24]

Exposure of these ecclesiastical fault lines fueled fears that repeated visits by African Americans could disrupt and possibly "break up" white churches. But for many white Christians in the South, the real threat posed by kneel-ins was not inconvenience, bad press, or church schism. Rather, visits by unwelcome visitors represented an invasion of sacred, familial space for profane purposes. For white Southerners, Sunday worship was "an intimate time with their God separated from the cares of the outside world," a place where they could "maintain comfortably the Southern Myth that racial relations were amiable and characterized by choice rather than coercion." As public accommodations and amenities were increasingly desegregated during the first half of the 1960s, churches became the "last bastion of white power and control," the only institutions blacks had not infiltrated.[25]

The consequences of failing to protect this preserve of white sanctity were described with varying degrees of hysteria, including references to the demise of Western civilization. When a pastor in Birmingham asked his elders to remember Christian principles as they dealt with kneel-ins at the church in 1963, one responded "to hell with Christian principles—we've got to save the church!" In the midst of a church visit campaign in Tuskegee, Alabama the following year, an elder responded to his pastor's use of Scripture in arguing for racial inclusion: "Leave the Bible out of this. Read *The Rise and Fall of the Roman Empire*, and you'll see what's happening here." Such sentiments help explain the lengths to which white Christians were willing to go in order to protect their sanctuaries—by blocking doors, locking them after services had begun, or physically removing unwanted visitors who somehow managed to slip past the church's sentries.[26]

The Question of Motives

What led visitors to risk these sorts of reactions? Bettye J. Williamson, a Spelman student who took part in the 1960 Atlanta kneel-ins, spoke for many students when she explained her motivation for visiting white churches. "I was taught that I should love my neighbor as myself," she said. "In my opinion, the first step towards such a goal would be to worship God with my neighbor whom we both say we love." Gwendolyn Harris, another participant in the Atlanta kneel-ins, described her worship experience at St. Mark Methodist Church in terms any visitor might use. "Deeply inspired by [the church's] Gothic structure and . . . intellectual atmosphere," she said, "the inspirational words of Bishop Smith carried me far beyond the realm of mere physical integration and I found myself experiencing true spiritual integration."[27]

John Gibson, a member of the Atlanta Committee on the Appeal for Human Rights, which in March 1960 indicted "churches which are ordained by God and claim to be the houses of all people [but] foster segregation," described his reasons for participating in the kneel-ins:

As I grew up here in Atlanta I heard constantly in Sunday School at Wheat Street Baptist Church and later in the Catholic schools I attended of the Fatherhood of God and the Brotherhood of Man. Unfortunately, I saw little of this as a reality in the relationships between white Christians and Negro Christians.... I had debated in my mind whether God-fearing creatures could with a clear conscience reject a sincere worshiper. For this reason I approached Grace Methodist Church not as a demonstrator, but as a believer in an eternal common Cause.[28]

It may be true, as Kip Kosek argues, that such "narratives of religious sincerity . . . were self-conscious attempts to win sympathy with a broader public." But there is little evidence for the claim, advanced by targeted churches across the South between 1960 and 1965, that unwelcome visitors were "agitators" or "publicity seekers" who lacked any genuine interest in Christian worship. For regardless of what church "testers" said or did not say about their motives, with very few exceptions these well-dressed, often Bible-toting men and women resembled and behaved like other worshippers. Uninterested in discerning the visitors' true intentions, white church people instinctively portrayed their presence as "political" or "sociological," while characterizing their own motives for excluding them as purely religious.[29]

As white Christians would discover, however, dependable religious justifications for preserving the racial status quo were difficult to come by. In fact, by 1960, biblical and theological warrants for segregation had been discredited by influential leaders in all the mainline denominations. Without a strong biblical basis for maintaining racial separation, many congregations could defend the exclusion of blacks only as a time-honored tradition embraced by their forebears, one that, they diffidently claimed, was not "unchristian." When denominational bodies condemned ecclesiastical segregation as theologically indefensible, conservatives complained that Church leaders were out of step with local congregations or were favoring one side in a complicated social debate in which Christians could respectfully disagree. Yet congregations that attempted to enforce segregation in public worship placed themselves on a collision course with Church powers. Under these circumstances, the safest way to avoid conflict and possible disciplinary action was to ignore segregation's theological or moral status and focus on impugning visitors' motives.[30]

Once exclusionary churches chose this path, they discovered that the Bible could indeed inform a Christian response to interlopers with unholy motives. The passage of choice in this regard was the story of Jesus's "cleansing of the Temple," which did not touch on race or separation but was claimed to reveal God's view of profane activity in the vicinity of God's House. In the story, which appears in slightly different versions in all four gospels, Jesus "drives out" those who buy, sell, or change money in the Temple precincts and proclaims, quoting Isaiah, "Is it not written, 'My house shall be called a house of prayer for all the nations'? But you have made it a den of robbers." In the absence of a reliable biblical warrant for enforced racial separation, Jesus's "cleansing of the Temple" was invoked repeatedly between 1960 and 1965 to characterize kneel-in partici- pants' unspiritual, perhaps even commercial, interests and to justify measures to keep them from profaning "the sacredness of the precincts of worship."[31]

Whether or not it was embellished with scriptural claims, the "questionable motives" justification for excluding kneel-in visitors was widely condemned as a cynical evasion of Christian duty. A *Christian Century* editorial that appeared within weeks of the Atlanta church protests opined that "so long as visitors to a Christian church conduct themselves with quietness and dignity it is not the privilege of any representative of the church to analyze the motives of communi- cants or refuse them admission." *Atlanta Constitution* editor Ralph McGill, meanwhile, warned that attempts to infer the motives of Sunday visitors could undermine a church's very identity:

> Whatever the motives of the kneel-ins, they have placed the Southern Christian Church in a position of choosing. Many of its leaders are deeply disturbed by the arrival of a time of decision. They are painfully aware that those churches which have ushers at the entrances, like doorkeepers at a secret lodge, instructed to make arbitrary decisions as to who is coming sincerely to worship and who isn't, are in an unten- able position bordering dangerously on the ridiculous. . . . Unless a church wishes, as it may, to become a private club with a private mem- bership list, it cannot continue in the preposterous posture of having a committee at the doors who will pass judgment on who is sincere and who isn't.[32]

Others noted that attempting to discern the intentions of would-be wor- shippers was a theological boomerang. An Episcopal priest in Savannah observed that if he "had to stand at the door each Sunday and check the mo- tives of each of our people seeking entrance, [he'd] have to turn a hefty per- centage away." An article in *The Presbyterian Outlook* imagined a fictitious church that had created a "motives committee" charged with excluding all those whose intentions were less than spiritual—including those who attended wor- ship to find a wife or "relax and sing." Arguments for exclusion based on visi- tors' putative motives were further undermined when collared Episcopal clergymen and Methodist bishops were among those turned away. Candid comments by church representatives, such as "we are not yet integrated," "this church was built by white people and white people worship here," and "if you want to worship there are nigger churches you can go to," were truer reflections of congregational sentiment.[33]

Because kneel-in participants seldom returned to targeted churches even when they had been admitted, it was natural for congregants to conclude that they had no interest in joining a white church or even attending regularly. But by their own accounts, "true worship"—that is, color-blind worship that reflected diversity in the body of Christ—was precisely what these visitors were seeking. Breaking the racial barrier was for them a way of "bringing God back into the worship at these churches . . . [and] restoring the authentic worship of God in these congregations and beyond." Two pieces of evidence reinforce this claim. First, newspaper accounts of kneel-ins unfailingly describe church visitors as "neat" and "well-dressed" in their Sunday best. Second, there are no reliable accounts of kneel-in participants creating any disturbance after being admitted to worship. Invariably, trouble arose when visitors were forcibly ejected from sanctuaries or arrested on municipal or state charges of "disturbing a worship service." In this sense, the concern that black visitors would disrupt divine services became a self-fulfilling prophecy.[34]

The First Wave

The high-water mark of activity in church desegregation campaigns was reached in the months following the Atlanta church visits. In April 1961, it was estimated that kneel-ins had been staged at two hundred churches nationwide. While the number of reported incidents was much smaller, there were complaints at the time that church protests "were possibly the most poorly reported aspect of the current Negro student demonstrations." Indeed, many of the campaigns to integrate white churches have apparently fallen through the cracks of history; but those that received media coverage or were written about by witnesses provide a fascinating glimpse of the kneel-in phenomenon. After exploring the Atlanta church visits in more detail, we will review first-wave church desegregation campaigns in Savannah and Memphis.[35]

Atlanta

As we have seen, the first organized attempts to test white churches' tolerance for integrated worship took place in Atlanta, Georgia, on August 7, 1960, when about twenty-five young people in small interracial groups visited six Atlanta churches—the Episcopal Cathedral of St. Philip, First Presbyterian, Grace Methodist, St. Mark Methodist, First Baptist, and Druid Hills Baptist. Although they were denied entrance only at the Baptist churches, the students' reception and their options for seating varied at each site.[36]

At First Presbyterian and the Cathedral of St. Philip, black students worshipped among white members of the congregation without incident. Visitors to Grace Methodist, who arrived after the service had begun, were seated in a Sunday school room outfitted with a loudspeaker. The experience was not unpleasant, however, as visitor John Gibson attests:

> We (there were seven students who went to Grace Methodist) were greeted at the entrance to the vestibule by a very polite usher who welcomed us to the church. Since we were five or ten minutes late, the church was already crowded, so we stood at the rear of the church until we were directed to a classroom which was being used to house the overflow crowd.[37]

In the classroom, according to Gibson, the black students "were not seated together or given any specific places to sit" and after the service were "greeted very warmly and with what seemed to be heart-felt sincerity." Three of the visitors were "cordially welcomed" by the pastor, who "expressed his gratitude that we had come," reported Gibson, "and hoped that when we returned we might be early enough to sit in the main body of the church."[38]

Students visiting St. Mark Methodist were seated in the aisles of a packed auditorium and following the service were introduced to guest preacher Bishop J. O. Smith, who thanked them for coming. Visitor Gwendolyn Harris reported being "deeply inspired" by the church's structure and atmosphere. At Druid Hills Baptist, ushers offered to clear a pew for black visitors in the rear of the sanctuary, but the accommodation was declined. Bettye J. Williamson said of the experience: "I was a very sad and disillusioned person when my neighbor told me that I needed reservations in order to kneel beside him and, together, worship our Maker. If my neighbor requires me to reserve seats in the House of the Lord, I wonder what he would require of me if he controlled the entrance to the Kingdom of the Lord?" At First Baptist, visiting students got only as far as the church foyer, from which spot they offered a mimeographed statement to congregants leaving the service.[39]

The campaign to integrate Atlanta churches continued on two subsequent Sundays. Remarkably, despite local and national media coverage of the kneel-ins, each week a larger proportion of targeted churches barred visiting interracial groups. After two of six churches refused to seat visitors on August 7, the following week half of the ten churches visited turned away student groups. Among them were the Baptist churches that had been called upon the previous Sunday and Grace Methodist, which a week earlier had actually welcomed black visitors. On August 21, student groups "left quietly without incident" after being barred from all three churches where they sought entrance—Grace Methodist, Westminster

Presbyterian, and First Christian. It appears that, initially at least, targeted churches felt little if any outside pressure to seat unwelcome visitors. And as the unpredictability at Grace Methodist indicates, accommodation of black visitors one week did not guarantee that a church's doors would be open the next.[40]

In Atlanta, Episcopalians seem to have had the best record of inclusivity and Baptists the worst. But one church's response to a kneel-in was not predictive of how black visitors and their fellow-travelers would be received at sister congregations. After parishioners at midtown's First Presbyterian welcomed kneel-in participants on August 7, Rev. Harry A. Fifield confided that he was "so proud of my people I don't know what to do." Two weeks later, however, suburban Westminster Presbyterian was among the churches that refused to admit black visitors. At Decatur Presbyterian, meanwhile, the very prospect of racial testing necessitated a "revision of policies" that, while keeping the church in theoretical compliance with its denomination's open-door policy, set aside a "specific pew for black visitors."[41]

Church spokesmen in Atlanta gave various reasons for their decision to bar blacks and their white colleagues. At First Baptist, head usher F. Joe Vining described visiting students as "just a bunch of agitators . . . [who] wanted to separate and sit where they pleased." At Grace Methodist, an usher told would-be worshippers they were "unwelcome because they are not Atlanta Negroes and are agitators not interested in truly worshipping as Christians." At Westminster Presbyterian and First Christian, church representatives informed black young people that the congregations were not yet integrated. Meanwhile First Christian's Rev. James W. Sosebee said that while he regretted anyone being excluded from worship, he also regretted that "our Negro citizens seek to use these methods of entry into the churches of the white people of Atlanta who have been their friends for many decades."[42]

The First Baptist usher's comment about kneel-ins being led by persons who were not "Atlanta Negroes" was accurate to some degree, for press accounts indicate that many participants in the Atlanta campaign hailed from historically black institutions outside the city. The group visiting the Episcopal Cathedral of St. Philip on August 7, for instance, included Frank James, a student at Philander Smith College in Little Rock, Arkansas, and Clarence Mitchell, who was premed at Morgan State College in Baltimore. Among those seeking entrance to First Baptist were Marion Barry, Jr., a student at Fisk University (and SNCC chairman) and Henry Thomas, a member of the Non-Violent Action Group at Howard University. The white students with them included Bonnie Kilstein, an Atlanta native enrolled at New York University, and James Laue, a Harvard graduate student.

But many of those who participated in the August kneel-ins lived in Atlanta or were attending college in the city. They included R. Kenneth Davis of Morehouse

College and Gwendolyn Harris, Bettye J. Williamson, and Ruby Doris Smith, students at Spelman College, which had recently been described in *The Nation* as a "finishing school for pickets." Smith would go on to participate in numerous sit-ins and freedom rides and spend time in Mississippi's notorious Parchman Penitentiary. Yet the 1960 kneel-ins left a lasting impression on this young Atlantan: "When I was refused admission to the church," she told a reporter, "I was stunned at first by the reaction of the ushers" who had blocked her entry. Smith pulled up a chair and worshipped in the lobby, from which spot she could glimpse the hateful looks of white worshippers.[43]

There was at least one other visit by black students to white Atlanta churches during the fall of 1960. On October 6, several Spelman women attended churches within walking distance of the campus. One group sought to enter Park Street Methodist, another West End Baptist. According to an account by student Angela G. Owen, the first group walked reverently into the Methodist church but were asked to leave before being seated. The second group was stopped in the driveway of the Baptist church by a deacon who instructed them to attend (black) Wheat Street Baptist Church and threatened to call police if they did not leave the property. When these women tried to join their peers at Park Street, they encountered "at least three or four men posted at each door." Asked if he would also be guarding the doors to the Kingdom of God, an elderly usher responded, "Yes, I'll be there and a host of others, and you won't get in there either." The Spelman women expressed their desire to "worship the God of ALL mankind in HIS holy temple," but their protestations were of no avail. They returned to campus, a story in the *Spelman Spotlight* related, "with tears silently falling from their eyes."[44]

Savannah

Lunch counter sit-ins came to the coastal city of Savannah, Georgia, in mid-March 1960, to be followed in the ensuing months by a boycott of downtown stores, protests at public beaches and parks, and visits to white churches. The Savannah kneel-in campaign commenced on August 21, when students affiliated with the local NAACP visited ten white churches. Newspaper reports identified this as the first occurrence of kneel-ins outside Atlanta, although in fact church desegregation campaigns had already begun in New Orleans and Norfolk and were getting under way in Memphis and other cities.[45]

Savannah was unique in at least one respect. It seems to have been the only locale in which there was a campaign to condemn kneel-ins before they began. On August 16, five days before the city's first church visits, Wesley Monumental Methodist Church adopted a statement denouncing kneel-ins as "deliberately provocative" and part of a coordinated effort "to use the churches as a staging

area for racial agitation." The statement went on to accuse those who would integrate white churches of coming "to intrude and disrupt . . . armed with carefully
planned publicity all ready for newspapers and wire services." "Since when is it
right to use the House of God as a stage to publicize and dramatize and adver-
tise?" the church asked.[46]

Although it was reported across the nation, the Wesley Monumental declaration did not deter young activists associated with the local NAACP. On August
21 they were welcomed at Christ Episcopal and Tabernacle Baptist churches,
while five others turned them away. In keeping with local tradition, three
churches offered visitors balcony seats, a compromise that was accepted at the
Lutheran Church of the Ascension after visitors were told that first-floor pews
had been reserved by church families "for generations." On August 28 black
groups were received by five Savannah churches, while six kept them out. Among
those targeted were three Episcopal congregations. One African American was
welcomed at Christ Church Episcopal and two more at Holy Apostles, whose
members invited the visitors to join them at the church coffee hour and afterward drove them home. However, at St. John's (the largest and wealthiest parish
in the Diocese of Georgia), several young people were told they could not enter
the church without "passes."[47]

As if to highlight the ludicrous nature of the exclusion at St. John's, the twenty-
eight-year-old rector at Holy Apostles made news by urging his congregation to
welcome anyone who appeared for worship. It is my "fervent prayer," wrote Rev.
Albert H. Hatch, that "the members of this congregation . . . will put the worship
of God above all other considerations." Although Hatch reported receiving
phone calls telling him "where he could go," he promised to address the issue in
his sermons. St. John's, however, was unyielding. In 1965, after interracial groups
had repeatedly been barred from entering the church, the bishop reminded the
parish's segregationist priest that since 1964 it had been a violation of canon law
to exclude any communicant or baptized member of the Episcopal Church from
worship or membership "because of race, color or ethnic origin." After prohibit-
ing a racially mixed group of Episcopalians from entering the church on Easter
1965, Rector Ernest Risley led St. John's out of the Episcopal Church.[48]

Memphis

In March 1960 the Memphis Freedom Movement was launched by students at
historically black LeMoyne and Owen colleges who had been mentored in nonviolent protest by Marion Barry (LeMoyne '58) and James M. Lawson, Jr.,
among others. The students contacted NAACP leaders only when their visits to
segregated local venues landed them in jail. But the organization embraced their
cause and the students were soon joined by adults from every stratum of black

society in Memphis, including professionals who picketed and sat in on busses and in restaurants. In August, having targeted the city's library system, art museum, zoo, busses, theaters, and downtown stores, the student protestors took aim at local white churches. On Sunday, August 21, nine black students successfully worshipped at two Catholic churches—Immaculate Conception and St. Peter's. The following Sunday black college and high school students visited Bellevue Baptist, Idlewild Presbyterian, First Assembly of God, and First Church of Christ, Scientist. All but the last barred the students, who encountered varying degrees of hostility.[49]

At First Assembly, services were suspended until the unwelcome visitors had vacated the premises. At Bellevue Baptist, about fifty congregants left the building when they saw African Americans arguing with ushers in the church vestibule. While most of the large congregation seemed not to notice the students, who "left peacefully" after declining an offer to occupy seats in the third-floor balcony, a policeman directing traffic nearby responded to "the disturbance" by arresting Nathaniel Exum of Memphis and William Freeman of Swansea, Massachusetts. In court, where Bellevue members had been subpoenaed as witnesses, the assistant city attorney described a "calculated scheme" to disrupt services at Bellevue and asked for a state warrant on charges of interfering with public worship. The students' attorney, future NAACP Executive Director Benjamin L. Hooks, called the arrest "Gestapo"-like, but was unsuccessful in having the charges dismissed. The judge fined the two men for disorderly conduct and held them on the state charge, setting bail at $500.[50]

Ushers at Idlewild Presbyterian responded to the appearance of four black students by offering them transportation to a "Negro Presbyterian church." When Rev. Paul Tudor Jones, who had been away from the church on vacation, addressed the matter the following Sunday, he confessed that he was "most appalled" by the "unfortunate incident at the doors of [the] church" the previous week. "Whose church is it?" he asked. "It is not mine. It is not yours. If it isn't Christ's church, it is not a church at all. And it has never been a question of whom I want and whom I don't want, but whom Christ wants and who will receive his welcome." By far the most welcoming church targeted on August 28 was the First Church of Christ, Scientist. According to one of four visiting students, "members of the church walked up to us, shook our hands, told us we were welcome, and to come when ever we felt like it." Even this remarkable reception was qualified, however, as the visitors were seated in a roped-off section of the sanctuary. A church representative explained that since there were no "Negro" Christian Science churches in town, separate seating was the congregation's policy.[51]

Students who participated in the 1960 Memphis kneel-ins were determined to find out where prominent white congregations stood with regard to segregation in the body of Christ. What they learned is that black visitors at white churches could provoke a range of reactions. They might be admitted without fanfare (the Catholic churches); worship might be suspended (First Assembly of God); church ushers might arrange transportation to a black church of the same denomination (Idlewild Presbyterian); they might be offered seating in a special (that is, segregated) section of the sanctuary (Bellevue Baptist and First Church of Christ, Scientist); or they might be detained and arrested by over-zealous law-enforcement officers.

But none of these experiences prepared the students for what they would experience when they crashed a religious rally at a local park. On Tuesday, August 30, two days after the second round of Sunday church visitations, fourteen black young people entered a youth rally sponsored by the Memphis Christian Youth Organization of the Assemblies of God. The venue was Overton Park, a 342-acre urban green space that is home to the Memphis Zoo and Brooks Memorial Art Gallery, both of which had been sites of nonviolent protests during the previous months. The Overton Park Shell where the youth rally was held had been the site of Elvis Presley's first paid concert in 1954. But on this occasion no symbolic blending of Memphis cultures would be tolerated.

Since a newspaper announcement of the rally had indicated that "the public may attend," a group of black students under the leadership of Evander Ford decided to find out whether the Assembly of God's conception of "the public" included African Americans. Arriving late, Ford and the others were informed that they had entered a "whites only" gathering. When the students insisted they had come to worship, ushers relented but requested that they sit together in the back. Once inside, however, the students spread out and found seats among the six hundred or so white attendees. When pastor T. E. Scruggs noted the presence of the unwelcome visitors, he called police. Ten men and women between the ages of nineteen and twenty-two were arrested (four members of the group were juveniles) and booked on charges of disorderly conduct and loitering. One of the students, Johnnie Mae Rodgers, spent the night in jail because her previous record of sit-in arrests marked her as a "habitual criminal."[52]

The following day the students found themselves before Judge Beverly Boushe, well known among activists for equating nonviolent direct action with "mob rule by intimidation" that bred "contempt for the law." Lawyer Benjamin Hooks maintained that the young people had been arrested solely because their "black face[s] showed up in a white audience." But Boushe, after characterizing the students' actions as "a shocking and new low in political chicanery," levied fines of $51. These convictions were appealed on the grounds that the students had intended to participate in the rally, not disrupt it. Indeed, the young people had made a point of dressing well and behaving politely. But witnesses testified that they had "barged in," caused an "uproar" in which several dozen people left the rally, and "scattered" on Ford's instruction. The students' convictions were upheld when the judge determined they had engaged in "rude conduct."[53]

Although Assembly of God officials had requested that police remove the black young people from the rally, they were hesitant to have them arrested and were even more hesitant to press charges (according to one of the defendants, the police "practically insisted" that they do so). However, prosecutors and judges were determined to make examples of the students. After being convicted of violating a city ordinance that made it a crime to disrupt a religious service, the students were charged under a corresponding Tennessee law. A year after the fateful rally, seven of the defendants were convicted on state felony charges by an all-white jury that had deliberated for twenty minutes. The judge levied $200 fines and sixty-day jail sentences.[54]

In March 1962, after the Supreme Court of Tennessee upheld these convictions and issued arrest warrants, the students' defense team appealed to the U.S. Supreme Court. Although the Court refused to overturn the fines and sentences meted out in state court, an order that the students be taken into custody was blocked by a federal stay that allowed them to remain free as they awaited a political intervention. It finally came in July 1965 when Tennessee Governor Frank G. Clement, acting on recommendation of the Tennessee Board of Pardons, Paroles and Probation, commuted the students' sentences through executive clemency. Clement had been led to understand that unless the students were pardoned he could not count on black support in his upcoming campaign for the U.S. Senate. Significantly, the students' documents of commutation noted that the pardons board had found "no evidence of rudeness, jostling, profanity or boisterousness . . . [or] willful disregard of the rights of others."[55]

The Overton Park "kneel-in" gave rise to a five-year legal odyssey that resulted in the only felony convictions arising from the Memphis Freedom Movement, and the only movement charges of any kind that were not eventually dismissed. Johnnie Rodgers Turner and Katie Jean Robertson Mallory (LeMoyne '62) had to wait three years before securing the teaching jobs for which they had prepared in college. Even after their sentences were commuted, legal consequences dogged some of the students. Protestor Alfred O'Neal Gross was denied a job promotion when a background check revealed he had a criminal record, and Evander Ford, the group's leader, was prevented from graduating from LeMoyne College. In a case of long-delayed justice, Ford's degree was finally granted in 2004.[56]

It is remarkable that these students' appearance at an outdoor youth rally to which "the public" had been invited could provoke such a legal firestorm. Apparently, whites in Memphis—pastors, church members, prosecutors, and judges alike—believed that blacks who chose to attend white church services were engaging in an egregious form of social disruption. This mindset is easier to understand when we remember that boundary-crossing behavior of this sort provoked deep-seated fears among whites that the interaction of young people across racial lines would lead to miscegenation. Fraternization with whites of the opposite sex was far from the minds of the black students who attended the Overton Park rally in August 1960. But, as would be the case four years later at Second Presbyterian Church, the mingling of white and black young people in a religious setting triggered visceral reactions.[57]

‖ 2 ‖

"Christ Did Not Build any Racial Walls"

Church Desegregation Campaigns, 1961–65

The first wave of kneel-ins emanating outward from Atlanta in 1960 would reach as far as Alexandria, Jacksonville, and New Orleans, and nonviolent church protests would continue to make news for the next five years. Kneel-ins occurred in towns and cities across the South, including Rock Hill, South Carolina; Tallahassee, Florida; and Augusta, Georgia, in 1961; Durham, North Carolina; Talladega, Alabama; and Albany, Georgia, in 1962; Birmingham, Alabama; Jackson, Mississippi; Atlanta, Georgia; Farmville, Virginia; Raleigh, North Carolina; and Houston, Texas, in 1963; St. Augustine, Florida; Memphis and Jackson, Tennessee; Tuskegee, Alabama; Lynchburg, Virginia; and Wilson, North Carolina, in 1964; and Selma and Montgomery, Alabama; and Americus, Georgia, in 1965. Many of these efforts at church desegregation received little media coverage at the time. But a reliable picture of the kneel-in phenomenon can be recreated from what we know about church testings in some of the larger locations.[1]

Albany, 1962

The Albany Movement began as a collaboration between several organizations, including SNCC, the NAACP, and the local black ministerial alliance. In November 1961, the movement's leadership launched a series of demonstrations and marches to which local law enforcement responded with mass arrests. Through the winter and spring of 1962, demonstrators were arrested at the city's library, bus depot, train station, downtown stores and in front of City Hall.[2]

Martin Luther King, Jr. and Ralph Abernathy lent spiritual support to the movement in Albany, and in July 1962 joined those who had been arrested there. After being convicted of parading without a permit and disturbing the peace, the two ministers chose to serve jail time rather than pay the fine levied on them. As this and other developments placed the southwest Georgia city on the national radar, sit-ins at lunch counters and visits to segregated libraries and parks were met with more arrests. In September, seventy-five Protestants, Catholics, and Jews from outside the state traveled to Albany to support the nonviolent movement there. They were arrested while praying in front of City Hall and shuttled to jails in surrounding counties.

Given the involvement of King and Abernathy and the role played by public prayer in the Albany Movement, it is not surprising that churches became targets of nonviolent protest. Rumors of kneel-ins circulated as early as December 1961, but it was not until August 12, 1962, that blacks—alone and in small groups—presented themselves for worship at white churches. Reactions to these surprise visits broke down along denominational lines: they were admitted at Catholic and Episcopal churches, but refused by the Methodists and Baptists.

When the visits resumed the following Sunday, seven churches in the Episcopal, Presbyterian, Methodist, Baptist, and Church of Christ traditions were targeted by African Americans in groups of three or four. The visitors carried a mimeographed statement that reminded Christians of their call "to a ministry of reconciliation, breaking down the walls of hostility that separate man from his brother and from God." If anything, however, the walls of hostility had become higher in the week since the initial visits. Doris Derby of Yonkers, New York, who had entered St. Paul's Episcopal the previous Sunday without provoking stares or "dirty looks," was refused admittance when she returned. The most hostile reception, however, was reserved for Rev. Robert Kenloch, Unita Tumblen, and Johnny Mae Cooper, who were arrested while standing on the steps of First Baptist Church. A church usher to whom the black visitors handed a copy of their statement of Christian reconciliation summoned a nearby policeman, who arrested them for loitering.[3]

In a city where arrests were the community's primary response to nonviolent protests, the episode in front of First Baptist was not unusual. What was unexpected, however, particularly given the virtual nonexistence of white support for the movement in Albany, was the reaction of First Baptist pastor Brooks Ramsey when he learned of the visitors' ordeal. "This is Christ's church," Ramsey told an Atlanta newspaper. "And I can't build any walls around it that Christ did not build. And Christ did not build any racial walls. . . . The church doctrine of love to all men transcends any racial consideration." Ramsey told the paper that he did not endorse kneel-ins as a strategy for racial reconciliation, but he was adamant that Christian courtesy demanded all be admitted to the church.[4]

This was a conclusion Ramsey had reached long before he arrived in Albany. It was based, in fact, on experiences that had shaped Ramsey while he was a seminarian. Raised in a fundamentalist environment in Memphis, Ramsey enrolled at Southwestern Baptist Theological Seminary in Ft. Worth, Texas, in 1958. Two encounters there permanently altered his understanding of race relations. One was a course with T. B. Maston (1897–1988), who had studied ethics with H. Richard Niebuhr at Yale and adapted the Social Gospel tradition for Southern Baptists. At a time when most white Southerners accepted segregation as compatible with Christian morality, Maston concluded that the practice "inevitably involves discrimination [and] is contrary to the spirit and teachings of Christ." In church publications like "'Of One': A Study of Christian Principles and Race Relations" (1946) and books such as *The Bible and Race* (1959), Maston rebutted the scriptural arguments for segregation and white superiority that were popular among Southern Baptists.[5]

Ramsey's other formative experience at Southwestern was the relationship he developed with the seminary's first black student, and a memorable conversation they had on the steps of the administration building:

> He said, "Brooks, it doesn't seem fair to me that I can't live in the dormitory. But over in the dormitory there's an ex-Japanese pilot who tried to destroy this country in World War II." He pulled up his pants leg and showed me shrapnel wounds. He said, "I got these wounds in the South Pacific. It just doesn't seem fair that I, who fought for this country, do not have the same privileges as one who fought against this country."[6]

Fifty years later, Ramsey describes the conversation as "an emotional event" that precipitated a life-altering decision: "I gotta be on the right side of this," he concluded. "I gotta fight for justice."

Ramsey arrived in Albany to pastor 2,700-member First Baptist Church in 1959. Aware that his views on race were not in the mainstream of the Southern Baptist Convention, Ramsey informed the pulpit committee that he was committed to breaking down racial walls. Committee members assured him that "we love our colored people" and Ramsey took the job in good conscience. But after arriving in Albany Ramsey learned that, however fond white Georgians might be of their "colored people," they were determined to keep their children from attending school with them. When the Sibley Commission came to Albany in early 1960 to canvass citizens' views on whether Georgia should comply with federal integration orders or discontinue public education, Ramsey and a few ministerial colleagues appealed for open schools. Despite severe criticism from their congregations, the white pastors formed a committee to encourage reconciliation with their black colleagues.[7]

In December 1961, as racial tensions in Albany were rising and church kneel-ins were rumored to be imminent, Ramsey pressed his deacon board to declare First Baptist an "open church" without racial barriers. When the resolution was voted down, Ramsey suggested that the board adopt the policy that black visitors would be seated either in the church balcony or in an overflow auditorium in the basement. In the end, however, all Ramsey was able to secure from the church's lay leaders was a promise that no visitors would be arrested unless they were provoking violence. As we have seen, however, not even this agreement would be honored.

Increasingly, Ramsey's statements and actions triggered suspicion within the congregation. During a convention of black Baptist Sunday School workers, Ramsey led some of the attending ministers on a tour of First Baptist's sanctuary. When word got around that several of them had stood in the church's pulpit, "all hell broke loose."[8]

On August 19 the feared visitations came to pass when blacks visited First Baptist and six other churches with a petition they asked be read to the congregations. Only after the worship service, when his ten-year-old son asked him, "Daddy, what did they do with those colored people today?" did Ramsey learn there had been an incident at First Baptist that morning. Concerned, he hurried to the front of the church and found a young black man standing on the sidewalk. He recalls their conversation:

> He said, "Are you Doctor Ramsey?" I said, "Well, I'm Brooks Ramsey, I'm not Doctor Ramsey yet. I'm the minister." And he said, "Well, I'm Andrew Young. I've been waiting for you to tell you that we didn't intend this to happen to you because we know you're one of the best friends we've got in Albany. But the irony is that we went to six other churches, at which the ministers are segregationists and at not one of those places were we arrested."[9]

Retiring to Ramsey's office, the two men ascertained that the three black visitors had been arrested on a charge of vagrancy. Soon afterward Ramsey received a call from the *Atlanta Journal*'s Walter Rugaber, who was working on a feature story about racial unrest in Albany. Rugaber asked Ramsey to comment on the arrest of the "colored people" at his church that morning, to which he responded that he could not build any walls around Christ's church that Christ himself did not build. This statement would be published on Monday afternoon, while Ramsey was in Panama City, Florida, with the church's youth group. On Tuesday morning, the park ranger found Ramsey to tell him he "must have a hundred phone calls." When he learned that one of them was from a television station in New York City, Ramsey knew his days in Albany were numbered.

After two First Baptist deacons drove to Panama City to inform their pastor that it was not safe for him to return to Albany, Ramsey and his wife headed to Atlanta to explore other job opportunities. But fearing that church leaders might declare the pulpit at First Baptist vacant if he did not return to Albany by the weekend, Ramsey informed the chairman of the deacon board that he would be preaching that Sunday. "Right after the Doxology's sung," he told the man, "I'm going to go to the pulpit and say that you and I are calling a meeting of the board of deacons this afternoon to discuss my future ministry."[10]

That Sunday evening—August 25—the church was host to journalists from around the country who were eagerly awaiting news that a moderate Baptist minister had been dismissed by his rabidly segregationist congregation. When the reporters learned that the board had voted unanimously to retain Ramsey and affirmed "the right of individual members of this church and its pastor to arrive at their own Christian convictions on all spiritual matters which may or may not be in agreement with the customs of this church," they were incredulous. Although he was not aware of it at the time, the intervention of an influential Atlanta banker had tipped the scales in Ramsey's favor. Although the mysterious intercession saved his job, it also kept Ramsey from receiving what would have been a generous severance package. A reporter from *Look* told Ramsey, "You just lost $50,000. That's what we were prepared to offer for the story of your firing."[11]

As it turned out, however, not everyone at First Baptist supported Ramsey's right to arrive at his "own Christian convictions." A lawyer in the congregation challenged the pastor to a race debate, nailing to the church door "95 theses" on white superiority, which included the declaration "that racial segregation as traditionally practiced is consistent with love and morality . . . and that a total . . . continuance of such practice of segregation shall and will prevail at all times on the Church premises." But the bigger story, the church's unlikely decision to retain Ramsey, resonated among Baptists at home and abroad. In October 1962, Baptist missionaries in Rhodesia wrote "An Open Letter to First Baptist Church of Albany, Ga." commending the church for its bravery. "You make our work easier," they wrote, "when you take such courageous actions," because "racial incidents from the States are given such prominence" in Africa.[12]

While Ramsey was certainly pleased to have Baptist support in southern Africa, he found very little in South Georgia. He knew, in fact, that First Baptist's deacon board included active members of the Ku Klux Klan and he was regularly reminded that some of his congregants could not tolerate his racial views. After services one Sunday, one of these men placed in Ramsey's hand a printed card that read, "I Have Just Paid Your Membership Dues in the NAACP. You Are Now An Honorary Nigger." Yet not all his memories of the period are bad. One day while Ramsey was attending a meeting in a local black church, the resident pastor announced that "Dr. King" was upstairs. King did not want to cause the white ministers embarrassment or trouble, the pastor said, but he would like to come down and join their discussion. Ramsey fondly recalls those "two-and-a-half hours talking theology and politics and philosophy with Martin Luther King."[13]

Atlanta, 1963

Despite a flurry of church testings in the fall of 1960, kneel-ins at segregated churches apparently did not resume in Atlanta until 1963. That spring, 6,000-member First Baptist Church was the site of several visits by students associated with the Committee on Appeal for Human Rights. In the wake of kneel-ins three years earlier, First Baptist's board of deacons had voted to seat blacks who presented themselves for worship in an auxiliary auditorium located in the church basement. But the plan was thwarted in April 1963 when five Morehouse College students entered the church through a side door and proceeded to take seats in the main sanctuary. Responding to what an associate minister called the students' "commando tactics," ushers confronted the visitors and, in a dramatic spectacle of exclusion, carried three of them from the building.[14]

Atlanta's First Baptist was a prominent church whose pastor Roy O. McLain *Newsweek* had recognized in 1955 as one of America's ten "Greatest Preachers." By local standards, McLain was a racial moderate, having joined fellow religious leaders in 1957 to sign the Atlanta Manifesto, which counseled against massive resistance to school desegregation. In 1961 McLain had written that Jesus was "colorblind." Obviously, this description did not apply to the ushers who physically removed visiting Morehouse students from the church in 1963. But when white students at First Baptist responded to the incident by meeting with some of the excluded African Americans, church authorities encouraged them to sit with their black counterparts in the auxiliary auditorium, thereby creating an "integrated" space within the church.[15]

Hopes of a peaceful solution to the integration problem at First Baptist were shattered in June, however, when Rev. Ashton Jones, a sixty-six-year-old clergyman from San Gabriel, California, with a history of dramatic racial gestures, thrust the church into the national headlines. Jones had recently been released from jail after serving twenty-two days for violating Georgia's anti-trespass law. When not incarcerated, the Butler, Georgia, native and graduate of Emory Divinity School was enlisting white undergraduates to protest segregation in the city. On June 30, Jones demonstrated his commitment to a desegregated Church by entering First Baptist along with "a 17-year old Negro youth and an unidentified white woman." Although refused admittance, the three found their way into the building through an unguarded entrance. Church members reenacted March's spectacle of exclusion when they seized the intruders and dragged them down the church steps. Although the incident was observed by two uniformed policemen, no arrests were made.[16]

That evening Jones returned to First Baptist with another racially mixed group. Despite their access to the building being blocked by wary church members, the visitors once again were able to locate an unguarded entrance. After once again being forcibly ejected from the sanctuary, Jones sat down on the church steps where, according to court testimony, he obstructed the entrance. Rev. McLain then summoned police to have the clergyman removed from church property. At his arraignment before Superior Court Judge Durwood T. Pye, the arresting officer claimed Jones bit and scratched him and "laid down in the floor and started kicking, screaming and hollering." Representing himself at the initial hearing, Jones was charged with contempt after implying that he was being "railroaded in a kangaroo court." Judge Pye ordered him held without bond on charges of "disorderly conduct—disturbing public worship" and "disorderly conduct—demented."[17]

When the case came to trial in August, a pastor, a deacon, and two congregants from First Baptist testified for the prosecution, as did the arresting officers. Witnesses claimed that Jones had called out to those entering the sanctuary, "Step right in, folks: worship a segregated God in a segregated church!" and had "screamed and raved about the evils of segregation." For his part, Jones testified that a member of the church's "hospitality committee" had dragged him down the church steps by the feet and that he had not resisted arrest. Jones's legal team, which included lawyers from the NAACP Defense and Education Fund, filed a motion to disqualify Judge Pye for "repeated denunciation of the Negro race." Nevertheless, on August 28 the defendant was convicted of disrupting a religious service and received the maximum sentence for a misdemeanor in Georgia—a $1,000 fine and eighteen months in prison, six at hard labor. Jones's appeal bond was set at $20,000 (later reduced to $5,000 by the Georgia Supreme Court). In pronouncing sentence, Judge Pye declared that "men have died on a thousand fields of battle for [the] precious right . . . to worship a segregated God in a segregated church if they please."[18]

While he languished in prison and suffered mistreatment at the hands of guards and other prisoners, Jones's cause was taken up by a number of church and civil rights organizations. *The Christian Century* printed a sympathetic story, the National Council of Churches formed an Ashton Jones Defense Committee, and the United Church of Christ offered to post Jones's bail (Judge Pye refused the offer). Appeals were made to Georgia Governor Carl Sanders, who received over 5,000 letters in support of Jones, and a U.S. senator from California requested that the Department of Justice investigate the case. Philosopher Bertrand Russell, who had previously drawn attention to Jones's multiple arrests, called the clergyman's treatment in Georgia "appalling and barbaric."[19]

Embarrassed by weeks of interracial picketing in front of the church, in December First Baptist rescinded its policy of segregating worshippers and Rev. McLain appealed for Jones's release. In a sermon, the pastor noted that even though Jones and the other visitors had not come to worship, "if our doors had been open [in June] there would have been no pickets." When the *Atlanta Constitution* published an appeal from Jones's wife and a favorable editorial, the combative clergyman's bail was posted by a local white woman with no connection to the case. "As a decent Atlanta citizen," she explained, "I'm just ashamed of all the publicity we're getting." A few weeks later, in a subdued and long-delayed spectacle of embrace, Jones and a few black companions entered First Baptist's main sanctuary without incident.[20]

Jones was released on bond in March 1964 after serving 188 days behind bars; yet the case against him for disorderly conduct was still pending. A year later, after the U.S. Supreme Court upheld Judge Pye's decision in the case, Jones was called back to Atlanta for sentencing. In the meantime, however, he and Martin Luther King, Jr. had met with First Baptist's McLain, who personally apologized to Jones, explained that his congregation had voted to end its policy of segregation, and offered to help him in any way he could. McLain upheld his promise in April 1965 when he testified before the Georgia Pardons and Paroles Board against sending Jones back to jail. Jones had served fifty-eight days of an 18-month sentence when the parole board granted him executive clemency on May 25, 1965. This was the first time a jailed civil rights worker had received clemency in Georgia.[21]

As leader of a nonviolent campaign to desegregate a prominent church, Ashton Jones was quite atypical. He stood out not only as a white man of retirement age, but as a veteran of a thirty-year national campaign to advance "equality for Negroes" that had taken him across the country in a series of "world brotherhood cars" bearing the image of black and white hands clasped in handshake. In the midst of this lonely crusade the itinerant preacher had been kidnapped and beaten, shot at and nearly lynched. Many Atlantans could not imagine a sane white person risking life and limb to protest segregation. Jones's history of flamboyant protests made it that much easier for his opponents in Georgia to portray him as religiously marginal and mentally unstable.[22]

Birmingham, 1963

In the spring of 1963 Birmingham became the site of a massive campaign of nonviolent direct action orchestrated by local leaders and the SCLC. In addition to sit-ins and mass demonstrations, the Birmingham campaign featured coordinated visits to white churches. Originally planned for Palm Sunday, the visits were postponed until Easter—"the holiest day of the Christian church," protest leader Wyatt Tee Walker reminded the press. On Easter Sunday (April 14), as Martin Luther King, Jr. languished in the Birmingham City Jail for parading without a permit, well-dressed church visitors ("the men in dark suits, the women in bright dresses and fancy Easter bonnets") met to pray and receive their assignments and instructions. Walker prayed that all would be blessed, "whether or not these white Christian churches admit your children." At least nine churches were visited by interracial groups that morning, including First Christian, where two black women were admitted, and Sixth Avenue Presbyterian, where three black teenagers who "walked up the white stone steps in brilliant sunlight" were met with the Easter message that "this church was built by white people and white people worship here."[23]

Among the targeted congregations were two prominent downtown churches— First Baptist and First Presbyterian—for whose senior pastors the Easter kneel-ins would have career-altering consequences. Earl Stallings had arrived at First Baptist Church just over a year earlier with a vision for reversing the proud church's decline. As historian Jonathan Bass observes, up until that fateful Easter Sunday "everything seemed to be going well." Less than an hour before the church's main service was to begin, however, Stallings received word that First Baptist would have black visitors that morning. When King aide Andrew Young and two college-aged black women arrived, an usher directed them to a reserved pew near the back of the sanctuary. Seventy worshippers left in protest; but the black visitors remained, placing money in the collection plate and joining the congregation in singing "Jesus Christ Is Risen Today." Following the service, Stallings warmly greeted Young and his female colleagues and accepted a letter explaining that they had come to worship in a house of prayer "for all people."[24]

As in Albany, reporters expressed disappointment that First Baptist's surprise visitors had precipitated no controversy. But they need only have waited. When a photograph of Stallings greeting one of the black women was picked up by several papers, including the *New York Times*, a firestorm ensued. Young, the *Times* reported, had "attempted to shake hands with the usher at the door and give him an envelope with the contribution. Both gestures were ignored." But above the story was an image of a gesture that could not be ignored—Stallings's hand clasp with a black woman on the steps of Birmingham's First Baptist Church. Stallings's decision to welcome black worshippers was commended by Martin Luther King in his letter from Birmingham Jail and brought messages of encouragement from friends, fellow pastors, and foreign missionaries. But it outraged segregationists inside and outside the congregation. "Confused Kennedy Baptist" was the kindest epithet directed at Stallings by co-religionists whom the photograph had offended. Members of one of First Baptist's adult Sunday School classes opined that since the visitors had come to advance the aims of an organization rather than to worship, the most Christ-like response would have been to drive them out as Jesus had driven the money-changers from the temple.[25]

The following Sunday, April 21, black worshippers were quietly admitted at four white Birmingham churches, while others were turned away by at least five, including two Baptist churches. Sixth Avenue Presbyterian, which had successfully repelled black guests on Easter Sunday, embraced three visitors who were "welcomed with a handshake at the door" and seated at the front of the church. But when a group of African Americans were ushered into First Baptist, segregationists in the congregation were moved to action. At a meeting to reconsider the church's open-door policy, in effect since 1954, Stallings argued that the central issue was not visitors' motives but whether or not the congregation would "do the Christian thing." After a motion to affirm the church's policy of admitting all to worship passed 16–10 and was subsequently endorsed by the congregation 182–136, Stallings began receiving threatening letters and harassing phone calls.[26]

In a sermon titled "Pilate's Wash Bowl," Stallings likened himself and his parishioners to the Roman governor who expediently turned Jesus over for crucifixion. Pilate "wanted nothing to upset his little kingdom," Stallings noted, and then asked, "are we any different? Ah, Pilate, we condemn you because your position, your security, meant more to you than truth. But, are we any better?" Apparently they were not. By the fall of 1963, well-organized racial hard-liners within the church were holding secret meetings, circulating a petition to rescind the church's open-door policy, and setting members of Stallings's staff against him. "The last citadel of segregation was their church," Bass notes, "and they determined never to see that tradition end." Stallings endured the emotional strain of ministering at First Baptist for two years before leaving in 1965 to accept a call in Marietta, Georgia. In 1970, Birmingham's First Baptist Church split in the midst of ongoing racial strife.[27]

Nearby First Presbyterian Church was also called on by black would-be worshippers on Easter Sunday, 1963. During the opening hymn, two black women were escorted down the center aisle to seats near the front of the sanctuary. Although a few congregants left the church in protest, others "most cordially" greeted the women, who were invited by Rev. Edward Ramage to come again. Ramage had been the senior minister at First Presbyterian since 1946; but his longevity at the church made him no safer from attack than Earl Stallings. "Almost immediately," Bass writes, "Ramage began receiving death threats."[28]

A committee of laypersons at First Presbyterian vowed to "get rid of the Communists," including Rev. Ramage. When the pastor told his session that the church's doors should be open to all and noted that church unity should not come at the price of Christian principles, an elder responded, "To hell with Christian principles—we've got to save the church!" Ramage had hoped to retire at First Presbyterian, but it became clear in the months following the kneel-ins that the congregation might suffer a split unless he moved on. In the fall of 1963 he accepted a call to Houston and suffered a heart attack soon after his arrival there.[29]

Jackson, 1963

Church kneel-ins in Jackson, Mississippi, were distinctive in several respects, including that they occurred over two and a half years and were orchestrated by a white minister. Rev. Edwin King was a native of Vicksburg, Mississippi, who had joined an interracial fellowship while attending Methodist-related Millsaps College during the 1950s. King later pursued graduate work in theology at Boston University, "a hotbed of social gospel teaching" where he was exposed to the thought of Paul Tillich, Reinhold Niebuhr, and Howard Thurman, as well as Christian pacifism and the religious imperative for racial reconciliation. In March 1960, King returned to the Deep South to work as a pastoral liaison between activists and white church people in Montgomery, Alabama. After he was convicted of disorderly conduct in Alabama, King's parents left Mississippi under the burden of responsibility for raising a "communist sympathizer and champion of black revolutionary activity."[30]

King returned to Mississippi in January 1963 to assume the chaplaincy at Tougaloo College, a Methodist-related historically black institution in Jackson. Having noted the "subversive and symbolic possibilities" of kneel-ins in Birmingham, King intended to make church visits an integral part of his ministry. He was not the only Methodist pastor in Mississippi who believed the churches should exemplify God's reconciling love. But as a college chaplain King enjoyed "freedom of the pulpit" to an extent his colleagues could only dream of. The same month King began his chaplaincy at Tougaloo, twenty-eight white Methodist pastors, all Mississippi natives, signed a statement titled "Born of Conviction" in which they affirmed that "Our Lord Jesus Christ . . . permits no discrimination because of race, color, or creed." Despite stressing their "unflinching opposition to Communism," within a year over half the signees had left the state under duress.[31]

It was in this environment of strict religious conformity that in May 1963 King donned clerical garb and conducted a biracial pray-in on the steps of Jackson's downtown post office. In June, just days before NAACP field secretary Medgar Evers was murdered, King organized the city's first church visits. Over the next two Sundays, black and white students in mixed groups were refused admittance at First Baptist, Capitol Street Methodist, Central Presbyterian, and First Christian, while others were welcomed at St. Peter's Catholic and St. Andrew's Episcopal. First Baptist, whose pastor, Douglas Hudgins, had turned down King's request for a meeting, adopted a resolution lamenting "the present social unrest brought about by agitators who would drive a wedge of hate and distrust between white and colored friends."[32]

Anne Moody, a Tougaloo student who participated in the Jackson kneel-ins, recalls that the churches were prepared "with armed policemen, paddy wagons and dogs—which would be used in case we refused to leave after 'ushers' had read us the prepared resolutions." Yet, as in other locales, these visits precipitated conflict inside as well as outside targeted churches. After black students were turned away from Galloway United Methodist on June 9, senior minister W. B. Selah declared that he could not "judge the motives of people who come to worship in this church. Only God can do that." The beloved pastor, who had led Galloway for nearly two decades, announced that he would ask the bishop for another appointment. Selah told his congregation, which included Jackson's mayor and officials of the White Citizens Council, that he knew "in conscience there can be no color bar in a Christian church."[33]

The Jackson kneel-ins resumed on July 21 when ushers at five white churches—including Trinity Lutheran and West Capitol Street Church of Christ—turned away racially mixed groups attending a conference at Tougaloo sponsored by the World Council of Churches. The same Sunday, an usher at Galloway informed Ed King that "this is a Christian church and we intend to keep it that way. We will not admit Negroes." By that fall, arrests at Jackson churches became routine. The first to be taken into custody were Bettye Poole, Ida Hannah, and Julie Zaugg—two black Southerners and a white Northerner— who, in a striking spectacle of exclusion, were turned away from Capitol Street Methodist on Worldwide Communion Sunday. After engaging church ushers in conversation, the three women were apprehended and charged with disturbing a worship service and refusing to leave private property. Even after being convicted and receiving one-year prison sentences and $1,000 fines, however, they returned to Capitol Street the following Sunday and were arrested along with nine companions, including four Methodist ministers. Before any of the cases could go to trial, a federal appeals court intervened and ordered a district judge to remove the accused from state custody.[34]

W. B. Selah's replacement at Galloway Methodist was W. J. Cunningham, a native Mississippian who assumed the task of conciliation within the historic congregation. Cunningham sought to ease Galloway into recognizing what he called the "Great Absolute—the indubitable fact that the doors [of the church] must be opened in accord with Methodist law." But his best intentions would be crushed between the righteous zeal of Ed King and the intransigence of Galloway's lay leaders. Cunningham later acknowledged that, despite several decades of ministerial experience, he had come to Galloway full of naivety about the power of racial conflict to "sever cherished friendships."[35]

Soon after arriving in Jackson, Cunningham learned that Galloway's Official Board had not only resolved to keep blacks out of the sanctuary, but had devised a rotational system for guarding the church doors on Sunday mornings. Side and back entrances were locked so that "the Color Guard," as the ushers were known, could control access to the building. In addition to these self-appointed gatekeepers, unwelcome visitors were met by a paddy wagon and a uniformed policeman wielding a billy club. Yet none of this deterred Ed King and his accomplices. In the fall of 1963, when startled ushers at Galloway formed a human barricade at the chapel entrance to repel King and a carload of Tougaloo students, the would-be visitors leaned over the men's outstretched arms and banged their fists on locked doors.[36]

Because it was the largest Methodist congregation in Mississippi, Galloway's determination to repel black visitors made it a target for those who felt called to condemn racial exclusion in the church. Often Cunningham would meet these persons on Saturday afternoon when they came to discuss the church's closed-door policy, and encounter them again the following afternoon when he visited the city jail to ask for their release. These sojourners from New York and Chicago wished only to enter the church for worship or, if excluded, render silent protest. Inevitably, however, they were arrested, whether or not church officials lodged a complaint.

In November 1963, the arrest of Methodist clergy outside Galloway led the denomination's Council of Bishops to adopt a resolution calling the detention of persons attempting to worship at Methodist churches an "outrage." While the "hit-and-run" visits that precipitated the resolution only sealed the doors at Galloway more tightly, they publicized the determination of Jackson's black community to achieve justice as well as the inability of local whites to grasp the problem: "I have Nigras working for me. We have real affection for Nigras. We love our Nigras and they wouldn't be demonstrating if communists and northern agitators would leave them alone" were some of the comments reported by visiting Methodist clergy. The detention of Yankee interlopers continued in December, when four New York-area Methodist ministers were arrested at Capitol Street and Galloway.[37]

On Palm Sunday, 1964, five members of an integrated group slipped undetected into Galloway Methodist through a side entrance. As ushers tried quietly to escort them out of the building, one of the group announced that she was a native of India and offered to produce her passport. In a report submitted to the Indian Embassy in Washington, the interim professor at Tougaloo claimed that "two tall men . . . came running and one of them took hold of my arms and started abruptly pushing me outside. I was infuriated, stunned, shocked, and rudely awakened to the brutalities of these people," she wrote. Such events made Galloway notorious in Methodist circles, including foreign mission fields. In

1964, the church received a letter from a Methodist missionary in Hiroshima, Japan, decrying its "denial of our universal fellowship in Christ."[38]

On Easter Sunday, while seven northern seminary professors were arrested attempting to enter Capitol Street alongside local blacks, two Methodist bishops—one black and one white—appeared at Galloway dressed in clerical garb. Despite Cunningham's protestations, the prelates were turned away and referred to a black Methodist church. In an open letter to the congregation, the bishops had written that "if we are not admitted we shall feel no ill-will toward those who may feel compelled to turn us away.... [but we shall] wonder at those who presume to speak and act for God in turning worshippers away from *His* house." The Easter incident did not break the color line at Galloway, although it did heighten internal resentment toward Cunningham and the denomination.[39]

Controversy at Galloway erupted again in October 1965 when a visiting Methodist bishop from California requested that his preaching services be open to black clergymen and their wives. Church leaders agreed to temporarily suspend Galloway's closed-door policy, but this decision did not sit well with many parishioners. Anonymous circulars began to appear throughout the city claiming that the California bishop had sponsored a reception for a "known communist" at the home of Sammy Davis, Jr. When one of the preaching services brought a racially mixed group of young people to the church, the doors were immediately closed to African Americans. According to the *Christian Century*, a black woman who came to hear one of the bishop's sermons was informed that those who had "crashed" the previous evening's service made it impossible for her to enter. In response to an usher's declaration that the church admitted only "Christian Methodists," the woman recited a litany of her service on national church boards.[40]

By Easter 1964, Cunningham writes in his memoir, "the mental and emotional stress of my ministry ... had become almost unbearable" and he knew it was time for him to move on. But before he resigned in late 1965 under pressure from the church's Pastoral Relations Committee, Cunningham would see a large part of the congregation depart. In June 1965, many of Galloway's leading members met to withdraw from the Methodist Church and establish a new denomination. Galloway would not witness a spectacle of embrace until early 1966, when twenty-two young blacks entered the church on a Sunday morning and were seated throughout the sanctuary.

Cunningham's memoir of this period in the history of Galloway Methodist Church, appropriately titled *Agony at Galloway*, opens a unique window on the struggles of a pastor charged with leading a congregation that is deeply resistant to racial change in a denomination that has embraced it. In particular, Cunningham's account illuminates the institutional and personal traumas that extended church kneel-in campaigns could inflict on church communities and their leaders.[41]

St. Augustine, 1964

Like other cities that became sites of direct action campaigns, St. Augustine, Florida, saw its share of church kneel-ins. The movement in St. Augustine commenced in the summer of 1963 with street protests and sit-ins and by September the city was playing host to mass civil rights demonstrations and Klan rallies. In March 1964 Martin Luther King, Jr. came to St. Augustine, where he was joined by prominent white Northerners, including Mary Peabody, Esther Burgess, and Hester Campbell. All three were married to Episcopal bishops and Peabody was the mother of the governor of Massachusetts. When the women were arrested on March 31 for dining at a local restaurant in a racially mixed group, the St. Augustine movement appeared on the nation's radar screen.[42]

Before their arrest the women had been involved in St. Augustine's fledgling kneel-in campaign. On Easter Sunday, March 29, several mixed groups attempted to enter white churches in the city. All were turned away. Two days later, a few hours before they were arrested for biracial dining, Peabody and Campbell accompanied a group of African Americans to Trinity Episcopal Church for a communion service. Church leaders had been tipped off to the biracial group's visit, however, and they found the doors locked and the sheriff standing guard alongside the church's rector. Rev. Charles Seymour explained that the church vestry had been forced to cancel the service for fear of a disturbance after determining that seventy-three-year-old Mary Peabody's attendance would constitute a "demonstration."[43]

Further attempts to integrate Trinity followed, with ushers claiming that members of visiting biracial groups were *ipso facto* demonstrators and could not be admitted. On April 5, Bishop Hamilton West intervened, instructing churches in his diocese to admit all persons presenting themselves for worship, and a week later five black Episcopalians worshipped at Trinity in a move orchestrated by the parish's clergy. Members of the vestry responded with a resolution "deploring the participation of Church Officials and laity in any activities, [or] demonstrations . . . which [violate] or willfully ignore the law, or which [disregard] the property rights of others, or make a mockery of the Church by using it as a tool." Then in May, the church's governing body voted 9–3 to withhold funds pledged to the diocese until it withdrew support from the National Council of Churches, which was assisting King and the SCLC in St. Augustine.[44]

On June 14, Trinity was approached by a racially mixed group accompanied by newsmen and television cameras. When a visiting black cleric pointed out a sign that read "The Episcopal Church Welcomes You," he was informed that the message did not apply to black people, who could worship at the local "Negro" Episcopal church. In a dramatic incident symbolizing the congregation's internal divisions, vestrymen blocked the church entrance as Seymour and his assistant rector prepared to escort the visitors into the sanctuary. An incensed vestryman refused to move out of the group's path and threw a stack of bulletins to the floor before storming away. After the service, local youths who had gathered outside the church yelled "nigger lover" at a priest accompanying the group.[45]

On June 23, the Trinity vestry voted 9–1 to seek their rector's resignation. When Seymour refused to quit, the vestry asked Bishop West to remove him on the basis of "irreconcilable differences." West responded by voicing his complete support of Seymour, rebuking those who had locked out, turned away, and otherwise abused church visitors, and threatening the recalcitrant vestrymen with suspension or excommunication. In the wake of a failed motion to take the parish out of the Episcopal Church, three vestrymen resigned, one of them complaining that he was being forced to decide between being an American and being an Episcopalian. With his bishop's support, Seymour had prevailed over Trinity's vestry. But the congregation was too divided for him to exercise effective pastoral leadership, and by summer's end he accepted a transfer out of the state.[46]

As the drama over integration raged at Trinity Episcopal, St. Augustine's Methodist churches became sites for multiple spectacles of exclusion and embrace. After turning black visitors away on Easter Sunday 1964 (March 29), Grace Methodist welcomed eight African Americans to its sanctuary the following week. Pastor John Gill said things "went right smoothly," despite reports that ushers had "slammed a door in the faces of the integrationists." Apparently there was no consensus at Grace Methodist on how to respond to kneel-ins, for on May 31 another group of black visitors was turned away at the church doors. An exasperated church member told would-be worshippers that "we just want to be left alone in peace."[47]

The same Sunday, mixed groups were turned away at several other white churches, including First Methodist, where seven visitors (all black but one) were arrested and charged with trespass with malicious intent, breach of the peace, and conspiracy. On June 28, one white person and four blacks were again barred from entering First Methodist. Although St. Augustine police were summoned when the unwelcome visitors refused to leave, officers were reluctant to make arrests when they found members of the biracial group kneeling in prayer. Two ministers at First Methodist, along with the pastor of Flagler Memorial Presbyterian Church, eventually lost their congregations for supporting church desegregation in St. Augustine.[48]

The St. Augustine church campaign lasted for over a year and involved at least five churches representing four denominations. Yet it could hardly be called a success. On April 22, 1965—over a year after the initial attempt to integrate worship at Trinity Episcopal—black teenagers were refused admission to

Grace Methodist and Ancient City Baptist churches. In fact, visiting a white church in St. Augustine could be dangerous even when its doors were known to be open. After worshipping at Trinity one Sunday, a group of black young people were pelted with eggs thrown by white teenagers.[49]

Selma, 1965

As in Savannah and St. Augustine, in Selma, Alabama, an Episcopal congregation became the focus of attempts to cross the color line on Sunday mornings. As the Selma voting rights campaign unfolded, progressive Episcopalians used the media spotlight trained on the city to illumine the problem of church segregation. Their target was St. Paul's, a wealthy and influential congregation housed in a beautiful Gothic Revival building and led by a group of staunch segregationists that included Rector T. Frank Mathews. During the week of March 7, 1965, in the aftermath of the abortive Selma-to-Montgomery march known as "Bloody Sunday," over five hundred Episcopalians from around the nation converged on the small Alabama city. Two weekday attempts to enter St. Paul's *en masse* were averted. Then, on Sunday, March 14, a group of visitors whose entrance to the church had been blocked by ushers knelt on the steps for corporate prayer.

When Bishop Charles Carpenter was informed of plans to conduct an interracial service at St. Paul's the following Saturday, he refused to grant permission and had the church doors locked. Nevertheless, on the appointed day a group of nearly two hundred Episcopal clergy set out for St. Paul's from Brown Chapel AME Church, staging point for the Selma-to-Montgomery marches. After being turned away by police, the group returned to Brown Chapel, where they celebrated the Eucharist on the sidewalk. Feeling pressure from national church representatives, Carpenter and Matthews prevailed upon the St. Paul's vestry to honor denominational policy and welcome blacks to worship. On March 28, sixteen black and white visitors, most of them Episcopal clergymen, were seated in the church's front row as Mathews preached a sermon on reconciliation. One visitor called the integrated service "the first breakthrough in Selma not induced by a court order."[50]

The *New York Times* covered the interracial worship service at St. Paul's in a front-page article. But it soon became clear that many parishioners viewed the integrated gathering as a one-time affair. On Palm Sunday (April 11), members of a racially mixed group that included two white seminarians and a half-dozen local blacks were stopped from entering St. Paul's for 7:30 a.m. worship. When police arrived, Mathews took the ushers aside to negotiate a compromise: The visitors would be allowed to enter the sanctuary, but they would sit in the back row and receive communion after the other parishioners. Almost no one was satisfied by the arrangement, which was repeated Easter Sunday.

Interracial visits to St. Paul's resumed on August 1 when a white seminarian named Jonathan Daniels accompanied a black woman to the 11 a.m. service. Shock reverberated through the congregation, in part because this was the first time an African American had dared to attend the main service of Holy Communion at St. Paul's. Mathews complained to diocesan leaders that the visit had precipitated a "crisis situation" in the parish. But the crisis was soon overshadowed by the tragedy of Daniels's murder in Hayneville, Alabama. In October, the woman who had visited St. Paul's with Daniels three months earlier returned alone to the church, accompanied by "a hushed suspension of worship."[51]

Montgomery, 1965

As in Selma, church-based protest came rather late to Montgomery. When it finally arrived, a main target was Trinity Presbyterian, which was the largest Southern Presbyterian congregation in Alabama and for years had been "in the eye of the storm" over race in that denomination.[52]

In a June 1957 letter to the PCUS Board of Christian Education, Trinity's session issued a strong protest against the presence of "racial and other liberal issues" in church literature. The church's ruling elders saw no reason why "this question of race relations should continually be injected into our literature and programs and presented in such a manner as to give only one side of the question." In 1962, the church once again complained of "liberalism" in PCUS-sponsored educational literature and asked that publication of the *Layman's Bible Commentary* be suspended. And when the 1964 General Assembly directed East Alabama Presbytery to incorporate local black churches, there was overwhelming opposition at Trinity, whose session claimed to oppose ecclesiastical desegregation on constitutional grounds.[53]

In late March 1965, a few days after battered civil rights marchers arrived in the Alabama capitol, Trinity's session determined that the church's deacons should urge visiting African Americans to find another place of worship, although if they refused, deacons were to let them "sit in the rear of the sanctuary and join the church service." While the statement implied that Trinity's doors would be open to insistent blacks, there seems to have been tacit agreement within the church that visitors of color could be barred if deacons determined they were "demonstrators." This is precisely what happened less than a week later on April 4, when Trinity's policy was tested by six black students who sought entry to Sunday worship. In a sermon, senior minister Robert Strong described the visitors' reception:[54]

They were met by a few of our officers at the church steps. Our spokesman could not have been better chosen; he was Deacon Winton Blount. Mr. Blount explained to the young people that they had arrived so late for the service that they could not help disturb it if they went in. He said that this late arrival made it all the more obvious that their intention in coming to Trinity Church was not really to worship. He explained the policy of the church that our officers were not willing to permit it to become an arena for sociological causes. The young people turned away.[55]

The same Sunday a mixed group participated in a communion service at Memorial Presbyterian Church, while another was turned away at St. James Methodist. On April 11, Palm Sunday, Memorial Presbyterian, St. John's Episcopal, First Methodist, and Dexter Avenue Methodist admitted black visitors, as First Presbyterian, St. James Methodist, and Frazer Memorial Methodist refused them.[56]

Repeated attempts to desegregate Montgomery churches necessitated a biblical response, and Trinity's Strong obliged in a Palm Sunday sermon titled "Holy Week and the Civil Rights Demonstrations at the Churches," which considered "contemporary happenings . . . in light of what our Lord did on the Monday before He suffered for us on the cross." Before casting the Montgomery church visits in the light of Jesus's final days, Strong waxed autobiographical. He claimed that as a transplanted Northerner whose ancestors had fought for the Union in the Civil War, he could fairly "claim to have no prejudice based on skin color."[57]

Nevertheless, Strong said, he recognized the "great resentment in the hearts of southern citizens" caused by Reconstruction, the unique racial demographics of the South, and "the enormous gap" existing between the white Southern population and "most of our southern Negroes"—a gap with cultural, moral, educational, psychological, and hygienic dimensions. Strong congratulated his parishioners for their "enlightened" attitude on race issues (evidenced in their willingness to take on a "heavy portion of blame" for neglecting black education and allowing discrimination in voting laws) and their disapproval of the sort of violence that had been on display in Selma and Birmingham. Strong went on to claim that at Trinity there had never been "the slightest sense of tension about Negroes" until the U.S. Supreme Court decision in Brown, and asserted that "to this day there is no real opposition to their presence in our church" at weddings and funerals. Indeed, they would be welcome at worship, Strong said, "if it were genuinely the case that their motive in coming was a desire to seek the Lord."[58]

Given the fact, recently clarified by the PCUS General Assembly, that churches could not exclude persons from worship on the basis of race, Strong had to ask whether Trinity's policy put it "in a position of rebellion" that is "unchristian." To this he replied that civil rights demonstrators constitute "a separate case" to which the denomination's constitution did not apply. This was a view shared by the church's ruling elders, who two days after the initial visit by black students had declared that

> sociological demonstrators are not sincere in their protestation that they have come to worship and . . . therefore they are not welcome at Trinity Church. The session is not willing to see this church sanctuary or church plant made an area of sociological demonstrations or an outsider's means to the end of furthering merely social causes.[59]

Elaborating this position, Strong averred that those approaching the sanctuary "as groups of Negroes or as mixed groups of Negroes and whites are in fact [he might well have said "by definition"] sociological demonstrators."[60]

Given such unspiritual motives, Strong declared, the church's decision to bar black visitors and their white colleagues was perfectly Christ-like:

> Twice in his ministry our Lord Jesus Christ entered the temple of God and saw it defiled . . . The second time he did this was on the Monday of Holy Week. You see how I came to give the particular title it bears to this address. When our Lord drove the profaners of the temple away, he quoted the prophet Isaiah from the 56th chapter saying, "Is it not written, for my house shall be called of all nations a house of prayer? But ye have made it a den of thieves." That verse in the Gospel of Mark is often used out of context, as though our Lord said, "My house shall be made a house of prayer *for all people.*" That is bad interpretation. What our Lord said was, "My house shall be for all people a *house of prayer.*" His emphasis was on the sacredness of the precincts of worship, that the temple is a place for prayer and not for money-making.[61]

According to Strong, proper interpretation of this passage revealed that "the motive of sincerity enters into the proper approach to God's house," whether it is the Temple in Jerusalem or a church sanctuary in Montgomery. Thus, on the basis of a "Scriptural application of the Holy Week incident in the temple, the officers of the Church judge that it is proper to say to sociological demonstrators, 'You are not welcome.'" This was clever, if nefarious, exegesis, for it allowed the church to claim that it "respected [blacks] as persons and accorded their proper dignity," while perpetually barring them from worship.

Strong concluded his sermon by referring to conversations he had carried on during the week with demonstrators and members of the media. In an effort to establish their lack of sincerity, Strong said, he had questioned black young people (whom he claimed were "obviously playing hookey from school") about their knowledge of Presbyterian doctrine. In discussion with a representative of the SCLC, Strong went on, he had impugned Martin Luther King, Jr. as a "religious hypocrite" who was "using the churches in the interest of a sociological movement," a charge he illumined by referring to Acts 5. According to Strong, God's decision to strike down Ananias and Sapphira for withholding some of the proceeds from land they had sold "shows what God thinks of hypocrisy."[62]

Although it was communicated with some eloquence by Strong, Trinity's rationale for Christian exclusion could sound contrived and contradictory when articulated by those entrusted with implementing church policy. According to a report in the *Presbyterian Outlook*, a racially mixed group of five Presbyterian elders and clergymen sought to enter Trinity on June 20, 1965. A church deacon they engaged in conversation was forced to admit that, while the visitors clearly intended to worship rather than to demonstrate, allowing them into the sanctuary "would disrupt the congregation at worship and split the church." When asked whether a traveling African American unfamiliar with the situation in Montgomery would be admitted to Trinity, the deacon responded that "it would be impossible to see how anyone could be unaware of the situation; he would be a demonstrator and not admitted."[63]

The question was not hypothetical, for that very Sunday church representatives barred a black visitor who was not affiliated with the group seeking entry to Trinity. Enoch Fears, an airman stationed at Craig A.F.B. in Selma, had come to Trinity to hear guest preacher Leighton Ford, an associate of Billy Graham. (Ford was part of the Graham crusade team preparing to launch Montgomery's first interracial evangelistic effort, a crusade Strong would co-chair.) In a letter published in the *Outlook*, Fears related how carelessly the motives of would-be worshippers were assessed at Trinity. "When I came within a few feet of the church," he wrote, "I was approached by a church officer and was directed to join a racially mixed group of Presbyterian ministers and members who were being told that they could not be admitted to the church because the pastor was afraid that our presence would create a chaotic situation." Fears's letter ended starkly: "I am not a member of any church. I am enroute to Vietnam." The *Outlook* drew the obvious conclusion: "A testing of motives of churchgoers is beyond the province of men."[64]

Such incidents gave the lie to claims that the exclusion of blacks from church sanctuaries was a response to their insincere motives. Despite Strong's nimble biblical interpretation, the circulation of his sermon by the tens of thousands, and the confident stand of Trinity's session, it soon became clear that the church was rationalizing its own "sociological" resistance to integration. The Synod of Alabama concluded as much when it condemned Trinity for turning away

Southern Presbyterian deacons, elders, pastors, and denominational officers in mixed groups.[65]

1966 and After

Although very few churches underwent genuine integration during the first half of the 1960s, kneel-ins became much less frequent after 1965. When they did occur, however, they typically received a good deal of news coverage. In the spring of 1966, as Methodist churches in Montgomery were once again being targeted by racially mixed groups, the print and visual media captured repeated spectacles of exclusion as local churches turned away the would-be worshippers. Then on Easter Sunday, with television cameras rolling, Rev. Charles Prestwood led a public spectacle of embrace when he welcomed a large group of African Americans to morning worship at Montgomery's Whitfield Memorial Methodist Church.[66]

In what would be the final kneel-in event of the decade, just before Christmas 1969 two black students from Morris College in Sumter, South Carolina, were refused entrance to that city's First Presbyterian Church. The students were turned away again in January, although this time they tried to push past the men who blocked their entrance. A shoving incident ensued, police were called, and the students were arrested and charged with disorderly conduct. One elder said he believed the students, "neatly dressed and carrying Bibles," might have come to demand reparations or read the Black Manifesto. Several weeks later, in a spectacle that symbolized changing attitudes at the church, the students were admitted without incident, greeted by ushers and escorted to the front of the sanctuary.[67]

Although each kneel-in protest was unique, as efforts at church desegregation spread across the South there emerged a general pattern of action and response. As we shall see in the following chapter, the Memphis kneel-ins of 1964–65 reflected many aspects of this general pattern, while remaining distinctive in important respects.

PART TWO

CONTEXTS OF A KNEEL-IN MOVEMENT

‖ 3 ‖

"This Spectacle of a Church with Guarded Doors"

The Memphis Campaign of 1964

The story of the kneel-in campaign at Memphis's Second Presbyterian Church begins in 1963, when Memphis NAACP Executive Secretary Maxine Smith met with representatives of Owen College, LeMoyne College, and Memphis State University to discuss establishing a citywide intercollegiate chapter of the organization. A meeting at LeMoyne in March was attended by thirty students and faculty advisors from the organizing institutions, along with student representatives from Southwestern, Memphis's all-white Presbyterian college. At first the NAACP's intercollegiate chapter met irregularly and, to Smith's surprise, attracted more white students than black. As a way of broadening involvement and sharpening focus, the group formed committees on Non-Violence, Voter Registration, and Publicity, each meeting weekly and reporting to the larger body.[1]

In the early months of 1964, the intercollegiate NAACP chapter's Non-Violent Committee, chaired by Southwestern senior Howard Romaine, launched a campaign of church testings. Group members paired up to visit white and black congregations and were welcomed (if not embraced) at a number of downtown and midtown churches. No incidents were reported, although at some churches the visits exposed internal divisions. At Idlewild Presbyterian, for instance, visiting students were seated but their appearance precipitated an emergency meeting of the church's elders and deacons. The officers' discussion concerned not whether racially mixed groups should be admitted to worship, but whether they should be seated in a special section of the sanctuary. After much debate, it was decided that all guests presenting themselves peaceably would be seated without regard to race.[2]

The most fateful of these NAACP-sanctioned church visits would occur on March 22, when Joe Purdy (a black student at Memphis State University) and Jim Bullock (a white Southwesterner) attempted to worship at Second Presbyterian Church (SPC) in suburban East Memphis. Fearing that the congregation might be targeted for interracial visits, the SPC session had arranged for several men to stand guard. As the students approached the church's main entrance, Purdy was asked if he was "African." When he answered, "No. I'm an American, but I'm black," Purdy and Bullock were told they could not enter the sanctuary.

Since they had decided they were willing to be arrested, the young men continued toward the church's entrance. Seeing their path blocked by men in suits and police approaching from the rear, they knelt to pray. When the police saw Purdy and Bullock assume a position of prayer, they stepped back and allowed them to leave the premises without incident. But while the young men were relieved to avoid arrest, they were also determined to return to SPC. They did so a week later—on Easter Sunday—with other members of the NAACP's intercollegiate group. While inside the church a special offering was taken up for "victims of disaster, destitution and hunger," the students "stood in a rainstorm and prayed for one hour while the officers of the church jeered at them."[3]

All told, racially mixed groups sought unsuccessfully to enter SPC for morning worship on eight consecutive Sunday mornings between March 22 and May 10, 1964. The weekly drama outside the church featured between five and forty well-dressed students hoping to enter the sanctuary, a line of churchmen stationed in front of the entrance to keep them out, members peering out from inside the church or entering through side doors, and the unwelcome visitors holding a "vigil" outside the church and praying whenever police approached. Meanwhile, curious onlookers gathered to take in the spectacle.

The Local Press Catches On

In early April the *Press-Scimitar*, Memphis's afternoon daily, began carrying brief reports of the weekly standoff in front of SPC. The April 4 edition announced that on three previous Sundays members of the NAACP intercollegiate chapter had been barred from SPC "by a phalanx of men accompanied by police officers." Several weeks later the paper noted that a group of "both white and negro men and women" had tried unsuccessfully to enter SPC for the sixth consecutive Sunday. These brief news blurbs, based on NAACP press releases, included no reporting from the church or comments from witnesses. They were buried in the newspaper's back pages alongside ads for fresh produce and hemorrhoid cream.[4]

The first substantive reporting on the church visits at SPC appeared in late April in Memphis's independent black weeklies, the *Memphis World* and *Tri-State Defender*. The *World's* April 25 issue described a racially mixed student group standing on a sidewalk outside the church entrance, "barred by Second Presbyterian officials who formed a human barricade on the steps." According to the paper, a motorcycle policeman reminded "the patient collegians" not to block the path of churchgoers while "special cops" roamed the church grounds. The *World* also noted the presence of spectators and slowly passing motorists. Citing "a very reliable source," the article stated that some in the church, including the senior pastor, favored opening the doors to the students.[5]

The same week's issue of the *Tri-State Defender* printed the fullest description yet of the protests. It described church officials standing "shoulder to shoulder at the entrance of the church" and "gun toting guards stationed at various points on the church grounds to keep the unwanted from entering." According to the paper, an elderly man whose connection to the church was unclear told those driving by: "You should have seen them last Sunday. Today they are back and have brought a 'coon' with them to take their picture." The article also noted the presence of a church photographer who "kept himself busy taking pictures of everyone in the [student] group."[6]

In their May 2 issues, both black weeklies published follow-up stories on the kneel-ins at SPC. In a front-page article, the *World* described a "human barricade of church officers" and noted that several students whom police had removed from church property "quickly returned to take their stand with the group." The lead article in the *Defender* was accompanied by four photographs, including one of Southwestern student Howard Romaine being forcibly removed from church property. The *Defender* reported that although the students had been "pushed around" the previous Sunday, they remained "just outside the front door despite threats of arrest." The article ended with an ominous description of a man photographing students "who wears dark glasses every week, despite the fact the sun has not shined during the time he is doing his work at the spot."[7]

These news articles in the *Memphis World* and *Tri-State Defender*, the first to be based on eyewitness reports from the church, emphasized the presence of NAACP adult leaders—Executive Secretary Maxine Smith, her husband Vice President Vasco Smith, and President Jesse H. Turner—and their interactions with church representatives. One article noted, for instance, that Vasco and Maxine Smith had insisted the church's hired guards "keep their hands off of her." But in focusing on these familiar black leaders, the papers gave the impression that the kneel-ins were being directed by the NAACP's adult officers. Another article identified Vasco Smith as the group's leader, despite quoting Smith himself to the effect that adults were only providing moral support to a movement conceived by members of the NAACP's inter-collegiate chapter.[8]

From the beginning, some SPC members believed that these visits to their church were no more than efforts to garner publicity. If so, they were a dismal failure, because for the first six weeks of the campaign the city's daily papers paid the kneel-ins no more than cursory attention. In the case of the *Press-Scimitar*, it is odd that the paper virtually ignored these kneel-ins at a prominent church located at a major city intersection when a few months earlier it had given front-page coverage—complete with photographs—to a protest occurring on the Southwestern campus.[9]

The *Commercial Appeal's* silence is even more curious, since Religion Editor Elinor Kelley had been reporting on the General Assembly of the Presbyterian Church in the United States (PCUS) since April 11. The meeting of the Church's highest court at the Montreat Conference Center in North Carolina had attracted more than the usual local interest because it was scheduled to be held the following year in Memphis—at SPC, in fact. Going into the Assembly, it appeared that the most divisive issues would be a proposal to ordain women as elders and ministers and an effort to force the denomination to withdraw from the National Council of Churches. From the first day of the week-long assembly, however, Kelley reported that a faction of delegates was pushing for a change of venue for the 1965 General Assembly based on accusations that the host church—SPC—was "forcibly segregated." Oddly, Kelley filed several reports on the ecclesiastical debate over whether to relocate the 1965 Assembly before the kneel-ins at the heart of the debate were acknowledged by her newspaper.[10]

Some of the protesting students interpreted the local papers' lack of attention to their kneel-ins during March and April 1964 as evidence of a news "blackout," perhaps the result of pressure applied by SPC representatives. But while it is true that the church's session sought to limit the press's access to information, the fact is that Memphis's daily newspapers had a history of underreporting civil rights demonstrations. Editors of both dailies were of the opinion that racial harmony was best promoted through the principle of "quietness," which dictated that only desegregation efforts sanctioned by the civic establishment were reported, and only *after* they had been successful. As a result, the SPC kneel-ins received the same treatment given the spontaneously erupting sit-in demonstrations of 1960, the scope of which most Memphians remained unaware because the daily papers relegated them to the back pages.[11]

No doubt this tendency to minimize the attention paid to incidents of nonviolent direct action reflected more than a concern for social harmony. As Benjamin Muse noted at the time, neither daily paper was an "unqualified champion of civil rights" and both were opposed to passage of a federal civil rights bill.

Indicative of attitudes at the *Commercial Appeal* was the fact that, despite having won a Pulitzer Prize in the 1920s for its campaign against the Ku Klux Klan, during the 1960s the paper continued to feature "Hambone's Meditations," a cartoon "reproducing degrading caricatures of blacks and silly homilies associated with the bygone days of minstrel shows."[12]

Whatever the reasons behind the mainstream press's silence on the SPC kneel-ins, it ended abruptly on May 4, when reports on the previous morning's events at the church appeared in both daily papers. In her weekly "A Visitor in Church" column, the *Commercial Appeal's* Kelley described a visit to SPC during which she witnessed a confrontation between church officials and a national Presbyterian leader who had traveled to Memphis to support the students' cause. Standing with a group of "about 20 Negro and white students," Rev. Carl Pritchett of Bethesda, Maryland, told the men guarding the church doors that he had come to SPC out of concern for "the influence of the racial policies of your church on the Christian witness and reputation of the Presbyterian Church of which I am a minister."[13]

According to Kelley, Pritchett urged the men "in the name of Christ to welcome his group," whose purpose, he said, was "to worship quietly and in reverence and demonstrate that the grace of Christ can overcome race prejudice." Accompanied by a television crew, Pritchett then mounted the steps, made his appeal, and walked away. Kelley wrote that after she entered the church SPC Elder John Cleghorn read a letter to the congregation claiming that the students' only interest was "social mixing" and reaffirming the session's intention to repel "with determination the use of our buildings as theaters for demonstrators." When Kelley got up to check on events outside the church, she was instructed to return to her seat or leave.[14]

By the end of that week, papers that had virtually ignored the SPC kneel-ins were reflecting a range of opinions on the matter. A *Press-Scimitar* editorial, reviewing the "difficult situation" that had unfolded over the previous six weeks as "biracial groups" were repeatedly denied entrance to the church, lamented that these things were occurring in a city that "has prided itself on the peaceful and friendly way racial relations have been handled here." A letter to the editor in the *Commercial Appeal* assessed matters rather differently. Reflecting nostalgically on the days in Memphis when "no one, white or colored, in his right mind would have advocated integration," the author recalled the SPC of his youth, where a special section of the balcony was reserved for "the dignified old darkies in their high hats" who had driven their employers to church in horse-drawn carriages. This was a time, the writer commented, when people were sensible about race relations and it was possible for black and white to live and work together "through kindness, courtesy and genuine respect and esteem."[15]

The Church Responds

While SPC clearly had its supporters, the church's leaders concluded that the situation called for more than wistful reminiscences of the "dignified old darkies" who once graced the church balcony. As at other white churches that had been targeted for racial testing, deterrent strategies employed at SPC ranged from forming human barricades to portraying visitors as "demonstrators" to making veiled threats of violence. Students recall one churchman who concealed a gun in his boot and another who bragged that he had one in his car. But the chief disincentive used at SPC was sending letters and photographs to the parents of Southwestern students who had taken part in the kneel-ins.[16]

When the visits began, students willingly gave their names to church representatives. When they refused to do so, their names and permanent addresses were obtained using Southwestern yearbooks and automobile registration records. Incriminating letters were then mailed to their parents. A typical letter, dated April 7, 1964, was written by SPC Elder Robert J. Hussey on C. W. Hussey & Co. stationery to the man he mistakenly assumed was Southwestern student Hayden Kaden's father. Writing from "one father to another," Hussey related that

> for several Sundays a group of white boys and white girls have been coming to the doors of our church here, bringing with them negro boys and girls, and among them was a car load in a Triumph car registered in [your] name. The white girls seem to pair off with the negro boys and the white boys pair off with the negro girls. They approach our church doors, which they know to be a segregated church, and demand that they be admitted; they are arrogant and offensive and say that they come NOT to worship but to enforce their civil rights.

Hussey expressed the hope that his letter would be received "in the spirit it is written," adding he would be grateful if someone were to inform him of similar actions on the part of his own college-aged son.[17]

Within days Hussey received a response from Kaden's stepfather C. Rodney Sunday, a 50-year-old Presbyterian pastor who since 1961 had been senior minister at The Pines Presbyterian Church in Houston. After thanking Hussey for his letter and explaining that Kaden's biological father had been killed in action during World War II, Sunday informed him that he both approved of and admired his stepson's behavior. "It has been a source of gladness to me," Sunday wrote, "that Hayden has a fine and sensitive social, Christian conscience. He seems to take quite seriously the basic thrusts of our Constitution and Bill of Rights. And he also takes seriously the Christian Gospel and its implications concerning the Church."[18]

As for Hussey's reference to "a segregated church," Sunday expressed his conviction that this was an oxymoron: "If it is segregated it is not a Church; if it is a Church it is not segregated," he wrote. Sunday then offered some advice rooted in his pastoral experience:

> In my former church, where I was pastor for almost 12 years, Negroes came 3 times. The ushers greeted them, gave them bulletins, and then seated them just as they did any other worshippers. We decided to do this for two reasons: (1) We felt that since this is Christ's church, not ours, that we must do what we believed He would want us to do. And we felt that He would not ever want anyone barred from His Church, and (2) we felt that in situations where people came just "to see if they could get in" that admitting them without any incident was the expedient and wise course of action. This proved to be true, for in such cases they never returned. I'm sure that if we had refused admittance, they would have returned again and again.[19]

A letter Sunday mailed to Kaden the same day reveals that, despite his spirited defense of his stepson's behavior, the pastor was no social radical. He told Kaden that using the church to enforce civil rights was "unrealistic and improper" and that he was disturbed by Hussey's charge that the students had acted rudely. "If you and the group have been arrogant and offensive, I am disappointed," Sunday wrote.[20]

No doubt feeling the sting of Sunday's rebuke, Hussey wrote the Texas minister again on April 13 to clarify SPC's position. "As a child," Hussey related, "I grew up seeing and being [seen] by Negroes sitting in our balcony with us who came into our church to truly worship." No African American, he said, was "ever turned away from our church until the NAACP organization started trying to force their way into churches." Hussey then elaborated on the charge that the Southwestern students had behaved offensively:

> Only yesterday one of the white boys, after having been requested in a gracious way not to disturb our worship stated to one of our elders, when he would enter into an argument with the boy, "you are either stupid or too dumb to enter into a discussion with us." This is one of the many insulting remarks, that are made each Sunday.

It does not help the students' cause, Hussey continued, that they "come up the front walk with a Negro boy putting his arm around the waist of a white girl."[21]

Hussey claimed there were pictures of such incidents; indeed, such pictures soon began to appear in the mailboxes of Southwestern students' parents. The photographer was Willis E. Ayers, Jr., known locally for a resolution he submitted to the Memphis City Commission in 1958 that would have empowered city officials to demand information from any organization regarding its membership, contributors, etc. The "Ayers ordinance," as it came to be known, resembled hundreds of statutes passed by Southern legislatures in the late 1950s specifically designed to inhibit the work of the NAACP. In the spring of 1964, Ayers turned his attention to documenting the kneel-ins at SPC using a Polaroid "instant camera" (probably a Land Model 100, which began production in 1963). His color photos were carefully framed to capture black and white students of different genders standing side by side. Ayers then mailed these photographs to the white students' parents, attached to brief letters.[22]

On May 2 Hayden Kaden's mother received one of these letters, accompanied by a photo of her son standing in the rain alongside, and holding an umbrella over, an unidentified young black woman. The accompanying note, typewritten on stationery bearing Ayers's name and address, read: "During the years, as our children grow up we have the habit of taking photographs of them to place in the album. Then as the years go on we can thumb through it and remember when. Attached is a picture of your son Hayden taken recently while attending a church service." We do not know if Ayers expected a direct response from Kaden's mother. But if he did, it could not have been the one he received a few days later. "I am so glad," she wrote,

> that you sent me the picture of Hayden and his friend attending a church service. This picture will very definitely be one of the most cherished ones in the album. And, I expect he will show it to his children, as they come along, with a degree of justifiable pride. Certainly his father and I are proud of him. Not every young man is so courageously loyal to Christ that he is willing to undergo ridicule, abuse, and insults because of his Christian convictions.

"If you have any more pictures," Kaden's mother wrote in conclusion, "I would certainly appreciate having them."[23]

These letters and photographs were mailed with the expectation that shocked parents would forbid their children from further participation in kneel-ins at SPC. Hayden Kaden's parents defied this expectation, expressing pride in their child, along with condemnation of the church and barely concealed ridicule of the tactics to which it had resorted. But in many cases the church's attempts to apply parental pressure on Southwestern students had dire consequences. Howard Romaine, whose mother and father were told by SPC representatives that he "had been walking hand-in-hand with Negro girls," told the *Tri-State Defender* that his parents were "quite upset." Female students in particular faced questions from angry and fearful family members.[24]

These letters and photographs are a remarkable and probably unique feature of the Memphis kneel-ins. In their determination to end church visits by racially mixed groups, a few SPC representatives were willing to go to great lengths to deter white students who were engaged in these visits. They did so without apparent shame, writing on personal or company stationery above their own signatures. It was not the only occasion on which Southern segregationists attempted to intimidate their opponents. But the time and effort expended on these tactics indicates a great deal of resentment toward Southwestern students who were participating in the SPC kneel-ins. How do we explain such animus toward young people whose religious and cultural identities were so similar to those of church members and who were students at a college with which the church had close historical ties?

Robert Hussey's letters to Rev. Sunday suggest that church leaders took particular offense at what they regarded as the students' lack of respect—expressed, in Hussey's view, by their "demand" to be admitted to the church, their "arrogant and offensive" demeanor, and their "many insulting remarks." While these charges cannot be dismissed out of hand, they do not align with what we know of the students' training in nonviolent protest, with newspaper reports of the kneel-ins, or with the students' own accounts of their encounters with church people. At the time, in fact, a spokesman for the students claimed they were the ones subjected to insults and dismissed as "lies" charges that they had "rudely demanded" admission to the church. An independent (though hardly neutral) witness, Carl Pritchett emphasized that in his time with the students he had witnessed no disrespect or misbehavior.[25]

Another charge lodged by church representatives was that the visiting students were coming to SPC to make a social statement rather than to engage in worship. But Pritchett was struck by the fact that the students with whom he visited SPC were invariably "short-haired" and well-dressed, and that anyone joining them had to adhere to the dress code of Southern churchgoers. It appears that what really irritated church members was not the students' demeanor or their dress, but the perception that they had "paired off" across racial lines. Given the social mores of the time, the students' adult advocates could not ignore the charge that there were "biracial couples" among them. Pritchett's explanation was that when pictures were taken, "a Negro boy just might be innocently standing by a white girl. If the picture showed only these two together it looked like an 'integrated couple.'" He conceded that "one or two of them in the excess of youthful zeal . . . [may] have been indiscreet in some of their public actions"; yet he was willing to stake his reputation on the fact that the "integrated couples" accusation was false.[26]

The College Responds

If most of the students could dismiss or explain away these attempts at coercion by church representatives, their status with the college was more precarious. The most visible kneel-in leaders were seniors who were scheduled to graduate in a matter of weeks. How would the Southwestern administration respond to the students' public humiliation of a church with which it had close ties?

Because SPC and its members were among Southwestern's chief financial supporters, the students had placed college officials in a very awkward position. On one hand, administrators quietly made students aware of their actions' possible consequences (albeit in a way that did not provoke the faculty who quietly supported the kneel-ins). On the other hand, because they had not intervened to stop the kneel-in campaign, college leaders were perceived as supporting, or at least tolerating, it. Dissatisfaction with the administration's inaction was communicated in a private meeting between SPC representatives and members of the Southwestern faculty and staff, including President Peyton Rhodes.

The meeting's dynamics were complicated: SPC had been instrumental in relocating Southwestern to Memphis in 1925, had led all local churches in supporting it financially, and had funded a chair in the Department of Bible. Naturally, these historical and financial ties came with expectations about the kind of Presbyterian college Southwestern should be. However, because the college was governed by a board of trustees elected by PCUS synods in the surrounding states, it was not directly accountable to individual congregations. Furthermore, while Peyton Rhodes was an active Presbyterian elder who embraced the college's denominational affiliation, he was also a committed academic dedicated to preserving Southwestern's identity as a liberal arts college.[27]

According to Dean Jameson Jones, who attended the fateful meeting with SPC representatives in the Southwestern board room, college officials were "coated and tied, somewhat tight-lipped, but ready to hear the protests of [their] fellow Presbyterians." The five or six church members who made up the visiting delegation indicated that they were "surprised and offended that students had assumed the right to sit in judgment on them." Sympathy was expressed and the conversation "progressed with some civility," according to Jones, until the churchmen sought assurance that there would be no further demonstrations. Because such an assurance would, in Jones's words, "imply punishments and sanctions which our group could not promise," the conversation reached a stalemate. Eventually, one of the church members declared that unless they were assured that the demonstrations would cease, the church would withdraw its financial support.[28]

According to Jones, "a silence of some moments followed his threat, and then President Rhodes said coolly and distinctly, 'The College is not for sale.'" "No one wanted to add to or demur from his words," Jones recalls, "and after he spoke nothing more was said." President Rhodes was not generally viewed as an advocate of social change. Many Southwestern students blamed him, in fact, for the slow pace of the college's movement toward integration. But Rhodes's response to the visiting SPC delegation indicated that, when push came to shove, he was willing to defend the college's independence from attempts at financial manipulation, even if he was troubled by the actions that were provoking the threats.

As word of the kneel-in controversy spread, other constituencies, particularly alumni/ae, expressed concern about the prominent role played by Southwestern students. Dean of Alumni and Development Alfred O. Canon was compelled to address the kneel-ins at SPC in the summer issue of the College's alumni newsletter. Although Canon significantly underestimated the number of Southwesterners who had participated in the kneel-ins as "some half dozen," he acknowledged that these students' actions had raised questions in the minds of Southwestern alumni. By letter and telephone, he reported, alums been inquiring whether Southwestern students had a "right" to participate in such demonstrations, to what extent those who did so represented the College, why Southwestern didn't expel, or at least discipline, them, and if the college had in any way encouraged their activities.[29]

Canon responded by noting that Southwestern did not presume to suggest to any church what its policies should be in the matter of race relations or otherwise; that no college representative had encouraged students to participate in the demonstrations; and that members of the administration and faculty had met with the students on at least three occasions in an effort to point out "the unhappy ramifications and consequences of their actions" and remind them that their statements and behaviors must be represented as "purely personal and private." However, Canon wrote, since "it is an essential part of a college education that each student be encouraged to search for the truth . . . to establish a personal system of moral values . . . [and to become] an independent person," the student must be granted freedom to exercise independent judgment, as long as this "does not result in the flagrant and consistent violation of the laws of the community or infringe on the rights of his fellow students." Finally, Canon reminded his readers, it is not the role of administrators and faculty at a Christian college to "impose their own personal convictions on students, especially in the political arena."[30]

Explaining the College's position to its alumni base was part of Canon's job, of course. But doing so put him in an uncomfortable position, as he himself was active at SPC, where he taught the Men's Bible Class. Given his familiarity to church members, it is not surprising that Canon was among those contacted when SPC representatives tried to convince the college administration to rein in the protesters. Student Winton Smith was present in Canon's office when the Dean received a telephone call from a church member. According to Smith, when Canon was told to "clean the situation up or the money stops," he made it clear that such an intervention would not be possible.[31]

Despite Canon's careful explanation of the college's position in the alumni newsletter and attempts by administrators to distance themselves from the student protestors, many church members felt betrayed by the institution they had supported faithfully for forty years. This sense of betrayal was reflected almost immediately in the college's fundraising efforts. In 1965, as the Southwestern Class of 1940 prepared for its twenty-fifth reunion, the financially strapped institution set up a friendly fundraising competition among the returning classes. Catherine Freeberg ('40) volunteered to solicit contributions from her former classmates. Forty-four years later, at the age of eighty-nine, Freeberg vividly recalls that she "didn't get a dime" from her classmates who attended SPC or sided with the church. They were "mad, mad, mad," she says, that Southwestern had not expelled the offending students.[32]

Summer at Last

In mid-May, a resolution to the kneel-in crisis at SPC seemed at hand. The local papers reported that visits to the church by "biracial" groups would be halted for thirty days and that Southwestern students had written a letter to SPC senior minister Henry "Jeb" Russell "expressing a hope of eventual reconciliation." The story fell out of the news as leaders of the campaign dispersed after graduation. But the kneel-ins had set the stage for an ecclesiastical showdown that could not be averted.[33]

In May and June, the unresolved racial crisis at the church scheduled to host the 1965 meeting of the PCUS General Assembly led presbyteries and synods across the denomination—from Texas to Missouri to Maryland—to go on record urging SPC to change its policy with regard to black visitors. The matter was of particular concern for the Synod of Tennessee, which, as if to highlight the matter that would dominate the week's business, met in June on the campus of Southwestern. The synod addressed the kneel-in crisis on theological principle, resolving that since "Christ did not hesitate to cut across the social customs of segregation of His day . . . the ground is always level where Christ stands. To exclude from worship, therefore, any believer, whether black or white, is to exclude the Christ who dwells within him." The synod's resolution also made the procedural point that defiance of injunctions from higher church courts is a repudiation of the ordination vows taken by pastors and elders and brings "ecclesiastical anarchy and congregationalism."[34]

A less direct but no less relevant response to the SPC situation was offered by retiring synod moderator and Southwestern alumnus Paul Tudor Jones ('32), whose keynote address was titled "The College-Related Church." Elaborating the college's task of rescuing the church from her "suburban captivity," Jones seemed to allude to recent attempts to exert financial pressure on his alma mater (his brother was Jameson Jones, Academic Dean at Southwestern). The goal of Christian education, Jones stressed, is to provide students an opportunity for developing "the habit of making decisions in the context of the highest Christian values." The church that supports such a mission, according to Jones, must be free from "the bludgeoning shadow of churchmen who say to the church related college—'no more of my money unless you teach sociology like my sainted father believed; no more of my money unless you teach the anthropology for which my God-fearing grand-father fell under the confederate flag at Shiloh.'" Put simply, the day had passed when the church could dictate to its colleges how students should be educated.[35]

Synod delegates could draw their own conclusions about the bearing of Jones's address on the SPC crisis. But there was less room for interpretation in a communication from First Presbyterian Elder Robert M. Hasselle, who charged that his son Robert M. ("Bob") Hasselle, Jr. ('64) and a Southwestern classmate had been "ejected" from the SPC sanctuary on Sunday morning, May 24. According to a statement signed by Bob Hasselle, he and Bert Ringold ('64)

> entered the Church, just before services. Bert had just arrived in town from Winona, Mississippi, and had brought no coat with him. He wore a shirt and tie. Only a couple of seconds after entering the door, we were approached by a man who asked us if we were looking for someone. We said no. Then Mr. Rives Manker motioned us over to the door. After we got near the side door, Mr. Manker grabbed my arm and forced us to leave the church. He insulted Bert Ringold by telling him that he could not enter the church services without a coat, which was the excuse he used for escorting us outside. He then told me that I had a lot of nerve coming in to Church. I told him I didn't understand; and he refused to elaborate. Then he and some other older men followed us around, apparently to make sure we didn't enter the Church.[36]

According to Hasselle, his ejection was not only "inexcusable," but ironic, since he had attended Sunday evening services at SPC for years and was included on a list of its college graduates published by the church in June 1964.[37]

Hasselle admitted that he had been present during some of the kneel-ins for the purpose of "observing and drawing sketches," but insisted that he had never participated. However, after experiencing the "rudeness, intolerance and prejudice" of SPC representatives, Hasselle's days as a bystander were over: "I plan to go back and stand outside with the other people, negro and white," he wrote, "who have been refused admission to Second Presbyterian Church, and wait to be admitted only when they are admitted."[38]

By the time of the synod meeting, Bob Hasselle had returned to SPC and been warmly received for worship. The issue festered, however, because Hasselle's father had received no apology or explanation from SPC senior pastor Jeb Russell, whom he had written to express concern about his son's ejection from the church. Hasselle sent a letter to the church's session denouncing the "men responsible for this perfidious act," complaining of the prejudice suffered by two young men "even with the right color of skin," and pointing out that "when the doors of the Church are closed [it is difficult] to say whether God is on the inside or the outside." The matter might have been resolved on the floor of synod if Robert Hasselle had not interpreted comments by SPC Elder Robert Hussey as impugning his son's character. Only after Hussey wrote an apologetic letter to the younger Hasselle did the matter die.[39]

As it unfolded in a series of charges and countercharges, the Hasselle incident revealed just how tense relations among Memphis Presbyterians had become in the summer of 1964. Local leaders were determined to exercise the authority vested in church courts to resolve the kneel-in crisis and spare the denomination further embarrassment. SPC's leaders were just as determined to resist what they regarded as meddling in their internal affairs. And old grievances—as the population of Memphis moved toward the suburbs, downtown First Presbyterian Church had lost its music director and most of its choir to Second Presbyterian— were finding new outlets for expression.

By the time representatives of the area's sixty-plus churches convened for the quarterly meeting of Memphis Presbytery on July 21, SPC's ongoing refusal to conform to denominational policy had become a matter of grave concern. This is not to say the presbytery was a stronghold of progressivism. Of the 120 laymen and ministers who were charter members of a PCUS group of racial moderates calling themselves A Fellowship of Concern, only one—Paul Tudor Jones— hailed from Memphis. Furthermore, there was a good deal of concern within the presbytery about the pro-integration positions taken by denominational boards and agencies considered out of line with the Church's spiritual mission. Nevertheless, Southern Presbyterian loyalists in Memphis were committed to a connectional polity that severely limited the autonomy of individual congregations.[40]

Presbyteries and synods across the denomination had gone on record urging SPC to welcome all comers or forfeit its right to host the upcoming meeting of the General Assembly. It would be Memphis Presbytery's task to convince the wayward congregation to accede to the will of the larger Church. Naturally, the body's first impulse was to appoint a committee, which it charged to consult with the church and report at the presbytery's next stated meeting. According to Lewis Donelson, a layman appointed to the five-member committee, the group convened only once. After a solemn invocation of God's blessing, the mood in the room abruptly shifted when an SPC representative declared that the church had spent $2 million on its sanctuary and didn't want "any goddamn niggers desecrating it." The meeting ended and further negotiations between church and presbytery took place behind the scenes.[41]

New Year, Old Controversy

In January 1965—after eight months of editorials in church publications, debates and resolutions in church courts, and discussions in private—matters between SPC and its denomination remained at an impasse. As time ran short for making a decision to move April's meeting of the General Assembly, Southwestern student activists once again took aim at SPC's policy of exclusion. In the January 8 issue of *The Sou'wester* (Southwestern's campus newspaper), Roger Hart wrote that even though students had stayed away from SPC during the fall in order not to "upset a delicate situation of discussion and negotiation," they had not lost interest in the controversy. Hart promised, in fact, that if the General Assembly were to go on at SPC before the church's session announced a change in policy, "scores of ministers and laymen, as well as seminary and college students [would] be quietly protesting during the Assembly meetings."[42]

As if to reiterate the threat, kneel-ins at the church resumed the following Sunday (January 10) and continued for at least three weeks. While renewal of the desegregation campaign did not faze session hard-liners, it did move the church's pastors to action, as we will see in a later chapter. It also caught the attention of local papers, which did not hesitate to report and editorialize on the renewed church visits. "It will be good news," opined the *Press-Scimitar*, "when Second Church joins other Memphis churches which have opened their doors to Negroes." This advocacy of inclusion brought responses from local citizens, who defended the prerogative of church members to decide with whom they wanted to worship. The notion that blacks should be encouraged to enter "the most private of all the white citizens' assemblies," one *Press-Scimitar* reader responded, might be expected in "Pravda or the New York Times," but was out of place in a newspaper serving "a community of decent white Southern Americans." Another letter writer claimed that freedom of the press did not confer the right to pressure a church to adopt a specific policy, particularly, he maintained, since the people of SPC "have only the friendliest feeling for peoples of all races and denominations."[43]

Despite the resumption of kneel-ins at SPC, however, it appeared that the impasse at the church would be broken only by the threat of ecclesiastical intervention. A showdown was set for the January 26 meeting of Memphis

Presbytery, which attracted visiting lay persons and ministers from as far away as California. The tone of the meeting was set in the opening sermon, which was based on the early church's fateful decision to embrace Gentile believers. When the committee appointed to counsel with SPC relayed the church's position that it had no problems it was "not able to handle," the response was an ultimatum: SPC's session was directed to meet not later than February 1, 1965, to consider the presbytery's request that it immediately bring its policy with regard to admitting worshippers into accordance with General Assembly guidelines. If it could not do so, it should release the General Assembly from its promise to meet at the church in April. If neither of these options were acted upon, the presbytery would request that the Church's Moderator make other arrangements.[44]

The ultimatum revealed that a majority of delegates to the meeting perceived SPC's recalcitrance as a threat to the Church's system of connectional government, not to mention its credibility in an environment of increasing sensitivity to racial discrimination. If SPC chose to ignore its ultimatum, the presbytery did possess a "nuclear" option, which would allow it to dissolve the SPC session and take over governance of the church. But such a move was not likely in the case of a congregation as large and powerful as SPC. In fact, Memphis Presbytery had no interest in alienating a church to which nearly 20% of the region's Presbyterians belonged and whose voluntary contribution to the presbytery's work represented nearly one third of its annual budget. Ultimately, however, whether the presbytery was willing to play its trump card was a moot point. Before its ultimatum was even announced, the denomination's Moderator stepped in to move the site of the 1965 General Assembly.[45]

When word of the decision reached Memphis, the public crisis receded, only to give way to a gut-wrenching internal struggle for the soul of SPC. This struggle led, two months later, to a clarification of the church's policy on segregation, a change in lay leadership, and a painful schism. Although the kneel-in controversy had finally been resolved, the impact of events on the church and its members was only beginning to be felt.

|| 4 ||

"Like a Child That Had Been Unfaithful"

A Church-Related College and a College-Related Church

Memphis is not like other American cities, even other cities in the South. It is not Atlanta or Birmingham, and it is certainly not Nashville. The city's distinctiveness is reflected in many paradoxes: It is an urban area with rural flavor. It is outside the Deep South, but deeply rooted in cotton culture. It is not a seat of state government, yet functions as the *de facto* capital of western Tennessee, eastern Arkansas, and northern Mississippi. It influences global culture, yet its citizens suffer from an inferiority complex. It is home to the National Civil Rights Museum and the Stax Museum of American Soul Music, as well as Confederate Park and an equestrian monument honoring Nathan Bedford Forrest—slave trader, Confederate general, and the first Grand Wizard of the Ku Klux Klan.[1]

Another Memphis paradox is that despite being branded with the stigma of Martin Luther King, Jr.'s murder, prior to 1968 Memphis's path toward desegregation had been remarkably peaceful. Memphians had no direct experience of firebombed churches, murdered civil rights workers, or demonstrators subdued by police dogs and fire hoses. The Bluff City had escaped the fate of Albany and Birmingham, and there was widespread optimism that Memphis was on its way to realizing interracial harmony in a new social order. Writing for the Southern Regional Council in 1964, Benjamin Muse called Memphis's progress toward the elimination of race discrimination "remarkable," its desegregation of public facilities advanced "well beyond the token stage," its eschewal of violence heartening. Muse's conclusion that Memphis had begun to "shine as a beacon of reason and decency for the Deep South" was echoed by the *New York Times*, which reported that the city, despite having "all the ingredients to make it a racial trouble spot," had made more progress toward desegregation with less strife than any other major Southern city.[2]

Given Memphis's reputation as a place where segregation was being system-atically dismantled with the support of enlightened community leaders and co-operative businessmen, it is ironic indeed that one of the longest and most strident struggles over church desegregation began there the very year Muse's study was published. How do we explain this entrenched conflict over church integration in a city that was known for peacefully desegregating its businesses and public amenities? Part of the answer must be found in the historical relation-ship between Second Presbyterian Church (SPC) and Southwestern College.

The Church

Organized in 1844, SPC spent five years in a brick warehouse in South Memphis before inhabiting its first dedicated structure, a Greek Revival sanctuary equipped with slave galleries on either side of the choir loft. At the outbreak of the Civil War, SPC's pastor was Robert C. Grundy, a Northerner of unionist sentiment who was an outspoken critic of Southern Presbyterians' theological warrants for slavery and secession. There was no open breach between pastor and congregation, however, until Gundy protested the elders' decision to donate the church bell for conversion into Confederate cannons.[3]

Nor was SPC members' dedication to the Confederate war effort limited to the contribution of raw materials. Untiring practical assistance to the Confed-eracy was offered by the women of the church under the leadership of Sallie Chapman Gordon Law, who began making uniforms for the Tennessee Volun-teers even before the state had seceded from the Union. After the war began, Law organized the Southern Mothers' Hospital to demonstrate compassion for sick and wounded Confederate soldiers passing through Memphis. Hailed as "the Mother of the Confederacy," Law reportedly lamented that she did not have "fifty sons to lay at the altar of [her] beloved country."[4]

Such expressions of Southern nationalism led to the church being occupied by Union forces after the fall of Memphis in June 1862 on the ground that its members were disloyal to the U.S. government. "Union Chapel," as SPC's building became known, was subsequently used as a hospital, stable, and place of prayer for convalescing soldiers and citizens loyal to the Union. Gen. Ulysses S. Grant told a church elder who requested that the building be restored to its owners that "it will be at your service when you recall Dr. Grundy to the pulpit." Members of the congregation appealed to President Lincoln, who on March 4, 1864, instructed military authorities to return the church to its trustees. Lincoln wrote that "if the Military have military need for the church building, let them keep it; otherwise let them get out of it and leave it, and its owners alone, except for causes that justify the arrest of anyone."[5]

By the 1880s, the church's location at the intersection of Main and Beale streets had become part of the city's business district. A building committee selected a residential site a few blocks to the southeast, at the corner of Hernando and Pontotoc. There a building distinguished by a magnificent spire—reportedly the largest church structure in America south of the Ohio River—was completed in 1892. During the long pastorate of Albert B. Curry (1903–31) the church gained 2,300 members and organized five daughter churches. Steady growth continued under Robert H. McCaslin (1932–1941), during whose pastorate another twelve hundred members were added to the rolls. Curry and McCaslin shaped a congregation that became known for evangelism, foreign missions, education, and benevolence. Though it was a gathering place for "the well-to-do and the socially prominent," the church was proud of its works of mercy, including a Settlement School for neighborhood children and their mothers. SPC was a place, according to a brochure from the 1930s, "whose open doors of welcome and vaulted roof speak of divine love and refuge."[6]

During the 1920s and 1930s SPC was a source of civic pride throughout Memphis. Local papers frequently celebrated the church's history and touted its accomplishments, including the steady growth in its membership, the stability and distinction of its pastors, the "important" churches to which it had given birth, the quality of its choir (featuring "some of the most prominent soloists in the city"), and its debt-free status. They also noted contributions to benevolent causes, attendance at Sunday school, missionaries supported by the church, and congregants who had been members for at least 50 years. Since these articles were based on documents commissioned by the church's session, they reveal concern at SPC with the church's status among peer congregations.[7]

In fact, SPC frequently boasted of a membership that contained "a large number of the most prominent men of affairs of the city . . . a list of which would include the men and women who have had a large share in building the city and shaping its progress for nearly a century." In the 1930s, this social prominence seemed perfectly compatible with the church's location in the heart of the city. A 1934 brochure provided a rebuttal to those who argued that SPC's downtown location was a handicap. Rather, the brochure said, "we look upon it as an asset":

> Here is a Church located where the population is densest and human need the greatest. It is not a church in some sylvan retreat; not a temple in some lonely solitude far removed from the walks of life and attended only by the children of privilege, but Second Church is one whose doorstep is on the pavement, against whose walls beat and lap the tide of labor, whose hymns mingle with the rattle of carts and the groans of traffic, whose seats are within easy reach of men falling under heavy

burdens, and whose altars are hallowed by the prayers of people who feel the need of divine strength.[8]

Over time, however, the church's attraction for the prominent and wealthy would wane as the surrounding neighborhood slowly transformed into "a business and slum area." Younger members began to move to neighborhoods east of downtown and the number of baptisms dropped accordingly.[9]

The decision to forsake the city's pavement for a "sylvan retreat" came in 1943, when the congregation voted to relocate to a "high class residential section" at the city's eastern edge. In explaining the decision, the church's historian notes of the location at Beale and Pontotoc that "what territory was not turned over to . . . rather seedy business . . . was being occupied by Negroes." SPC was certainly not alone in choosing to follow its younger members to the suburbs. It was conforming, in fact, to a pattern identified by sociologist Frank Loescher in 1946—resisting a "Negro invasion" as long as possible before moving to the suburbs and selling its church property to a black denomination—which SPC did in 1949.[10]

The move east was realized under Anthony B. Dick (1947–58), a man of unusual energy and passion for church growth. Under Dick's leadership SPC broke ground in 1948 on a 7.5-acre tract of land at the corner of Goodlett and Poplar in East Memphis. The new church plant, which would eventually feature five buildings in the Colonial style, was envisioned with tennis courts and an air-conditioned movie theater. A new 1,450-seat sanctuary was dedicated in 1952, and by 1957, when the church completed a "combination fellowship-hall-dining room-gymnasium" that included handball courts, the congregation had gained 1,000 new members and weekly Sunday School attendance was over 1,600. A church representative boasted that SPC's campus included "probably the most complete church facilities" in Memphis.[11]

As Memphis continued to expand eastward, SPC grew in size and influence. Much of the credit belongs to Rev. Dick, a personable leader with a gift for fundraising. But Dick was haunted by private demons. After tirelessly overseeing SPC's massive building program, he suffered a "nervous breakdown" in 1957 and died the following year from a self-inflicted gunshot. The congregation honored him by dedicating SPC's completed fellowship hall in his honor.[12]

Dick was followed at SPC by Henry Edward Russell, who would pastor the church until 1975. "Jeb" Russell was the thirteenth child of Richard Brevard Russell, a successful lawyer who became chief justice of Georgia's Supreme Court. Jeb was also the younger brother of Richard B. Russell, who after one term as Governor of Georgia was elected to the U.S. Senate, where he served from 1933 to 1971. Jeb Russell did not flaunt his family name or seek the spotlight himself. But as the pastor of prominent churches in Montgomery

(1944–58) and Memphis (1958–75) during the civil rights era, he was exposed to the events and personalities that were shaping the region's history.

In Montgomery Russell would experience the bus boycott of 1955–56 at close range. Although he was not one to court controversy, Russell was appointed to the Mayor's Citizens Committee, a biracial group tasked with negotiating a resolution to the crisis. In Montgomery Russell also came to know civil rights icons Frank M. Johnson, Rosa Parks, and Martin Luther King, Jr. Johnson, the federal judge who would be responsible for deciding a series of landmark desegregation cases between 1955 and 1979, was a member of Russell's congregation at Trinity Presbyterian. Parks was employed by the Russell family as a seamstress, and King's aunt had worked as a domestic in the Russell home in Atlanta in the 1940s. When Martin King was called to Montgomery's Dexter Avenue Baptist Church in 1954, Russell's former housekeeper wrote him requesting that he "be good" to her nephew. Russell seems to have done so. When King encountered Russell at a meeting of the Mayor's Citizens Committee in 1955, he was impressed by "the heartiness of his smile and the warmth of his handclasp." The men's paths would intersect again in 1968, when King led his last civil rights campaign in Memphis.[13]

When SPC called the forty-nine-year-old Jeb Russell as its senior pastor in 1958, it was getting a man from a leading Southern family who was widely respected in Presbyterian circles and had guided a prominent Deep South congregation through the turbulent waters of social change. In addition to his successful pastorate in Montgomery at one of the denomination's larger and wealthier churches, Russell had been Moderator of the Synod of Alabama and a member of the PCUS Board of World Missions. He seemed on track, in fact, to become the sixth SPC pastor to be elected Moderator of the PCUS General Assembly. But before this dream could be realized, he would stand with SPC at a "crossroads in its history . . . unequaled since Union forces occupied the Southern church's buildings." Ironically, SPC was brought to this crossroads by representatives of an institution with which the church had enjoyed close ties for forty years.[14]

The College

The institution known today as Rhodes College was organized in Clarksville, Tennessee, in 1848. Founded under Masonic auspices, the college was purchased by the Presbyterian Synod of Nashville in 1855 and named Stewart College in honor of scientist and philanthropist William Stewart, a Presbyterian elder from Philadelphia with a vision for making the frontier college a Princeton for the South. Despite strong leadership and fine prospects, however, Stewart College became a casualty of the War Between the States.[15]

At the outbreak of hostilities, most of the college's students and faculty volunteered for military service and the buildings and grounds were turned over to the Confederate government and employed as a hospital. But as the Union army swept into central Tennessee in early 1862, the campus was occupied by hostile forces; when finally returned to the college trustees in 1866, Stewart College was in a state of near ruin. The institution tentatively reopened in 1870 with five faculty members and 100 students, but during the next few years enrollment steadily declined. Meanwhile, influential Presbyterians began to agitate for a "Southern Presbyterian University" to be supported by church people throughout the region. In 1875 Stewart College, the only Presbyterian institution of higher education then operating in the Mississippi Valley, was re-chartered as Southwestern Presbyterian University (SPU).[16]

From 1875 until America's entry into the Great War, SPU remained the sort of conservative Southern institution its founding fathers envisioned. But the university's identity began to change when Charles E. Diehl assumed the presidency in 1917. Diehl was a West Virginian trained at Johns Hopkins, which he described as "the first real university in this country." He went on to earn degrees from Princeton Theological Seminary and Princeton University, where he studied under Woodrow Wilson. After pastorates in Kentucky and Mississippi, Diehl arrived in Clarksville, Tennessee, in 1907. Ten years into his ministry at First Presbyterian Church, there he was, invited to assume leadership of the city's struggling university.

A few months into Diehl's presidency, about half of SPU's students dropped out to enter military service in the world war. Diehl promptly closed the Divinity School, initiated a new course in engineering, and announced that the university would place special emphasis on the sciences. But Diehl's most fateful initiative as SPU president was his effort to relocate the school. In 1920, responding to the Memphis Chamber of Commerce's offer to raise $500,000 for the university if it would move there, the SPU board decided to act. The Tennessee Supreme Court finally approved the removal in 1924 and the college opened in Memphis the following year, shortening its name to "Southwestern." Diehl's ambitious plan to establish a first-rate college of the liberal arts in Memphis quickly earned the enthusiastic support of city leaders.[17]

In the 1920s, Southwestern based its appeal on a careful mix of religion and scholarship. It advertised a faculty boasting "seven graduates of Oxford University, six of whom were former Rhodes Scholars [including Robert Penn Warren], and . . . four ordained ministers of the Presbyterian Church." Entrust your children to a church college that will mold their mind and character, expose them to the finest teaching in the English tutorial tradition, and prepare them for leadership in the wider world: This was the essence of Diehl's appeal to Southern Presbyterians. It was an inspired vision, but one destined to lead him afoul of conservative churchmen.

In 1930, a few weeks after the college had celebrated retirement of its $700,000 mortgage debt with a bond-burning ceremony, four Presbyterian ministers appeared in Diehl's office. Accusing the Southwestern president of unsound faith, reckless financial administration, and failure to monitor the dress and behavior of students, the clergymen asked for his resignation. When Diehl refused, the men circulated a petition that was signed by the ministers of eleven local congregations representing one third of Presbyterians in Memphis. Perceiving that the city's newspapers were against them—one editorial opined that without Diehl Southwestern "might not remain what it is very long"—and realizing that their target audience was spread over four states, Diehl's opponents launched a pamphlet war. Their crusade to "save Southwestern" was waged in publications with titles such as "Southwestern at the Cross-Roads" and "Needed Changes in Southwestern College," while Diehl's supporters countered with "Facts about the Southwestern Controversy" and "Give the Truth and Southwestern a Chance."[18]

The claim potentially most damaging for Diehl—and the one reiterated most often by his opponents—was that he was a theological Modernist who did not adhere to traditional Presbyterian beliefs, including "full inspiration" of the Scriptures. Diehl's opponents pressed their case at a hearing before the Southwestern Board of Trustees in February 1931. Points of church doctrine upon which Diehl was allegedly heterodox included his views of the atonement (he conceded that he had "no set theory"), the fate of the heathen (he could not imagine Plato in "an undying hell"), and divine inspiration of the Bible. Diehl's concept of biblical inspiration came under scrutiny because he had expressed doubts about the historical and scientific value of the early chapters of Genesis, judged the imprecatory psalms to be unchristian in spirit, and denied that God instructed Joshua to utterly destroy the Canaanites. In Diehl's view, although the Bible was an infallible rule of faith and practice, it was "not a library of universal knowledge . . . [with] parts of equal value." This understanding was compatible with the confessional standards of his denomination, he maintained, which did not demand a "verbal inerrancy theory of interpretation."[19]

Compelled to respond to Diehl's critics, the Southwestern trustees concluded that the president did, in fact, embrace "the system of doctrine contained in the Confession of Faith and Catechism of our Church." But they were loath to become mired in theological controversy. "The battle today," the board emphasized, "is not a struggle in the eddies, but a mighty conflict in midstream. It does not have to do with the petty differences of sects, but with the life of religion itself. It is a war between atheism and materialism on the one hand and religion on the other. Civilization itself is at stake." If Southwestern became entangled in sectarian disputes, the trustees warned, it might become submerged in a cultural backwater and bypassed by the tide of national destiny.[20]

The Southwestern board's desire to avoid theological disputes should not obscure the fact that the Diehl Affair was essentially a reprise of the fundamentalist–modernist controversy that shook American Protestantism during the 1920s. In fact, as the *St. Louis Post-Dispatch* noted, the controversy involved many of the issues that had been on display in the Scopes "monkey trial," which had taken place three hundred miles to the east in 1925. For traditionalists who were dedicated to ensuring that Southwestern remain a safe place for the education of Presbyterian young people, there could be no compromise with a man who was suspected of harboring "insidious and pernicious rationalism," a man whose supporters were making the school "about as pagan as any state university."[21]

Diehl's endorsement by the Southwestern board saved his job, but it did not end the crusade against him. In fact, the petitioners' campaign to defend Southwestern "from rationalism and worldliness" was still making news in 1934. A persistent concern was the spiritual influence the president and faculty were exercising on the student body. Rev. J. P. Robertson, the main spokesman for the ministers who had begun seeking to oust Diehl in 1930, emphasized this concern as he rallied Presbyterians "to demand a faculty sound in faith to guide our beloved youth aright." Robertson was particularly troubled that teaching of the Bible at Southwestern had been infected by "the blighting Rationalism of Central Europe"—a colorful reference to higher biblical criticism. Teaching both sides of religious questions, Presbyterian conservatives charged, was causing students at Southwestern to question their faith and candidates to abandon preparation for the ministry.[22]

Diehl's supporters characterized his adversaries as demagogic inquisitors with a medieval pedagogy. Indeed, it was easy to portray these zealous men as "sectarians" who wished to turn Southwestern into "an institute for propaganda." But the charge of theological modernism presented a serious problem for the leader of a church college in the South. Thus, after he had won the backing of Southwestern's trustees, Diehl submitted himself to a heresy trial in his home presbytery. Although he was vindicated as "a true minister of Jesus Christ," Diehl's opponents were essentially correct in viewing him as a modernist who infused traditional concepts with novel meaning. In subsequent years, in fact, Diehl would come to sound more and more like a liberal Protestant, as "the Fatherhood of God, and the Brotherhood of Man, the infinite value of the human soul and personality, and love as the law and life of the universe" became recurrent themes in his sermons.[23]

In the wake of attacks on his character, leadership, and religious orthodoxy, Diehl received many expressions of support from Southwestern faculty and students, college alumni, clergymen, educators, foundation representatives, businessmen, and national luminaries, including William A. Percy (uncle of novelist

Walker Percy). Yet it was probably true, as one of his opponents charged, that not a single Presbyterian pastor in Memphis shared Diehl's theological views. For this reason alone, perceptions of Southwestern as a place unfriendly to faith were difficult to combat. By the late 1930s, they had become so acute that the college solicited testimonials from local Presbyterian pastors who defended its wholesome religious influence.[24]

Despite their zealous efforts on behalf of "true Presbyterians," Diehl's opponents failed to "clean house" at Southwestern and the college flourished under the president's leadership during the 1940s as an institution devoted to preserving the Western tradition from the threat of barbarism. To meet the challenge, in September 1945 Southwestern inaugurated a humanities course titled "Man in the Light of Western History and Religion." The tutorial plan, honors courses, and the "Man" sequence were offered as examples of the "distinctive and progressive" educational policies adopted by the college. None of this displaced Southwestern's emphasis on the Bible, which according to Diehl contained "the root principle of democracy, [which is] the infinite worth of the individual." But it did require that the Bible be recast as "the classic of classics," a knowledge of which was required to produce "educated, well-rounded persons."[25]

After physicist and Presbyterian Elder Peyton Rhodes assumed the presidency of Southwestern in 1949, the college continued to lift Diehl's distinctive banner of "sound Christian liberal arts education." Although students were required to complete four semester courses in the Department of Bible with teachers who were ordained clergymen, Southwestern branded itself as a college with "accent on the academic, with Phi Beta Kappa, tutorial and honors courses, seminars, and [a] lively program of science research." It was a careful balancing act; what the college earned in academic respect it risked losing in the confidence of Southern Presbyterians, many of whom had long since ceased viewing Southwestern as "their" place.[26]

Traditionally, religious colleges were expected to build on the foundation laid by parents and home congregations by offering moral guidance and encouraging or requiring expressions of religious piety. But as with other church-related schools, Southwestern's role in sanctioning student religiosity shifted over time. In the 1870s, obligatory "religious exercises" at Southwestern Presbyterian University included daily chapel, Sunday Bible classes taught by professors, and weekly church attendance. (According to Chancellor John Waddel, religious instruction was one method of taming a student body that had become notoriously dissolute.)[27]

In the 1920s, Southwestern continued to require daily chapel, although Sunday church attendance was now pledged on the honor system. By the 1940s, religious activities at the college took on a more voluntary character, even though required chapel remained the mainstay of campus religious life. Chapel attendance was never a guarantee of genuine spirituality, of course. Even in the nineteenth century, morning prayer had often been the occasion for "some exhibition of low practical mischief." But mandatory chapel persisted into the 1960s because it was emblematic of the Christian atmosphere parents and supporters expected the college to support.[28]

Viewed against this background, the student rebellion against compulsory chapel that broke out at Southwestern in late 1963 reflected changing views of how much control over students' lives could be exercised by church colleges that aspired to be taken seriously as academic institutions. Most Southwestern students gave grudging assent to the tradition of required chapel. But when one of them wrote a letter defending the practice in *The Sou'wester*, he unwittingly tapped into a reservoir of campus resistance. A recurring theme in the year-long debate that followed was the view that Southwestern could not reach "the educational potential of the small liberal arts college while continuing its compulsory religious atmosphere." As one student put it, because required chapel was akin to censorship, it was not "compatible with the concept of Southwestern as a citadel of knowledge." "Since when has intellectual knowledge been nurtured by anything which is not voluntary?" he asked.[29]

Southwestern's chapel requirement would not be lifted until 1968. But by 1962, as the civil rights movement began to influence campus discourse, progressive students were already noting a "radical change in the political attitude and involvements" of their peers. In September of that year, the campus buzzed with news of James Meredith's attempt to enroll at Ole Miss and with reports that Southwestern students were "observing and/or participating in" the spectacle. In the aftermath of the Meredith affair, progressive students stated the moral case for integration at Southwestern in letters to the student newspaper and in dozens of conversations with President Rhodes.[30]

During 1963, growing student interest in life beyond Southwestern's gates gave rise to formal discussions of the proposed federal civil rights bill and speaking invitations to Ole Miss professor James W. Silver (whose exposé of his state's "segregation creed" in *Mississippi: The Closed Society* had earned him considerable notoriety), preacher-activist Will Campbell (the former Director of Religious Life at Ole Miss who had resigned amid death threats), and James Meredith, whose invitation to appear on campus was an open repudiation of the administration's judgment that he was not of "sufficient intellectual caliber" to warrant such an honor. In inviting Meredith, Campbell, and Silver to the Southwestern campus, students were honoring men who had been identified by the Mississippi State Sovereign Commission as among that state's most dangerous enemies.[31]

The first *bona fide* campus protest at Southwestern occurred in January 1964 when a handful of students organized a march to coincide with a visit by Senator

Herbert Walters (D-TN), who had not taken a position on the proposed civil rights bill. A few students carrying pickets demanded to know where the senator stood on civil rights legislation. By 1967, activism had spread even to the Southwestern football team, whose members led a successful boycott of a local steakhouse that refused to serve a black teammate. And in 1968, when the Memphis Sanitation Workers' strike brought civic unrest just a few blocks from campus, many students supported the workers' "I Am A Man" campaign and ignored the advice of parents and administrators by marching with Dr. King down Beale Street. Remarkably, one of the groups with which King was forced to negotiate was "The Invaders," a local black militant organization whose spokesman was Coby Smith ('68), a member of the first integrated class at Southwestern.[32]

As an institution, Southwestern approached integration very cautiously. By the time the college decided to accept African American students in the spring of 1963, the Presbyterian Church (US) had been encouraging integration at its colleges for almost a decade. And even then, President Rhodes's appeal to the college's trustees rested on financial necessity rather than moral or religious considerations. The college's policy of exclusion, Rhodes told the board, had disqualified it for support from large granting institutions like the Ford Foundation. The contrast between the cautious practicality of school administrators and the moral zeal of progressive students, who had campaigned for integration at the college since 1962, would be on full display during the Second Presbyterian kneel-in controversy.[33]

The Church–College Nexus

SPC had been a reliable source of support for Southwestern ever since the college moved to Memphis in 1925. Of the $137,000 Memphis Presbyterians were asked to raise for Southwestern at that time, more than $85,000 was contributed by SPC. In recognition of the church's largesse, the Southwestern board established a Chair of Bible in honor of SPC pastor A. B. Curry. Even in Curry's day, however, the church–college relationship was troubled by theological tensions.[34]

Curry was a Southwestern alumnus and a member of the board that exonerated Diehl in 1931. Yet he also figured prominently in the arguments of the president's opponents, who claimed that in a conversation with Curry Diehl had articulated his belief that only some parts of the Bible were inspired. Curry, it was reported, had called Diehl a modernist and characterized the president's views as "most dangerous." Curry defended the president at his board hearing, stressing that if not for Diehl's "zeal and faith," the college would have met financial ruin in 1930. Yet his testimony at the hearing seemed to contradict the president on the matter of what represented an acceptable view of biblical inspiration.[35]

The church–college relationship became more comfortable under pastor Robert McCaslin, who in 1938 testified to the wholesome effect of a Southwestern education on young Presbyterian men and women. "I have been pastor of Second Presbyterian Church of Memphis for the past six years," McCaslin wrote. "During that period scores of mothers have come to me, asking me to talk to their children who had gone off to college, state institutions and other colleges, who were upset in their religious life, but not once have I been asked to render a service of this kind by any mother whose child or children attended Southwestern." In the 1940s, the symbiotic relationship between the institutions was personified by Felix Gear, a Southwestern Bible professor who became SPC's senior pastor in 1943.[36]

During the 1950s and 1960s, the church maintained strong ties with the college, offering scholarships to SPC members who attended Southwestern and employing professors and administrators in the adult education program. But the relationship was attended by expectations on the part of the church that changes in American higher education would make increasingly difficult for Southwestern to fulfill. By 1964, in fact, there was growing disappointment at SPC that education at Southwestern was not more consciously faith-related. Some church members steered young people away from the college and there were repeated attempts to cut funding for the Curry Bible Chair. Charles Murphy, an SPC member who entered Southwestern in the fall of 1963, recalls being warned that the college would "take the Bible out of you." "There was a lot of pride in Southwestern," recalls church member John Clark, "but many viewed the college as "a child that had been unfaithful."[37]

The perception of Southwestern as a wayward child intensified during the fall of 1962, when a series of articles in *The Sou'wester* came to the attention of church leaders. In the midst of the Meredith affair in Oxford, Mississippi, a brief article titled "A Southwestern Student Prays" parodied a sort of piety the author believed was well represented at the college. "God, help James Meredith to see the error of his way," wrote the anonymous author. "Help him to understand that we are not used to sitting next to niggers in school and that he should retain a Christian attitude in accommodating this old custom, although he may have to give up his chance for education to do so." In a reference to Southwestern's tentative path toward integration, the prayer continued: "Dear God, above all don't let any niggers apply to Southwestern or there may not be any new towers or student centers or Gothic bird baths or anything because these are very important to the 'development of a society of individuals dominated by the Christian spirit.'" The prayer's conclusion was eerily prescient of the kneel-in campaign that would be led by Southwestern students two years later:

Dear God, please don't let the Communists or the wicked NAACP tempt Negroes to come to our church for we have some very rich members who are very touchy on this situation, and we have this new combination gym, tennis court, swimming pool, and club meeting building going up that's going to be so much fun, and the niggers would spoil everything.[38]

In subsequent weeks *The Sou'wester* carried a regular column titled "The Seeker," presumably by the same author, that was invariably vivid and inflammatory. One column described the beating of a "worthless, cursed, despicable black beast." Another mimicked biblical language in a presentation of supplemental commandments, the thirteenth of which was "let there be separate schools, and separate churches, and separate hotels. Woe to the evil black one who desires to enter therein." The most disturbing installment of "The Seeker," however, took the form of an allegory that depicted the college as a lady from a "fine and noble" Southern family at whose death a monument was inscribed with the words, "To an Outstanding Member of the Oldest Profession."[39]

After seven weekly installments, "The Seeker" disappeared in a cloud of sarcasm, but not before the column and its author had provoked a great deal of controversy on campus and beyond. Offended students referred to the pieces as "slander," "trash," and "pseudo-intellectual garbage," and they were not alone in taking umbrage. In November 1962, SPC senior pastor Jeb Russell wrote Southwestern President Peyton Rhodes to complain:

Recently articles in the South Wester [*sic*] have been called to my attention and the turbulence has been considerable, over some writer whose nomedeplume [*sic*] is unknown to me. But obviously he is the type of boy that used to like to write on toilet walls, or some individual who is frustrated because they didn't get in the Fraternity or Sorority that they desired. I have not seen the writings in recent weeks, but I did have someone bring a copy by the Study about two or three weeks ago. At our Family Night Supper on Thursday the 8th I discovered that a more recent issue was being shown to some of the Elders of the Church.[40]

There is probably never a good time for a college president to receive such a letter, but this was a particularly bad one, as it arrived one week before Southwestern was to host the church's pastors and elders in order to thank SPC for "its long sustained interest and generosity over the years."[41]

The significance of SPC's "generosity" can be fully appreciated only in light of Southwestern's tenuous financial position at the time. Opposition to Diehl on the part of conservative groups in the Presbyterian Church (US) had made it difficult for the college to raise funds in the supporting synods of Tennessee, Alabama, Mississippi, and Louisiana. Thus, since the 1930s the burden of financial support had fallen increasingly on the citizens of Memphis and on local congregations, particularly SPC. When Southwestern launched its Annual Sponsors' Campaign in early 1964, the financial partnership between college and church was very much in evidence. The campaign kickoff, in fact, was a banquet hosted by President Peyton Rhodes, board chair Van Pritchett, and SPC pastor Jeb Russell. Two weeks later, Southwestern students would begin kneeling-in at the church.[42]

5

"A Time When the Bare Souls of Men Are Revealed"

Southern Presbyterians Respond

By the end of April 1964, despite the fact that neither of the city's daily newspapers was paying much attention, news of the kneel-ins at SPC in Memphis had spread across a good part of the country. *The Presbyterian Outlook*, read by American Presbyterians North and South, was the first national publication to carry the story, which it summarized this way:

> A group of students in the Intercollegiate Chapter of the NAACP, including some Presbyterians, has been visiting various Memphis churches for some weeks. They were received with courtesy wherever they went—until they visited Second Presbyterian. For four successive Sundays they presented themselves and, according to newspaper accounts, were turned away. Witnesses said the students were barred by a line of church officers standing shoulder to shoulder on the church steps, backed up by uniformed officers with guns much in evidence. It was said that one student was threatened with arrest and another with a promise of even more serious treatment. Behind the scenes deeper forces were let loose—intimidation of various forms, with serious results to the students involved.[1]

This ominous account of the standoff in front of SPC was circulating among Presbyterian ministers and laypersons just as the 104th meeting of the General Assembly of the Presbyterian Church (US) was getting underway at Montreat, North Carolina. How would the kneel-in drama be interpreted in the wider ecclesial context of Southern Presbyterianism?

Race Relations and the Presbyterian Church (US)

Founded in 1861 as the Presbyterian Church in the Confederate States of America and confined almost entirely to the territory of the old Confederacy and border states, the Presbyterian Church (US) was deeply imprinted with white Southern values. As Donald W. Shriver noted in 1964, the denomination exemplified

> an almost unique combination of nationalist and regionalist thinking.... [Southern Presbyterians] have continued to maintain a peculiarly intimate tie between their feelings for their church and their feelings for the history of their region. They never quite forget that their denomination was born with the Confederacy but did not die with it.[2]

While the PCUS had never excluded African Americans, it had adopted the practices of segregation that came to define Southern culture after the 1870s. Black churches were placed in "Negro presbyteries" (which together made up a "Negro Synod") and would-be black Presbyterian ministers were directed to Stillman Institute in Alabama, established in 1874 for "the training of a colored ministry."[3]

Unlike other white denominations in the South, the PCUS did not relegate its black members to a separate Church. This made Southern Presbyterians the only regional denomination to receive African Americans at meetings of its governing bodies. But because black delegates slept and ate apart, the theological and moral contradictions of intra-church segregation were difficult to ignore. They were finally addressed at the denominational level following World War II. In 1950 the annual meeting of the General Assembly was finally desegregated and a year later the PCUS abolished Snedecor Memorial ("Negro") Synod, transferring existing Negro presbyteries to geographic synods. The dissolution of these same Negro presbyteries followed in 1964, when the synods of Alabama, Georgia, and Louisiana were instructed to "take into their membership and under their care" all ministers and churches within their bounds (responding to a backlash from the synods, the General Assembly amended "instruct" to "request"). As these changes were under way, incidents of ecclesiastical hospitality across racial lines were celebrated in the official church press.[4]

A watershed in the PCUS's public posture on race relations was reached in 1954 when the General Assembly adopted a report by the Church's Council of Christian Relations that made Southern Presbyterians the first Protestant group to formally endorse the Supreme Court's decision in *Brown v. Board of Education*. The report declared that "enforced segregation of the races is discrimination which is out of harmony with Christian theology and ethics," a sentence whose impact on the denomination, according to one scholar, "can never be measured." The report urged that PCUS camps, conferences, and institutions of higher education desegregate, and called upon sessions of local churches to admit persons to membership and fellowship "without reference to race." The report was adopted by only 59% of voting delegates at the 1954 General Assembly and had to survive repeated efforts to rescind it. But it represented an unequivocal condemnation of *de jure* segregation from which the denomination would never retreat.[5]

Traditionalists and Reformers

Few Presbyterians claimed a direct biblical mandate for segregation, but those who were committed to the practice strenuously rebutted the implication that it was un-Christian. Some traditionalists distinguished between *discrimination*, which they acknowledged was sinful, and *segregation*, which they claimed was essential to a well-ordered society in the South. Others argued that since Southern Presbyterians had "strong and sincere differences of opinion" on matters of race, it was inappropriate for Church boards, agencies, and courts to actively support integration and thus "leave the impression that to believe and think otherwise is un-Christian." Another resistance strategy was to link desegregation with other targets of strong opposition among PCUS conservatives, including the "Communist goal of amalgamation" (that is, racial intermarriage), civil rights organizations and the ecumenical bodies that supported them, plans for reunion with Northern Presbyterians (the Churches had split in 1861), and the denomination's educational curriculum.[6]

PCUS traditionalists who defied the denomination's increasingly progressive stands on social issues were opposed by reformers whose views began to gain ascendancy during the decade following the end of World War II. Reformers in the PCUS maintained that the social order was in need of conversion every bit as much as individuals and sought to leverage the Church's moral and financial resources to address social problems. Traditionalists viewed their reforming co-religionists as "young turks" who were out of touch with Presbyterians in the pew; some even intimated that control of the PCUS had been seized by "subversive powers in the upper echelons of our denomination." A commissioner to the 1964 meeting of the General Assembly expressed what many conservatives must have felt after attending meetings of higher church courts where reformers were well represented: "I'm going back to Mississippi and close the door behind me."[7]

Although they were always a minority in the PCUS, reformers were prominent on seminary faculties and occupied key positions on denominational boards.

They were united by the beliefs that the worldwide quest for civil rights could not be resisted "any more than we can turn back the tide," and that rather than retreat from a culture in transition, the Church should assert moral leadership. Their mouthpiece was *The Presbyterian Outlook* (circ. 9,000), which during the 1960s published articles by Martin Luther King, Jr., Benjamin Mays, and Ralph McGill, materials on race prepared by the much-maligned National Council of Churches, and numerous sermons and articles challenging the notion that segregation could be defended biblically.

PCUS traditionalists were alienated not only from the *Outlook*, but increasingly from the denomination's official magazine, *The Presbyterian Survey* (circ. 262,000), which fell afoul of conservatives for its general "liberalism" and for failing to reflect "both sides" of the segregation issue. The magazine's editor took the position that since the denomination had "relegated segregation to a level near heresy," allotting space to pro-segregationist viewpoints would validate them as Christian, which, he insisted, they were not. Southern Presbyterians who held "traditional and long established convictions" on race were incensed at being condemned by a presumably "churchwide" publication.[8]

Traditionalists rallied around a publication of their own—*The Presbyterian Journal* (circ. 45,000), whose acknowledged goals were combating liberalism within the denomination, defending the "integrity of the Scriptures," opposing the National Council of Churches (which was viewed in some parts of the Church as "aid[ing] the movements of Communism and atheism"), and fighting plans for reunion with Northern Presbyterians. During the 1950s and early 1960s, the *Journal* could be relied upon to oppose virtually any PCUS pronouncement on race relations. It did so, typically, not by denying the reality of black suffering, but by claiming that, from the Christian point of view, the black man's "plight is identical to that of the white man. *Both* need Jesus Christ." "The Biblical solution to the problem of race prejudice," according to this perspective, was the Holy Spirit's transformation of the individual, which in turn would increase harmony between the races. This and related views (e.g., that "materially, the American Negro is better off than most white people in the entire world") were routinely expressed in the *Journal's* pages. Significantly, in *Journal* articles the term "civil rights" was typically surrounded by quotation marks.[9]

On the question of segregation's theological status, the *Journal* tended to reflect the views of its co-founder, L. Nelson Bell, a former medical missionary to China and Billy Graham's father-in-law. Bell was an influential figure in the wider evangelical movement who was executive editor of *Christianity Today*, where for many years he published a column titled "A Layman and His Faith." Bell took the relatively moderate position that while racial separation had no biblical sanction, maintaining natural barriers through *voluntary* segregation was congruent with Christian charity (this was the *Journal's* official position after

1957). Whites could even welcome blacks to their churches, Bell believed, without supporting "forced" intermingling or "crusading" for desegregation.[10]

During the 1950s and 1960s, reformers often prevailed at the denominational level; but traditionalists remained a well-funded and determined PCUS constituency until a majority of them exited the denomination in 1973.

Spiritual vs. Social Conceptions of the Church

Chief among the complaints of PCUS traditionalists was that the Church's primary mission—"winning people to faith in Jesus Christ and nurturing them in the faith"—was being compromised by "over-emphasis on social, economic and political matters." Such sentiments were not uncommon among conservative Protestants. In 1967, *Time* reported that every major U.S. Protestant Church could be roughly divided between members who favored greater involvement in social issues and those who felt that the church should stick to helping individuals find salvation. But inside the PCUS this division was sharpened by conflicting attitudes toward the traditional Southern Presbyterian doctrine of the church's "spirituality."[11]

Forged during the antebellum period, the concept of "the spirituality of the church" received its classic formulation in the writings of South Carolinian James Henley Thornwell (1818–1862), who taught that the provinces of state and church were "perfectly distinct." According to Thornwell, the state "aims at social order; the Church at spiritual holiness." The doctrine's connection with the preservation of slavery was revealed in Thornwell's declaration that "whether slavery shall be perpetuated or not, whether arrangements shall be made to change or abolish it, whether it conduces to the prosperity of States or hinders the progress of a refined civilization," are questions not for ministers but for statesmen. "Christian men may discuss them as citizens and patriots," he wrote, "but not as members of the Church of Jesus Christ."[12]

Although fashioned to deflect criticism from a Church perceived as lending moral credibility to slavery, the "spirituality" doctrine survived the Civil War. Indeed, for seventy-five years this view of the Church's mission underlay not only the PCUS's silence on social issues (excepting Sabbath observance, intemperance, and worldly amusements), but its suspicion toward Northern Presbyterians who, from the Southern perspective, had been engaged in a fatal embrace with politics since 1861. As one Southern Presbyterian leader put it, "the great Scriptural truth of the spirituality of the Church [is] the distinctive principle upon which our Church rests its separate existence."[13]

Around 1930, however, the denomination began to rethink the normative Christian relationship to social concerns. The change was reflected in statements by the PCUS's Committee on Social and Moral Welfare, which in 1934 declared that it was the Church's duty to "interpret and present Christ's ideal for the individual and for society, [and] . . . warn men of the presence of sin and of its effects in the individual life and in the social life." The task of the Church, in other words, was to encourage and stimulate its members to realize the ideals of Christ "in their individual lives, in the life of each group of which they are participants and in the total life of the nation."[14]

Once the PCUS acknowledged "sin . . . in the social life," it was only a matter of time before it would directly address racial discrimination. In 1949, in a statement on "States Rights and Human Rights," the former Committee on Social and Moral Welfare (now the Council on Christian Relations) declared that American minorities' claims to full civil rights have a "sound moral and historical basis." Furthermore, in an implicit rejection of the church's "spirituality," the council concluded that "a church that tries to be neutral by keeping silent . . . will to that extent forfeit its redemptive power and influence among men." By 1966, when the General Assembly adopted a report proclaiming that the *essence* of sin is "political-social," the denomination's official perspective on its role in society had been "completely transformed."[15]

This revised understanding of the Church's relationship to civil society was regarded by many traditionalists as a fateful departure from the denomination's historical position. Whenever conservative Presbyterians claimed that laws could not change wicked hearts or drew a sharp distinction between Christian orthodoxy and the "liberalism" that presumed to replace evangelism with sociology, they testified to how deeply the "spirituality" doctrine continued to inform their understanding of the faith. Echoes of the doctrine were often audible, in fact, in debates over Church statements or programs concerned with civil rights, for instance when a layman from Birmingham contended that individuals are "changed and renewed by God's grace, not by the NAACP, CORE, NCC, or UN programs." Meanwhile, proponents of the denomination's social agenda pointed out the "spirituality" doctrine's theological shortcomings and emphasized its shameful provenance.[16]

Desegregation in PCUS Churches: Ideals and Reality

Given lingering fidelity to the idea of the church's "spirituality," intense opposition to the goals and tactics of the civil rights movement, and the congregationalist ethos that characterized many Southern Presbyterian churches, it is not surprising that during the 1950s and 1960s the most stubborn resistance to the ideal of desegregation embraced by the PCUS General Assembly was to be found in local churches. Nowhere was this resistance more evident than with regard to receiving blacks as worshippers and members. Although the PCUS had never had an official policy of racial exclusion, practice was not uniform. In fact, even after the General Assembly declared segregation to be un-Christian and urged that it be discontinued in all church-sanctioned environments, the synods of Mississippi and South Carolina resisted the General Assembly's authority to determine their practices.[17]

Segregation in individual congregations was generally not a denominational concern until the kneel-in era, when unwelcome visitors drew attention to exclusionary policies. The results of a 1963 study conducted by the denomination's Permanent Committee on Christian Relations illuminated the landscape of congregational attitudes. Of the nearly twelve hundred congregations surveyed, only twenty-eight had accepted blacks into membership and only forty-two indicated having had black members in the past. A more striking finding was that only 63% of congregations indicated a willingness to welcome blacks to Sunday morning worship (another 8% said they would do so on a segregated basis).[18]

The PCUS's official position on segregated worship, articulated by the General Assembly in 1865, stressed "the advantages of the colored people and the white being united together in the worship of God." But the 1963 survey revealed that a century later there was considerable latitude in congregational practice. This led in 1964 to an effort to amend the PCUS constitution to make explicit that "no one should be excluded from participation in public worship in the Lord's house on the grounds of race, color, or class." The amendment passed, was subsequently ratified by the presbyteries, and was officially adopted at the 1965 meeting of the General Assembly. In the meantime, however, confusion lingered at the local level over how much independence congregations had in deciding whom to admit to worship.[19]

Not everyone was confused, of course. In 1957 Ben Lacy Rose, a professor at Union Theological Seminary in Virginia, had thoroughly addressed the issue's biblical/theological and polity dimensions in an *Outlook* article that was subsequently published and distributed in pamphlet form. In *Racial Segregation in the Church*, Lacy stressed that while separation of the races had long been the custom in many Southern churches, the practice had no basis in the Bible or the PCUS's constitution and had never been sanctioned by the denomination. Rose conceded that silence on the matter during the first half of the twentieth century may have been interpreted as consent, but he emphasized that the General Assembly "has never spoken with any other voice than to condemn segregation of believers in the church."[20]

Lacy's exposition of the case for open worship notwithstanding, the reigning assumption in parts of the Church was that it was the prerogative of a congregation's "spiritual leaders" to decide who would be seated for worship, and where. In early 1964, Rose sought to clarify the matter in his "answer man" column in the *Survey*, where he wrote that "neither elders nor deacons have a right to determine who may worship God in his own house." Furthermore, Rose concluded, "for any man or group of men to judge whether any of his children may enter his house is the height of presumption." The question was raised more formally when a Virginia presbytery requested that the 1964 General Assembly address the matter of whether it is "proper for a Session . . . to exclude persons from public worship at the Lord's house on the grounds of race, color or class."[21]

This, then, is the polarized, contentious, and somewhat confused ecclesial environment in which the kneel-in controversy at SPC in Memphis erupted in March 1964. The presenting issue was whether SPC's leadership was obligated to admit a racially mixed group of students into its sanctuary for worship. But the controversy soon became another field of battle for PCUS traditionalists and reformers, their divergent perceptions of the civil rights movement, and their differing understandings of the denomination's authority to trump social custom and restrain individual preference.

The 1964 General Assembly

Planning for the 1964 PCUS General Assembly was in its final stages when word began to circulate that a kneel-in campaign was under way at the church scheduled to host the following year's meeting. The matter was met with concern by denominational leaders, particularly reformers like Rev. Carl R. Pritchett, a pastor from Bethesda, Maryland, who for years had tried to convince Southern Presbyterians that their Church should lead in the quest for racial justice. In 1946, for instance, Pritchett called for desegregation of the Montreat Conference Center, long before integration was a cause most white Southerners were willing to support. In 1963, he was one of about a hundred Southern Presbyterians who participated in the March on Washington, and two years later he joined a few other PCUS clergymen on the march from Selma to Montgomery.[22]

Pritchett headed to the 1964 General Assembly prepared to argue for the establishment of an Emergency Committee on Religion and Race that would guide the denomination's efforts to eliminate segregation and racial discrimination and mobilize Church resources to support pastors "in distress because of their faithful witness against racial injustice in the church and society." Given his agenda, it is not surprising that Pritchett was the one to place the SPC controversy before the General Assembly. He brought to the Standing Committee on Assembly Operation a resolution to "establish the policy of holding [the General Assembly's] annual meetings only in churches willing to accept all persons for worship and membership in the congregation regardless of race." After several hours of deliberation, the committee recommended implementation of the policy, but not until 1967. Following a vigorous debate that lasted until nearly 11 p.m., the committee's recommendation was approved by the full assembly 240–157.[23]

What seemed to a majority of commissioners like a reasonable compromise given that the General Assembly had already contracted with SPC to host the 1965 meeting in Memphis, others viewed as a bargain with the devil. Roscoe Nix, a black commissioner from Washington, D.C., called it "the most distressing moment of [his] life" and wondered if he should return home and drape his church in black. Those on the losing side of the vote could take solace, however, in the assembly's "unprecedented admonition" that

> In view of the pronouncements of this 104th General Assembly, and those of previous Assemblies and out of consideration for the feelings of our Negro and white commissioners who feel keenly on the issue of Christian unity and racial justice, and in view of the gravity of the racial struggle in the world, we request and urge the Second Presbyterian Church of Memphis, Tennessee, to reconsider any policies or pronouncements of its own which may be inconsistent with our Assembly's position on race and Christian unity, and which thereby may be an embarrassment to our Church.[24]

This request, along with overwhelming passage of a non-exclusion amendment to the Church's constitution, sent the clear message that SPC's refusal to admit black worshippers was unacceptable to a majority of those elected to speak for the denomination.[25]

A Personal Crusade

Nevertheless, denominational leaders who had sought a stronger stand on the issue expressed frustration and regret. Malcolm P. Calhoun of the PCUS Department of Education wrote to Southwestern student Hayden Kaden (an early participant in the SPC kneel-ins) of his "disappointment and feeling of revulsion" that the General Assembly had not acted to institute the new policy immediately. "Really, I was sick about it, and so were many others," he wrote.[26]

No one was sicker than Carl Pritchett. In a written assessment of the assembly circulated among friends, Pritchett lamented that by honoring a segregated church's bid to host the General Assembly, the denomination had failed to take a stand for truth at "a time when the bare souls of men are revealed." Pritchett acknowledged that the assembly had moved in the right direction on the race issue but believed it had failed to recognize its "moment of greatness" by declining to insist that the next meeting of the General Assembly be held in a church with no racial restrictions. The Assembly's decision to honor its contract with SPC, Pritchett wrote, had actually "jeopardized the honour of religion and the reputation of our church."[27]

The problem, as Pritchett saw it, was not what might happen in Memphis in 1965, but what was happening in front of SPC at present. Pritchett argued that even if the church were to suspend its exclusionary policy for the upcoming assembly, it would be "base and wrong" for the denomination to be hosted by a congregation so "unrepresentative of Presbyterianism even in Memphis." He worried that the message communicated to protesting students would be "the power of money and influence to control the Christian Church." And he warned that if SPC persisted in barring students who were protesting "the sin of segregation," their number would grow and include Presbyterian ministers and seminary students. In fact, Pritchett wrote, if the 1965 General Assembly were held at SPC he would personally "march around the church with a verse of scripture on a placard every day the Assembly is in session." He then predicted that

> if, through the open windows and doors of that beautiful and wealthy church, I hear men piously talking about unity, brotherhood and peace, I think I know what I will do. I will hurriedly lay aside my little piece of the Word of God and rush around that church looking for a place of privacy away from the crowd. I will kneel down as in prayer and vomit before God as a violent demonstration against my own church.[28]

Barely able to concentrate or sleep in the days following the assembly, Pritchett decided he could not sit back and watch events in Memphis unfold. On Friday, May 1, 1964, he composed a letter that would be read to his congregation the following Sunday. "As you are sitting here in this church," Pritchett wrote to his flock, "I expect to be standing before the door of the Second Presbyterian Church of Memphis, Tennessee, asking to be admitted to the House of God to worship." "If I can arrange it," Pritchett went on, "I hope to stand beside a Negro Elder and ask to be admitted to worship with my brother in Christ. . . . If I cannot get in the house of God with my negro brother, I intend to stand quietly at the door with him." Pritchett noted that as a white man and a friend of SPC's senior minister (Jeb Russell had been a classmate at Davidson College), he could enter the church at any time. But the possibility that he might be excluded if accompanied by a black man, even a Presbyterian elder, made going to Memphis an act of conscience he could not evade.[29]

When Pritchett returned to his pulpit the following Sunday, he provided a detailed report of his sojourn in Memphis. He described how a group of Southwestern students had met him at the airport and drove him past the church so he could visualize the following morning's events. In contrast to the Gothic fortress he had imagined, he beheld a suburban church in the colonial style. In conversation with the students, Pritchett came to realize that his image of a picket line was inaccurate as well. What the students described were "vigils" in front of the church during which they "engage[d] in meditation and unostentatious prayer." At the home of Vasco and Maxine Smith, Pritchett reported, the group drew up a statement of their reasons for appearing at SPC.[30]

Pritchett described the scene on Sunday morning, May 3, as students from across the city assembled at Southwestern before traveling to SPC:

> There were to be twenty-three of us in all. Dr. Vasco Smith and his attractive, cultured wife were to be there. . . . The rest were students. The statistics were as follows: As to race, thirteen of us were Negro and ten of us were white people. According to church affiliation, there were eleven Presbyterians, eight Methodists, four Baptists, one Episcopalian. Every single one of the students is a member of some Christian Church. There were five ministerial students and two who are thinking seriously of the ministry. Five of them have parents who are elders, deacons, or hold some other office in their local church. There were seven whose parents teach in the Church School or have some other responsibility in their churches.[31]

This was no "beatnik crowd," Pritchett emphasized, but a collection of "well-dressed and bright looking youngsters." He noted that "no one was in blue jeans. No one was angry. No one had a placard."[32]

After the students lined the sidewalk around the entrance, Pritchett recalled, he and Vasco Smith walked slowly toward the church doors as congregants came and went around them. There were news cameramen, but "no commotion or confusion." Pritchett read the prepared statement into a microphone placed before him by a member of the media. "I am at the door of your church because I am concerned about the influence of the racial policies of your church on the Christian witness and reputation of the Presbyterian Church of which I am a minister," it began. The statement urged church members to permit the group to worship with them "quietly and in reverence" as a demonstration that "the grace of Christ can overcome race prejudice." According to Pritchett, SPC Elder Robert Hussey replied: "Dr. Pritchett, I respectfully request you to leave. We are worshipping here. You are interfering with our worship. I respectfully request you to leave. You are creating a disturbance. You are trespassing. I respectfully request you to leave."[33]

The spectacle of exclusion concluded when Pritchett dramatically announced to the assembled students that "we cannot enter the House of God!" The group then repaired to Parkway Gardens Church, where pastor Lawrence Haygood invited Pritchett to address the congregation. "The white, local Christian churches," he preached, "may be the last voluntary refuge of segregation in our society; . . . the very honesty and integrity of the churches is on trial before a skeptical world."[34]

That evening Pritchett and Haygood enjoyed a meal together at an integrated Holiday Inn before watching television reports of the morning's confrontation in front of SPC. Pritchett left Memphis, he told his congregation in Maryland, with a great deal of admiration for the "sheer nerve and conviction" of the students and a sense that his trip had been worthwhile. In fact, Pritchett said, when he read in Monday morning's *Commercial Appeal* claims by SPC representatives that the students were "demonstrators" whose only interest was in promoting a cause, he lost all fear that he might have "interfered in a delicate situation and made it worse."[35]

Church Constituencies Weigh In

Pritchett was the only white Presbyterian minister willing to join the SPC kneel-ins. But there was growing evidence of denominational support for what the Memphis students were doing. A lesson in the spring 1964 issue of the PCUS's Quarterly for Older Youth instructed young people that "if the law says you may not picket or gather peaceably for purpose of protest, then you violate the law, appealing to a higher law to justify your actions. And, of course, you take the consequences." Similarly, a "pastoral letter on race" adopted by the 1964 General Assembly spoke approvingly of the "demonstrative" approach to achieving justice and observed that the marching, picketing, and boycotting conducted by civil rights advocates had been "remarkably peaceful and forceful." Around the same time, the *Survey's* "answer man" wrote that "when civil laws run contrary to the law of God, we have the necessary Christian duty of disobeying them."[36]

When an integrated student group was denied admission to SPC for the eighth time on the Sunday following adjournment of the 1964 General Assembly, regional governing bodies began to weigh in on the kneel-in controversy. Hanover Presbytery in Virginia was the first church court to take a position on events in Memphis. Its statement, featured in the May 18 issue of the *Outlook*, asked SPC's session to reconsider its policy regarding public worship, as it had "caused embarrassment to the General Assembly, to the Presbyterian Church in the U.S., [and] to the cause of Christ, at home and abroad." In an accompanying editorial, the *Outlook* referred to the spectacle that had been "broadcast to a nationwide audience" on May 3 and suggested that a special meeting of the General Assembly might be required to deal with the matter.[37]

At its May meeting, the Synod of Texas drafted a letter to SPC noting that "neither the Bible nor the Book of Church Order offers any ground for barring anyone from worship or from membership because of his race." Like other church bodies compelled to address the matter, the synod asked SPC to amend its policy or release the General Assembly from its contract to meet there in 1965, and offered to secure a location for the meeting within its bounds. According to newspaper reports, Houston's Pines Presbyterian Church (where Hayden Kaden's stepfather, C. Rodney Sunday, was pastor) was at the forefront of the synod's efforts to address the SPC situation.[38]

By the end of June, no fewer than nine synods and presbyteries had made known their views on the kneel-in controversy in Memphis, and by summer's end Southern Presbyterians at denominational seminaries, on college campuses, and on foreign mission fields had weighed in as well. In a letter addressed to the SPC session, sixty-eight members of the faculty and student body of Austin Presbyterian Theological Seminary asked the church to reconsider its "announced policy of segregated worship." "Your continued maintenance of this policy," members of the seminary community declared, "puts not only your church but our entire denomination in a most embarrassing position." Meanwhile, the Westminster Fellowship Council, which represented PCUS students at colleges and universities across the region, informed the General Assembly of its concern for the "segregated situation" at SPC.[39]

These communications had little if any effect on SPC's response to the growing controversy. But given its longstanding commitment to world evangelism, it was difficult for SPC to ignore censure from the Church's foreign missionary corps. Complaints began to be broadcast in April 1964, when over two hundred PCUS missionaries serving in South America, Asia, and Africa wrote the General Assembly to express "concern about the effect that the existence of various forms of racial segregation in the church has on the work of Christ in other lands." Identifying just the sort of spectacle of exclusion that was on display in Memphis that spring, the missionaries urged "the opening of the doors and fellowship of all churches to any person who comes to worship." "A picture of Negroes being turned away from a white church," the foreign workers explained, invariably becomes front-page news overseas.[40]

As the controversy in Memphis lingered into the fall, the *Outlook* and *Survey* published an "Open Letter to the Presbyterian Church, U.S. From the Congo Mission" that directly addressed the SPC kneel-ins. "Till recently," the mission's 119 members wrote, "we have deemed [the kneel-in controversy at SPC] to be your problem to be dealt with according to the dictates of the conscience of local congregations. [But] the question of the place of meeting of the 1965 General Assembly points up the fact that the action of one Session can undo the good effects of our Assembly's pronouncements." The situation at SPC presented the danger, the signatories alleged, "that certain actions, or failure to act, may wound your brothers, cheer the enemies of the gospel and bring discredit to the name of Christ."[41]

The letter from the PCUS's Congo mission was drafted by Hugh Farrior, M.D., who with his wife Ellen ran a hospital and school in a remote tribal area of the country. Farrior was quite familiar with the challenges faced by American Christians ministering in foreign lands. Raised by missionary parents in China before they were expelled from that country, Farrior was among a handful of American missionaries who remained in Congo throughout the nationalist rebellion of the early 1960s. After hearing of Carl Pritchett's visit to Memphis, Farrior decided to express his concerns directly to the SPC session in a letter that explained the damage racial prejudice in the American church could inflict on the Presbyterian mission in Africa. Session minutes indicate that his letter was read at a meeting on June 28, although Farrior received no response. The church's refusal to acknowledge his communication led Farrior to organize the letter from members of the Congo mission.[42]

Claims that racial discord in America could interfere with the gospel's spread in foreign lands were not new. Nor was it unprecedented for missionaries to comment on the affairs of particular congregations with which they were familiar. But for a denomination's entire mission corps in a foreign country to address a domestic controversy from 7,000 miles away was remarkable, and not easily dismissed. These statements by PCUS missionaries placed SPC hard-liners and their supporters in the unenviable position of being opposed by brothers and sisters whose dedication to the gospel was unimpeachable.[43]

As these various church bodies and constituencies addressed the kneel-in controversy at SPC, denominational magazines did their part to inform and shape the opinions of 900,000 Southern Presbyterians, many of whom felt they had some stake in the outcome. The news source favored by the majority of Southern Presbyterians was *The Presbyterian Survey*, which as the denomination's official publication tended to emphasize the controversy's polity dimensions. In the summer of 1964, for instance, Ben Lacy Rose pointed out that the church's constitution gave "no right to refuse the privileges of worship in God's house to any man on the ground that he is Negro or on the ground that he came with improper motivation." Rose was no doubt aware that SPC representatives had downplayed the racial identity of excluded visitors and focused on their putative motivations.[44]

The Presbyterian Outlook, mouthpiece for PCUS reformers, began reporting the kneel-in story in April, and was consistently critical of SPC's position. In an editorial published while the 1964 General Assembly was still in session, the *Outlook* concluded that the 1965 meeting of the assembly should not be held in a church that "declines, with force, to open its doors to all who seek to worship there." Among those who addressed the SPC situation in the *Outlook*'s pages was Union Theological Seminary professor John H. Leith, who observed that when race is made a condition for membership or worship "the line is clearly drawn between apostasy and obedience, between heresy and orthodoxy, between pretentious fraud and the reality of the church."[45]

The conservative-leaning *Presbyterian Journal*, meanwhile, expressed sympathy for SPC's ongoing attempts to "deal with the racial issue" and accepted the church's justification for its refusal to admit visitors, which it described as opposition to "the use of church buildings as theaters for demonstrations." In fact, the *Journal* tended to cast SPC not as a renegade but a victim of liberal intolerance. Following the decision to relocate the 1965 meeting of the General Assembly, a *Journal* editorial claimed that despite "signs of progress toward an ideal resolution of difficulties within Second Church," some within the PCUS do not wish to see the "triumph of reconciliation" in a conservative congregation. "It is hard to avoid the feeling," the editorial concluded, that "the most vocal minority within the Church—the 'young turks' of liberal bent—are out to alienate and divide, to punish and to destroy. And what better target than a great evangelical congregation with a tremendous (and embarrassing) evangelistic and missionary testimony?"[46]

The Role of the Moderator

How these various Presbyterian publications would interpret the SPC crisis was fairly predictable. But the role played by the Moderator of the PCUS General Assembly in resolving the crisis was not. When Felix Gear was elected to a one-year term as Moderator in April 1964, Presbyterians across the political spectrum had reasons to be hopeful. To progressives, Gear was "a man of sensitivity and awareness to change going on in the world." Moderates saw in this seminary professor a safe and sensible man who would guide from the center. Traditionalists had reason to be optimistic as well. Although the SPC issue was far from resolved when commissioners left the 1964 General Assembly, it bode well that the new moderator was a former senior pastor of the church in the vortex of the kneel-in controversy. Surely Gear would sympathize with his former congregants and would refrain from embarrassing or punishing the church. At the very least, many believed, Gear's familiarity with the congregation and its leading personalities would make it possible for him to quietly negotiate a resolution to the crisis.

Gear was quite aware that his stint at SPC in the 1940s uniquely positioned him to mediate in the controversy; but he was determined to move cautiously. In May 1964 he wrote to a friend that he was already "in negotiation" with the church and hoped it would "quietly withdraw" its invitation to host the General Assembly so as to "end this unsavory situation and the possibility of future notoriety." Gear lamented that a meeting with the SPC session had been temporarily postponed due to some comments he had made regarding the country's need for "something in the way of a civil rights bill." Nevertheless, he said, he was corresponding with the elder who seemed to be the church's spokesman, a man with whom he had been "very good friends," and was weighing "whether it would be wise to do anything that may further estrange them from me at this time."[47]

Gear's itinerary as PCUS Moderator took him to Memphis in June and again in September 1964. On these occasions he conferred with the SPC session and local Presbyterian leaders, both of whom he had engaged in ongoing conversations. Memphis Presbytery representatives wrote to ask Gear how long they should wait before "taking some action," while SPC leaders sought private conversations with the Moderator. Elder Charles Gillespie invited Gear to call him at home "collect," adding that "we are very proud of you as Moderator . . . and we pray that God may continue to use and guide you as His servant." Gear was also in quiet but regular contact with SPC senior minister Jeb Russell, although his primary interest in these conversations was in ascertaining whether SPC would discontinue actions that were interpreted as reflecting a ban on black worshippers.[48]

To appreciate Gear's role in the kneel-in crisis, it is important to understand that SPC was not the only Memphis institution with which he had a personal connection. Before being called to the church in 1943, Gear had served for ten years as Professor of Bible at Southwestern. It is not known whether Gear held any particular sympathy with the Southwestern students who were being turned away from SPC in 1964. But he was certainly familiar with the sort of pressures conservative churchmen could bring to bear on church-related colleges. Gear had arrived at Southwestern in 1934 in the immediate aftermath of the Diehl Affair. As a Bible professor under the embattled president—a man Gear praised for being "willing to fight alone and against terrific odds" without lowering his ideals—Gear no doubt learned that maintaining theological integrity sometimes required one to offend popular sentiment.[49]

As the kneel-in crisis dragged on, it became increasingly likely that the moderator would be called on to intervene in some way. Where would Gear come down in the controversy that pitted his former church against his former college? Those who remembered his days in Memphis could be confident of one thing: Gear would not hesitate to condemn the "Southern way" when he judged it to be incompatible with Christian charity. In 1946, for instance, he had preached a sermon at SPC, subsequently published in a local newspaper, condemning the bigotry of Mississippi Senator Theodore Bilbo, of whom he wrote that "every Christian in the South must feel a real sense of shame." It would not become clear until early 1965 how these various aspects of Gear's experience and character would affect his handling of the kneel-in crisis at SPC.[50]

PART THREE

MEMORIES OF A KNEEL-IN MOVEMENT

‖ 6 ‖

"You're Going to Have
to Go Out There Yourself"

Church People

To understand why the SPC leadership reacted as it did to the presence of racially mixed groups at its doors during the spring of 1964, we need more than an over-view of the church's history and an introduction to how PCUS traditionalists viewed the denomination's social pronouncements. We need to explore SPC's response to the prospect of ecclesiastical integration as racial boundaries within the PCUS steadily eroded during the 1950s.

At SPC the point of active resistance was reached in August 1957, when the church's session considered a request that African Americans be permitted to attend an upcoming meeting of Presbyterian women hosted by the church. Elder Robert Hussey moved that the request be denied and that the session go on record as being "opposed to integration in our conferences and institutions; and further, that our staff be instructed not to attend or promote any integrated meetings, nor send any funds to any conferences or institutions that are practicing integration." The motion carried, though five elders—including Marion S. Boyd, the federal judge who would erect many roadblocks on the path to school desegregation in Memphis—abstained.[1]

Although it was introduced in response to a specific challenge—the presence of black women on the SPC campus—Hussey's motion had larger implications. At a session meeting October 7, these were enumerated in an eleven-paragraph "Statement of Policy," which began:

> In view of repeated plans and programs for the holding of integrated meetings of the white and negro races in our local churches, camps and conferences, at all age levels, the Session of the Second Presbyterian Church feels that the time has come for a definite statement of policy in regard to this question.

> Many learned and devout Christian men have debated pro and con
> the question of segregation being Scriptural. This is a moot question. It is
> the current decision of the Session of Second Presbyterian church that
> this Church will adhere to the policy of segregation in all of its endeavors.[2]

To ensure that this "clear, honest Christian" declaration would not be ignored or misunderstood, Hussey's proposal called for establishment of a Policy Committee and provided for a copy of the statement to be placed in the hands of staff members and those "employed in any executive position or capacity" at the church. After an extended discussion, the motion to adopt carried with only two dissenting votes. News of the policy was forwarded to Memphis's daily papers.[3]

It is not at all clear why an all-white church in a thoroughly segregated city, a church whose racial homogeneity was not under threat, would adopt an official policy of segregation in 1957. Part of the reason, no doubt, is that in the fall of that year eyes in Memphis and around the nation were fixed on Little Rock, Arkansas, where nine black students had enrolled at the formerly all-white Central High School. Under orders from Governor Orval Faubus, members of the Arkansas National Guard blocked the "Little Rock Nine" from entering Central. In response, President Dwight Eisenhower federalized the state guard and dispatched the U.S. Army's 101st Airborne Division to keep order and protect the students. The federal government's willingness to enforce court-ordered desegregation by "sending in the troops" worried many white Southerners, including the citizens of Memphis, which is only a two-hour drive from Little Rock.[4]

The fact that SPC's segregation policy was adopted just two weeks after the army arrived in Little Rock suggests that events there influenced session members to make their position clear. Yet the threat that most concerned SPC's elders came not from their government, but from their denomination, which, as the "Statement of Policy" lamented, had overseen "a gradual promotion of integration into the life of [the] church." Indeed, since the first non-segregated meeting of the PCUS General Assembly in 1950, the prospect of interaction with black Presbyterians in church courts had become increasingly real. The system of internal segregation implemented through "Negro" presbyteries and synods was being dismantled and most of the black churches founded since World War II— including Memphis's Parkway Gardens (1952)—had been placed in geographic presbyteries. This meant that at every level of church life beyond the individual congregation white Presbyterians might find themselves in contact with African Americans.[5]

As was the case among white Southerners more generally, conservative Presbyterians were particularly troubled by the breakdown of racial barriers in places where young people congregated. PCUS seminaries integrated in 1951 and church-affiliated colleges were urged to do so as well beginning in 1954. More disturbingly, some camps for young people had also begun to integrate. Although Montreat youth conferences continued to operate on a segregated basis, stories circulated of black workers at the conference center associating with white conferees. All this fueled a concern to protect Presbyterian youth from the dark threat of race mixing. This concern was explicit in SPC's "Statement of Policy," which declared that

> the decision to allow, and the planning for and promotion and encouragement of mixed dancing between whites and negroes at our conference grounds, leaves us no choice but to rule that no members or groups shall, as official representatives of the church, attend any such integrated meetings.[6]

The SPC session's anxiety around "mixed dancing" was no doubt rooted in concerns, common among white Southerners at the time, that social relations of this sort could lead to miscegenation. This deep-seated fear helps explain church representatives' strong reactions when mixed groups congregated in front of the church in 1964.[7]

SPC's 1957 "Statement of Policy" illumines another dimension of the church's response to students who visited seven years after its adoption. The statement denied that the church's segregation policy was un-Christian, arguing that SPC had "proven itself for over a hundred years to be a benefactor of mankind over the whole world, carrying the Gospel of Jesus Christ to every man, regardless of race, color or creed." In other words, the church's session argued, SPC might discriminate on the basis of race in its domestic endeavors, but its love for all people was evident in its colorblind commitment to world evangelization.[8]

The same mindset was in evidence at SPC in 1964. In January, the church's first-ever World Missions Conference resulted in the commissioning of fourteen new missionaries, six of them to Africa. Two months later, black Memphis State University student Joe Purdy was excluded from worship when he identified himself as "American." To some of the church's lay leaders, visiting blacks from foreign lands were symbols of the church's missionary outreach, while visiting African Americans represented a subversion of the social order.[9]

The 1957 "Statement of Policy" also anticipates the weak theological position in which the session would find itself when it was forced to defend its exclusion of black visitors in 1964. The statement's sidestepping of the "question of segregation being Scriptural" is remarkable for a document composed by group of evangelical Protestants. Increasingly, however, this evasive position was one Southern Christians in mainline denominations were forced to take. David L. Chappell has observed that, in contrast to the earnestness with which Southerners had argued for "biblical" slavery a century earlier, in the 1950s even avid segregationists were reluctant to claim biblical sanction for separation of the races. This reluctance was particularly evident among Southern Presbyterians. A year before SPC adopted its segregation policy, a special committee of East Alabama Presbytery, one of the denomination's most conservative regional bodies, conceded there was "no Scriptural basis for racial segregation in the Church."[10]

Yet despite the SPC session's admission that a defense of segregation could not be based in the Bible, its "Statement of Policy" did offer a religious defense of racial separation. Segregation was a Christian necessity, the statement emphasized, because "one of the leading forces for integration is godless communism, which we believe to be the greatest present day foe of Christianity." This claim reflects a tendency in the post-*Brown* era for Southerners to express resistance to integration in the idiom of anti-communism. In this language of moral defiance, integration was characterized as part of a plot to "Sovietize the South," perpetrated by NAACP activists who dwelt in "the seedy underworld of communist subversion."[11]

The Policy Evolves

The SPC session's fear that the church would be forced to deal with the integration of PCUS-owned camps was realized in 1962 when it learned that Memphis Presbytery had approved inviting all local churches (including Parkway Gardens) to participate in presbytery-sponsored programs of Christian Education at Nacome, a denominational camp near Pleasantville, Tennessee, which offered a summer camping program for youth. The announcement provoked a motion that SPC's senior pastor "inform the members of our congregation who have children, of the action of Presbytery to integrate all meetings of Nacome."[12]

In June 1963 a meeting of the SPC session was called to hear a report by the committee responsible for overseeing the 1957 "Statement of Policy." The Policy Committee had met for several hours the previous day "to consider recommended changes in the Session's previous instructions as to the seating of visitors," apparently in response to rumored attempts to integrate the church. Elder Horace Hull related that "after much discussion and prayerful thought," the committee had concluded that "if visitors of the colored race" presented themselves for worship on Sunday, June 16, "they would be coming for demonstration purposes, accompanied by the Press, television cameras, movie cameras, etc." Apparently in order to avoid unfavorable publicity, the committee moved that

> due to changes in the current situation, the former directions given by
> the Session concerning admission of visitors or members be tempo-
> rarily suspended for the period of the next three months, and that the

handling of such matters in emergency be left to the discretion of the pastor and the officers in charge on duty in the narthex, they being authorized to have guests sign the guest register or guest cards and to seat them at their discretion.[13]

With respect to black visitors, the committee advised that they be "seated in two rows of pews set aside for this purpose, without fanfare." Yet even this temporary suspension of the 1957 policy was not acceptable to the session's hard-liners, including Robert Hussey. After Hussey questioned whether the meeting itself was in order, Elder Rives Manker successfully moved that the Policy Committee's motion be tabled.[14]

What led the SPC session to believe that the church might have "visitors of the colored race" in June 1963 is not known. But it is clear that at the time a majority of session members were uncomfortable with any suspension of the 1957 policy. Session minutes also reveal that the majority of elders expected what was then being referred to as the "'Statement of Policy' on integration" to be observed in all the church's activities. At a meeting in January 1964, a motion was adopted reiterating the obligations of the church's ministers to advise all staff members of the segregation policy and instructing the Chairman of the Christian Education Committee to review it "with every staff member in that department and advise them that they must adhere to that Policy in both spirit and practice and if they cannot do so to tender their resignations."[15]

Who Would Guard the Church?

The first direct challenge to SPC's segregation policy came in March 1964, when students in racially mixed groups appeared at the doors of the church intent on entering together. The fateful mingling of sex and race that the SPC session had feared might take place at PCUS conference grounds was now on display at the very threshold of the church sanctuary. Words—even strong words linking integration to "godless communism"—were not a sufficient response to this threat. The students' entrance to the church had to be thwarted.

The task fell to the church's junior deacons, a group of younger men whose job it was to usher worshippers to their seats on Sunday mornings. In 1964, the chairman of SPC's junior deacons was thirty-year-old John Adamson. In a telephone call from Elder Robert Hussey, Adamson learned that the session had been tipped off to impending attempts to integrate the church. But when Hussey instructed him to keep the unwelcome visitors out, Adamson said he would resign his position before refusing anyone entrance to God's House. To Hussey's assertion that the students would be coming to demonstrate rather than to worship,

Adamson responded that he was not in a position to judge their motives. "If you want to keep people out," he remembers telling Hussey, "you're going to have to go out there yourself."[16]

Adamson would not relent, but neither would those who wanted the junior deacons to protect the church from unwelcome visitors. Hussey warned Adamson that if SPC were to admit blacks, Parkway Gardens church "would shut down and they would all move over here." Adamson regarded such fears as unfounded, but realized that the position taken by session hard-liners was rooted in a profound fear of change. "They really believed that things should stay as they had been all during their lifetime," Adamson says. He adds that many of the church's elders were entrepreneurs and business owners who were used to being in charge. "They felt like this was their church," he explains, "and they could run it the way they wanted to." Adamson stresses that while these men were widely respected within the church, the majority of the congregation wanted to open the church's doors to all comers. "Anyone under forty years old felt that way. We had grown up in a different era."[17]

Bill Weber was another SPC member who was serving as a junior deacon in 1964. Weber, a 1959 graduate of Southwestern, remembers being asked not only to guard the sanctuary doors, but to "secure the campus." He refused on both counts, and recalls that the elders who were forced to assume responsibility for the church's security carried walkie-talkies and stationed themselves around the perimeter of the property, "like sentries on the lookout." Weber also remembers students being placed inside cars that pulled up beside the church. Initially he thought they were being arrested; then someone explained that they were being transported to Parkway Gardens church, "a place where they would have an opportunity to worship." Although Weber was "horrified" by the treatment given these visitors, he emphasizes that the church had fallen victim to the misguided decisions of "a handful of men who were segregationists." The experience led Weber to reevaluate his own feelings about race; however, when the church's policy changed and the students did not return to worship, Weber felt SPC had been "set up."[18]

John Clark was another younger SPC member who served as a junior deacon in 1964. He does not remember being asked to guard the church doors, but he does recall catching glimpses of the kneel-ins while moving between his Sunday School class and the 11 a.m. worship service. Clark says that while many SPC members felt instinctively that the church doors should be open to all, they took offense at the students' behavior. "The girls and boys were walking back and forth in front of the church," he says, "and had a certain degree of fraternization going on between them." One example Clark recalls is "a black girl and a blonde girl" in a walking embrace. He remembers church members commenting on such scenes and believes that photographs of these "intentional provocations" may have circulated in the church.[19]

At forty-three, Don McClure, Sr. was one of the older members of SPC's junior deacon corps. In 1964, he had been a church member for a good while, having "married into" an SPC family in the 1940s. Interviewed at age eighty-eight, McClure's memories remain vivid and succinct: "They were real upset about the prospect of these people coming to our church and they told me to go stand on the front porch and shoo 'em away. And I wouldn't do it," he recalls. McClure even wrote to one of the elders expressing his disappointment with the session's actions. He did not receive a response, he says.[20]

Not all SPC junior deacons resisted or evaded the session's charge to repel unwelcome visitors. In 1964, Milton Knowlton was a twenty-eight-year-old member of an SPC family that traced its roots in the church back to 1850. "I stood outside on the church steps along with some others; I guess I was asked to do it," he says. "One or two spokesmen were out on the sidewalk and they just said 'you're not welcome here, we don't want you on our property; we'd appreciate it if you would leave.' Their feeling was that this was political. And I felt that way, too." Although Knowlton witnessed no "misbehavior" on the part of students, his sense that they had come only to make a social comment was confirmed a year later when a group of black visitors were welcomed into the church, seated in the front pew, and never seen again.[21]

Like others, Knowlton blames the lingering crisis at SPC on a small group of men in their seventies and eighties whose stance was opposed by the great majority of the church's membership. But Knowlton's own story reveals that hard-line elders could find support from younger men who, though lacking an ideological commitment to segregation, were determined to protect their church from an invasion of "demonstrators." Claiming that God does not recognize "black, white or purple or whatever," Knowlton denies that the decision to exclude the students was racially motivated. What was it, then, that marked the students as demonstrators? Like the older men standing alongside him on the church steps, Knowlton seems to have found it impossible to believe that students in mixed groups trying to enter a church where they were unwanted could be motivated by religious conviction.[22]

Having been a Southwestern student himself only a few years earlier, Knowlton thought he might be in a position to mediate in the lingering conflict between church and college. In a conversation with Southwestern Dean Jameson Jones, he suggested that Jones ask the students to "back off for three or four weeks" so the church could resolve matters internally. Knowlton was shocked when Jones responded that "he didn't have any control over what the students did off campus." An incredulous Knowlton replied that "if I had gone off campus and made a fool of myself and embarrassed the College I would have been called before you and probably kicked out of school. So if you want to tell me that you don't *want* to do anything about this, then I'll believe you." Church members like

Knowlton who had attended Southwestern and other church-related colleges before 1960 naturally expected the school's administration to exercise its *in loco parentis* role by "reining in" protesting students. Whatever their view of the session's treatment of the young visitors, they could scarcely conceive of a church college that could not regulate student behavior.[23]

Justin Towner was enrolled in what he calls the SPC "cradle roll" in 1931. He is one of just a handful of current SPC members who attended the church when it was located in downtown Memphis. After leaving for college, dental school, and military service, Towner returned to his native Memphis in 1956. He did not hold a leadership position at SPC in 1964, but he became involved in the kneel-in controversy nevertheless. "I don't like to remember it because I'm not proud of it," he says, "but I was one of the ones who stood at the doors to keep demonstrators out. And I guess the feeling was that those coming were not serious, just making a political racial point. I don't know how we came to judge that but that is what it clearly was."[24]

Forty-five years later, Towner remains troubled by his decision to stand between visiting students and the church's sanctuary:

> You felt you were correct . . . but it wasn't long before you realized that it wouldn't have been a big deal just to let them come on in. I can remember when we did there was an elderly African American down in the front of the sanctuary, and at the proper time he would give a good "Amen" to the pastor and the pastor's response at that time was "You know that's not bad, I kind of need that." So I don't know, you would have to feel wrong and many did feel wrong at that time. The majority of the church did.[25]

Dissent From Within

If a majority of church members "felt wrong" about SPC's response to the kneel-ins that began in March 1964, there is little evidence of internal dissent before the following January. As protesting student Hortense Spillers recalls, what she and other visitors did not see on Sunday mornings spoke as loudly as what they did see:

> I never heard of, never saw, never heard about any member of the church coming out saying to those people "you need to stop this. These people are obviously dressed to go to church. And they are not out here cussing and yelling and throwing Molotov cocktails and bricks, so I

think we can assume that they are peaceful, and they look pretty civilized to me. So why are you doing this?" I don't know anybody who ever did that. . . . It's possible that there were people in the congregation who didn't agree with what was going on. But as far as I know they never made themselves known. They never came out of the crowd. But they knew that we were there, I guess. And we were trying to guess what was going on behind those locked doors.[26]

What *was* going on "behind those locked doors"? Interviews with church members reveal that, along with soul searching, there were attempts to reason with session members and plans to place limits on their power. As chairman-elect of SPC's Board of Deacons in 1964, Zeno Yeates was disturbed by talk of hiring armed security guards and bringing guns to church. While many members shared his concerns, he says, dissent within the church was initially muted by the widespread belief that the students wanted "to disrupt the service and make a public stand." Yet even after the spring kneel-ins had ended and the session's intransigence was gaining notoriety, there was little vocal opposition within the church. "If more people at Second had been more opinionated and more involved and taken a stand," Yeates says, "I wasn't aware of it. And that bothered me no end."[27]

Another church member disturbed by the unfolding controversy was Millen Darnell, whose family had been active at SPC since the 1890s. Darnell was a former Sunday School teacher and junior deacon who in 1964 was serving in Ecuador as an SPC-supported missionary. As we have seen, news of the SPC kneel-ins made its way to many foreign lands where PCUS missionaries were serving. Darnell was kept apprised of events by his mother, who was employed at the church. By the time the kneel-in story reached Ecuador, however, it had undergone considerable embellishment. Darnell "remembers" that the rebuffed students "went to the newspapers . . . all over America. People were flying in from all over the United States to integrate [the church]. . . . They were marching around it." Even if it was difficult to get an accurate picture of events from twenty-five hundred miles away, the basic problem was clear: A racial controversy was tarnishing the reputation of Darnell's beloved home church in Memphis and beyond.[28]

Although Darnell had grown up in thoroughly segregated communities in Memphis and the Mississippi Delta, his experiences in the Andean Mountains had sensitized him to race relations back home. Thinking he might be able to help some old friends think through the issues, while home on furlough Darnell visited session members with whom he had some influence. He asked Elder Horace Hull, part of the session's hard-line faction, to consider "just let[ting] the blacks come in and worship." Hull's response was that he had no problem worshipping with blacks; after all, he said, he conducted devotions with the servants he employed in his home. Aware of the uphill battle he was facing, Darnell made no further visits.[29]

The only effective internal resistance to the session's majority would come from a small group of SPC's younger leaders led by William S. Craddock, Jr. a third-generation church member who was a deacon in 1964. From the beginning of the protests, Craddock had felt that, because the church belonged to God, anyone who wanted to worship should be welcomed. He watched incredulously as elders patrolled the perimeter of the church property and communicated on the movement of student visitors via handheld radio. Craddock was not asked to help guard the church ("they were scared to ask me," he says), but he did have many conversations with session members who hoped to capitalize on his influence among the church's younger men. One elder, he says, took him into the sanctuary, pointed to the last two or three pews, and suggested that the controversy be resolved by setting them aside for black visitors.[30]

Open opposition to these men, Craddock stresses, was suppressed by the fact that some were "very prominent people in town." Nevertheless, determination to do something grew along with the negative publicity they were attracting to the church. In early 1965, convinced that the session's position was opposed by "all the Deacons and the majority of the church," Craddock began meeting with a small group of concerned men that included Elder Clifton Kirkpatrick and Deacons Thomas C. Farnsworth and James H. Wetter. Together they devised a strategy to end the controversy by delimiting the power of the pro-segregation faction controlling the SPC session.[31]

Presbyterian ruling elders and deacons are ordained to their offices for life, although once ordained they must be elected to active service in a congregation. Traditionally the sessions of PCUS churches included all ordained elders within the congregation, but in the 1960s the trend was toward rotating elders in and out of active service according to what was known as the "limited service plan." If SPC were to adopt this plan, Craddock and the others concluded, the church's longest-serving elders could be replaced on the session by men of the congregation's choosing, men who could dramatically alter the body's balance of power. PCUS polity stipulated that a rotational plan for church officers could be adopted by a simple majority of the membership but only at a congregational meeting called for that purpose. Requests for such meetings had to be directed to the session by petition of at least one fourth of a church's membership.[32]

This was the strategy settled upon by Craddock's group (which came to be known as the Accord Committee) and the one that eventually brought an end to the kneel-in crisis at SPC. Craddock and the others believed that a majority of congregants would support elder rotation. But they knew their opponents would not relinquish their influence on the session without a fight. One key to the

Accord Committee's success was its ability to splinter the session majority by enlisting the support of Elder John Cleghorn, erstwhile spokesman for session hard-liners. Craddock and others took Cleghorn to lunch, "read the riot act to him," and convinced him that the session's intransigence was not serving the church's long-term interests. The Accord Committee even prevailed on Cleghorn to speak in favor of elder rotation at a fateful congregational meeting at the end of February 1965.[33]

The Pastors

There were four pastors on the staff of 3,650-member SPC in 1964. Serving alongside Senior Minister Jeb Russell were two associate ministers—C. Phil Esty and W. James Hazelwood—and an assistant minister, Edward J. Knox. The fifty-five-year-old Hazelwood had been a seminary classmate of Russell's and was recruited to SPC in 1961 after spending most of his pastoral career in Georgia. Like the other ministers on the church's staff, Hazelwood was a graduate of Columbia Theological Seminary in Decatur, Georgia, reputedly the denomination's most conservative seminary, although it had recently come under attack for its supposed "liberalism."

Forty-one-year-old Phil Esty had come to SPC in 1959 after seven years in a solo pastorate in Athens, Georgia. With considerable experience as a senior minister, Esty became Russell's "number-two man." Although he had no personal encounters with protesting students, Esty was quite familiar with how the church's leadership viewed them. "Somehow," he recalls, "word leaked out to us that Southwestern students were coming to demonstrate because they heard that blacks would not be allowed in. So some of the older men were really upset. And they thought it would upset worship and said 'we'll just stand at the doors and let them know that if they've come to demonstrate that we do not want them in.'"[34]

Esty does not defend the session's hard-liners, many of whom, he says, were "what we would call racists." He even acknowledges that elders who claimed they were acting to protect the church from disruption were themselves a disruptive influence. But Esty maintains that these men were "godly people [who] loved the Lord and really supported missions and evangelism and the church"; furthermore, he says, blame for the crisis must be shared by Southwestern students, whom he accuses of being in search of media attention. Esty goes so far as to suggest that if blacks had come to the church without white Southwestern students, they would not have been refused entrance.[35]

Esty's memories provide a rare glimpse of how the church's pastors interpreted the crisis in the months during which they were publicly silent. According to Esty, the ministers discussed the issue often and prayed for guidance in dealing with a session that refused to follow their guidance. The pastoral staff believed that eventually even the "hot heads and racists" would do the right thing, but they feared that divergent perceptions of the kneel-ins could split the church. This fear was fueled by comments like the one made by an elder who threatened to "go and build a sanctuary bigger than Second"; it was inflamed by the fact that the man had the money to do it.[36]

Ed Knox was a native Tennessean who, at thirty-one, was considerably younger than the other clergymen serving SPC. His portfolio included ministry to the church's youth and collegians. Hired during the fall of 1964 when the kneel-in controversy was far from resolved, Knox's interview naturally included questions regarding his racial views. When he had finished addressing the topic, an older elder asked Knox whether he was "a segregationist or an integrationist." Knox responded that he did not believe there would be segregation in heaven. In that sense, he said, "you can call me an integrationist." Knox was certain this admission would cost him the SPC job, in part because he knew a candidate who had been dropped from consideration after his own "race talk" with the session. Thus Knox was shocked when Russell called to offer him the position; he was reassured when told it was only a matter of time before the race issue at SPC was settled.[37]

Knox never witnessed the kneel-ins that took place outside the SPC sanctuary. But he was well aware of the discontent they were creating among the church's own collegians. Although he wisely refrained from openly criticizing the session or its actions, Knox was sympathetic to the protesting students and viewed the elders who were guarding the church as "basically rednecks." Eventually Knox concluded that holding the party line was undermining his credibility among SPC's young people. His personal turning point came in January 1965: "I got up one morning and told my wife, 'I've got to talk to Dr. Russell today; I've got to tell him that if he wants me to leave, we'll leave, but I'm going to have to start [talking] with the college kids . . . saying here's where we stand on this thing."[38]

Before Knox could act on this resolution he was summoned to Russell's office, where he found the other pastors assembled and in the process of "writing a letter to the congregation, going around the session." Dated January 21, 1965, and addressed "Dear Friends in Christ," the letter was brief, but unequivocal:

> Some of our members have been asking for months how your ministers feel about the turning away of people from our Church. Your pastors want the congregation to know that we cannot in Christian conscience approve the policy of excluding people from our Worship Services. We cannot find support for this policy in the Word of God. We cannot find

support for it in the history of our beloved congregation, and this policy
is out of harmony with our Presbytery, Synod and General Assembly.[39]

Going on record as opposing the decisions of the church's governing body was a
bold move for Russell and his colleagues. And once the threshold of open resistance had been crossed, there could be no going back. Knox was counseled not
to sign the letter because as an assistant minister and the newest hire, he was the
most vulnerable to retaliation. But he insisted on adding his signature nevertheless. "What would the college kids think if I didn't sign it?" Knox recalls asking.
While he would keep his job, Knox's decision to stand with the other ministers
brought consequences. One elder told the young pastor he would never again
come to hear him preach.[40]

The Women

How did the majority of SPC members who were women view the kneel-in controversy that consumed their church between March 1964 and March 1965? It
will be recalled that SPC's segregation policy was adopted in response to a church-
woman's request that African Americans be allowed to attend a presbytery-wide
meeting at the church. The request indicates that at least some churchwomen had
a more racially inclusive vision of the church than their male counterparts. This
was certainly the case at the denominational level, where historically women and
students had been the catalysts for desegregating camps and conferences.

Some SPC women instinctively followed the lead of the church's male leadership, while others expressed open dissent; many women, however, particularly
young mothers whose primary focus at the time was raising children, simply
hoped the matter would be resolved with a minimum of disruption. Pat Clark
was among those who wanted to "come to church and have our service and go
home" and were relieved when the controversy came to an end. "I just remember, along with the sadness of different people leaving that I really loved," says
Clark, "also just this feeling of relief, a tremendous relief!"[41]

For churchwomen who believed that the session was mismanaging the crisis,
there were few sanctioned means of expressing their views. Even so, women had
always found avenues for making their influence felt at SPC. An oft-cited example is a congregational meeting in the late 1940s at which two women serving
on the committee tasked with finding a new location for the church were able to
persuade the congregation to vote against the committee's official recommendation. During the kneel-in crisis, however, church policy was determined solely
by the session, a body in which women had no voice. If individual women were
fortunate enough to have an elder in their extended family, their opinions might

gain a hearing. Alternatively, they could follow the example of women like Elsie Yeates, who "fussed at" elders blocking the church entrance, telling them "you have no right to keep people from the church."[42]

Yet women's power was most effective at SPC when it was mobilized behind the scenes. When members of the Accord Committee needed to collect nine hundred signatures in order to formally request a congregational meeting where elder rotation would be considered, they enlisted the help of SPC's women. Margaret Askew, May Patton, Betty Hutton, Jeanne Craddock, and Elizabeth Kirkpatrick were among those who mailed and collected the petitions and, according to Craddock, "were very efficient in doing so." "You want to get something done," Craddock says reflecting on the collaboration, "you get a bunch of dedicated women and they'll get it done."[43]

The official women's organization in PCUS churches was the Women of the Church (WOC). At Second Presbyterian the WOC included over a thousand women assigned to thirty-one "circles" that met monthly in members' homes. The organization was led by an executive board and its work was overseen by several committees. In addition, each circle had its own "chairman," "co-chairman," secretary, treasurer, and, of course, telephone chair. While we can only imagine the conversations that took place in these circles over tea and cheese straws, there is evidence that by early 1965 strong resistance to the actions of the SPC session had grown up within the WOC. In February, for instance, the *Press-Scimitar* reported that when Pastor Jeb Russell told women attending a WOC meeting that "the church must draw all to worship, even atheists, if this be possible," the response was applause and cries of "Amen" and "Hallelujah." Further indications of dissent may be found in the WOC's annual congregational histories for 1964 and 1965.[44]

In contrast to the official history of SPC published in 1971, which did not so much as mention the SPC kneel-ins, the WOC's congregational history for 1964 devoted over two of its eight pages to the crisis. The narrative began by citing an invitation that had appeared in the SPC worship bulletin on the first Sunday of each quarter in 1964: "To all who sin and need a Saviour . . . this Church opens the door and makes free a place, and in the name of Jesus Christ, our Lord, says 'Welcome!'" The author of the WOC history, Mrs. K. William Chandler, commented that "Second Presbyterian Church comes to wonder in this trying year of 1964 if this expressed invitation is the true feeling of the congregation or not." During the spring, Chandler related, the church had encountered

> one of the most grave problems it has faced in it's [sic] entire history. It had to do with the admittance of Negroes to the Worship Service. Beginning in March and going on through early June, interracial groups were turned away from the 11:00 A. M. Worship Service by members of the Session. These people were in the most part college students,

some belonging to the Intercollegiate Chapter of the National Association for the Advancement of Colored People.[45]

Significantly, the WOC's chronicle of the kneel-ins ignored the claim, so vociferously advanced by the church's session and its supporters, that the students were "demonstrators" whose goals were political rather than spiritual.

The kneel-in controversy dominated the church history compiled by the WOC for 1965, covering four of its six typewritten pages. After noting that beneath the church's "confident façade of serenity lay an unsolved problem, that of integration of races in our Church," the narrative delved into the history of race relations at SPC. "It is very surprising to many members of our Church to learn," Chandler wrote, "that Scipio, the man-servant of Miss L. C. Boyd was one of the twenty-one [charter] members of Second Presbyterian Church." Until the church moved to its present location, she went on,

> a few Negroes were generally in attendance at the Sunday morning service. They were welcomed and seated in the balcony. These Negroes were servants, carriage drivers, or chauffeurs of our white members and many present members of our congregation recall with happiness the lovely singing coming from the balcony. However, when our Church moved to its present location, there was never an instance of a Negro in the Church, except in the case of marriages, funerals, baptisms, graduation and commencement exercises when servants and Negro friends of our families were invited and welcomed. Also, of course, when large meetings were held in our Church in which delegations from various churches were represented, the negro delegations were equally welcomed as the white.[46]

Just beneath the surface of this seemingly wistful recollection of a time when happy Negroes sang from the church balcony lay the charge that the controversy engulfing the church had been precipitated by a departure from congregational tradition.

The narrative located the fateful turn in the church's attitude toward black visitors in the pastorate of Rev. Anthony Dick. "Fearing that our Church might be a target for racial integration," the historian asserted, Dick "led the Session, their being mostly in agreement, in making a statement of policy concerning this matter." Chandler then pointed out that the body that had adopted the 1957 segregation policy was "almost entirely the same Session who thwarted the demonstrators in the Spring of 1964 and who faced again the problem in 1965." In this way the WOC narrative cast serious doubt on the session's claim that its response to student visitors had been unrelated to race.[47]

The 1965 WOC church history also warned that the lingering integration crisis had threatened to undermine SPC's commitment to the missionary enterprise. According to the narrative, speakers and guests at SPC's World Missions Conference in early 1965 had condemned the church's policy of excluding blacks from worship. "Missionaries said it was difficult to preach Christian love for all mankind to African natives, etc., when white Christians will not even accept other races in their worship," Chandler noted. "Many others said it was non-scriptural and some had social reasons."[48]

How widespread was the dissent expressed in the WOC chronicles for 1964 and 1965? Chandler suggests that a majority of church members ultimately came to oppose the position taken by the session, although she acknowledges that "for many, a strong endorsement of the Session superseded their love and loyalty to their Church." SPC's women were no doubt divided by the crisis; but it appears that the WOC's leadership was more open-minded, more pragmatic, and more concerned with the church's broader Christian witness than the men who were determining church policy at the time.[49]

Deference, Collusion, and the Convergence of Memory

Even if they had reservations about the visiting students' motives, as the kneel-ins continued many SPC members seem to have decided there was more to be lost than gained by keeping them out of their church. By the fall of 1964, news of the standoff had spread across the nation and beyond; pressure was being applied from all sectors of the denomination; the prospect of losing the upcoming meeting of the General Assembly was increasingly real; and looming on the horizon was the specter of an intervention by Memphis Presbytery that could dissolve the church's relationship with its elders and/or pastors.[50]

But if, as interviews and documentary evidence indicate, a majority of church members believed that the session's stance was damaging SPC and the cause of Christ, how is it that there was so little dissent before January 1965, ten months after the kneel-ins began? One factor seems to have been the high esteem in which rank-and-file members held their leaders, men widely respected in the church and in the city, despite their espousal of racial views that were deemed "old fashioned." Natural deference became near-reverence when it encountered the aura of spirituality in which the SPC session packaged its statements during the crisis. For example, the session's letter to the congregation on May 3, 1964—the day the kneel-ins were being broadcast to a national television audience—stressed that despite differences in age and conviction, members of the body were united by "a sincere love of the Lord Jesus Christ, a deep love and loyalty for his church and a prayerful devotion to the cause of spreading God's gospel to all people and all nations." Throughout the kneel-in crisis, in fact, session spokespersons portrayed the church's elders as "almost continually in prayer, asking God's will and guidance in this matter."[51]

Such expressions of piety appear to have delayed the congregational opposition that would eventually bring an end to the controversy. John Clark's sentiments were no doubt typical. Although he opposed the views of the session's leadership, he was convinced that each of these men was "an outstanding person, in his own personal, and Christian, and business life." It seems to have been extremely difficult for younger church members to openly defy men whom they regarded as pillars of the local community, generous supporters of the church and its ministries, and paragons of personal piety.

The tendency to defer to age and status was evident even within the session itself. From the beginning of the crisis, in fact, two factions had wrestled to control the body, and thus the direction of the church: senior elders who wanted to maintain the old ways and resist pressure from "outside groups" (including church courts), and more junior elders who, whatever their personal preferences regarding association with African Americans, believed that the church should undergo token integration in order to protect what was left of its reputation. This faction was represented by moderates like Charles Gillespie, who were hopeful that given sufficient time the church's "Ross Barnetts and Gov. Wallaces" would come around. In the meantime, however, the intransigence of these Barnetts and Wallaces was enabled by a cautiousness rooted in younger men's deference to age and concern for their livelihoods.[52]

Even taking these factors into account, however, it is difficult to escape the conclusion that church members' responses to segregationists on the session involved collusion as well as deference. Interviews reveal that while there was very little sentiment in the congregation for maintaining racial purity, many rank-and-file members heartily supported the session's determination to repel "demonstrators." In doing so, they accepted an interpretation of the students' motives that was contradicted by easily verifiable facts—for instance, that the kneel-ins had begun not with "demonstrations" but with an attempt by two local young men to attend church together, and that the returning visitors were invariably well-dressed and well-behaved and did not engage in disruptive behavior while on church grounds.

Session hard-liners no doubt worked hard to convince church members that the visiting students wished to disrupt rather than participate in worship. But their task was made easier because most members did not bother to gather first-hand information about the students or their goals, choosing instead to enter the sanctuary through side doors while the main entrance was guarded by men whose racial outlook they supposedly did not share. The decision to avoid direct contact with the students kept church people stuck in a pattern of circular thinking that cast the visitors as demonstrators because, having been excluded from the sanctuary, they chose to stand outside and "demonstrate."

Some members acknowledge having had feelings of uncertainty regarding the students' true intentions. Jack Connors, for instance, says he "didn't know whether they really wanted in or they just wanted to cause trouble or whether they were peaceful Christians that wanted to just be able to participate." But most members repressed this ambiguity and accepted the session's version of the visitors' goals, despite the lack of any precedent for publicly questioning church-goers' motives. As Carl Pritchett observed when he visited Memphis in May 1964, "if a white man appears in the company of a Negro Christian these days the officials seem suddenly interested in the motives of such people. At other times they are glad to have anyone who is white whether he has any faith or character or not."[53]

Church members' failure to independently analyze events made them suscep-tible not only to misapprehensions of the students' motives but also to efforts at minimizing the kneel-ins' significance, efforts that were under way soon after the visits began. On May 3, 1964, for instance—as a network television crew was filming outside the church—a session representative pleaded with the congrega-tion to "avoid exaggeration of this situation and not to be influenced by those who will try to distort these incidents out of all proportion to their importance."

Four decades later, some church members who experienced the kneel-ins con-tinue to downplay their significance. "It didn't amount to a hill of beans, really," says S. Herbert Rhea, a moderate member of the session in 1964. "It was more smoke than fire. When we opened the doors nobody showed up." Similarly, the extent of the kneel-ins at SPC is often seriously underestimated, with some wit-nesses collapsing the year-long controversy into a couple of Sunday visits. To some extent, such failures of memory are products of time and age. But it is telling that, even after being informed that the kneel-ins continued for eight consecutive weeks in 1964 and resumed for another six in early 1965, church members who lived through the events remain doubtful.[54]

Another common theme in interviews with SPC members who were active in 1964 is the claim that the kneel-ins only *appeared* to be about race. According to Herbert Rhea, for example, the controversy should be understood as a power struggle between the church and presbytery, which was "getting away from the Bible and doing political type things we didn't agree with." Even when the kneel-ins' obvious racial overtones are acknowledged, some church members deflect blame from SPC by claiming that segregationist sentiments were confined to the men and women who left to form Independent Presbyterian Church in 1965. In this view, the controversy concluded in a self-purging of the church's racist ele-ment. As long-time member Jack Connors puts it, "a group of people here who were very conservative thinkers . . . split because they thought that the church here was going to open the doors and welcome the blacks."[55]

Blaming racism at SPC on men who resigned from the session in 1965 is no more an invitation to honest self-analysis than are other dubious aspects of "official" church memory, including mischaracterization of the visitors' motives, minimization of the kneel-ins' significance, and outright denial of the controversy's racial dimensions. Each interferes with the kind of personal and institutional soul searching that is required to grow beyond such experiences. It is a testimony to the church's overall health that in recent years its leadership has insisted that the congregation be engaged in just such soul searching.[56]

"Our Presence at the Church Is Itself an Act of Worship"

White Visitors

At the beginning of 1964 the sleepy segregated college known as Southwestern was one of the last places in Memphis one expected to encounter civil rights activism. A front-page article in the *Press-Scimitar* acknowledged as much. In a story describing how Sen. Herbert Walters (D-TN) had been met at Southwestern by students marching and carrying placards, the county chairman of the Democratic Party commented: "Well, this is certainly a surprise . . . at such a sedate place as Southwestern. . . . wow . . . what is this world coming to?"[1]

Contrary to popular perception, however, the flower of activism at Southwestern did not spring *de novo* from a desert of social apathy. As we have seen, the civil rights movement had entered the consciousness of many Southwestern students via the violent reaction to James Meredith's attempt to enroll at Ole Miss. Also crucial for the students who would eventually join the kneel-in campaign at SPC was their involvement in the NAACP's local intercollegiate chapter, formed in the spring of 1963. Participation in the NAACP group brought these Southwestern undergraduates into contact not only with black students from across the city, but with local civil rights leaders Maxine Smith, Vasco Smith, and James M. Lawson, Jr.

The Organizer

Jim Bullock ('64) was the senior Southwestern student whose visit to SPC with Joe Purdy on March 22, 1964, launched the kneel-in campaign there. Bullock had long been known as a campus activist. In 1962, he was among the students who swamped the appointment schedule of Southwestern President Peyton

Rhodes hoping to convince him to integrate the college, and in early 1964 he led the placard-carrying student group into the campus auditorium where Sen. Herbert Walters was speaking.[2]

Bullock came by his courage honestly. His father, James Randolph Bullock, was pastor of First Presbyterian Church in Jackson, Tennessee, where in 1958 he had welcomed an integrated group to Sunday-morning worship. When the session met that night and voted to close the church's doors to African Americans, the pastor had his dissent recorded in the session minutes. Weathering the controversy that followed, Bullock "loved and preached his way through those segregated walls" for the next eighteen years. "He was one of these preachers," Jim Bullock recalls of his father, "who felt called to preach that God loves all people; and he got a lot of grief for that, but you know . . . the church opened its doors to everybody. And the community changed. . . . And that's what I knew of the civil rights movement before I came to [Southwestern] in 1960."[3]

Bullock's own commitment to social justice deepened during his years at Southwestern, in part as a result of his participation in the 1961 PCUS Youth Triennium. "The folks there were talking about justice for all people," Bullock recalls, "and I sort of became conscious that this segregated society was an unjust society. And on the way back [from the Triennium] we became concerned that Afro-Americans we'd been with at the conference couldn't eat with us." After returning to Memphis, Bullock decided he would disregard local segregation statutes. "I began to sit in the back of the bus on my own," he recalls. "I began to really not abide by the drinking fountain and the restroom deals—all that."[4]

In 1963, Southwestern student body president Steve Richardson invited Bullock to LeMoyne College for a meeting of the intercollegiate chapter of the Memphis NAACP. Much to his surprise, Bullock was elected vice president. "They needed a white and somebody had seen me at church camp or something," he recalls. Participation in the NAACP "opened a whole new world" for Bullock, who like most whites at the time had rarely been in black homes or churches or interacted with African Americans as peers.[5]

Michael Braswell, the Memphis State student who served as the intercollegiate chapter president, was committed to pressuring local businesses to adopt nondiscriminatory hiring practices. But several chapter members, including Bullock, wanted to launch a church visitation campaign. It was decided that black and white group members would pair up on Sundays and visit each other's congregations. Joe Purdy took Bullock to Parkway Gardens Presbyterian Church; Bullock returned the favor by inviting Purdy to SPC, where he had visited a few times. "It was not a targeted thing," he says. "It was sort of like, 'let's choose a church.'"[6]

Bullock was shocked when he and Purdy were prevented from entering SPC. But he had been preparing for this moment for several years under the tutelage of his parents, Maxine and Vasco Smith, and Jim Lawson, from whom he learned "the use of non-violence as a way of opening up places for all God's people." Upon arriving at the church, Bullock saw uniformed law enforcement officers with guns and night sticks. "I remember my legs wobbling," he says. "It was scary. And they started moving toward us and we began this prayer kind of thing. And it was amazing. They just moved back and nobody touched us. . . . And we were really innocent in our prayers, [you] were just saying what would come to your heart."[7]

After being turned away from SPC, Bullock returned to Southwestern and began to recruit others to return with him to the church. By his own admission, Bullock "hounded" his classmates to join the kneel-ins, addressing some with Bob Dylan's question: "How many roads must a man walk down before you can call him a man?" New recruits were asked to meet for prayer on Sunday mornings on the steps of the Southwestern library before proceeding to SPC. Bullock estimates that at the peak of the kneel-in campaign thirty Southwesterners participated.[8]

In Lawson's workshops, Bullock had invariably played the role of disciplinarian, helping would-be protestors maintain their poise and removing anyone who could not do so. Naturally, this was the role Bullock assumed on the sidewalk in front of SPC on Sunday mornings. His calm demeanor allowed Bullock to remain composed even on Easter Sunday when a young mother, her children in tow, came up to him cursing "every word you ever heard, and spitting in your face." Many church people accused the students of being confrontational, Bullock recalls. But he stresses that "we weren't there to hack our way in. The force we were using was love and we were really seeking to change the place. We really were very concerned about segregation not being just. And the churches should have been the last places on earth to be segregated, in our minds."[9]

Lawson had taught Bullock to appeal to the consciences of those on "the other side." This training came in handy at SPC, where Bullock engaged in conversations with the men guarding the church doors. "We were trained to personalize things . . . to get in a long conversation," he says. "We'd try to do active listening. We would try to make friends with them . . . We never were angry—if anybody got upset or angry we always just took them out of what we were doing. You've got to keep from becoming spiteful, even if somebody takes an umbrella and sticks it in somebody's shoe or threatens somebody with a gun."[10]

Looking back, Bullock figures he received more education in Jim Lawson's church and Maxine Smith's living room than in all the college classrooms in which he sat. Lawson, in particular, was "the spiritual force that guided us. . . . He helped us a lot in understanding what to do when we were out there on our own." Yet Bullock emphasizes that the decision to join the kneel-ins was an individual one. "Some people felt like SNCC had sort of wooed you into it or maybe the NAACP and Mrs. Smith or somebody. But it was never like that. We were really on our own a lot."[11]

Because of Bullock's leadership in the kneel-ins, he became a target for those who believed the students had gone too far. Although his family endorsed his activism (upon receiving a photograph of her son in front of SPC, Bullock's mother wrote the sender to say she wished she could join her son there), members of his father's church in Jackson were not so supportive. In retaliation for Jim's role in the kneel-ins, the Clerk of Session at Dr. Bullock's church, who also headed the county draft board, worked unsuccessfully to revoke Bullock's Peace Corp deferment.[12]

In part because it provoked such responses, Bullock's leadership in the SPC kneel-in campaign was formative for him. "I think it said to me, don't just accept that things have to stay the same. You can do something about it." For Bullock "doing something" has included advocating for the victims of corporate coal mining in Kentucky, integrating a youth group in rural Alabama, and becoming an advocate for children at risk in north-central Florida. "The events at SPC brought out some skills I didn't know I had. And I've used those skills all through life," he says.[13]

The Philosopher

As Jim Bullock and Joe Purdy were being turned away from SPC, Southwestern student Howard Romaine ('64) was sitting with an African American colleague in the back of Memphis's First Baptist Church. But as chair of the NAACP intercollegiate chapter subcommittee that had planned the church visits, Romaine soon became a spokesperson for the SPC protestors and a lightning rod for their opponents.

Romaine was a chemistry and philosophy double major from New Iberia, Louisiana, who had grown up in the Presbyterian Church. As was the case with many of his peers, the seeds of his racial awakening had been planted at a church youth camp. "The cooks and kitchen staff sang spirituals to the summer campers," he recalls, "to encourage tips I guess—or perhaps to speak to us in a language we couldn't understand at the time, but maybe worked its way into our souls or hearts, or something." At Southwestern Romaine was active in the PCUS-affiliated Westminster Fellowship, but the biggest influences on his spiritual development were the music of Bob Dylan and the momentous events of 1963, including the violent crackdown on a CORE-sponsored mass rally in Plaquemines, Louisiana.[14]

In September, when the national media reported that law enforcement officials in Plaquemines had attacked protestors with tear gas and fire hoses, Romaine drove his grandfather's Ford Falcon down to Iberville Parish. There he watched "dogs, tear gas, and state police on horses drive black folks into their churches, where they were running to escape the tear gas and cattle prods." In the midst of these traumatic extracurricular events, Romaine's formal education had begun to affect him in new ways. He was reading Heidegger, Wittgenstein, Bonhoeffer, Bultmann, and Barth, all of whom, he learned, had been personally affected by Nazi totalitarianism. Meanwhile, Romaine was digesting King's "Letter from Birmingham Jail," which he came to understand as a "local reaction to racist totalitarianism in Alabama." His conversion from philosophy to activism became complete in the wake of JFK's assassination in late 1963. In the aftermath of this national tragedy Romaine joined similarly minded peers in the NAACP intercollegiate chapter, where he was exposed to the nonviolent philosophies of Maxine Smith and Jim Lawson.[15]

Aware that he was not a regular churchgoer, Romaine's parents were doubly surprised when they received a letter in April 1964 claiming that he had been attending SPC with his "black girlfriend." As his mother sobbed in the background, Romaine's father called to ask whether he was "still riding those niggers around in [his] car." Indeed, Romaine was not only transporting fellow students to SPC on Sunday mornings, but engaging in conversation with the men guarding the doors, and being forcibly removed from church property. He was also assuming the role of group spokesman, eloquently describing the kneel-ins' moral rationale in the campus newspaper.[16]

In words that echoed those used by the architects of the first kneel-ins in 1960, Romaine described the spectacle he and others hoped to create outside SPC:

> We feel that our presence at the church is itself an act of worship, the presentation of our bodies a symbol of the church's tragic rejection of the gospel message of brotherhood and love. Our remaining outside the church, apart from it, symbolizes the separateness of our people, Negro from white, man from man, the separateness of the "church" from love. Although we come with this attitude of worship and hope, we have been met with hate, bitterness, recrimination and hired policemen—evidently "guarding" the "church." But we yet hope that this momentarily harsh confrontation will make visible a genuine reconciliation and brotherhood, and a refocusing of attention upon the role of the Southern church in the struggle for human dignity and freedom.[17]

Ironically, given his ability to articulate a theological rationale for Christian involvement in the struggle for civil rights, rumors circulated at SPC and beyond that Romaine was an atheist. In fact, few students at Southwestern were more concerned with the issue of God's existence in 1964. Romaine explored the matter in an honors thesis that considered René Descartes's ontological argument for God's existence through the lens of Albert North Whitehead's "process" philosophy.[18]

Yet despite working on his thesis, preparing for comprehensive exams, and running track, Romaine's activism intensified in the final months of his senior year. On April 13, while the SPC kneel-ins were still in progress, he was arrested for attempting to desegregate the Normal Tea Room near Memphis State. When Romaine returned to the Tea Room, he learned that citizens who opposed the restaurant's integration were much less restrained than the men who guarded the doors at SPC. In fact, Romaine and other picketers were chased by an angry mob and forced to take refuge in the Memphis State Catholic Center. Press coverage of this incident led to the eviction of Romaine and his roommate Bob Morris from their off-campus apartment.[19]

Then in early May, the *Press-Scimitar* published Romaine's rebuttal of SPC Elder John Cleghorn's claim that the visiting students lacked "a sincere desire to worship in our sanctuary, prompted by genuine spiritual motivation." After pointing out that church members had written "absurdly false, and to some degree, threatening letters to us and our parents," Romaine described Cleghorn's charges as "further proof of the bigotry which grips Second Presbyterian Church." "How can the members of such a church call themselves Christians?" he asked.[20]

As Romaine's words and actions garnered attention in the press, they began to create repercussions on campus. Southwestern's track and field coach encouraged him to desist from his involvement at SPC, as did President Rhodes, who asked Romaine to consider how his parents might react "if Negroes came to their front door in New Iberia." Despite the pressures, however, Romaine continued to protest at SPC until a truce was brokered by denominational representatives. After graduating from Southwestern in June 1964 and spending the summer in Mississippi as one of the few Southern white students to participate in Freedom Summer, Romaine began graduate studies in philosophy at the University of Virginia. In Charlottesville, he was deeply involved with the Southern Student Organizing Committee and was elected SSOC chairman for 1965–66.[21]

In 1965, Romaine spoke to a reporter from *Life* magazine with characteristic eloquence and passion: "People ask me what I am going to do when the civil rights cause runs out. I tell them it is not just a cause we arbitrarily picked just to do something. It is a feeling about humanity—any color, anywhere. And that won't change." For Romaine the "civil rights cause" has never "run out." After helping found an underground Atlanta newspaper called *The Great Speckled Bird*, Romaine embarked on a career in community organizing and legal advocacy. Among his proudest achievements is the file that bears his name in the papers of the Mississippi State Sovereignty Commission.[22]

The Seeker

After graduating from Southwestern in 1963 with a degree in French, Robert Morris enrolled at Princeton University as a Bayard Henry Fellow in Romance Languages. But following an aborted suicide attempt in January 1964, Morris found himself back in his hometown of Medina, Tennessee, a broken young man. In a humbling turn of affairs, he returned to Memphis and took a job with the Southwestern maintenance staff. Morris found lodging in an off-campus apartment with Howard Romaine, who suggested he attend meetings of the NAACP's intercollegiate chapter.[23]

Before he knew it, Morris was considering actions he never contemplated as an undergraduate. Meeting with Southwestern students who were preparing to kneel-in at SPC, he was asked to lead the group in prayer. At that juncture in his spiritual journey, the only higher power Morris could summon was "truth and social justice"; but it was enough to carry him to the steps of SPC with the others. When he arrived he witnessed a memorable exchange between Joe Purdy and one of the churchmen guarding the doors, who asked the light-skinned Purdy if he was from India. When Purdy said he was from "here," the response was "then you can't come in."[24]

Morris quickly realized that engaging in public action of this sort had real consequences. When his name appeared in news reports of a disturbance outside the Tea Room, he lost not only his apartment but his job at Southwestern as well. He also learned that his controversial activities would have repercussions in his home town. When Morris returned to Medina, the town's police chief told him some locals were planning to "jump" him and that he had no intention of stopping them. A few days later, the threat materialized when half-a-dozen young men encircled Morris and began taunting him with epithets, including "nigger lover." The situation was unexpectedly diffused when one of the boys spoke up and convinced the others that Morris "hadn't done anything wrong."[25]

After this whirlwind of Tennessee experiences, Morris headed back to Princeton to train for service in a federal anti-poverty program. His sense of purpose regained, Morris relocated to New York and spent the next decade as a Quaker volunteer in East Harlem. This was only one step in a remarkable spiritual journey that included a period of atheism and sojourns at Oral Roberts School of Theology and Missions and Jewish Theological Seminary of America.[26]

The Idealists

Bob Hall ('66) was a math and philosophy double major from Orlando, Florida, who had grown up attending First Presbyterian Church, where his mother worked as the pastor's secretary. At the church she was befriended by a couple who offered to send her four children to college, as long as they attended Presbyterian institutions. Bob Hall chose Southwestern, where he arrived in the fall of 1962.

As a working-class kid growing up in a wealthy congregation, Hall had long been aware of tension between Christian ideals and the reality of the institutional church, and this awareness only intensified at Southwestern. "I remember . . . coming back [to Orlando] and doing a Sunday service in the evening with the youth," Hall says. "I preached the sermon, and it was definitely one that embarrassed my mother because it was about hypocrisy in the church. It didn't go over well, but that was where I was coming from." When the SPC controversy arose toward the end of Hall's sophomore year, he saw an opportunity to witness against the sort of ecclesiastical hypocrisy he despised. In addition to visiting the church on Sunday mornings with black and white peers, Hall requested a meeting with SPC Senior Pastor Jeb Russell. Hall says that when Russell informed him that the church could not integrate because members could not tolerate race mixing among the young people, he responded by invoking the ideal of Christian brotherhood he had internalized as a child: "Red and yellow, black and white, they are precious in His sight."[27]

Because he viewed the exclusion of racially mixed groups as an obvious departure from Christian principle, Hall expressed frustration that so few of his Southwestern peers were protesting at SPC. In the May 8, 1964, issue of *The Sou'wester*, he complained that although events at the church were making national news, "the majority of Southwestern collegiates are still ignorant of the true situation that exists." Most of his fellow students, Hall wrote, believed it was hypocritical for worshippers of any color to be barred from entering the house of God; nevertheless, they viewed the kneel-ins as "ill-motivated and unjustified." Hall countered that, despite this lack of support, because "the barricade of prejudice and hate . . . is entirely contrary to every basic Christian principle," the students visiting SPC would "continue to worship . . . the Christ they believe would stand on their side of the 'blockade.'"[28]

Another Floridian in the Southwestern class of 1966 was Roger Hart, a history major from Gainesville who learned about Southwestern from his pastor and his high-school English teacher, both alums of the college. Like Hall, Hart entered Southwestern with strong ideals. Not long after arriving on campus in the fall of 1962, he wrote a letter to *The Sou'wester* calling for immediate integration of the campus. "The choice is clear-cut: right or wrong," he wrote. "Southwestern should not use race as a qualification for admission."[29]

During his sophomore year, Hart was among a handful of Southwestern students who participated in the campus protest against visiting U.S. senator Herbert Walters. In a photograph of the protest that appeared in a local paper, in fact, Hart was clearly visible holding a sign that read "End Racial Discrimination."

"This was regarded as a terribly radical and upsetting thing for us to do," he remembers. "Students walked by me and said things like 'how could you do this? How can you hurt Southwestern like this?'" As his activism evolved, however, Hart demonstrated not only his commitment to social change, but his belief that the Church had a role in effecting it. In a *Sou'wester* article, Hart critiqued the PCUS's traditional failure to offer a "co-ordinated attack on social problems":[30]

> A historical-theological reason for the [problem] may be found in the doctrine of the spirituality of the church, taken up a century ago by Southern Presbyterians unwilling to face the slavery issue squarely; their only escape was to proclaim that the church should confine itself to "religious" realms and not meddle in the "secular" world. This doctrine, combined with other factors, has had the result of making the Presbyterian Church, U.S., as a whole, quite irrelevant to the contemporary South and its revolutionary crises.[31]

Despite his concern for civil rights and his strong Presbyterian background, Hart did not immediately join the SPC kneel-ins because he was teaching Sunday School at another church. As the controversy wore on, however, Hart concluded that he had to get involved. As he recalls, "I wrote [the church] a letter and said that I was quitting being a Sunday school teacher so I could join my friends who were standing outside Second Presbyterian because of the segregation of the church. I didn't hear back from them." Hart remembers carpooling to SPC from the Southwestern campus, "leaving our . . . very warm, secure and comfortable community and going out into the cold hostile foreign territory of East Memphis. That was almost a foreign country out there."[32]

According to Hart, there was a great deal of hostility to the students' presence at SPC. Men stood with scowls on their faces, their arms folded and feet firmly planted, he says. "People would walk past us on the sidewalk as they were coming out from their cars and going to church. I remember one woman walked by me and she said in a Deep South voice 'Good mornin' Jackass!' Very respectable looking woman, but this anger just came out of her." Hart remembers being asked by someone at the church if the assembled students were being paid by the NAACP. One of them responded that, to the contrary, they were paying dues to belong to the organization. "And that was considered to be so ridiculous, that it was dismissed as absurd. There was a total lack of understanding that we would be there because we believed in something. It was beyond them."[33]

After graduating from Southwestern, Hart attended Louisville Presbyterian Theological Seminary. But he soon realized that the interests in theology and social action he had developed at Southwestern were not enough to sustain a pastoral vocation. "My own personal religious faith was either not there or so immature as to be not a basis to lead in ministry," he says. After a year in seminary Hart returned to Memphis to teach for three years at historically black LeMoyne Owen College. Afterward he began graduate study at Princeton University, returning to teach briefly at Southwestern in 1974. Later Hart joined the Foreign Service and worked for the State Department in Chad, Turkey, Russia, and Belgium. Eventually he earned a master's degree in public administration and went to work in the nonprofit sector. Hart now belongs to a Unitarian Universalist congregation.[34]

The Preachers' Kids

In the 1950s and 1960s Southwestern was a popular choice for Southern Presbyterian young people, particularly the sons and daughters of ministers, who received a tuition break from the college. Thus it is not surprising that several of those who would become engaged in the SPC kneel-ins were children of the manse.

Rocky Ward ('64) was the son of Rev. William B. Ward, a racial moderate who found himself in the minority on most issues that came before the presbyteries to which he belonged. Rocky Ward spent his early childhood in Spartanburg, South Carolina, where his father served First Presbyterian Church. One of his formative memories involves a family outing to see "The Robe" at a downtown Spartanburg cinema, an excursion on which Doris, the Ward's black live-in housekeeper, was invited as a matter of course. After buying their tickets and taking their seats, the Wards were approached by the theater manager, who informed them that Doris would have to sit in the balcony. Bill Ward responded that Doris was "part of the family" and would be sitting with them. According to Rocky, the incident created a "firestorm" in Spartanburg—he remembers newspaper articles, phone calls, and a furor at the church. Reflecting on the controversy over fifty years later, Ward says, "I didn't understand everything that was going on, but I knew that something was wrong and I was proud of my father for standing against it."[35]

When he arrived at Southwestern, Ward took advantage of his newfound freedom to sleep in on Sunday mornings. But he "came back" to the church through Southwestern's Westminster Fellowship. Along with his roommate Jim Bullock, Ward became involved in the NAACP intercollegiate chapter and was "fired up" when the SPC protests got under way. He vividly remembers facing church officers who were standing shoulder-to-shoulder on the steps. "If what I've been taught to believe in my home and church has any truth at all," he thought, "then I need to be here" in order to press the question whether there was going to be justice in the church. Ward's experience at SPC created uncertainty about his own future in the Presbyterian Church. Eventually, however, he concluded that it was the place for pursuing his vocation and he began a long career in ministry.[36]

Hayden Kaden ('64) was another Southwestern participant in the SPC kneel-ins who was the child of a Presbyterian minister. Like Ward, Kaden was prepared for church activism by what he witnessed at home. In the late 1950s, while his stepfather, C. Rodney Sunday, was pastor at Houston's St. Andrew's Presbyterian Church, Kaden watched Sunday welcome black visitors from a conviction that "this is Christ's church . . . and He would not ever want anyone barred from His Church." As a teenager, Kaden visited African American churches in the Houston area and made black friends at an integrated youth conference.[37]

After spending his junior year at Southwestern in France, Kaden adopted something of a bohemian identity, driving a Triumph he had purchased overseas and taking up residence with his French girlfriend in an off-campus artist's studio. But when the SPC kneel-ins began, Kaden decided to join his peers on Sunday mornings in front of the church. Although he tried to maintain a low profile, church representatives used his vehicle registration information to identify his parents, who were sent accusatory letters and photographs. When their responses revealed that Kaden was the stepson of a Presbyterian minister, this only confirmed some church members' suspicions that the Southwestern students were paid agitators. As Kaden tells the story,

> I got a call one day from the Memphis *Commercial Appeal*, one of the editors, who said they had a letter to the editor from a man. . . . who wrote that Hayden Kaden was obviously being paid to agitate (by communists I suppose). His proof was that I went to expensive Southwestern and that my father was a preacher in Texas, so how could he afford to pay so much for my education on a minister's salary. I also drove an expensive sports car. How could my parents possibly afford that if I wasn't on the payroll of outside agitators. I explained that my actual father, Capt. James Kaden, had been killed during the Second World War and that my mother had saved all of the money that was sent to me by the government from the time I was a year old until I was 18. That money, along with the discount I got at Southwestern for being a Presbyterian minister's stepson, paid for my education and for the car that I bought in England at the Triumph factory for $2,400 while I was on my junior year abroad in Aix-en-Provence. So, the editor and I had a laugh at the expense of the letter writer and he said that the letter would not be published.[38]

After college, the trajectory of Kaden's life maintained a progressive arc. In law school at the University of Texas he joined Students for a Democratic Society

(SDS) and was active in anti-war protests. Eventually, he helped start a chapter of the American Civil Liberties Union in Alaska. According to Kaden, the legacy of his involvement in events at SPC is "courage to stand up and speak out."[39]

Southwestern student Elizabeth Currie ('64) was the daughter, grand-daughter, and niece of Presbyterian ministers. She recalls that her grandfather, Thomas White Currie, who became president of Austin Presbyterian Theological Seminary and moderator of the PCUS General Assembly, was "very eager for racial reconciliation and for the Presbyterian churches in the north and south to reunite." During Currie's childhood, her father, Thomas White Currie, Jr., was pastor of St. Paul's Presbyterian Church in Houston. "There would be black people that would come to our home as guests and my dad was very involved in starting Presbyterian churches in the black community," she recalls. "And none of that seemed strange to me, but it was pretty strange to most of my classmates."[40]

Currie connected with other students from relatively progressive back-grounds in her classes and in Southwestern's Westminster Fellowship. She was also influenced by larger events that were difficult to ignore, even in the cocoon of a private college. "We knew that things were heating up in Mississippi," she says, "and I remember when the guy who wrote *Mississippi: The Closed Society* [James Silver] came up to speak at Southwestern and that was a moving experi-ence." During her senior year, Currie joined the church visitation campaign led by members of the NAACP intercollegiate group. Her initial experience, at First Baptist Church, was uneventful. But when she heard that students were being turned away from SPC, she felt she had to join them.[41]

Yet Currie regrets not becoming more involved in the fight for civil rights while at Southwestern. "I didn't have anyone who was going to punish me; if anything . . . the people who cared about me would have been more excited if I had been more daring. And I don't know if that was typical of my classmates." After leaving Southwestern, Currie joined the civil rights struggle in Prince Edward County, Virginia, first as a worker in an anti-poverty program and then as a teacher in a high school that had been shuttered for five years as part of the county's "massive resistance" to federally mandated school desegregation. Un-like her brothers, Currie did not join the "family business" and become a Presby-terian minister. She did, however, become the first woman to chair the board of trustees at Austin Presbyterian Theological Seminary.[42]

Not all the preachers' kids at Southwestern felt free to protest in favor of church desegregation, even if it was a cause they supported. Dossett Foster ('64), whose father was pastor of Highland Heights Presbyterian Church in Memphis, was a liberal-minded young man, in part because his favorite baseball team—the Brooklyn Dodgers—had led in integrating the sport. His progressivism blos-somed at Southwestern and he became instrumental in extending speaking invi-tations to James Meredith and James W. Silver. But his father was "old school,"

Foster says, having attended Ole Miss in the 1930s and having spent most of his pastoral career in the Deep South. Moreover, Rev. Foster was a close friend of SPC Senior Pastor Jeb Russell. Although Foster felt drawn to the kneel-ins at SPC, he decided not to risk embarrassing his father by joining them.[43]

The Seminarians

If pastors' kids who became involved in church desegregation efforts were subject to special pressures, students who were preparing for ministry had to be careful as well. Like many of his male classmates, Kyser Cowart ("K.C.") Ptomey ('64) was a few months from enrolling in seminary when the Memphis kneel-in campaign broke out. Ptomey hailed from Birmingham and was the child of "deep southerners" who had never lived outside Alabama. But at Southwestern, Ptomey says, he was "exposed to a lot of things . . . that kind of broke me open." A formative influence was Paul Tudor Jones, pastor at Idlewild Presbyterian Church and Memphis Presbytery's leading racial moderate.[44]

Ptomey felt drawn to the protests at SPC, but his father, who did not have the benefit of a college education, was fearful of anything that might sidetrack his son so close to graduation. "When all the racial stuff started in Memphis . . . I was coming home on breaks and talking with him about all this stuff, [and] he was really afraid," Ptomey says. But Howard Romaine and Jim Bullock kept working on Ptomey, who was president of the Southwestern Honor Council. "I was a high visibility kind of guy, and I think they needed me," he says. They finally prevailed on Ptomey to participate in a nonviolence workshop.[45]

Ptomey found himself increasingly conflicted. "On one hand, my dad was begging me not to get publicly involved and on the other hand I felt a sense of conscience to be a part of it, in particular because of the segregated church being [part of] my denomination, and the General Assembly was going to meet there." When Ptomey heard that SPC had sought to avert the crisis by agreeing to admit black commissioners to the General Assembly without changing its exclusive worship policy, he was "infuriated by the hypocrisy." So in the midst of studying for comprehensive exams and preparing to enroll at Louisville Presbyterian Theological Seminary, Ptomey decided to "stick his toe in the water" at SPC.[46]

With twelve or fifteen others, he appeared at the church entrance:

> I walked up on that porch with a big ol' black guy; I can't remember his name. . . . And there was an elder standing at the door who put an umbrella across my chest and said, "You, you can come in, but he can't." And I said, "Well, isn't this a Presbyterian church?" (I was kind of a smart ass, you know). And he said, "Yes." So I started kind of reciting some of

the policies of the Presbyterian Church US at that time. And he stopped me and said, "Son, I am not going to argue with you. . . . If you want to come in, you can come in. But he cannot come in." Then he turned to this African American guy and he said, "You, are you from Africa?" The guy said, "No." He said, "Well, are you a foreigner?" And the guy said, "No, I'm an American." He said, "Well then you can't come in."[47]

At the time Ptomey decided not to relate this experience to his family, but it gave him much to reflect upon. He was still reflecting when he delivered his senior sermon at Louisville Seminary in late 1966. Titled "The Other Side of Discipleship," the sermon included a sober reappraisal of the prophetic zeal Ptomey and his peers had brought to the steps of SPC:

On a bright Sunday morning in the early spring of 1964, several students walked up the sidewalk and mounted the three steps to the porch of one of the largest Presbyterian churches in the South. As the students crossed the porch to the front door, they were met by several ushers who blocked their way.

A short conversation took place between one of the ushers and one of the students. It went something like this:

"You can't come in."

"Why not?"

"Because we don't want any trouble here."

"Is this a Presbyterian church?"

"Yes."

"Are you aware of what the General Assembly has said about a church opening its doors to all men?"

"We don't take orders from anyone."

"Is this a Church of Jesus Christ?"

"Look, son, we're not here to discuss theology. Y'all can't come in."

I look back on that occasion with mixed emotions. At the time there was no question in my mind. These students were not only within their rights, but they had an obligation to make known to the world the deplorable situation, which existed at that particular church. It was within the realm of their discipleship to stand with the Negro students who were being excluded from worship.

But the question which has haunted my soul ever since that Sunday in 1964 has been this: How much concern and love was I expressing for the usher who blocked the way? Had I not aroused such animosity and fear in his heart that he had become unable to hear my case, as righteous and good as it might have been? In my pompous self-righteousness,

wasn't I kicking sand in his face instead of seeking to remove the cata-
racts of prejudice from his eyes?

On the one hand there was the overwhelming feeling of responsibility to stand with those students who were being discriminated
against. On the other hand there was the agonizing recognition of the
responsibility for getting the "word" of truth through to the man whom
I was alienating by my very act of "demonstrating."

"What does taking up a cross mean?" Ptomey asked in conclusion. "Does it
mean taking up a 'cause,' or taking up a sign, or demonstrating? Maybe. But isn't
there more to it than that?"[48]

No one was more intrigued by this vignette than Ptomey's father. After his
first visit to SPC, Ptomey had called home to say he was "thinking about" participating in the kneel-ins. The response from his father was a stern warning. "If
you've ever thought about being a minister," he said, "this will be on your record
forever and no church will ever call you." With these words ringing in his ears,
Ptomey decided against telling his father that he had already gone to the church.
When Mr. Ptomey heard K. C.'s senior sermon three years later, the pieces of the
story came together. "You'd already done it when you called me that day, hadn't
you," he said to his son.[49]

Cam Murchison ('65) was a Southwestern pre-ministry student who had
transferred to the school from LSU. In Baton Rouge a campus pastor had challenged Murchison to read Martin Luther King, Jr.'s "Letter from Birmingham
Jail," which he did. But the letter's full impact was not revealed until Murchison
attended one of Jim Lawson's workshops on Christian nonviolence. With workshop participants of both races, Murchison planned to visit local churches. But
he missed the rendezvous with his African American partner, and his sense of
"guilty relief" remained vivid forty-five years later:

> On a frosty Sunday morning in . . . 1964 . . . two white students waited
> the arrival of their African American colleague with whom they would
> attend worship in a white congregation, unannounced and probably
> unwelcome. In some small way, it represented a youthful intention to
> take the cost of discipleship with new seriousness, amidst the justice
> challenges of the civil rights movement.
>
> For reasons unknown, the African American student never made it
> to the rendezvous point. To be sure, the cost of discipleship for that
> student was by all odds higher than that for the two white students. But
> what is known is the almost shameful relief the two white students felt
> as it became clear that they could refocus their plans and attend wor-
> ship elsewhere that day without risk. One can only ponder the fear they

might have felt if, just as they had departed for the safer worship experience, they had received a call that the young colleague was waiting for
them on the steps of the sanctuary in which they had agreed to worship
together.[50]

In the Bible commentary for preachers in which this reminiscence is published,
Murchison connects his experience on that "frosty Sunday morning" to Mark's
account of Jesus's resurrection. In both, he notes, "a tension is manifest between
the trustworthiness of the message of God's present and powerful reign in the
world and the fearful response of disciples more ready to make peace with the
death of the gospel than to enter into its promise."[51]

Although Murchison never joined his peers in protesting church segregation,
he remembers the controversy at SPC as "part of the larger experience that era
spawned for many of us at Southwestern that set a course that has been pretty
influential thereafter." Following college, Murchison attended Union Theological Seminary in Virginia before studying theology at Yale. His career in the
church has included stints as a congregational minister, seminary professor,
and academic dean.[52]

Winton Smith ('66) was another Southwestern student who would head to
seminary following graduation. Smith did not participate in the SPC kneel-ins,
but he was close to many who did, particularly Jim Bullock, whom he knew from
their hometown of Jackson, Tennessee. Like Bullock, Smith was raised by racially moderate parents whom he never heard use the word "nigger." Furthermore, Smith says, "I had the good fortune to grow up in a family where my dad's
business was in the black community." This socialization, along with his love for
the black woman who helped raise him and his exposure to Andrew Young at a
Cumberland Presbyterian youth assembly around 1960, molded Smith's outlook on race relations.[53]

Yet as Smith contemplated joining his peers in front of SPC, concern for his
father's grocery business caused him to hesitate. When Bullock asked Smith to
accompany him to the church, he offered to use his influence on the Southwestern student council to pass a resolution in support of the protesting students. To
his shame, however, Smith decided not to join them because his parents had recently bought a grocery store in the wealthier part of Jackson. "I remember
thinking . . . if I go, it will kill my parents' business." When asked if he believes
word of his activities would have traveled the ninety miles to Jackson, Smith
laughs and says, "in a New York minute."[54]

Robert Wells ('64), a philosophy major from Oak Ridge, Tennessee, was also
preparing to enter the ministry after graduation from Southwestern. Like most
Southerners, Wells had grown up with segregation. He recalls drinking from a water
fountain in his hometown bus station, seeing the "colored" sign on an adjacent

fountain, and asking his mother to explain "colored water." Wells gained a more mature perspective on racial discrimination when twelve brave young people from Clinton, Tennessee (eleven miles northeast of Oak Ridge), became the first black students in the Southeast to integrate a public school. In 1958, after their building was dynamited, Clinton High students were bused to Oak Ridge. "Rather than integrate," Wells recalls, "somebody blew the school up."[55]

After this experience, passionate resistance to integration did not surprise Wells. But when he stood in front of SPC and saw a black Presbyterian minister being denied entrance to the church, he was indignant. "It was like going to a kindergarten and seeing little kids puffed up, saying 'You can't play with my ball.'" Wells was further outraged when he realized that church people were photographing the visiting students from angles that suggested they had paired off in interracial couples. "It was so childish I couldn't take it seriously," he recalls. His experience at SPC challenged Wells to stand up for what he said he believed. "Never had to do that before. Never had to put my body where my mind was, you know." Doing so was formative, he says.[56]

After graduation, Wells joined the Peace Corps in East Africa. Three years later he entered seminary in Chicago, where he and wife Rose Mary Hoye Wells ('64) were active in a number of activist causes.[57]

"She's Fallen In with a Bad Crowd"

As we have seen, male students who joined the SPC kneel-ins were subjected to many forms of pressure, including warnings that they could be jeopardizing a career in the church. Their female counterparts may have been less vulnerable to threats of professional insecurity; but they were more susceptible to coercion from family members and peers. Students like Liz Currie, who had inherited a legacy of public support for social justice, did not worry about familial backlash. But most Southwestern co-eds were not so fortunate.

Ervin Haas, a sophomore in the spring of 1964, hailed from Mobile, Alabama. "Can't get much more Southern than that," she says. Although she was familiar with militant white racism—she had an "uncle" who was a KKK Grand Dragon—Haas belonged to the relatively moderate, Episcopalian side of the family. She describes her father as an Atticus Finch figure who insisted his children call black women "ladies." When most of Haas's friends were being sent to private schools, he reminded her that blacks had "as much right to a good education" as she did. In Mobile in the early 1960s, however, racial moderates faced opposition in every local institution, public and private. "My senior year [in high school] we were supposed to write a term paper," Haas recalls, "and the only two books required were both by Barry Goldwater." As for the influence of her church, Haas remembers that among her Sunday School teachers was a member of the local school board who assured her she would never be forced to attend school with African Americans.[58]

Exercising the freedom she enjoyed as a college student four hundred miles from home, at Southwestern Haas began attending meetings of the NAACP intercollegiate chapter with boyfriend Jim Bullock, whom she would later marry. "The first meeting I went to . . . [Memphis State student] Joe Purdy immediately put on some music and said, 'You've got to get over dancing with a black man.' And he just started to dance with me and I thought, 'Well this is something.' It was; it was a huge step for me." Through meetings of the NAACP and nonviolence training with Jim Lawson, Haas befriended black students, including Vivian Carter, with whom she occasionally attended church. Having transgressed the boundary that separated black and white congregations, Haas took aim at the racial barrier between black Memphis and her segregated college. When she invited Carter to spend the night in her dorm room at Southwestern, Haas recalls, "none of the girls on the floor cared." The same cannot be said of alumnae of her sorority and members of the college administration.[59]

In January 1964, Southwestern's Dean of Women called Haas's parents to inform them that she had fallen in with a "bad crowd." If they wished to remove her from school, the dean said, they might be eligible for a tuition refund. Haas's parents were troubled by her behavior, to say the least. She was summoned home, where her father had begun a hunger strike. "He didn't eat the whole time I was home, for five days. And they weren't going to let me go back." After sending in Haas's older brother to tell her she was "killing them," her parents outlined the path they had in mind for their wayward daughter. "They said, 'you know, we just want you to be happy and go up to the University of Alabama and meet some nice college football player or something. . . .' And I said, 'You don't want to send me to Tuscaloosa. . . . If I get to doing what I'm doing at Tuscaloosa, you really will have crosses burned on your lawn." Haas says she was allowed to return to Southwestern only on the condition that she promise not to do anything that would reflect badly on her family.[60]

Because she had sworn to stay out of trouble, Haas held a low profile as the SPC kneel-ins began, standing in the church narthex rather than on the steps. "I would go inside and I'd take notes," she says. "But I was not part of the demonstration. That was an agreement with my family." Although she could not stand with her classmates, Haas could hear the hymns and prayers emanating from inside the church as her peers maintained a vigil outside. Among her vivid memories are church women cursing the students and a man pulling up his pant leg to reveal a gun tucked into his boot.[61]

Though technically she was not a participant in the kneel-ins, Haas's association with the protestors had consequences in both Mobile and Memphis. It kept her younger brother from joining a high school fraternity, she says. And alumnae of her college sorority were quite disturbed by the company she was keeping. When they met with the intention of expelling her, Haas displayed her usual moxie:

> They called a meeting and I went to it [even though] they didn't want me to be there. And then they wanted me to leave the room while they discussed it. And I said, "No, anything you've got to say I think I ought to be here to hear." So they talked about it and they wanted to vote. And they wanted me to leave the room. I said, "No, I think I have a right to see how you're going to vote." And I stayed, and then they wanted me to put my head down and I said, "No, I want to watch you vote." Well, they didn't vote to kick me out cause I was right there.[62]

Haas left Southwestern at the end of the school year, but her experiences in Memphis set her on a path of escalating activism. "When I went to Glasgow University [in the fall of 1964], I started going to all these debates and I started looking for places to plug into," she says. "I started demonstrating against the war in Vietnam, that was '64, that was pretty early." Today Haas is an "ardent activist" who works for the Presbyterian Church (USA) in the area of peace advocacy. Her father died in 1966 still troubled by her activism; but in 1988 her mother accompanied her to a peace conference where she walked around proudly announcing that her daughter was the organizer.[63]

Another female student who became intimately involved in SPC kneel-ins is Jacquelyn Dowd ('65), a religion and mathematics double major who had grown up a Presbyterian in Oklahoma. Deeply influenced by the high ideals honored in the Southwestern curriculum, Dowd began to look for ways to implement them. Shortly after Howard Romaine invited her to a meeting of the NAACP intercollegiate chapter at a local black church, Dowd found herself among the students traveling to SPC on Sunday mornings. "We would get dressed up and go down and just stand there very respectfully and quietly and prayerfully," she recalls. The child of a Presbyterian deacon, Dowd was shocked at the sight of church leaders barring students' way into the church.[64]

Dowd's experience at SPC had a lasting impact, part of which is lingering disillusionment with Southwestern's response to the controversy. If what she and her classmates were doing was "an expression of what we were being taught," she wondered, then why wasn't the college administration more supportive? Although the Southwestern students who participated in the kneel-ins were not disciplined, they did experience subtle acts of retaliation, she says. For instance, when Dowd was $100 short on her tuition payment the semester following the church visits, Southwestern's Dean of Women told her she would have to leave school. "Icy and hostile are the words that come to mind" when she recalls administrators' reactions to her and other kneel-in participants. "It was made clear to us that we were no longer the darling children that we had been just a few months before."[65]

Like many of her peers, Dowd was pushed by the SPC controversy "toward questioning authority and being willing to do much more confrontational things in the years to come." At the same time, however, the events took a toll on her religious faith. In the midst of the controversy, Dowd had been elected chair of Southwestern's Protestant Religious Council. But she returned to school in the fall of 1964 a "different person" and felt she could not assume the post. Relationships were strained as well. Her boyfriend at the time of the kneel-ins drove her to the church, waited for her in the car, and drove her home; but he would not participate. Looking back, Dowd says that his failure to become involved "was symbolic of things between us that in the end really kept us from going on together." After college, Dowd would follow Bob Hall ('64) to New York, where she pursued graduate work in history at Columbia while Hall studied at Union Theological Seminary. Jackie Hall is now a prominent historian at the University of North Carolina at Chapel Hill and past president of the American Historical Association.[66]

Martha Overholser ('66) was a reluctant protestor. The sophomore from Lewisburg, Tennessee, grew up in the Presbyterian Church, where she was active in youth activities. A friend she had made at Presbyterian summer camp was a Memphian who attended SPC and whose family "adopted" her when Overholser arrived at Southwestern. In the spring of her sophomore year, as Overholser learned what was happening at the church, she began discussing events with Jim Bullock (whom she remembers as a "one-man consciousness raising committee"). She decided to get involved; but not before trying to convince her adoptive father—who happened to be an SPC elder—that the visiting students should be admitted to worship. When they discussed the matter in his office, Overholser was shocked and disappointed. Going beyond the party line that the church was only repelling "demonstrators," her friend's father shared his conviction that blacks were inherently inferior to whites. "Because I loved that family," she says, "it was only after it became clear that he would not change his position that I stood outside on Sunday mornings."[67]

Rose Mary Hoye ('64) grew up in Shreveport, Louisiana, in a family that was at once "strongly Presbyterian" and "strongly Southern." On her mother's side were moderate Presbyterians, including an uncle who was president of Louisville Presbyterian Theological Seminary and later PCUS Moderator. Her father, however, despite being "a wonderful, wonderful man," was a staunch racist. Hoye's conviction that "it was wrong to separate black people from white people" grew under her mother's influence and her relationship with the black domestic who worked for her family. She knew instinctively that it was "wrong to discrim-inate against anyone who I loved as much as I loved Ella."[68]

Hoye arrived at Southwestern in the fall of 1960 with strong convictions about human dignity and deep attachments to a black maternal figure, but virtu-ally no experience of social contact with African Americans. This held true until her senior year when, through the influence of boyfriend and future husband Bob Wells ('64), Hoye began attending meetings of the intercollegiate NAACP chapter. For Hoye and other Southwestern students who had known blacks pri-marily as nannies and common laborers, meeting in the homes of black Mem-phians and holding hands while singing "We Shall Overcome" was a heady experience. With encouragement from Wells and others, Hoye became involved in the kneel-in campaign at SPC.[69]

Hoye admits she was not terribly aware of conditions in Memphis beyond the Southwestern campus, but she felt strongly that what was happening at SPC was "unconscionable." In her mind, the issue was the prospective exclusion of black Presbyterian ministers should the General Assembly honor its commitment to meet at SPC in 1965. "That was just wrong. How could a Presbyterian minister say 'no' to another Presbyterian minister, no matter what color they were?" Once the theological dimension of the kneel-in controversy came into focus, Hoye says, she "couldn't not be there." Although she was familiar with Southern resis-tance to integration, what she found when she arrived at SPC shocked her. "As we started walking toward the front of the church," she recalls, "men just materi-alized across the front at the top of the steps, and just were lined up there, some with their arms crossed, some with their arms behind them. . . . It was at first kind of a standoff and then as we got to the steps there were some questions thrown at us . . . 'what are you doing here?' 'why are you here?' . . . And I think only once did I have the courage to speak up and say . . ., 'we're here to come to church.'"[70]

It was not long before someone identified Hoye and a letter reached her par-ents in Shreveport. "My daddy got the letter and he called me and he said 'you stop that right now,'" Hoye recalls. And I said, "but I really believe it's the right thing to do, daddy." And he said, "if you don't stop right now you will have no more money from me for remaining at that pinko, communist school." Hoye also felt pressure from peers at Southwestern. After her first visit to SPC, the presi-dent of her sorority told her that because she had brought embarrassment on the sisterhood, she needed to "turn in her pin." Hoye's response was not one her sisters were expecting: "I remember telling her that I had been thinking seriously . . . about disassociating myself from the sorority because of its exclu-sive policies. . . . But that I had just changed my mind, and that I thought I could do more good by doing what I felt was right while wearing my pin. From there on I wore my Tri-Delt pin to everything that I did, and I continued to wear it in Chicago when Robert and I marched in anti-nuclear marches."[71]

Hoye doesn't recall the names of the black students who stood with her in front of SPC in 1964. But the experience laid the foundation for a fuller commitment to social justice and human rights. "I wanted to put myself on the line and say, 'this is the right thing to do,'" she says. After considering joining Wells in Tanzania with the Peace Corps, Hoye became a Vista volunteer working primarily with African American migrants. Today Rose Mary Hoye Wells calls her experience at SPC the "bedrock of my now forty-year involvement in diversity."[72]

The financial threats and relationship strains these women endured are a memorable legacy of their decision to leave their comfortable co-ed lives and transgress the boundaries that circumscribed white Southern womanhood. As we shall see in the next chapter, black students who participated in the Memphis kneel-ins faced their own distinct set of challenges.

8

"You Will Only Know My Motivation When You Open the Door"

Black Visitors

The Mentor

James M. Lawson, Jr.'s impact on the civil rights movement in Memphis is typically viewed through the prism of his leadership in the Sanitation Workers' strike. Prior to 1968, however, Lawson's greatest contribution to civil rights in the Bluff City was probably to be found among the young people he introduced to the theory and practice of nonviolent direct action, many of whom became involved in the church kneel-ins of 1964. These men and women had never encountered anyone quite like Jim Lawson. He was, in the words of David Halberstam, "a black middle-class Christian disciple of a Hindu activist" who had spent three years in India studying Gandhian nonviolence. He was also a committed ecumenist who did not shy away from positions or activities that led others to question his patriotism. Nor was he shy about criticizing traditional approaches to securing black civil rights.[1]

In fact, by the time Lawson arrived in Memphis in 1962 to pastor Centenary United Methodist Church, his attacks on the NAACP as "the voice of the black bourgeoisie" were notorious. The youth-led sit-in movement, he claimed, had been "a judgment upon the middle-class conventional, half-way efforts to deal with radical social evil." So how would Lawson be received in a city where the NAACP was the undisputed representative of black interests, particularly given his outspoken view that Memphis's black leaders failed to possess a precise understanding of nonviolent direct action and as a result were willing to settle with concessions rather than demanding structural change?[2]

Lawson acknowledges that his relationship with the civil rights establishment in Memphis was always tenuous—in part because he was regarded as an "intruder," in part because he pastored a large congregation in a "white" denomination, in part because he was a theoretician and tactician at a time when religious leaders generally did not engage in serious analysis of the black predicament. Nevertheless, he maintained a "gracious" and "cordial" association with Maxine and Vasco Smith and played an essential role in training and mentoring members of the NAACP intercollegiate group who would participate in the Memphis kneel-ins.[3]

Sensing the students' discomfort with holding interracial meetings at LeMoyne or Southwestern, Lawson offered to host the intercollegiate group at his church. Once introduced to Lawson, many students returned to Centenary to study the theory and practice of nonviolent direct action in his "Christian Non-Violence" workshops. These were essentially the same workshops Lawson had conducted in Nashville in 1959 in preparation for the sit-in movement there, as well as in Albany in 1962 and Birmingham in 1963. In these workshops Gandhian methodology was presented in a Christian theological context, with Jesus's ministry supplying the template for a life of nonviolent action. Along with gospel stories like Luke 4:28–30, in which Jesus walks through a "lynch mob" and is not harmed, Lawson identified biblical examples of nonviolent action in Exodus and the dramatic public enactments of the Hebrew prophets. He traced the history of nonviolent practice in America from Roger Williams to the Montgomery bus boycott, the Freedom Rides, and the civil rights campaigns in Albany and Birmingham. And he introduced a number of role-playing exercises. In one, participants tried to provoke one another with hostile words; in another, group members simulated a physical assault on those who played the role of "demonstrators."[4]

Lawson deeply impressed the young men and women he encountered in Memphis. As students, they were accustomed to his academic manner; as children of the Church, they resonated with his characterization of segregation as sin and of biblical figures like Moses, Jeremiah, and Jesus as "demonstrators." When Lawson claimed that "the Christian favors the breaking down of racial barriers because the redeemed community of which he is already a citizen recognizes no barriers dividing humanity," many of the Memphis students heard a call to "radical Christian obedience" they could not ignore.[5]

And unlike most of the professors and ministers they had known, Lawson unflinchingly spoke truth to power. The consequences he had endured included a prison sentence for refusing military service and expulsion from Vanderbilt Divinity School for his role in the Nashville sit-ins. If his own story was not enough to convince the students that the road to justice was paved with personal sacrifice, Lawson asked them to sign a pledge that delineated the connection:[6]

I HEREBY PLEDGE MYSELF—MY PERSON AND MY BODY—
TO THE NONVIOLENT EFFORT IN MEMPHIS. I WILL THERE-
FORE KEEP, THINK ABOUT AND LEARN THE FOLLOWING
COMMANDMENTS:

1. *MEDITATE* daily on the life and teachings of Jesus.

2. *REMEMBER* always that the nonviolent movement seeks justice
and reconciliation—not victory over others.

3. *WALK AND TALK* in the manner of love—"For, God is Love."

4. *PRAY* daily to be used by God in the struggle to set men free.

5. *SACRIFICE* personal wishes in order to work for this struggle.

6. *OBSERVE* with both friend and foe the ordinary rules of courtesy.

7. *SEEK* to perform regular service for others and the world.

8. *REFRAIN* from violence of fist, tongue, and heart.

9. *STRIVE* to be in good spiritual and bodily health.

10. *FOLLOW* the directions of the group leader on a demonstration
and be obedient to the direction of the movement once you agree to
join it.

(The demonstrator is asked to keep this and memorize it.)[7]

Although they were probably unaware of it, in pledging their persons and bodies
to the nonviolent movement in Memphis, these would-be activists were standing
in the footsteps of hundreds of students and civil rights workers who since 1957
had studied the principles of nonviolence at Lawson's feet. They may have been
intimidated by the spiritual and physical demands implied in his "ten commandments," but they could not have been better prepared for the reception that
awaited them at SPC.[8]

The Elder

Vasco Smith is less well known than the other adults who supported and mentored the students who protested at SPC—Maxine Smith, Jim Lawson, and Carl
Pritchett. But his part in the Memphis kneel-in campaign cannot be overlooked
because he brought a unique set of experiences and connections to his role as
advisor to these young people.

Smith was personally familiar, for instance, with many of the leading civil
rights figures in the mid-South. He and wife Maxine had hosted James Meredith
as he prepared to enroll at the University of Mississippi in 1962. He was with
Medgar Evers on the night of his assassination in Jackson, Mississippi, in 1963.
And he was a veteran of the nonviolent campaign to end segregation in Memphis. "I went to jail six times," Smith says of his experience in the early 1960s.

Despite being slightly built and mild-mannered, Smith proved himself time and again to be a tenacious crusader for civil rights.[9]

Smith realized rather quickly that as a lay leader at Parkway Gardens Presbyterian Church he was uniquely positioned to support the students who were attempting to worship at SPC. He recalls thinking, "Well I am an elder in the Presbyterian Church; matter of fact, I'm an officer of the presbytery. Dang it, I had represented the Memphis Presbytery in Washington before the United Nations." So along with wife Maxine, who also was active at Parkway Gardens, Smith gave credence to the students' claims that they had come to SPC to participate in worship. Smith was under no delusion, however, that the group would be welcomed simply because he was present. "After all," he says, "I was not welcome to many of the activities of the Memphis Presbytery, so why should they accept me at Second Presbyterian?"[10]

In fact, when the Smiths arrived at SPC the first time, they were treated exactly as the students had been. Their path was blocked by men in suits "arm in arm, linked, basically saying 'you shall not pass.'" "There was an armed guard there," Smith recalls. "*Armed* guard. And he said we were gonna be arrested. Well, I weigh 145 pounds but I told him I'm not gonna be arrested. And don't you put your hand on me." Smith surmised that the guard's job was to intimidate rather than arrest the visitors. So he informed him that the young people were determined to say a prayer on church property and there was nothing he could do about it. Of the church members' intentions, however, Smith was less certain. "One of the [church] officers clearly stated, 'Y'all know that I have a gun in my pocket.' I heard that with my own ears and I know his name, I know his name. Anyway, we went on to the church grounds and we prayed. It was a very moving experience. And after prayer, we were gonna move along cause we didn't want things to get out of hand."[11]

One of Smith's essential contributions to the Memphis kneel-in campaign was his role as liaison between protesting students and denominational officials. Particularly when the movement to relocate the 1965 meeting of the General Assembly was gaining momentum, Smith kept Presbyterian leaders informed of the kneel-ins' progress. But what Memphians appreciated most in Smith was his remarkable willingness to suffer for justice. In a sermon preached in June 1964, Parkway Gardens Pastor Lawrence Haygood made a fitting tribute to Smith's example of nonviolent protest: "He has emptied himself," Haygood proclaimed, "into the captivity and enslavement of his white brother for the purpose of bringing about liberation and hope in his behalf. By seeking admission to the Second Church, he is attempting to save his white brother from the captivity of fear, bigotry, prejudice and suspicion. Through such humble men the cancerous sore of racial segregation will be healed."[12]

The Organizer

Among the black students who participated in the kneel-ins at SPC, several died relatively young. Among them is Joe Purdy, whose visit to the church with Jim Bullock on March 22, 1964, launched the kneel-in campaign there.[13]

Like Bullock, Purdy was a college senior. He was several years older than his peers, however, because after graduating from Manassas High School in 1956 he had spent four years in the Air Force. Following his discharge from the military, Purdy enrolled at Owen College and later transferred to Memphis State, where his life experience and natural leadership ability made him a campus organizer. Purdy became active in the NAACP intercollegiate chapter, where he encountered the white Southwestern students with whom he would protest at SPC. By all accounts, Purdy was particularly comfortable around white students who had had little exposure to African Americans. Thus it is not surprising that in early 1964 he was invited to address the Westminster Fellowship at Southwestern in preparation for that school's impending integration.[14]

While the SPC kneel-ins were still under way, Purdy was involved in a campaign to desegregate the Normal Tea Room, a popular eatery near the Memphis State campus. On April 13, 1964, he was one of four black and two white young men (Southwesterners Howard Romaine and Bob Morris) who occupied a booth at the restaurant and demanded service. All six were arrested on state charges of interfering with trade and commerce. Additionally, Purdy faced a charge of extortion for writing a letter to the restaurant's proprietor requesting that he open his business to all without regard to race. "If this cannot be accomplished," Purdy wrote,

> we will be forced to dramatize this failure to comply with the basic tenets under our Christian and democratic heritage. This will be done in accordance with the tenets of non-violence in whatever form we deem necessary and desirable. It is our hope that you will meet with us before the end of the week to work out plans whereby desegregation will be accomplished with as little damage to your business as possible.[15]

The extortion charge, however, was soon overshadowed by a major disturbance outside the Tea Room. A small group picketing the restaurant in early May was opposed by a mob of students who jeered, threw objects, and chased them through the Memphis State campus. Nevertheless, the picketers returned and resumed their protests until the restaurant's management decided to integrate. By July Purdy had called off the demonstrations at the request of the Memphis Committee on Community Relations and local papers were reporting that the Tea Room was serving black patrons.[16]

Several of those who participated in the SPC kneel-ins retain vivid memories of Joe Purdy. Maxine Smith remembers him as a tireless activist. During the spring of 1964 she was helping the Memphis State senior land a job. "He had applied at a bottling company and they were ready to hire him and we had to run find him on the picket line [at the Tea Room] and tell him to go for his job interview," she recalls. Classmate Vivian Carter Dillihunt remembers Purdy as "very much involved in the demonstrations, as well as organizing the African American students." Another classmate, Hortense Spillers, adds that Purdy was "extraordinarily dynamic. . . . He was probably one of those people for whom the description charisma really is true."[17]

Spillers relates a story that reflects the way Purdy's charisma was combined with courage. At a time when racial tensions at Memphis State were elevated, an African American woman was knocked down by a football player. A group of black students, including Spillers and Purdy, asked to meet with university administrators. Spillers vividly recalls Purdy's message to the president and the dean of students: "Write this down: this is the last time that you will touch any one of us—and especially a black woman—on this campus. You will not do it. If this happens again, you've got a war. You need to tell your people that. Keep them away from us!"[18]

Purdy's siblings (he was one of seven children) remember him fondly as a man who drew people "like a magnet," in part because he loved to converse on matters of religion and philosophy. After graduating from Memphis State with a degree in psychology, Purdy took a job with Pepsi Cola Company, where he became the company's first black regional manager.[19]

The Militant

If Vasco Smith was uniquely positioned between the student protestors and the denomination being rocked by their actions, Coby Smith (no relation) stood at the nexus between the Southwestern students who had come late to the civil rights movement and the black students born and raised in Memphis who were veterans of the struggle. In 1964 Smith was president of the student council and a member of the National Honor Society at Manassas High School, and the only Jr. ROTC cadet in Memphis to receive the American Legion's Legion of Valor Award. During his final semester of high school, Smith stood with Southwestern students in front of SPC as a member of the NAACP Youth Council. A few months later, after his appointment to West Point was blocked by a segregationist congressman, he would become part of the first integrated class at the Presbyterian college.[20]

Smith recalls his first impressions of the Southwesterners he encountered in the kneel-in campaign. They were "wrestling inside with trying to be true to . . . the values that their families had taught them," he says. Smith remembers Southwestern students telling their black peers: "Come go to my church. We're going to demand that the spirit of Jesus be reflected in what they do today. And the way to prove that is your being admitted to this church." But according to Smith, his white counterparts did not appreciate the risks he and other black visitors faced. "A black kid is thinking 'I'm going in there and they could kill me.' White kids didn't think that. They thought, 'Here's a test and we've got to present ourselves in order to be true to the test.' The police weren't gonna drag them off to jail. They weren't gonna be beaten and possibly killed."[21]

White students may have run different risks, but Smith is quick to concede that they were real enough. "You're nineteen years old and somebody says, 'Are you willing to go over there and do that?' Your reputation is on the line. And you're going to walk into the church beside a black woman and everybody sitting down in that congregation is thinking that that means you're having sex with 'em. Because that was what the deal was." What integration boiled down to for whites, Smith declares, was fear that black men wanted to marry their daughters. "It wasn't about attending the same schools or anything else," he says. The concern was that if young people mingled across the racial divide, "the purity of the races" would be destroyed.

Smith came by these insights honestly, having grown up in North Memphis with white folks living nearby. The odd thing about segregation, he says, is that

> you could live right next to white people. You could grow up with them. You could be in their house. They could be in yours. You could eat off the same table. But when the girls got to be ten, twelve years old, when the boys got to be teenagers, you couldn't have close personal relationships. . . . You couldn't go to the same school. You couldn't date.[22]

Because Smith was one of two African Americans chosen to integrate Southwestern in the fall of 1964, there was a great deal of hope that this outstanding young man would open the school's doors even further for local blacks. But as he came under the influence of the Black Power movement, Smith made many white Memphians, including members of the Southwestern administration, uncomfortable. He reached a personal turning point in June 1966 as he participated in James Meredith's "March against Fear" from Memphis to Jackson, Mississippi. Like other student activists in Memphis, Smith had come under the sway of Jim Lawson and his message of nonviolence. "I, like everybody else, admired and loved the man," he says. But as he was influenced by the militant movement that was energizing younger activists, Smith became frustrated that Memphis's civil rights establishment was ignoring the contributions young people could make in the quest for social change.[23]

While on the "March against Fear," Smith watched the reactions of Martin Luther King, Jr. and Stokely Carmichael as police beat and tear gassed black marchers "until blood and tears rolled down their faces." Concluding that the putative divisions between violent and nonviolent black leaders were superficial, he began to view nonviolence as a tactic, one most effective, no doubt, when whites feared black counter-violence. In 1967, Smith took time off from his studies at Southwestern and moved to Atlanta. He returned to Memphis determined to create a "black united front" that would pose a "credible threat of violence." In this spirit, Smith and Memphis-born antiwar activist Charles Cabbage formed the Black Organizing Project (BOP) for younger activists in Memphis. The militant wing of the BOP was the Invaders, a black-power–oriented group consisting mostly of young men. Smith and other Invaders played on white fears of black rebellion to strengthen their role in the larger movement for civil rights. By the time of the 1968 Sanitation Workers' strike, the Invaders had become a local force with which King and his lieutenants had to reckon. The attractive and articulate Smith became a spokesman for the group, appearing on television in his Invaders jacket and red beret.[24]

Smith's militant persona complicated his relationships with members of the civil rights establishment and created discomfort on the Southwestern campus. He recalls that

> one day [Dean] Jameson Jones came to me and said, "Coby, I'm sorry that I have to ask you this. But there is a rumor out that you're gonna burn the campus down. And the rest of the administration wanted me to come and talk to you. They feel like you and I have a rapport." And I said, "Well, sir, Dean Jones. I couldn't burn this place down. It's made out of stone. You'd have to blow it up." And he said, "I'm so relieved."[25]

The Intellectual

Hortense Spillers is a native Memphian and a 1960 graduate of Melrose High School. After a year spent attending college in North Carolina, Spillers returned to the Bluff City and attempted to enroll at Southwestern. A college official told her the school did not intend to integrate its classrooms for another three years. "I beg your pardon," Spillers said. "But I'll be done by then." She ended up at Memphis State, which had integrated two years earlier. Looking back, Spillers sees a missed opportunity for the liberal arts college:

> They had a model opportunity to be progressive and forward and they did not take that chance. The handwriting was on the wall. It was time,

it was past time. It was six years past *Brown v. Board* and state universities were integrating, private schools were opening up. They could
have been forward, progressive and they are a school run by a religious
denomination traditionally. That should have given them some courage.
They had none.[26]

Spillers would not meet Southwestern students in the classroom, but she
would encounter some of them on the front lines of the Memphis movement.
Like other students with activist leanings, she became involved in the NAACP
intercollegiate chapter. "Jim Lawson was one of our mentors," she recalls. "He
encouraged the church visitations that students in the intercollegiate group were
undertaking," helping them with "the whole attitude and posture toward nonviolence." When Spillers heard that some of her peers had been turned away from
SPC, she decided to join them.[27]

Spillers remembers the men guarding the church as "bold-faced, adamant—as
if they were doing something brave resisting, I suppose, what they called their
way of life." The scene she recalls as peaceful, the quiet punctuated only by conversations between individual protestors and church members. Spillers says she
wanted to worship at SPC in order "to raise the consciousness [at the church]
because apparently it needed raising." For her, the underlying issue was not the
site of the upcoming PCUS General Assembly, but justice: "All my history and
religion told me that there was no way in the world that they could be right. All
the laws said that they were wrong—both God's and man's law said that they were
wrong. I knew that we were in danger but that we had to persist and that we would
eventually prevail."[28]

Spillers contrasts her experience at SPC with that of the white students who
visited her church. When Southwesterners from the intercollegiate group
attended St. John Baptist, she recalls, "the black people were curious about who
they were, but weren't bent out of shape about it." They probably wondered,
Spillers says, "what these children were up to now." "But it was nothing like the
white audiences who refused to accept black parishioners and, you know, were
disgusted or frightened or whatever it was."[29]

Church kneel-ins were not the only acts of boundary crossing Spillers engaged
in at Memphis State. In May 1964 she was arrested while attempting to lunch in
a mixed group at the Normal Tea Room. Around the same time, she led a delegation of Memphis State students—consisting of herself and six white men—to
a Model United Nations conference in St. Louis. According to Spillers, "everybody was just appalled that I was going to pile in a car with a bunch of young
white men and go to St. Louis. And I said, 'what do you mean? I like these
people! They're not going to hurt me. We took classes together and we really had
a wonderful time with each other. And we just really liked each other a lot.' And
we said 'screw the customs, we're going!'"[30]

The lessons Spillers learned as a college activist served her well after leaving Memphis in 1966. "Somewhere along the way I learned that one of the most critical weapons in any struggle is language—the power to use it effectively, forcefully, eloquently and movingly, to argue well, and to know things. And so I became a professor and that's what I do, I write about my culture. I write about women's culture, because I think discourse and language are so important." After receiving a master's degree from Memphis State in 1966, Spillers taught at Kentucky State University before heading to graduate school at Brandeis. She later taught African American literature at Cornell and since 2006 has been Gertrude Conaway Vanderbilt Professor of English at Vanderbilt University.[31]

The Morehouse Man

In the spring of 1964, Harold Taylor was a senior at Memphis's Booker T. Washington High School. As president of the local NAACP Youth Council, Taylor was drafted into the church visit campaign undertaken by the intercollegiate group. Although he was one of the youngest participants, he possesses clear memories of how things worked on Sunday mornings:

> We would carpool to Southwestern. We would meet in their dining hall. We would decide who was going to what church. We would then go from there. We'd arrive at the churches about 15 minutes before the 11:00 service. At Second Pres we would be stopped at the steps every Sunday by the elders of the church. We would essentially have prayer service and sing songs right at the front of the church. We would sing anywhere from about 30–45 minutes, then disperse. Civil rights songs like "We Shall Overcome," and "I Shall Not Be Moved." Afterward we would go to Parkway Gardens.[32]

Taylor and other members of the Youth Council were prepared for the resistance they met at SPC because they had undergone nonviolence training at NAACP headquarters. There, under the tutelage of Jim Lawson, they considered questions such as "What's gonna happen if somebody hits you? What's gonna happen if somebody spits on you? What's gonna happen if somebody calls you 'nigger'? How are you gonna react? What you gonna do if today they open the door and they tell you to come in?" The training was intense, Taylor says, because it was paramount that sixteen-, seventeen-, and eighteen-year-olds learn that "the worst thing you can do is strike back."[33]

Taylor recalls that his parents supported his activism, even though it made his father vulnerable to retaliation:

My father was maitre d' at the Tennessee Club here in Memphis . . . an old style club for whites; so his livelihood depended on segregation, it really did. And with his son being active in civil rights he could lose his job. But he never tried to stop me and we never had any long philosophical discussions about it, you know. He never said, "Don't go." I came to realize later on that what I was doing really could jeopardize him. I didn't think of it at the time.[34]

The SPC kneel-ins were a crucial part of the experience Taylor took with him to Morehouse College in the fall of 1964. On one hand, "you had the sense that you were part of something that was going to help change America." On the other hand, Taylor says he was dismayed that Christians were making assumptions about the motivations of other Christians without giving them the opportunity to prove that their intentions were genuine. "You will only know [my motivation] when you open the door," he remembers thinking.[35]

Taylor returned to Memphis after college and became an oral surgeon. In the 1990s he began pursuing church reconciliation in a less confrontational way: For eight years he participated in a men's Bible Study that met at SPC. "What are you doing out there with them white folk?" some of his friends asked. "You're the same guy who stood on the steps and said 'let me in to worship.'" Taylor's response was that once the doors of the church had opened, he ought to be able to enter without being ostracized by his own community. "People of faith," he says, "have to understand that there's no color in your faith."[36]

The Disciple

Like Hortense Spillers, Earl Stanback attended Melrose High School, where in 1964 he was a senior active in the NAACP youth chapter. Also like Spillers, Stanback attended St. John Baptist Church, which he remembers as being full of people who had grown up under the boot-heel of racism and were not used to mixing religion and activism. This quietism was embodied by his mother, who one day told Stanback, "You better stop marching, you gonna get beat up and arrested and put in jail!" Despite such warnings, however, Stanback became a disciple of Jim Lawson and his philosophy of nonviolent direct action.[37]

Stanback's involvement in the SPC campaign began when some Southwestern students asked him to join them at the church. Stanback agreed, with the stipulation that they come to his church as well. Stanback's memories from his initial visit to SPC remain vivid:

So we hopped in the car, we went over there, parked, got out, and we walked up to the church. And the deacons met us, and said, "Where are ya'll going?" And we said, "We're going to church." "Well, what are you going to church for?" "You know, we're going to hear the message; our buddies invited us." [And they said] "ya'll are just troublemakers. Why don't you go to your own church?" And we looked at each other and I said, "Well, I heard your minister is pretty good, I wanna see how he speaks." And they said, "Why don't you go to your church? We built a multi-million church out here, and ya'll didn't even put a dime into the plate! Go on to your own church!"[38]

When Stanback related this encounter to Lawson, the churchman was incredulous. He told Stanback, "I'll tell you what. We're goin' to church next Sunday." Lawson did attend, according to Stanback, although his presence was undetected because of rainy weather. Afterward, Stanback says, Lawson recruited more students, whom he instructed to stand in front of the church in interracial pairs. He was adamant, however, that there be no pushing, shoving, or loud singing, lest church members have support for their claims that the students were rabble-rousers. "We would walk up [to the church] in a chain," Stanback recalls, "and of course we sang. We had prayer right there at the front of the church. We prayed for the church, we prayed for the deacons, we prayed for the pastor. And then we left."[39]

Stanback has one rather unique memory of his activism at SPC. One Sunday, he says, "the minister came out and said, 'How ya'll doin? How ya'll doin? Wish you the best of luck.' That's all he said!" While Stanback was touched by the gesture, he is critical of Jeb Russell's leadership in the crisis. "You know, he never preached about the issue, he never said anything, he never made a move—he was probably scared. He should have made a stand. He didn't." Stanback also recalls pictures being taken of students as they stood in front of the church. He believes SPC representatives asked the Southwestern administration to identify the students, write letters to their parents, and even expel them. He knows parents were sent pictures and letters containing "a bunch of lies," because he saw some of the letters Southwestern parents wrote to their children in response. Stanback was appalled at the behavior of church officials. "They lied. They lied, lied. I said, 'We got deacons of the church lying on students, talking about how we were violent and we come out here to rabble rouse.'"[40]

Stanback emphasizes that the kneel-in campaign at SPC happened "all by accident." "Some friends from the NAACP . . . just *happened* to go to church," he says. "And it went all over the nation as far as the Presbyterian Church is concerned." A friendly church exchange evolved into a direct action campaign, according to Stanback, because the church's response placed it on the wrong side of the day's great moral question.[41]

The Teachers

In 1964, Elaine Lee Turner was a sophomore at LeMoyne College. Her oldest sister Ernestine, also a LeMoyne student, had helped organize the 1960 Memphis sit-ins. In fact, by 1965 five members of the Lee family had been arrested for engaging in civil disobedience. Not surprisingly, Turner joined the NAACP Youth Council while in high school, later graduating to the intercollegiate chapter, where she met fellow activists from Memphis State and Southwestern.

Turner recalls that members of the intercollegiate group began their church visits in 1964 because, despite the significant gains made by the civil rights movement in Memphis, congregations in the city were still "very segregated." "The churches were basically the last battleground—how 'bout that?" Turner says. "And we found that one was as difficult as the others had been, surprisingly enough." Turner's introduction to the church visitation campaign came when she was invited by Southwestern students to attend Evergreen Presbyterian Church, a PCUS congregation adjacent to the campus. Evergreen embraced the visitors, but other churches, including Bellevue Baptist, were less welcoming. SPC stood out, according to Turner, as the "most hostile."[42]

Turner returned to SPC on several occasions, convinced that it was only a matter of time before the church opened its doors to welcome her and her peers. "The deacons . . . would form a line across the steps of the church," she recalls. "And they were not very kind at all. I remember some profanity . . . and I just wondered, 'What god are they serving in there?' Because we would talk to them and ask why we couldn't come in, and they had some very cruel things to say to us as they stood there all during the service." Because rank-and-file members tended to avoid the protestors, Turner saw no indication that anyone inside the church felt differently than those who were guarding the doors.[43]

Like many of the student activists, Turner was prepared for the kneel-ins at SPC through Jim Lawson's nonviolence workshops. "He would really drill us as to the kinds of things that we should do and how we should respond as to not provoke anyone and not to strike back and be violent ourselves." According to Turner, the students refrained from singing, so as not to give the church any basis for claiming they had disturbed the service. "We really stood peacefully and engaged in conversations sometimes," she recalls. "Just talking with them, seeing if we could prick their conscience at all, you know, if they would listen."[44]

Turner remembers pondering the theological meaning of her experiences in front of SPC on Sunday mornings. "This is the church," she reflected, "and I *know* that if they are worshipping the same God as we worship that they just need to be shown that . . . this is not God's way. And if they want to be Christians then I know they will change." If that hope could be realized, Turner reasoned, society could change as well: "If there were ministers who spoke out, then the politicians and judges and policemen who filled white churches might learn that God was not pleased with what they were doing."[45]

The whole experience was disorienting for this child of the black church. "In our churches," Turner says,

> we were taught that we are all equal under God's sight, that God was no respecter of persons and that he made us all and that we are to be treated as human beings. And so I just wondered what Bible they were reading from. I wondered what the minister said when he talked to them. Did he try to show them that their way of thinking was against God's principles?

Looking back, Turner finds it significant that churches represented the last barrier to integration in Memphis. "They had their laws in place and their tradition in place, and they were not going to have any students come and challenge that," she says. "I think it was the church saying that we are not going to give in like these public institutions. We don't have to because this is our church, and we are the law."[46]

Following college Turner worked as a teacher in Mississippi, Missouri, and Texas. Upon retirement from that profession, she and sister Joan Lee Nelson started Heritage Tours, a sightseeing company in Memphis that offers tours of Beale Street, historic Memphis churches, and "Slavehaven," an antebellum home that was once a stop on the Underground Railroad. "We talk about the history, we talk about the civil rights movement; we tell students today what it was like, walking them through that era and the things that happened in the past. I think that's what I'm supposed to do," Turner says.[47]

In the spring of 1964 Vivian Carter Dillihunt was a freshman at Memphis State and a neighbor of Vasco and Maxine Smith. After hearing about the SPC kneel-ins through the Memphis State grapevine, she attempted to enter the church on several Sundays. "There was a group of us. We got to the front door and we were turned away. We were told that we could not enter," she says. The students' response was to "praise, sing, just stand there . . . while the person who had been designated as our leader spoke with the person who was turning us away." Dillihunt emphasizes that the students were very respectful. "There was never a harsh word uttered by any of us. There was never anything done that was disrespectful, or anything that would cause any kind of disruption to the services that were going on inside."[48]

Although there was no violence at SPC, Dillihunt says, there was always fear—not only of physical attack but of academic retaliation, as black students at Memphis State believed that their grades suffered if they became identified as activists. Dillihunt does remember small acts of civility from church members—people saying "hello" or "good morning"—but is saddened by the absence of explicit signs of support. "No one ever started a conversation; no one ever said 'I support you.' No one ever said 'I hope you come back.' No one ever said 'I want you to get in.'" She believes that while the majority of church members may not have been in favor of what was happening, they were afraid to stand up and say "this is wrong."[49]

The civil rights movement had a profound effect on Dillihunt. "We have a number of white friends, we have a number of Jewish friends, and we have friends of all cultures that come out to our home . . . We don't see colors anymore. We see people." After thirty-five years working in the Memphis City Schools as a teacher, counselor, principal, and district administrator, Dillihunt is now an author and consultant. In 2007 she received a Distinguished Educator Award from the National Alliance of Black School Educators.[50]

Unlike other participants in the SPC kneel-ins, Lillian Hammond Brown was not a student at the time of the protests. In 1959 she had considered joining the first integrated class at Memphis State, but enrolled instead at Lincoln University, a predominantly black institution in Jefferson City, Missouri. Brown missed the 1960 Memphis sit-in movement and was not involved in integration efforts at Lincoln. When she returned to Memphis to take a teaching job in the summer of 1963, however, she went back to the congregation where she had grown up—Centenary United Methodist—and discovered that the church had a new pastor named Lawson.

"Just listening to him Sunday after Sunday and hearing his approach to trying to make a difference in our community inspired me to want to be a part of that," Brown recalls. Soon she was participating in Lawson's workshops on Christian nonviolence. "Whatever Jim Lawson was about, I was trying to be near," she says. Around the same time, Brown met Maxine Smith and became active in the local NAACP chapter. When the Smiths informed her about what was happening at SPC and invited her to accompany them to the church, she knew her activist moment had arrived. Brown recalls that on Sunday mornings she would wear a tan suit and a silk patterned blouse—"the first outfit I bought with my own money," she says.[51]

Not all her memories of the visits are pleasant, however. "The elders stood in the door. We just lingered. . . . I had no idea they were gonna tell us we couldn't get in. I thought that was horrible. It was a bad experience. It left a bad taste in your mouth." Nevertheless, Brown harbors no bitterness toward SPC. In fact, since getting to know some of the church's leaders through a program called "Life Focus," Brown has visited the church on occasion. She has even helped SPC come to terms with its history. In the early 1990s, when SPC Senior Minister Richard DeWitt preached at the church Brown then attended, the two dined together with their spouses. When Brown told DeWitt she had been kept out of his church in 1964, the "very troubled" pastor apologized on behalf of the congregation.[52]

Several years later, while at the home of an SPC member, Brown again shared her experience as a would-be worshipper at the church in 1964. Her host relayed the story to SPC's new pastor, Sanders "Sandy" Willson, who invited Brown to meet him for lunch. "I'd like you to come one Sunday and tell our members why they should open up more to minorities," Willson told her. Brown replied that "this is a new day. Now you need the members from within your congregation . . . to get up and tell their own family members. This is the way it has to be done now. . . . If you have members who feel that way sincerely, then it's time for them to stand up." The conversation was the beginning of an abiding friendship between Brown and Willson. "I listen to him [preach]; as a matter of fact, I'm tardy to my church sometimes because I'm trying to listen to him on TV," Brown says. She is impressed by Willson's commitment to "mov[ing] his members to a true Christian approach to humanity."[53]

The Student Experience: Similarities

To what extent did the experiences of young people who participated in the SPC kneel-ins during 1964–65 differ depending on their race? One commonality is that white and black students alike developed a genuine respect for colleagues on the other side of the racial divide. Elaine Lee Turner describes the lasting impact of standing alongside white students in the church visitation campaign:

> This was actually the first time that I had really gotten to know any white students at all. You know, I was in college at that time but I had no op- portunities to really interact with white students because everything was very segregated here. I think that was very positive because we were able to see that they were just like us; they're studying, they're going to school, they have ambitions, goals just like we do, so you know, that was really positive. And then they were willing to take a stand, you know, and that was something that was really good to see.[54]

Similarly, Coby Smith reflects that "when you go through these experiences with people, you have a genuine respect for them." On occasion, black and white students developed friendships that went beyond NAACP meetings and church protests. Vivian Carter Dillihunt and Ervin Haas Bullock both remember the night they con- travened social conventions and campus rules by sharing Haas's Southwestern dorm room. It's something the women recall with pride forty-five years later.

Both black and white kneel-in participants report, however, that lasting inter-racial friendships were quite rare. When asked if she remembers any of the African Americans with whom she protested, Southwestern student Liz Currie Williams confesses that she "can't remember the names of the black people very well. I actually don't remember being with them except on Sundays." Hortense Spillers, responding to a similar question, says, "you know, I don't but I should. If I saw faces I would remember." Vivian Carter Dillihunt describes the white students she met at SPC as "acquaintances" rather than friends. Robert Wells shares this assessment, lamenting that the protestors were only "acquaintances that gathered on Sunday morning over this issue." It is ironic that students whom church members assumed were emotionally and sexually intimate actually established very few long-term connections.[55]

Another similarity among white and black participants is their insistence that nothing in their dress, behavior, or speech indicated they had any intention other than entering SPC for Sunday-morning worship. Most of them had been trained, in fact, not to antagonize the defenders of segregation—whether policemen, restaurant owners, or church officers—and they were careful to avoid doing so at SPC. Furthermore, most of the students of both races were lifelong Christians who instinctively recognized the sanctity of church buildings and held church leaders in high esteem. Some kneel-in participants remember singing; others claim they remained silent; but all agree that they were prepared to endure abuse rather than respond in any way that would undermine their nonviolent witness.

Nevertheless, black and white students alike were accused of visiting the church from unspiritual motives. As the kneel-ins dragged on and SPC appeared increasingly inhospitable and exclusive, the church's beleaguered session worked hard to cast the student protestors as "agitators" who lacked any interest in Christian worship. In fact, many SPC members embraced the view that the students were "demonstrators" whose only aim was to create a public disturbance. It did not matter that they were dressed for Sunday morning in the South, or that they were well disciplined as a group and respectful individually. Their presence in a place where they were not welcome—and their interracial fraternization—labeled them as troublemakers.

Aware that their motives were under scrutiny, on at least one Sunday morning visiting students handed out copies of an article reprinted from *The Presbyterian Outlook* titled "Motives Committee." It referred to a memorandum that had been distributed to "colored people" attempting to worship at a white church in Charleston, South Carolina. After analyzing the memorandum's dubious assumptions, the author engaged in "a little fantasy":

If a church starts turning people from its doors on the ground that their motives are presumably bad, why stop with colored visitors? Why not examine the white folks on the same basis? Let us imagine . . . the church has appointed a Motives Committee. After they have had a few sessions, let us look over the secretary's shoulder at some items in the minutes.[56]

These "minutes" refer to several church members whom the committee votes to exclude—Mr. A, who comes not to worship but to seek a wife, Mrs. C, who comes to relax and sing, and so forth. The article concludes with a conversation between two angels on an "invisible inspection Team." As they discuss the Motives Committee's work, the younger angel asks how it is that the committee seems "to know the motives of the dark people without investigating at all." The older angel responds that "these people don't need to look into the heart. They can tell bad motives by the color of the skin."[57]

This attempt to turn the issue of motives back on church members had no discernible effect on the situation, and insistence that the students were agitators for social change continued to dominate official discourse at SPC. This conviction was undergirded by two popular explanations for the students' decision to "agitate" at SPC. One, encouraged by reports of the kneel-ins in newspapers and magazines, was that the campaign had been launched to embarrass Jeb Russell's brother, U.S. Senator Richard Russell, who at the time was leading Southern congressional resistance to federal civil rights legislation. A second explanation of choice was that the church had been targeted because it was slated to host the 1965 meeting of the PCUS General Assembly. The impending meeting provided an ideal opportunity, the argument went, to embarrass SPC by focusing attention on its longstanding segregation policy.[58]

Obviously, any reliable assessment of the students' motives must be informed by their own testimony, which clearly indicates that neither of these factors was decisive. The students became aware that Rev. Russell's brother was a U.S. Senator, they say, only after it was reported in the papers. Similarly, SPC's contract to host the 1965 PCUS General Assembly did not become well known until several weeks after the kneel-ins had begun. The truth is that SPC became a target of the church visit campaign only after it turned away Jim Bullock and Joe Purdy—two of the city's best-trained and most committed student organizers. Jeb Russell's prominent family and SPC's place in the denominational spotlight brought added attention to the kneel-ins once they were under way; but they do not explain why they occurred.

The relevant question, then, is not "why was SPC targeted by the students?" but "why did SPC respond to 'testing' by interracial pairs in a way that made it a target for repeated kneel-ins?" Answers to this question will be explored in a later chapter.

The Student Experience: Differences

There were also significant differences in the ways black and white students experienced the kneel-ins at SPC. For instance, with the exception of Vasco and Maxine Smith, the black protestors were unconcerned with the church's Presbyterian identity, which was not a factor in their decisions to join the kneel-ins. In this they differed from their white counterparts, all of whom were students at a Presbyterian-related college and most of whom were concerned to draw attention to racial attitudes in PCUS churches.

Furthermore, the experiences of black and white students differ in that many of the African Americans feared for their safety as they ventured into affluent East Memphis. Far from their neighborhoods in an area of the city where most people who looked like them were domestics or gardeners, the black protestors were confronted by prominent white men who were accustomed to exercising social control over African Americans of any age. Blocking the doors of the church seemed to SPC officials like a reasonable defensive action. But in the implacable faces of these umbrella-wielding elders some black students perceived the countenance of white supremacy, which in their experience often disguised violent intentions. As Hortense Spillers relates, although the protests remained peaceful, she feared that the black students—isolated from their families and communities—might be attacked by vigilantes.[59]

White students do not report being concerned with the threat of physical violence. They were, however, subject to attempts to silence them by appeals to the adults who paid their tuition and would sign their diplomas. These appeals, it was hoped, would create enough fallout at home and on campus that the Southwestern students would be forced to abandon their kneel-in campaign. But these efforts to influence the students' behavior, even when successful, proved insufficient; they had to be supplemented both with claims that the students were not true worshippers, and with accusations that they were not Christians.

The allegation that protestors who dared challenge segregation from within the orbit of white privilege were "atheists" was introduced at the end of April 1964. In a letter to the congregation, the SPC session wrote that church representatives had been "confronted" by two "admitted atheists," one of whom "said he was a member of the International Farm Youth Exchange, [who] at some length harangued several elders with traditional Marxist ideological doctrine." Given what we know of the students, their goals, and their training, the assertion that one of their number was a haranguing Marxist is less than credible. However, it is not at all surprising that white students' efforts to force integration on an unwilling church raised the twin specters of atheism and Marxism.[60]

At the time, in fact, many Southerners were convinced that racial integration was part of a communist plot to destabilize American society. And since communists were notoriously "godless," it followed that anyone fighting to end segregation was an atheist or a dupe of atheists. Or so the thinking went. Those at SPC who held such views pointed to the fact that the protesting students were affiliated with the NAACP, an organization that they assumed was communist-inspired and that was commonly referred to among segregationists as the National Association for the Advancement of the Communist Party. Like the belief that the NAACP was a front for communism, the conviction that the kneel-ins were led by atheists was impervious to rational argument. It was soon broadcast throughout the PCUS.[61]

By the end of April, caricatures of the presumably irreligious students had reached Maryland, where a member of Carl Pritchett's congregation confronted him with the accusation that the students kneeling-in at SPC were led by "a white boy who is . . . an avowed atheist." After returning from Memphis, Pritchett sought to refute the rumor by emphasizing that the students' motivation "came from their Christian faith and concern about racial injustice." He specifically mentioned Howard Romaine and Bob Morris, both of whom, he said, had been branded "atheists" by representatives of SPC. These young men, Pritchett told his congregation, were motivated not by anti-Christian animus but by "the lack of honesty in the church and the denial of brotherhood which is so evident." Relating what he knew of their religious outlooks, Pritchett spoke admiringly of the young men:

> I learned to have great respect of [Bob's] mind and spirit. Wherever his mind may lead him in his religious thinking, I know he will stand by it always and express it in the concrete situations of life. Howard expects to engage in the struggle for social justice in Mississippi this summer. I do hope he will be more careful than I think he will be. I consider him a friend and comrade now. This world can ill afford to lose such a man of God, whether he is sitting in the pew inside the walls of the institutional church or standing outside on the lawn of a fashionable church longing to enter the church with his Negro brother.[62]

Pritchett even quoted from Romaine's *Sou'wester* article in which he presented a theological rationale for church integration, adding "if this is atheism . . . I'll eat my hat!"

As further evidence that the Southwestern protesters were religiously motivated, Pritchett held up Jim Bullock, with whose father he had been in contact. Bullock "may be a member of the NAACP standing before the door of that church," Pritchett wrote, "but he did not learn why he ought to stand there from the meetings of the NAACP. He got it from his father and mother and the Word of God." Jackie Dowd Hall, whose religious background was similar to Bullock's, muses that the Southwestern students who participated in the kneel-ins were pushed toward atheism more by the church's reaction to their presence than by their own inclinations. "If they wanted us to *become* atheists they did a good job," she says. As we will see in the next chapter, these were not the only young people whose faith was challenged by the kneel-in crisis at SPC.[63]

"Mama, Why Don't They Just Let Them In?"

Children

A question rarely if ever asked is how kneel-ins were perceived by the young people who witnessed them from inside targeted churches. Particularly in cases where visitors were not admitted and kneel-in campaigns continued for several weeks, it was inevitable that a church's youth would be exposed to the controversy. W. J. Cunningham, pastor of Galloway Methodist Church in Jackson, Mississippi, which was rocked by racial dissent in the early 1960s, describes the sort of episode that undoubtedly left an impact on young people. On the evening of Palm Sunday 1964—the day that would mark the beginning of the kneel-ins at SPC—a woman from India working as an instructor at local Tougaloo College was forcibly ejected from Galloway in front of twenty-four of the church's young people who were about to be received as members. Cunningham wondered, with good reason, whether they would ever forget the incident.[1]

Youth at SPC were mentioned only once in newspaper reports of the kneel-ins in Memphis. In April 1964 the *Tri-State Defender* related that "young members of the church came out frequently from a side door [of the church] and peeped over the hedge to get a good look at the would-be worshippers." Similarly, only one interview with a student protestor includes any mention of children at the church. Jim Bullock recollects being told that "one of the kids came out, and he seemed to be president of the youth group, and he was crying for what he saw." Despite scarce references to reactions by the church's young people, however, the length of the SPC kneel-in controversy and the conflicts to which it gave rise inside the church suggest that attempts by SPC's youth to determine what was happening on Sunday mornings were probably quite common.[2]

What did curious young people see when they "peeped over the hedge" to catch a glimpse of the drama being staged in front of their church? What questions and emotions did these sights evoke in them? What were they told by their parents and Sunday School teachers? And what were the long-term effects of witnessing these traumatic events? This chapter answers these questions based on interviews conducted when former church youth were in their fifties and sixties.

Preachers' Kids

The children of pastors typically have little choice when it comes to their involvement in church activities. This was certainly the case with the three younger children of Rev. Jeb and Ala Jo Russell. By the time of the SPC kneel-ins, Joanna Russell Hogan had finished college and was raising a family. Harriette Russell Coleman, the second of the Russell children, was spending the spring of 1964 in France with students from Southwestern. Among the bits and pieces of the kneel-in story that made it across the Atlantic was the fact that her father was receiving "hate mail." "What I picked up," Coleman recalls, "is that a lot of the elders had a very old-time Southern plantation mentality and they were the problem."[3]

Cay Russell Davis, the Russell's third child, was a high-school junior in 1964. She doesn't remember much of the kneel-ins, in part because it was her habit to enter the sanctuary for worship directly from the Sunday School building. Davis does recall, however, someone in the church claiming that a protestor told him that "we don't want to worship with you, we just want to take these niggers into the church." Unlike his sister Cay, Henry "Jeb" Russell, Jr., who was fourteen at the time, has vivid memories of the protesters. "They didn't say anything to anybody," he recalls. "I walked down the sidewalk among them and entered the church without having any conversation; so I think they were pretty disciplined. I was pretty fascinated by it all." Jeb, Jr. also remembers fishing trips when his father would open up about events at SPC. Jeb Russell's attitude, his son recalls, was "whosoever will, may come; that is, no one should be prevented from coming, or even joining the church." Russell even remembers discussing the students' motives with his father. For all he knew, his father told him, some standing in front of the church had more character than some sitting in the pews.[4]

Howard Hazelwood, son of Associate Pastor James Hazelwood, was a fifteen-year-old high school sophomore in 1964. Initially, the kneel-in controversy was of little interest to him and his friends. But one Sunday morning Hazelwood decided to see for himself what was going on in front of his church. On that particular day, he saw

> a lot of people from the church standing around (this was prior to the service beginning), but I vividly remember on that particular Sunday

standing on the left side of the [church] entry on the step. . . . I had a
bird's eye view of the crowd, and there were some people who came up . . .
I'm assuming that they would have been from the session, who met
them at the entrance and talked to them . . . One of the students who
was participating in the demonstration made a comment to me that I
should be with them, to which I didn't respond.[5]

Hazelwood remembers a "standoff" between students and three or four elders
standing halfway between the front doors and the steps. There were no raised
voices, only an explanation of the church's policy.[6]

Hazelwood doesn't recall the kneel-ins being discussed in senior-high meetings on Sunday evenings or any other time. Nor does he remember the resumption of protests in 1965, the letter that went out over his father's signature, the
circulating petitions, or the congregational meeting that finally curbed the session's power. But Hazelwood does recall hearing that students were being kept
out of the church because they "only wanted to make trouble." He also vividly
remembers his father saying that he and Rev. Russell had recommended to the
session that "if anyone should come and want to be seated at the service, they
should be seated."[7]

Future Clergymen

Horace Houston convinced his parents to join SPC when he started attending
church-affiliated Presbyterian Day School at age six. Houston's chief memory of
the kneel-in controversy is from the spring of 1965, when the fifteen-year-old
accompanied his mother to church while home from boarding school.

"We went to church and the elders were standing in a semicircular ring around
the front door of the church, and I was very surprised," Houston recalls. "I
remember my mother taking my hand and leading me through that line of elders.
They parted to let us through and then resumed their stance." When Houston
told his mother he thought it was God's church and everyone should be welcomed, she responded that the students only wanted to stir up trouble and the
elders did not want the church used in that way. Protesters had targeted the
church in an attempt to disrupt services, she said, because Jeb Russell's brother
was a U.S. Senator.[8]

His experience of entering SPC through a phalanx of ushers who were guarding the doors left a lasting impression on the young Houston. It prepared him, in
fact, for subsequent church experiences in which race would play a role. After
studying for the ministry at Princeton Theological Seminary, Houston's first pastorate was a multiracial church in downtown Newark, New Jersey, which he

describes as "probably as different from Second as you could get." But when he returned to Memphis to take a church in 1990, it did not take long for him to find that white racism was alive and well in his home town.[9]

When it came to light that a student intern at the church was dating a black man, one of the elders pressured Houston to fire her, insisting that interracial dating was "unbiblical." Houston refused and influential church members were furious. The situation became so difficult that he resigned his pastorate and began graduate work in American history. Houston decided to write his dissertation on the Fugitive Slave Law, particularly the Southern Presbyterian divines who supported it. Today Houston sees all these experiences through the prism of his adolescent memories of a guarded church. "God can take something negative," Houston says, "and use it in creative ways."[10]

Clifton Kirkpatrick left Memphis and SPC for Davidson College in the fall of 1963. At the time, he shared the conservative outlook of most of his peers; but Davidson exposed him to a universe of new experiences, including a roommate who was an atheist and played the viola. "I wasn't sure which was worse," Kirkpatrick says. At Davidson Kirkpatrick encountered not only a new breed of young person, but a new perspective on the Bible as well. As a result, his worldview began to change. "I began understanding God's call to justice and civil rights," he says, and concluded there was a necessary connection between Christian faith and Jesus's "concern for the poor, the outcasts and the oppressed." Eventually, Kirkpatrick concluded that "the civil rights movement was a part of God's plan at this point in history."[11]

Kirkpatrick's new perspective on the Christian faith was tested when he returned to Memphis in the summer of 1964 and realized what had been happening at his church. As president of SPC's college fellowship, Kirkpatrick was involved in drafting and presenting a petition to the church session calling for all worshippers to be admitted, regardless of race. The students who signed the petition felt that segregation "was not what God intended for the church and the world," he says. The petition had no more effect on the church's official position than any of the pleas that preceded or followed it. But Kirkpatrick believes it may have inspired moderate elders eventually to stand up to session hard-liners.[12]

Among the men who would set the church's path out of the crisis was Kirkpatrick's father, Clifton Kirkpatrick, Sr. Father and son had many conversations that summer as they struggled to understand the civil rights movement from a Christian perspective. The kneel-in crisis at SPC proved a watershed for the elder Kirkpatrick, who, after concluding there had to be change in the South, decided to leave the church. For his part, the younger Kirkpatrick experienced the controversy as one of "two dramatic turns" in his life as a Christian (the other being his conversion). The kneel-ins at SPC left him with a deep sense of "unease" toward his religious tradition, Kirkpatrick says, and pushed him in the direction of a more ecumenical Christianity.[13]

Given his disenchantment with his home church, Kirkpatrick concluded that his call to ministry would have to be explored outside the PCUS. He headed to Yale Divinity School, where he became immersed in ecumenism, the anti-war movement, and civil rights work. After Yale, Kirkpatrick worked for a number of ecumenical organizations before reconnecting with his ecclesiastical roots by joining the PCUS program staff in the area of global ministries. He eventually served for twelve years as the Presbyterian Church (USA)'s Stated Clerk (CEO of the Office of the General Assembly). In 2004, he was elected President of the World Alliance of Reformed Churches.

Kirkpatrick has not been shy in referring to his experience of the SPC controversy and the role it played in his theological development. In 2007, he explained to a reporter for Presbyterian News Service that his "abiding passion for [church] unity" was based in "what I witnessed growing up in Second Presbyterian Church in Memphis." Watching that church be torn apart by theological conflict was "very painful," Kirkpatrick said, and "has made me utterly committed to the belief that there's room under the Lordship of Christ for more diversity in our church."[14]

Proving that the legacy of the SPC kneel-ins is still contested, the *Presbyterian Layman* published a response to Kirkpatrick's comments that claimed "what [he] would have 'witnessed growing up in Second Presbyterian Church in Memphis' was a church committed to historic Presbyterianism." It may be true, as the author of this response noted, that Kirkpatrick's name is "not exactly a household word" at SPC. But he is among several former church members who were deeply influenced by their experience of the kneel-ins and have gone on to achieve prominence in the larger Presbyterian world.[15]

Future Clergywomen

Despite its conservatism and commitment to traditional gender roles, in the 1960s SPC nurtured a number of young women who would become ministers and/or seminary professors. These women's early experiences at SPC set them on a path of service to the larger church. But it was a path shaped by the kneel-in crisis that rocked their congregation while they were in the formative stages of spiritual development.

In 1964 Elinor "Perky" Perkins was an eleven-year-old student at Lausanne Collegiate School who attended SPC with her family. After watching the Sunday-morning kneel-ins for several weeks from a safe distance, Perkins decided to leave the SPC chapel to get a better look. "I remember standing on the lawn," she says, "watching as elders of the church lined up to prevent black students from entering, and the college students there as protesters." Perkins recalls her "surprise that anyone who wanted to worship would not be allowed to do so."[16]

The protests and the controversy they engendered would form a significant milestone in Perkins's spiritual journey, as afterward she was inspired "to develop friendships across color lines, and to lead in trying to undo some of that damaging prejudice." Perkins eventually attended Agnes Scott College and became involved in music ministry at Presbyterian churches in Atlanta. In her thirties, despite never having heard a woman preach, Perkins answered a call to pastoral ministry and enrolled at Columbia Theological Seminary. She was ordained to the Presbyterian ministry in 1986 and would eventually pastor a congregation that included former Southwestern students who had protested at SPC when she was a child.[17]

In the spring of 1964, Elizabeth "Lib" Caldwell was a sixteen-year-old high school senior heavily involved in youth activities at SPC. Her recollections of the kneel-ins are hazy. "My memory is that there were people out there picketing and it was loud," she says. "Or maybe it was just their presence that made it seem loud." Avoiding the sanctuary's main doors, Caldwell did not witness the standoff in front of the church. But she did watch churchmen place African Americans in taxis that had been hired to transport them to "their own churches." This memory stands out, in part, because one of the men offering transportation to black visitors was a member of Caldwell's mother's family, which she describes as "deeply racist." Her maternal grandmother, in particular, sought to inculcate in Caldwell an attitude of racial superiority; these messages were counteracted, she says, by the influence of her father, a World War II veteran who felt passionately that "all people are equal."[18]

Caldwell recalls that at some point during the kneel-ins, session representatives decided it was time to address the situation with SPC's youth. According to Caldwell's recollection, the young people were "served the party line: 'This is why we're doing this' and 'this is why protesters should be taken away.'" Caldwell was treated to a more honest account of what was at stake for those who opposed integration at SPC when she asked her parents what would be "so wrong" with allowing black people to worship at their church. "And I just remember silence," she says. "And then the response, 'Well, then you might start to date.'" The comment suggests that the same fear of miscegenation that spurred the SPC session to adopt a segregation policy in 1957 was behind at least some church members' support for the session's position in 1964.[19]

Caldwell also has vivid memories of the congregational meeting of March 1965, at which church members voted to end lifetime active membership on the SPC session. Sitting in the back row of the sanctuary with her grandparents, Caldwell heard a lot of shouting, a lot of noise. I mean, normally those congregational meetings were always tidy. But this was not tidy. It was loud, and there were a lot of voices, and I don't know when I realized it, but at some point I knew this was not about rotation of elders. It was something much more.[20]

When told of Southwestern President Peyton Rhodes's rebuff of an SPC delegation with the declaration that the college was "not for sale," Caldwell reflects: "Well, I guess that explains what I was told about Southwestern when I applied the next year . . . which was . . . 'You will lose your faith.' 'You'll be brainwashed.' 'You have to watch out for those Bible professors.'" These warnings were, as it turns out, prescient of the impact Southwestern would have on Caldwell. "My world changed," she says, as she came to view the civil rights movement from the perspective of those whose rights had been systematically denied in the South.[21]

After graduating from Southwestern, Caldwell attended the Presbyterian School of Christian Education in Richmond before returning to Memphis to work as a church educator. She eventually received a Ph.D. from Northwestern University and was ordained to pastoral ministry in the Presbyterian Church (USA). Since 1984, Caldwell has taught pastoral theology at Chicago's McCormick Theological Seminary, where she pursues a scholarly interest in the spiritual lives of children.[22]

Ruth Duck joined SPC with her family in the summer of 1965, shortly after the controversy over integration at the church had been resolved. The kneel-in crisis, she says, was a "dangerous memory" that hid in the shadows of the church's collective psyche. This memory would take on increasing importance for Duck as she experienced a personal awakening to civil rights. After a year at Memphis State, Duck transferred to Southwestern in the fall of 1966, "virtually a fundamentalist." "But slowly all these good teachers and pastors were helping me broaden my understanding," she says. Energized by what she was learning in the school's required religion courses, Duck decided to major in social studies and Christian education.[23]

As her world expanded at Southwestern, Duck became alienated from her parents' outlook on race relations (her mother had taught her to wash her hands if she handled something that had been touched by a black person; her father feared his daughter would marry a Catholic or a "Nigra"). Her racial outlook broadening, Duck was "more and more appalled" with the stance her church had adopted in 1964. An opportunity to stake out her own position on civil rights would arrive when the Sanitation Workers' Strike erupted in Memphis in early 1968.[24]

Captivated by the marches, speeches, and public debate stirred up by the strike, Duck experienced what she calls "sort of a conversion through hearing

Martin Luther King speak." After King's assassination, she made her own contri-bution to racial reconciliation through a PCUS program called "Crisis in the Na-tion," which sent workers to cities that had experienced racial conflict, where they helped local churches engage the issues theologically and practically. SPC was chosen to participate in the program and Duck was able to open a dialogue between her church and civil rights leaders.[25]

Upon graduating from Southwestern in 1969, Duck attended Chicago Theo-logical Seminary, where she received a Master of Divinity degree in 1973. Expe-riencing difficulty finding a pastoral call in the PCUS (one church offered her a position that was part-time youth ministry, part-time secretarial work), she was finally ordained in the United Church of Christ. After ten years in pastoral ministry, Duck pursued graduate work leading to a Th. D. degree, and since 1988 has taught at Garrett Evangelical Theological Seminary, where she is Professor of Worship.[26]

Princeton Men

In 1964, Frank Jemison and John Slater were tenth-graders active in the SPC youth program. Jemison attended private Memphis University School, while Slater was a student at public White Station High (where his classmates included actress Kathy Bates and physicist Alan Lightman). Jemison and Slater were among the seven Memphians who entered Princeton University in the fall of 1966. Both returned to Memphis after graduating from Princeton, and neither has trouble remembering the events that transpired at SPC during their sopho-more year of high school.[27]

Slater recalls sometime in the spring of 1964 "walking in the sanctuary and seeing those folks standing out there in the rain. The guys barring the door were a bunch of old men and the protestors were well-dressed—suits and ties—very polite, and it just seemed very unchristian and I suspect others felt the same way about that." Slater also has vivid memories of the tense congregational meeting the following year. "I remember this one elder getting up in the midst of it and yelling something to the effect that, 'If you let a damn nigger in here, I'm gone' before walking out."[28]

Slater says he was dumbfounded by the determination to keep blacks out of SPC, particularly since he suspected that the student visitors had no desire to attend the church long term. At the time, he had concluded that integration was a foregone conclusion in the South. His attitude was based not only on the rela-tively trouble-free integration of his high school the previous year, but the dehu-manizing reality of segregation he had witnessed first-hand as a child. Around 1960, while at the Memphis Fairgrounds with his family, Slater saw a black man turned away from the gate on "whites only" night. "The man literally broke down and cried," Slater recalls. "Mother tried to talk them into letting him in, which they wouldn't do. That was probably the most dramatic thing I ever saw growing up."[29]

Frank Jemison's family was active at SPC in 1964, though he admits that at the time he was fairly oblivious to tensions in the church and only "semi-conscious" of injustice in the South. Jemison's father was a Holiday Inn franchisee who was uncomfortable managing segregated hotels but believed he had to do so to stay in business. Jemison remembers seeing racially mixed groups of protestors in front of SPC and recalls that they handed out leaflets (most likely copies of "Motives Committee," the article several protesting students remember bringing to the church). His chief memory from the congregational meeting of March 1965 is of a respected elder saying not only did he support rotation of session members, but he would be glad to be the first to go on the inactive list.[30]

The effects of the kneel-in crisis on the sixteen-year-old Jemison were not immediately apparent. But the experience contributed to a gradual transformation in his awareness of racial injustice in Memphis. In fact, Jemison has become a strong advocate of SPC's role as a force for racial reconciliation in the city. Today his real-estate company is the leading renter of subsidized housing in Memphis. Indeed, his understanding of and sympathy with the struggles of Memphis's black underclass far exceed that of most white Christians, evangelical or otherwise. In this sense Jemison personifies the new SPC, which is committed to addressing the social and economic problems that plague the Bluff City.[31]

In 1964, Ed Beasley was a high-school junior whose family had been at SPC for four generations. Beasley, too, would end up in Princeton, but as a student at the Presbyterian seminary after his graduation from Southern Methodist University. Beasley's memories of the kneel-ins at his church remain vivid and include "a lot of white men in blue suits" milling about in the church narthex, "black folks out in the front yard of the church," and white students with beards, which, he says, qualified them as "beatniks." Beasley also remembers the emotions these scenes evoked in him. "I was afraid of beatniks and I was afraid of black folks being around the front door of the church unless they were there as chauffeurs," he says.[32]

Beasley felt, as did his parents, that the student visitors were "just troublemakers. . . . that the whole thing was people just stirring up trouble." In his view, the races were meant to occupy separate worlds, worlds that in Beasley's experience overlapped only when "black people cleaned our house and ironed my father's shirts." Beasley regarded this worldview as morally sound until its uglier side was revealed as the kneel-in controversy dragged on. The congregational meeting of March 1965 was a wakeup call for Beasley and his parents, who were dismayed to hear church members express "ugly" (i.e., racist) sentiments.

Around the same time, his mother resigned from her neighborhood Garden Club to protest the group's rejection of a Jewish woman she had nominated for membership.[33]

Beasley's worldview received a further jolt when he went off to SMU in 1965 and was enrolled in classes that challenged his views of humanity, God, and the Bible. By his junior year in college, Beasley was reading radical New Testament critic Rudolf Bultmann and questioning the facticity of the Resurrection. Despite making adjustments to his theology, however, he was leaning toward a career in ministry and seeking encouragement from his home church. But in a deflating luncheon at Memphis Country Club, Beasley was told by one of SPC's pastors that he shouldn't be considering seminary because he had not been sufficiently involved in the church's youth group. Finding support at another local church, Beasley headed off to Princeton Seminary. But after field experience revealed that he was not cut out for the life of a pastor, Beasley decided to pursue a career in elementary education. He married and returned to Memphis, where he taught fifth grade in an inner-city school.[34]

Beasley does not hesitate in describing the role of the SPC kneel-in controversy in his spiritual development: "I think it probably was the pivotal event that made me begin to understand how my faith should interact with social problems. And it has given me at least a measure of ability to check my own racism," he reflects. "Memphis is a very tough place to live without being a racist. Because we're still very segregated. But those events keep me from giving up like a lot of my friends have done."[35]

Between Church and College

Suspended in the emotional space between the students who were hoping to be admitted to SPC and the young people who saw these hopes frustrated were Southwestern students like Carole Branyon, Dale Seay Kasab, and Charles Murphy. Having grown up at SPC, they found themselves torn between loyalty to their church and solidarity with their college peers.

Carole Branyan ('67) was a Southwestern freshman in the spring of 1964. She was quite aware of the kneel-in controversy at the church, as her father was a member of the SPC session. Too ill to attend session meetings, Branyan's father was visited at home by elders who sought his support in maintaining the church's segregation policy. When he refused to espouse their cause, Branyan recalls, friendships ended. For her part, Branyan thought the controversy was unnecessary. If the students were admitted to the church, more than likely they would not be back. And if they really wanted to worship, Branyan reasoned, "they probably would have tried another door." But as a Southwestern student with a lifelong affiliation at SPC, Branyan felt caught in the middle. "Church people were looking at you," she says, "like 'How could you go to school there and worship here?' and 'What do you think about the folks standing out front?'"[36]

Dale Seay Kasab ('65) had been active at SPC since the first grade. Although she was not a regular at worship during her years at Southwestern, she kept up with church developments through her parents (her father chaired the SPC Board of Deacons). Explanations for the kneel-ins Kasab remembers hearing were some of the standard ones—that students had targeted SPC because Rev. Jeb Russell's brother was a U.S. Senator and because the church was scheduled to host the 1965 PCUS General Assembly. From her contacts on campus, however, Kasab learned that the kneel-ins at SPC were part of a citywide church testing initiative. She knew, moreover, that the students' goal was not to make a political statement but to be "silent witnesses to what was happening" at the church.[37]

The more Kasab learned of the kneel-ins from her classmates who were participating, the greater was her embarrassment over SPC's response. A fellow student who was a Fulbright scholar from Germany called late one evening to inform her that a church member had identified him among the protesters and was threatening to have him deported. (Kasab got her father involved and the threat was averted.) Another of her Southwestern friends, Ted Morris ('65), shared with Kasab that his family in Alabama had been informed of his involvement in the kneel-ins and was pressuring him to desist. Yet despite being horrified at the treatment of her peers, Kasab did not feel she could join them. One side or the other would regard her as a "turncoat," she concluded, "whether [she] went inside or stayed outside."[38]

Kasab became an eyewitness to the spectacle of exclusion on display in front of SPC when she attended the church with her parents on Mother's Day, May 10, 1964. Walking up the front steps, Kasab recognized some of her peers standing on the sidewalk. "It was raining, with people standing under umbrellas. There was no sound, but it was very sad, and sort of theatrical," she recalls. Elders stood shoulder to shoulder on the steps, one "defending the church" with a folded umbrella. Kasab remembers slinking into the sanctuary, overcome by shame. Even though she knew her parents did not support the session's stand, Kasab told them she could not return to the church with them.[39]

Charles Murphy ('67) was another Southwestern student who had grown up at SPC. Long before the kneel-in campaign began during his freshman year, Murphy was aware of tensions between church and college. SPC members had discouraged Murphy from attending Southwestern, in fact, warning him that "they would try to knock the Bible out of you." Murphy discovered on his own that Southwestern "was a tremendous challenge to a person trying to maintain a biblically oriented faith," although he persevered and found spiritual support in a campus prayer group he started.[40]

Murphy recalls that during the spring of 1964 someone at the college asked him to explain what was going on at his home church. He had no idea what they were referring to and was stunned when he learned the details. So one Sunday he set out to see for himself what was taking place in front of SPC:

> As I got out of a car . . . the scene hit me like a punch in the stomach. The session stood shoulder to shoulder across the main entrance of the sanctuary, blocking everyone, including a group of 30–40 black and white college students, from entering the sanctuary. (The members knew other doors to use.) I do not know how many elders did not participate nor how [those who did] were pressured to stand there and shame themselves. Many of these were men I had known and respected as leaders and examples for our church.
>
> I went in the sanctuary through a side door and came out on the back side of the elders, facing the "visitors." I was very disturbed and curious. Since no one stopped me, I wanted to get close enough to hear what was going on. One of the students, Howard Romaine, recognized me and asked what I thought of all this. I had not been in on the conversation and was unwise to step in at that moment. I blurted out something like, "I do not think you ought to be forcing things, but I don't see why they can't let you in." [SPC Elder] Mr. Rives Manker was in front of me and "jumped me with both feet" for having no business here and for trying to interfere. I was very humiliated.[41]

In retrospect, Murphy says, Manker did him a favor. For in that moment he decided that he did "have business" at the church. After discussing the matter with Howard Romaine and Coby Smith, Murphy believed he might make a contribution to resolving the controversy:

> I prayed and thought a lot about what it meant that I am in both "camps," the school and the church. I was not a prominent figure in all this. But I decided to try bringing some "visitors" to meet some elders and see if that sort of communication might help. . . . I took a fellow student named Tony and his girl friend to the home of Mr. Clifton Kirkpatrick (father of my friend Cliff who became Stated clerk of the denomination—1996–2008) to see if that could help. They would at least see that the elders are not all closed red-necks, and that the demonstrators were not all angry trouble-makers.[42]

Murphy played the role of mediator on the Southwestern campus as well. Judging that events at SPC were being viewed there with a mixture of self-righteousness and silliness (during the kneel-in crisis his dormitory phone was being answered, "Memphis chapter, NAACP"), Murphy offered a sober and balanced view of the protests in an article he wrote for the *Sou'wester*. He lamented that there was "much ill feeling around school about Second Presbyterian Church and at Second about Southwestern," yet he sided neither with the church nor its "front lawn worshippers." He did try to remind his peers, however, that SPC was a church "with God very much a part of it" that had spawned other successful congregations and maintained a vibrant youth program. "Innumerable people have met Christ through this church and the dedicated Christians in it, who are working quietly and behind the scenes on this problem," he wrote. Murphy encouraged his fellow students to discuss the matter "with the Lord and with directly involved folks on both sides a little more before acting or denouncing."[43]

Nearly five decades later, Murphy remains ambivalent about the events of 1964. He believes that the attempt to integrate SPC "was not a very godly crusade," in that it did nothing to change hearts or create understanding. Nor was it godly, he adds, to keep people from worshipping because their motives were in doubt. One of the lessons Murphy gleaned from the experience is that heroes often turn out to have clay feet. "I just remember thinking many times," Murphy says, "how remarkable that men who [were] noted racists could be unchallenged leaders of a church."[44]

Jim Williamson, a high-school senior who would later attend Southwestern, experienced a similar disillusionment with SPC's adult leaders. Williamson was active in the Boy Scout troop that met at SPC, as well as the church's youth group. He recalls that in the spring of 1964 word got around that students would be coming to the church "to stage a political demonstration." His curiosity piqued, Williamson stood outside the church one Sunday morning and waited to see what would happen. He watched as a bus pulled up and unloaded a group of students, all of whom were "extremely well-dressed." According to Williamson,

> they began walking together up to the front steps of the sanctuary and as they approached . . . the doors to the church opened and out came a group of men who I recognized as members of the session . . . and they spread out across the front portico of the sanctuary, sort of shoulder-to-shoulder, made a wall essentially. So the group of demonstrators walked up and stopped at the foot of the stairs and their spokesman said . . . that they were there to worship. . . . The guy went back down and the elders stood there, and as it got closer to 11 o'clock and members of the church came up to attend the service . . . the line would part, sort of like the Red

Sea, you know, and these members of the church would walk into the
sanctuary and then the line would close down again.[45]

Williamson watched as the "standoff" continued in absolute silence for the duration of the worship hour. Then the doors opened and the line of elders parted
once again as congregants left the church.

Williamson felt that what he had witnessed "went against everything I had ever
been taught about what the church believed." He concluded, in fact, that if Jesus had
been present that morning, "he would have been on the bus." But these sentiments
were not shared by his peers. At a meeting of the SPC youth group that evening,
Williamson expressed his opinion that the church's session should have handled
things differently. When some of his friends argued that the visiting students were
"up to no good" and were probably "communists," he felt "utterly isolated." Afterward, a session member offered him a ride home. In Williamson's driveway, the
elder spoke to him about that morning's events and the session's response:

> He said, "you know, we really didn't have any choice because those
> people weren't there to worship." And then he started into the whole
> standard argument that was used at that time to justify segregation . . .
> [and used] parts of the Bible to defend slavery. . . . He talked about how
> our society was about to be disrupted by radicals and communists and
> it had finally come to Memphis and it was our duty as Christians to
> stand up against it. And to my horror—to this day it makes my flesh
> crawl—I just sat there and listened to it.[46]

Although Williamson "knew in his heart" the man was wrong, he could not
come up with an argument to refute him. Afterward he resolved that he would
never again be intimidated by someone who could out-argue him. "That was a
great watershed for me intellectually," he says.

Fifty years later Williamson is still processing these events, which he refers to
as his "first exposure to what I would call evil, in a first-hand way." His second
novel, which is set in a small town in Mississippi in the 1950s, includes a church
standoff similar to the one he witnessed at SPC.[47]

Family Vibrations

Young church members, even if they had no direct experience of the kneel-ins
that were taking place at SPC, sometimes felt them reverberate through their
extended families. In 1964, Alex Thompson and Minna Thompson Glenn were

deeply involved at the church. The children's grandfather was an elder, their father a deacon, and their mother president of the Women of the Church. In part because the Thompson children lived next door to their grandparents, they were more aware than most young people of goings on at SPC. They knew, for instance, that the kneel-in controversy was taking a physical toll on their grandfather, Elder Buck Potts. Glenn says he was "sick with worry about the situation" and died shortly afterward.[48]

When nine-year-old Alex Thompson heard about the kneel-ins, he asked his mother why college students coming to the church was such a "big deal." She explained that some church leaders felt the "guests" were there to cause a disturbance rather than to worship. Thompson found this confusing, since he had heard her say on more than one occasion that the church was "a hospital for sinners, not a temple for saints." He suspects his mother believed that "our motives were just as suspect as theirs and we had no right to close the door to any worshippers" but was being diplomatic for fear of contradicting session hard-liners.[49]

Minna Thompson Glenn, sixteen at the time, has no personal memories of the protests. But she does remember the day the controversy became more than a vague cloud hanging over the church, discussed in hushed tones. In the first congregational meeting at which Glenn was old enough to vote, the race question came to the fore in a proposal to create a separate worship space for blacks at the rear of the sanctuary. The "no" vote was overwhelming, recalls Glenn, who says she'd "never heard as loud a sound in that sanctuary." At that moment, Glenn realized for the first time that the vast majority of SPC members had become opposed to any sort of segregation in the church.[50]

John McKee was another child of SPC who felt more of the controversy than he saw. Like many kids growing up in the South at the time, the ten-year-old McKee "had to go to church every Sunday of my life." He retains vague memories of well-dressed young people of both races standing around in front of the church. What sticks in his mind, interestingly, is the hats worn by the black men—"hats that you thought were reserved for white people." Just as vivid as his mental image of men in fedora hats is the sense of dread that permeated the church as the controversy unfolded. The entire congregation seemed "on edge," says McKee, who was reminded by his elders to act respectfully because the press "was watching."[51]

Like many adult church members, McKee's parents thought the protestors were "too much in your face"; but they were also uncomfortable with the racist sentiments expressed by some SPC leaders. This was particularly true of McKee's mother. When asked by her son, "mama, why don't they just let them in?" she responded that the students were "rabble rousers." Nevertheless, in 1965, when

McKee's father was recruited by men who were leaving to start a rival church, she demanded that her husband tell them the family was staying at SPC. At the time, McKee shared the ambivalence of his parents, though for reasons that were intensely personal. He could not separate his feelings about the protestors, he says, from his affection for "Bunny," the family's domestic, with whom he continues to maintain contact. Today his perceptions of what transpired at the church in 1964 are informed by an understanding of the history through which he was living. "Bottom line," he says, "it was all about race, and I think everyone understands that."[52]

In 1964, Elizabeth Cleghorn Wall was a twenty-one-year-old woman preoccupied with planning her impending wedding. She has little memory of what she refers to as "the Sunday [when] some people . . . came to the front door of the church." But she does recall the impact the kneel-in controversy had on her parents. As was discussed in a previous chapter, her father, Elder John Cleghorn, switched sides in the midst of the kneel-in crisis. A spokesman for the session's policy of excluding student visitors in 1964, by early 1965 he became an advocate of limiting the power of hard-line session members through elder rotation. But Wall also witnessed a profound change in her mother, whose views on race had been shaped by her own parents. Wall says of her grandmother, a North Mississippi native born in the nineteenth century: "She was taught that black men could not control their sexual urges as well as white men; therefore you had to be very, very careful and keep your distance. And she taught that to my mother, who taught it to me."[53]

Wall tells two stories to frame the transformation of her mother's racial outlook:

> My parents were at a business conference [in the late 1950s] on the West Coast and there were some black people at the table. And my mother said to my father, "I don't want to hurt anyone's feelings. I'll sit here but I don't think I can eat." And then [in the late 1960s] they were at a Christian conference and they saw a black couple sitting at a table for four, and my mother said, "John, let's go over there and make sure they feel welcome."[54]

The change in her mother indirectly influenced Wall's own racial views. Her epiphany took place one day while turning into her driveway, when "suddenly it hit me that God loved everyone the same, and he would not be in favor of segregation. . . . And it was a huge revelation to me." Thus the kneel-in controversy at SPC had a lasting impact on three members of the Cleghorn family, only one of whom was directly involved.[55]

Contested Memory

SPC has been able to successfully face its troubled racial past in part because so many younger members who experienced the kneel-in crisis continue to attend the church today. But not all veterans of the controversy view it in the same way. For many, it is a turning point in the church's history when members fought to wrest control of their church from racist leaders who had lost sight of the gospel. For others, however, the episode is but a brief detour on a consistent path of evangelical faithfulness.

Fred Flinn was a high-school junior in 1964 and remains an active church member. Unlike most SPC youth, who kept their distance from the main sanctuary doors on Sunday mornings while kneel-ins were under way, Flinn was an eyewitness to the standoff between students and churchmen. Even at the time, he regarded claims that the students were coming to disrupt worship as "clearly wrong." Yet even if that had been their intent, Flinn says today, it would not have justified excluding them. Discrimination on the basis of inferred motives, Flinn stresses, has "no biblical basis, and the Bible is our standard for faith and practice." The visiting students were kept from entering the church, he believes, because what they were doing was "culturally not acceptable."[56]

One influence on Flinn's perception of events at the time was Assistant Pastor Phil Esty's view that "Christianity is not about color." Another was his observation that the "demonstration" he witnessed was obviously intended to be peaceful. Indeed, he was struck by the fact that "these were people who otherwise looked as if they would fit in at this type of church; they were well dressed, clean and neat." The realization that he had much in common with those who would spend the worship hour standing outside on the sidewalk had a lasting impact on Flinn. "I'm going in and these people aren't," he remembers thinking as he entered the church, "and there's no reason that these people shouldn't be going in."[57]

For other current members, however, recollections of the kneel-in controversy have little to do with race or justice. Like Fred Flinn, in 1964 John Housholder was a high-school junior very involved in the church's youth program. After graduating from Vanderbilt University and spending two years in the Navy, he returned to Memphis and SPC, where he has been active ever since. Housholder's memories of the integration controversy of 1964–65 conform largely to the official view disseminated at the time by the church's session. Central to Housholder's interpretation of events, in fact, is the judgment that the church "was open to anybody who had a sincere desire to worship. But we were not open to someone saying 'open the doors, we're coming in.'" He claims that people at SPC bore no ill will toward the students but were determined that the church should not be made a venue for demonstrations.[58]

Housholder emphasizes that opposition to the visiting students was not a case of rank-and-file members blindly following their leaders. It was clear to everyone, he says, that the standoff was a result of unreasonable demands by pushy students. Had they been genuine worshippers, Housholder reasons, everything would have been different:

> The church would have come together and gotten with our leaders and said "wait a minute, fellas, we need to reconsider this"; don't just point us down this road here if they really want to become part of our congre-gation, if these people really want to worship here. But I got the idea that it was just a short-term protest and basically . . . to go in and say "this is how closed this church is, or how closed the society is, this is the kind of reaction we expected," and then just . . . disappear.[59]

Housholder's explanation recalls the ones favored by many adult members at the time. They reflect the tendency to minimize the extent and significance of the kneel-ins (they "just seemed to disappear") and the inclination to ascribe un-spiritual motives to the visitors.[60]

Young people at SPC in 1964 were in a difficult position. Adults they trusted were offering a version of events that on the surface appeared quite reasonable and their access to information was limited. Even skeptical youth were left to piece together an explanation of the kneel-ins from brief glimpses, walk-pasts, and tidbits of conversations. Naturally, SPC's adults wanted to shield the church's youth from exposure to the less-than-spiritual aspects of church life. But this did not keep most of them from being touched by institutional trauma or from con-cluding that their spiritual leaders had failed them.

PART FOUR

AFTERMATH OF A KNEEL-IN MOVEMENT

"The Greatest Crisis in the 120-Year History of Our Church"

Defiance, Intervention, and Schism

As the kneel-in crisis at SPC escalated and the session's resistance to what it regarded as outside interference grew apace, tensions within the church increased as well. As this chapter delineates, these tensions were reflected in attempts by various church constituencies to influence the session, in the senior minister's public repudiation of the church's ruling elders, in the creation of an ad hoc group dedicated to restoring peace and repairing the church's reputation, in a congregational meeting that was the occasion for a showdown between church factions, and in a painful church split—all occurring under the intense glare of media scrutiny.

The Session Digs in its Heels

On March 23, 1964, the day after students Jim Bullock and Joe Purdy were blocked from entering SPC together, the church's session convened to consider its response to the incident and to prepare for future visits by students in "mixed groups." The obvious starting point for pondering these matters was the decision, adopted by the SPC session in 1957, that the church would "adhere to the policy of segregation in all of its endeavors." Robert Hussey, a driving force behind the original policy, made the connection explicit when he moved that an expanded Policy Committee be appointed to consider "all matters of integration in this Church in conformity with the Statement of Policy as adopted October 7, 1957." The passing of this motion initiated a year-long effort by the session to weather the kneel-in storm without succumbing to the rising tide of integration. This effort would require dozens of "called" meetings at which the church visits and their fallout dominated the agenda; and it would test session members' patience and goodwill.[1]

By the time the SPC session gathered on April 29, 1964 to hear the Policy Committee's report, the church was facing a full-scale kneel-in campaign that had become a magnet for negative publicity. In a statement to be read at worship the following Sunday, May 3, the committee invoked the church's 1957 "statement of policy," while carefully avoiding any mention of its segregationist intent. According to the document, the policy had been adopted out of concern that the church might one day be singled out "as a target for demonstrations." With this concern in mind, the statement claimed, the session had wished to go on record as opposing "with determination the use of Second Presbyterian Church buildings as a theater for demonstrations which are obviously and specifically and admittedly designed to promote a social cause and to further the interests of a political and racial organization."[2]

This statement, which had been approved by the full session, indicated a significant shift in strategy on the part of those who would be responsible for defending the church's practice of segregation in the new crisis. Although the session remained determined to prevent "race mixing" among young people, its emphasis would shift from avoiding integrated meetings, camps, and conferences to fending off racially mixed groups of young people who, it was argued, wished to make SPC a site for "demonstrations . . . to promote a social cause." The Policy Committee's statement indicated how this strategy would be applied in the current situation. Since elders who had been "confronted by this group of demonstrators" had witnessed no evidence of a "sincere desire to worship in our sanctuary, prompted by genuine spiritual motivation," they had been forced to conclude that the students' purpose was "to promote the cause of social mixing of the races," their ultimate goal "to walk arm in arm down the central aisle of our sanctuary and sit among our people."[3]

There were obvious advantages in representing opposition to integration in terms of a principled defense of the church from social demonstrations. For one thing, the session could avoid the stigma of endorsing a practice that its denomination had repeatedly condemned as un-Christian. Furthermore, this approach was sensitive to the fact that congregational support for a policy of racial segregation was withering under scrutiny from local and national media and assault from fellow Southern Presbyterians. Finally, Scripture could now be appealed to more confidently than had been the case in 1957's "Statement of Policy." As other racially exclusive churches had done during the kneel-in era, the SPC session invoked the story of Jesus's cleansing of the Temple as both precedent and justification for their position:

> As Christ in spectacular fashion denounced the use of the Lord's house
> by money changers, so we believe your Session has the duty to reject

attempts to make this congregation a cats-paw in the hands of those seeking to advance a secular position, through demonstration and maneuver which then be nationally publicized.[4]

The congregational letter ended with a plea to "avoid exaggeration of this situation and not to be influenced by those who will try to distort these incidents out of all proportion to their importance."[5]

Facing a kneel-in campaign that showed no signs of abating, hard-liners on the SPC session wagered that the church's 1957 policy could best be defended by raising the threat of "social mixing" inside the church's sanctuary. Yet the line of reasoning in which these threats were employed was clearly disingenuous, a fact that can be inferred from the session's own deliberations. Not only was the plan for responding to the kneel-ins immediately taken up by the committee that had been established in 1957 to enforce the church's segregation policy, but in subsequent discussions the session's own minutes would refer repeatedly to the "integration problem." Furthermore, when the May 3 statement was read to the congregation the session had already voted down a motion that the church rescind its segregation policy while continuing to exclude "atheistic demonstrators from disturbing the worship of our congregation."[6]

While the session's explanation of its actions seems to have been accepted, at least temporarily, by a majority of church members, it did not put the matter to rest. The week following the reading of its statement to the congregation, SPC's session met twice to discuss communications from the Stated Clerk of the General Assembly and officials of the PCUS's Board of Christian Education, along with sixty letters and telegrams, over forty of them from SPC members. Indeed, although the weekly spectacles of exclusion in front of SPC would end in mid-May, the controversy they had initiated was only beginning.[7]

The Assembly in the Balance

During the summer and fall of 1964, presbyteries, synods, and denominational officials were pleading with SPC's session to admit black worshippers or relinquish the church's right to host the meeting of the PCUS General Assembly the following spring. The session, meanwhile, was defiantly refusing to do either.

Hosting the General Assembly was a significant honor for which SPC had been preparing for several years. But some elders seemed willing to sacrifice this honor in exchange for a perpetual ban on admitting blacks to worship and continued freedom to govern their own affairs. In May 1964, Robert Hussey proposed that, rather than alter its segregation policy or admit black worshippers, the church preserve its independence in racial matters by simply withdrawing its invitation to host the upcoming General Assembly. Following "lengthy discussion" of the resolution and prayer for "God's guidance and blessing," Hussey was convinced to withdraw his motion in exchange for agreement that no final action with regard to the 1957 Statement of Policy would be taken before September's stated meeting.[8]

Discussion of the church's segregation policy might be deferred until the fall, but the kneel-in crisis could not be. In June, members of the SPC session learned that PCUS Moderator Felix Gear had advised the church to withdraw its General Assembly invitation in order to spare the denomination and the church further embarrassment. A session motion to do so was narrowly defeated 19–17, suggesting that many elders were still hopeful of a compromise that would allow the assembly to meet in Memphis as planned. Bringing his reputation as a trusted PCUS evangelical, L. Nelson Bell visited the session in July with a list of suggestions for resolving the crisis.[9]

However, neither quiet diplomacy nor public censure could convince the SPC session to reconsider its stance. It chose to wait out the crisis by indefinitely tabling motions, all the while repeating assurances that it was seeking divine guidance. In September, when the agreement to postpone action on the 1957 Statement of Policy was set to expire, Horace Hull moved that it be extended until May 1, 1965. This motion, which carried unanimously, meant that without concurrence of a majority of the session and thirty-day written notice, the segregation policy would not be revisited until after the 1965 General Assembly had concluded.[10]

With the church's policy now off the table, there was another attempt to avoid a showdown with the denomination by giving up the 1965 General Assembly. At a session meeting October 21, Robert Hussey moved "with reluctance and regret" that the church withdraw its invitation to host the meeting. This time Hussey's motion would carry by a vote of 15–12; nevertheless, doubts remained. Four days later the session met again to consider whether, given the absence of eight elders at its previous meeting, the action taken needed to be reaffirmed by a second vote. In addition to concerns about the vote's constitutionality, there was hope that "more prayerful . . . consideration" might preserve the session's harmony.[11]

When the session met on November 23 to take final action on the matter of hosting the General Assembly, the window for making a decision about the meeting's location was rapidly closing. In hopes of achieving a decisive verdict free of constitutional ambiguities, Rev. Jeb Russell announced a ruling by PCUS Stated Clerk James A. Millard that elders emeritus would not be eligible to vote on the matter. In keeping with its tradition of fierce independence, however, the session decided that the votes of elders emeritus would indeed be counted. In an unusually well-attended meeting, the invitation to host the General Assembly was sustained by a vote of 28–22; the press was informed that there had been "no change in [the church's] present position."[12]

With the fate of the invitation left in other hands, attention turned once again to the church's policy with regard to black visitors. On November 30, a motion to revisit the matter was defeated 24–14. Still, the policy generated a great deal of interest among newer session members, who apparently knew very little about it; nor were those responsible for its adoption seven years earlier eager to submit it to scrutiny. A motion to have copies of the policy distributed to all session members was defeated. As a compromise, four copies were placed in binders that were not to be removed from the church.[13]

Meanwhile, the patience of denominational staff had been exhausted. At a meeting January 18, 1965, session members were greeted by a letter from Felix Gear, who inquired tersely, "What is the official policy of the Session on the question of segregation?" and "What action has been taken and what decisions have been made by your Session in response to the request of the General Assembly to your Church concerning the racial question?" The session responded in what by now had become typical fashion, informing Gear that while there had been no policy changes, the group had been "giving constant study and prayer to the request of the General Assembly to continue to study our Policy." With neither of his questions answered, Gear was forced to conclude that the segregation crisis at SPC would not be resolved internally.[14]

Russell Speaks Out

One of the mysteries of the SPC kneel-in controversy is the public silence maintained by Senior Minister Jeb Russell between March 1964 and January 1965. From the beginning, Russell seems to have been aware that the visits had the potential to precipitate a major crisis in his congregation. After the initial wave of kneel-ins had ended, Russell wrote to his daughter Harriette (who was studying in France) that the quiet Sundays he was enjoying were "probably only a lull before a greater storm." Nevertheless, it would be six months before the local papers had anything to report from SPC's pastor other than "Dr. Russell had no comment."[15]

Given the fact that he was the younger brother of U.S. Senator Richard Russell (D-GA), it is tempting to interpret Jeb Russell's reticence during the kneel-in controversy as evidence that he shared the well-publicized anti-integrationist commitments of the senator. In 1956, Richard Russell had co-authored the Southern Manifesto, which famously referred to the U.S. Supreme Court's decision in *Brown v. Board of Education* as an "unwarranted exercise of power by the Court, contrary to the Constitution . . . [which] is destroying the amicable relations between the white and Negro races that have been created through 90 years of patient effort by the good people of both races." In 1964, as the kneel-in campaign at SPC got underway, the senator was leading a filibuster against the federal civil rights act, which, he warned, would bring about the sort of "intermingling and amalgamation of the races" so feared by some of SPC's leaders.[16]

In fact, however, although Jeb Russell had campaigned extensively for his brother in Georgia during the 1930s and 1940s, he was not a political man and seems to have had an aversion to public controversy. Given his influence in the prominent churches he pastored, some ministerial colleagues regarded this as a failure of leadership on Russell's part. A pastor who worked alongside him in Montgomery during the 1950s describes Russell as an inveterate "vote counter" who dreaded the prospect of having to assume an unpopular stand. "The word among the brethren," says another pastoral associate, "was that every time Memphis Presbytery took a close vote, Jeb was in the bathroom." But it was precisely this ability to avoid being identified with one side of polarizing issues that helped make Russell a successful tall-steeple minister. His diplomacy and resilience were a particularly good match, it seems, for an SPC session that many observers believed had contributed to his predecessor's suicide. Russell's job was "to keep everybody happy," says a former church member. And he was probably one of the few men in the PCUS with the skills and personality to do it.[17]

Without doubt, Russell's conciliatory style would have affected his willingness to speak out on matters of race. As pastor of a prominent white church in the South, he knew the quickest way to become embroiled in controversy was to espouse racial views that members of his congregation found threatening. It was well known, in fact, that PCUS ministers who took a "prophetic" stand against segregation had suffered alienation from friends and neighbors, congregational disruptions, harassment, and threats of physical violence. Among those who had been targeted for abuse was William O'Neal, Russell's former assistant in Montgomery, who in the early 1960s had suffered KKK harassment after preaching at a black church in Baton Rouge.[18]

As the SPC kneel-ins got under way, in fact, the costs of identification with the movement for civil rights were being felt within Russell's extended family. In 1960, Jeb's nephew, William Russell, had left the employ of his uncle, Sen. Richard Russell, to study for the ministry at Columbia Theological Seminary. In the spring of 1964, as he awaited his first ministerial call, William Russell signed a petition urging passage of the civil rights act that at the time was being debated on Capitol Hill. Within a few hours, he received a telephone call from an Associated Press reporter asking if he was the nephew of Sen. Russell and giving him an opportunity to clarify his position on the civil rights act.[19]

Russell confirmed his support for the legislation, which was reported on the 11 p.m. television news; by midnight, he was receiving death threats. When the

AP story appeared in print, Presbyterians from across the region mailed him copies of the article across which were scrawled comments such as, "you'll never have a church in our town." Prank callers telephoned the hospital where Russell worked as a chaplain and asked to speak with "the nigger lover"; anonymous letter writers explained that God had killed JFK and would kill him, too. Despite support from the senator, the episode had a lasting impact on William Russell's career in the Southern Presbyterian Church. When it became clear he would not have his own congregation, Russell joined the faculty of Union Theological Seminary in Richmond.[20]

At SPC, the consequences of breaking rank on the issue of race were only hinted at; but the hints were chilling. Messages of disapproval were communicated anonymously via internal "hate mail," some of it clipped inside the pastors' preaching robes on Sunday mornings. Such warnings were not lost on Jeb Russell, and the climate they created took a physical and spiritual toll on SPC's senior pastor. As the controversy lingered, the man known for his colorful similes was heard likening his job to placing his head in a meat grinder and turning the handle himself, or to donning a Union tunic and Confederate trousers and being shot at by both sides.[21]

Russell's public silence during 1964, then, was most likely a result of his belief that the best way to forestall a traumatic church split at SPC was to keep his job, and the best way to keep his job was to work behind the scenes toward a resolution of the crisis. If, as some believe, Russell aspired to be elected Moderator of the PCUS General Assembly when it met in Memphis in 1965, he would have had extra motivation to resolve the kneel-in controversy quietly and diplomatically.

Another factor contributing to Russell's low profile during the controversy was his hope that, under pastoral guidance, SPC's elders would decide in "good clear Christian conscience" that they could no longer exclude persons from worship. But as the months wore on and it became clear that the course being pursued by the session could end in catastrophe for the church, Russell concluded that the time for hope, diplomacy, and self-preservation had passed. The moment had come for taking sides, and there was no question which side he must take. In early 1965, while being pressed by Moderator Gear for "an interpretation of the action of [the] Session concerning admission of Negroes," Russell took an unequivocal public stand in favor of opening the church doors to all who wished to enter.[22]

Several days after he and his fellow pastors had drafted a congregational letter registering their dissent from the session's handling of the crisis, Russell addressed the situation in his weekly sermon January 24. Deceptively titled "On Achieving a Christian Mind" (Phil. 2:5), the homily was woven of scriptural arguments, references to the congregation's history, reminders of denominational policy, and refutations of claims being made by advocates of exclusion. Russell began by acknowledging what everyone listening knew—that SPC was in the midst of "the greatest crisis in the 120-year history of our church," a crisis that had tarnished the church's reputation in many quarters.[23]

Responsibility for the crisis Russell assigned to the session's ongoing efforts to obfuscate the segregation issue by impugning the visiting students' motives. "It has been argued in the session," Russell noted, that the church's policy "excludes no one from worship or from hearing the gospel preached." However, he declared, this argument has been contradicted each time a person of color has approached the church doors over the previous months. "It is easy enough to say that there are other doors that are open, so why knock at ours?" Russell said in reference to the view that blacks should attend black churches. But he claimed that this attitude reflected more about the church's view of "Negroes" than its view of Christ. Finally, Russell argued that even if church representatives were correct in judging the intentions of would-be guests, these persons' unworthy motives should not determine their welcome.[24]

Turning to the church's history, Russell reminded his listeners that a slave was among SPC's charter members and that blacks had freely attended worship services when the church was located in downtown Memphis. He also noted that if blacks occasionally entered the East Memphis sanctuary for weddings, funerals, and baptisms, it was difficult to understand how they could be "forbidden to hear the gospel preached." Russell then held up the doctrinal standards of the Presbyterian Church (US). "To exclude any who come because they are of another race, or because they are not suitably dressed, or because they are socialist or atheist, or communist," he declared, "is contrary to, and in defiance of our history, standards and pronouncements."[25]

By continuing to exclude blacks, Russell continued, SPC was out of accord not only with its own history and the pronouncements of presbyteries, synods, and General Assemblies, but with the Bible itself. Whatever part of the Bible we turn to, he asserted, Scripture testifies with one voice to God's non-discriminatory invitation. Invoking Isaiah 56:7 ("for my house shall be called an house of prayer for all people") and Matthew 11:28 ("come unto me all ye that labor and are heavy laden"), Russell reminded his auditors that God is no respecter of persons and warns those who would presume to judge others.[26]

Finally, Russell appealed to his flock's concerns for SPC's witness, locally and around the globe. Every Christian who hears the Great Commission, he declared, "must be moved when some 200 missionaries, some of them our very own, sign and send a petition directed at us and plead that we change our policy." Recent word from an African missionary supported by SPC, Russell added, had confirmed that "the publicity given in the Congo of our action cripples the work of Christ." The minister then reminded his congregants that more than once they had heard from the congregation's young people "disapproval of this spectacle of a church with guarded doors." Russell concluded his sermon by asking church members to search the Scriptures, pray, and discuss this matter with their ministers and elders, whose names he read aloud.[27]

Russell's message of inclusion—"we can't serve Christ with shut doors about the Cross"—was clear and bold. Sadly, however, it was contradicted by the spectacle of exclusion on display that very morning when several African Americans were turned away from the church. But if Russell's message had little if any impact on the session's deliberations or the church's official response to visitors, at least it modeled the courageous habit of speaking truth to power.

The Moderator Intervenes

On January 19, 1965, as Russell and his fellow pastors were preparing to publicize their opposition to SPC's session, PCUS Moderator Felix Gear received two pieces of mail that would precipitate an unprecedented move on his part. One was a registered letter from John Randolph Taylor, pastor of the Church of the Pilgrims in Washington, D.C. and a leading PCUS progressive, which contained a signed petition calling for a special meeting of the General Assembly to reconsider the location of the annual meeting in April. The other was a communication from SPC's Clerk of Session Granville Sherman informing Gear that the church's policy with regard to segregation had not changed.[28]

In the absence of any movement by SPC's session and facing the prospect of a public showdown between PCUS factions in a called meeting of the General Assembly, on January 23 Gear exercised his prerogative under the church's constitution and relocated the upcoming meeting of the General Assembly to the Montreat Conference Center in North Carolina. The Associated Press noted that the annual gathering had not been moved since 1862, when relocation—from Memphis, no less—was necessitated by the presence of warring armies. In a public statement, Gear said "the continued sharpening and deepening of the controversy" had created an atmosphere in which the General Assembly might find it difficult to function.[29]

Gear communicated his decision by letter to SPC's session. He wrote that as a former pastor of the church he had been reluctant to take this action, which was made only after "consultation with hundreds of people in our Church and mission fields." Gear was convinced that his decision to move the General Assembly was necessary because the SPC controversy concerned nothing less than the nature of the church. But he knew that it would be regarded in segments of the denomination as a punitive measure taken against an evangelical church that refused to accede to the denomination's social agenda.[30]

In fact, if his experience as PCUS moderator during 1964–65 had taught Gear anything, it was that a vocal minority of Southern Presbyterians viewed the civil rights movement as a communist-inspired plot to destroy the Southern way of life. Gear's ecumenical commitments and his emphasis on the denomination's role in responding to the social revolution had led some of these traditionalists to vilify him in extraordinary terms—as "a defender of beatniks, promoter of the new culture to come, advocate . . . of the great experiment with humanity," "race traitor," and "dictator" of "our once Christian Presbyterian Church."[31]

To deal with the flood of complaints he received from Presbyterians displeased by the Church's unequivocal denunciation of segregated congregations, Gear had composed a form letter, which read, in part:

> I am sorry that you do not agree with the actions of the General Assembly on these matters, but I would respectfully point out to you that . . . the Presbyterian Church has never officially sanctioned segregated churches. . . . Further, at no time has the General Assembly of the Presbyterian Church in the U.S. ever upheld the exclusion of a Negro from a church court or from membership on the ground of color or race. . . . Because we have accepted the policy of segregation for so many years, we have come to think that the Presbyterian Church is actually a segregated church constitutionally—this has never been true.[32]

Gear reminded his fellow Southern Presbyterians that since Reconstruction the denomination had held fast to the position that "exclusion on the basis of race or color of anyone from membership in the Church is unscriptural and therefore wrong." To those who believed otherwise, he mailed a copy of the 1865 General Assembly resolution that determined the church's stance on the issue.

Yet even before he was elected moderator of the denomination, Gear was quite familiar with the intransigence of racial hard-liners in the PCUS. By 1964, in fact, his son-in-law, Abel McIver "Mac" Hart, had become identified with the travail of racially progressive clergy in the Deep South. Hart and his wife, Muriel, Gear's daughter, had been called to Trinity Presbyterian Church in Meridian, Mississippi, in 1962. But Central Mississippi Presbytery had repeatedly refused to confirm Hart's call to the church on suspicions that he was pro-integration and favored reunion with Northern Presbyterians. After twice examining him in the areas of experiential religion, theology and sacraments, and church government, the presbytery judged Hart to be unqualified and refused to receive him as a member, effectively nullifying his call to Trinity.

It was not surprising that Mac Hart's racial views were out of step with those of many ministers and elders in Central Mississippi Presbytery. But the charges of heterodoxy leveled against the young minister revealed just how far dedicated segregationists would go to resist change in the Church. Gear's first-hand experience of the "Hart case" certainly prepared him for the resistance he would meet among racial hard-liners at SPC.[33]

Defiant to the End

When they entered the fray in late January 1965, SPC's pastors no doubt hoped to influence wavering elders, shift the balance of power on the session enough to secure an agreement to open the church's doors, and preempt the moderator's threat to intervene. Sadly, however, they had acted too late. Even as Russell was putting the finishing touches on the sermon that would mark his personal Rubicon, Gear moved to revoke the church's right to host the 1965 General Assembly.

Still, all was not lost. Obviously conflicted over his decision, Gear told a Memphis newspaper that he was open to further discussion of the matter should there be a quick and decisive change of direction at SPC. How quick was not clear, but any change of direction appeared unlikely when Elder Robert Hussey responded to the pastoral letter circulating among SPC members with his own letter recounting the session's justifications for the exclusion of "demonstrators" and accusing Russell of misleading the congregation. Nor was there any indication of changed attitudes the following Sunday, when one white and two black students were turned away from worship by an elder who asked them not to "disturb the service."[34]

At this point Memphis's local dailies began routinely reporting on the controversy and editorializing against the stand taken by SPC's session. The *Press-Scimitar* noted that among the "demonstrators" recently turned away from the church were "a Negro Presbyterian minister and two white boys in shirt sleeves." Commenting on the church's refusal to recognize visitors in mixed groups as worshippers, the paper asked whether it would not be better "to welcome all who wish to come into the house of God, and for whom there is room, hoping that whatever their motives might be they would get spiritual benefit from the services." The *Press-Scimitar* also commented on the paradox that in early February SPC would begin a week-long World Mission Conference. "It is embarrassing to a great church," the paper noted, that the race matter had not been settled before missionary leaders gathered at the church to celebrate preaching the gospel to "all mankind, regardless of color."[35]

Under the pressure of continuing visits from racially mixed groups, growing internal dissent, and public censure, the SPC session was presented with a final opportunity to fall in line with denominational policy by complying with an ultimatum delivered by Memphis Presbytery at its meeting January 26. Session members who gathered four days later to consider a response to the ultimatum received the further news that their support in the congregation was dwindling. Nearly 90% of letters recently received from church members, they were informed, supported a change in policy. Yet this evidence of their increasing isolation was not enough to move hard-liners from the position they had stubbornly occupied for the previous ten months. After considering a number of motions, the session commissioned a seven-member "special committee" to study a resolution by Elder Stuart McCloy and report back within fifteen days.[36]

The McCloy resolution began by depicting the church as a victim of "widespread misunderstanding of [its] position on the racial question" and of efforts "to embarrass and humiliate [the] church . . . and to detract from its long history of service to the Presbyterian Church in the United States and to all mankind." While these attacks had been borne "in silence, with great patience and with diligent attention to the dignity and the great traditions of this historic church," the resolution claimed, the session was obliged to inform the presbytery's Moderator and Stated Clerk that the church was engaged in no practice inconsistent with any "present official policy" of the General Assembly, Synod of Tennessee, or Memphis Presbytery; that "no individual, white or black" would be turned away from the church's doors as long as they presented themselves "as subject to the Church's policy and as amenable in Christian Spirit to the peace, purity and unity of our church"; and that the purpose of mixed racial visits was clearly to embarrass the church and disturb its worship services.[37]

The McCloy resolution is remarkable not only for its defiant reiteration of views that had come to be rejected by nearly everyone but session hard-liners, but also for its acknowledgment that for over a century the church had maintained "a policy of segregation in all of its endeavors," a policy providing for "separate seating for the races" at worship services. This was the first open admission that the 1957 segregation policy was guiding the session's actions during the kneel-in crisis; it was also the first mention in the session's minutes of the possibility that the crisis might be resolved through separate seating for African Americans inside the sanctuary. But, of course, even separate seating would require that blacks be admitted to the church. When a motion to end "exclusion from our public worship services because of race, creed or class" was voted down, it became clear that a majority of the session had no intention of letting this happen.[38]

Upon recommendation of the special committee established to review the McCloy resolution, it was adopted by the full session on February 8. The 19–15 vote revealed that, despite mounting resistance, a majority of SPC ruling elders remained determined to fight integration at all costs. While the McCloy resolution sought to obscure the race issue by distinguishing between genuine worshippers and those engaged in "group and mixed racial demonstrations," it unequivocally revealed the majority's segregationist mindset. Acknowledging this fact, the headline over the *Press-Scimitar's* story on February 10 was "Second Presbyterian Church Vote Keeps Segregation Policy." Rev. Russell called the session's decision "a most imprudent act."[39]

The Opposition Organizes

From the beginning, there were indications that the kneel-ins at SPC were dividing the congregation. In April 1964, the *Tri-State Defender* related that some members were so disturbed by the spectacle of exclusion in front of their church that they left before the sermon, while one woman "went to each one of [the visitors] and shook hands." The following week the same paper reported that Southwestern student Howard Romaine had been escorted from the property after attempting to speak with a woman who "upbraided the elders for their policy of strict segregation." Most ominously, the article noted, "church members who talk to the protestors are photographed by a man who wears dark glasses every week, despite the fact the sun has not shined during the time he is doing his work at the spot."[40]

Given the intimidating responses that even nominal expressions of support for the students could engender, it is not surprising that for many months dissent was sporadic and unorganized. The first statement of opposition from an official church constituency was not penned until November 1964, when twelve (of seventy-three) SPC deacons signed a letter addressed to the session. While expressing sympathy for the concerns undergirding the elders' stand, the letter argued that a change in policy would be in the church's best interest. "As officers who are in part responsible for our Church's witness," the deacons wrote, "we feel that a maintenance of our present policy of barring anyone from general worship services inevitably will bring calamitous injury to Second Church." The deacons asked that the "present rigid, untenable policy be altered."[41]

While blaming the controversy on "radical racial agitators with their unchristian approach," the deacons warned of "a great rift in Second Church with all of its fearsome spiritual consequences," including a weakening in zeal among the church's young people. They reasoned that the church was "better off running the very remote risk" of untoward social consequences resulting from the admittance of black visitors than facing "the very real risk of tearing it apart." In an effort to mollify concerns over a black invasion, the deacons cited the experience of leaders at Memphis's First Baptist Church. This congregation, they wrote, had opened its doors to blacks and after a few weeks "had no more colored visitors." First Baptist members, according to the church's pastor, "swallowed hard a few times, [and] one Church officer threatened to leave, but after a short time all was harmonious again."[42]

The deacons' letter carefully blended theological and practical arguments. It warned that "inordinate preoccupation with racial pride can lead to sinful pride and wrongful action" and pointed out that "closing the door to the House of God . . . is not sanctioned biblically." But it also asked session members to consider the possibility that its present path might actually force it to negotiate with the NAACP. "These liberals" were unlikely to desist, the deacons warned, because they were aware they could cause a "fateful cleavage" in the church.

There is no evidence that the deacons' plea—remarkable for its prescience regarding the possibility of a rupture in the congregation—received any official response. But the concerns that animated it only grew as the controversy wore on and the session's intransigence subjected the church to more embarrassment and recrimination. At some point in early 1965, concerned moderates at SPC concluded that the only way to forestall the sort of ecclesiastical rift described in the deacons' plea was to effect a shift in the session's balance of power by replacing the longest-serving elders with younger, more pragmatic men.

The first attempt to do so actually came from within the session itself. In early February, Elder Theron Lemly moved that "in view of the Session's inability to establish unity and accord within its own ranks, with the Diaconate, with the congregation, with the ministers, with Presbytery, and with the General Assembly," it adopt a policy of rotation of one fifth of session members each year, "the order of rotation for individual members to be based on length of service in the Session, in descending order." This motion was ruled out of order before the body voted to adopt the aforementioned McCloy resolution.[43]

If SPC's elders would not vote to limit their terms of service, obviously the congregation would have to find a way to do so. In mid-February, a group calling itself the Accord Committee emerged with a strategy to implement what was known in PCUS churches as a "limited service plan" for service on the session. The group's stated goals were to remain in the denomination, to open the church's doors for public worship and remove guards from "God's house," and to restore the church's witness "to its former place in the community, nation, and world, on a true scriptural basis." In a letter addressed to all church members, the Accord Committee requested support for a petition to call a congregational meeting for the purpose of limiting elders' terms of service. The letter complained of "a cloak of secrecy over the actions taking place within your session" and noted that sixteen of nineteen local Presbyterian churches had already adopted a limited service plan.[44]

When the Accord Committee's strategy became known, there was immediate pushback from the men whose power was under threat. A newspaper article published on the morning of Sunday, February 14—which in 1965 was not only Valentine's Day but Race Relations Sunday—reported Robert Hussey's accusation that "some of the minority [at SPC] are playing power politics." Adding to the drama, Jeb Russell announced from the pulpit that morning that unspecified charges were to be filed against him with the local presbytery. These charges would be withheld, Russell had been told, if he "would seek to quell the 'rebellion' of the Accord Committee." As far as Rev. Russell was concerned, the gloves were off. "I know of no church in this community," he told the congregation, "which does not admit any who come, regardless of race or class, except ours . . . as a result of our obdurate session majority."[45]

At their regular session meeting February 15, elders were greeted by growing evidence of an emboldened church opposition. The Clerk of Session reported receiving 299 new communications dealing with the current crisis, nearly 80% of which supported the ministers in their "stand to open our doors to all worshippers." Furthermore, it was reported, the Board of Deacons had gone on record to commend "the spiritual leadership and guidance of our ministers as set forth in [their] letter and in Dr. Russell's comments at worship on January 24th." Most significant, however, was a communication from the "Accord Committee of Second Presbyterian Church" announcing that it had received signed petitions from "considerably more" than the one fourth of the congregation required to request a congregational meeting, the purpose of which would be to consider a resolution

> that the Session adopt a policy of rotation which will provide for rotation of one-fifth (1/5) of the Session members each year. The order of rotation for individual members is to be based on length of service in the Session in descending order. . . . Elders rotated off active service are not to be renominated for service for two years from date of rotation. Voting to be by written ballot. It is directed that this policy be placed in practice within thirty (30) days after passage.[46]

Among the benefits of adopting this rotational system for service on the SPC session, the Accord Committee's letter cited new approaches and personalities on the session, restoration of harmony between the church and denominational courts, and removal of "the cloak of secrecy" from policy decisions. The petition was accompanied by a notary public's certification that "there are more than 950 signatures on the petitions bearing names contained in the [SPC] Year Book and additions from the Church Roll." The petition soon became national news.[47]

Thus, just one week after making what it regarded as a final statement on the matter of integration at SPC, the session majority was being pressured to call a congregational meeting at which their continued leadership in the church would be subject to popular vote. Even as the meeting was set for February 28, session hard-liners were mulling their options. Maurice Miller protested approval of the petition on the grounds that "there is no way any auditor can prove whether [it] was signed under duress," to which Rev. Russell responded by appointing a "Detail Examination Committee" charged with certifying signatures. Rives Manker moved that, in addition to the Accord Committee's plan, the congregation be presented with the option of making the shortest-serving elders inactive first. Stuart McCloy moved for adoption of a statement he hoped would quell the congregational rebellion by satisfying Memphis Presbytery's insistence that the church "admit all persons desiring to attend divine services":

> The entire balcony in our sanctuary, or such part thereof as may be necessary, [shall] be reserved for the seating of non-communing negro persons presenting themselves at our doors individually or in groups, racially mixed or otherwise, and that our church ushers, officers and committees be instructed to seat them in the space reserved for them, a separate portion of which will also be reserved and provided for any white persons accompanying them, all of which is in accordance with this Church's long established policy providing separate seating for the white and negro races.[48]

After this motion carried, Forbes Barton made a last-ditch effort to forestall a vote on rotation by moving to override Russell's ruling that the called congregational meeting was in order. He was defeated 19–5.

Press reports of the February 15 session meeting gave the misleading impression that the church "had voted to admit Negroes" without restriction. An editorial the following day commended the church for "changing its [segregation] policy" and expressed the hope that peace would "descend on this great church." Apparently, the team of elders designated "to divulge news items to the Press" had neglected to mention that black visitors and any whites accompanying them would be relegated to the sanctuary's balcony. Meanwhile, church members began receiving letters from a group calling itself "Elders for the Preservation of Our Church." Opposed to "those who wish to integrate" SPC, the group solicited signatures to halt the upcoming congregational meeting. However, at worship February 21 it was announced that the meeting would be held as scheduled the following Sunday. Russell's sermon, titled "How to Change Your Mind," dealt with making difficult decisions.[49]

The Congregation Triumphs

Most congregational meetings in Presbyterian churches are brief, orderly, and predictable. Typical agenda items include approval of clergy pay raises and adoption of candidate slates for church offices. But the meeting at SPC on February

28, 1965, would be anything but typical. From both sides of the ideological gulf created by the kneel-in crisis, the very future of the church appeared to hang in the balance.[50]

Realizing it was imperative that there be no procedural irregularities that could be used to contest the meeting's results, members of the Accord Committee invited PCUS Stated Clerk James A. Millard to attend in an advisory role. It was agreed that spokesmen for and against elder rotation would take seats at the front of the sanctuary and that each side would be allotted ten minutes to present its case and five minutes for rebuttal. Written ballots would be marked, folded, placed in envelopes, and sealed with the voter's name printed on the outside. *Roberts' Rules of Order* would be meticulously followed and the meeting would reflect the Presbyterian ideal that church business be conducted "decently and in order."

The day before the meeting, SPC's Accord Committee issued a press release announcing that its petition had received over 1,500 signatures, representing nearly half the church's membership, and clarifying that the group's goal was not to "retire" elders (a term that had appeared in newspaper accounts) but to limit their terms, which under the proposed plan could be renewed after two years of inactivity. The Committee expressed the hope that the following day's meeting would proceed "with a minimum of argument and without bitterness or strife." The service bulletin on the morning of the meeting struck a similar tone, asking members to "prepare for this vital Meeting with earnest prayer." It also noted that special arrangements had been made for care of children, and that overflow seating would be available in the Session Room and Chapel. Jeb Russell's sermon, which reminded his auditors that Jesus was considered scandalous for the way he "fraternized with publicans and sinners and many other people despised by many," offered food for thought.[51]

Following the service, the congregational meeting was opened with prayer and yet another plea for civility. Russell asked everyone present to conduct themselves "in a quiet and orderly manner and to refrain from expressions of approval and disapproval." Speaking in favor of the motion to implement a rotational system, Clifton Kirkpatrick claimed that the elders' failure to resolve their problems was damaging the church's witness. John Cleghorn, the former hard-liner who had been won over to the side of the Accord Committee, contended that rotation would not only bring harmony to the session but would broaden the church's leadership base. Cleghorn also noted the toll the crisis had taken on session members, some of whom had become physically ill, he said.[52]

The anti-rotation group, aided by a team of lawyers, offered a number of arguments for maintaining the status quo. Rives Manker pointed out that congressmen's terms of office were not limited. Similarly, Luther Keeton, who saw in the motion to rotate "a power thrust and grab" by pastors who wished to usurp the power of ruling elders, observed that the twelve Apostles were not appointed for a set time. Marvin Ellis claimed that the church had prospered under the leadership of older men who should not be "put on the shelf." Maurice Miller went on the offensive, charging members of the Accord Committee with hypocrisy:

> There has been a lot of pious talk in this Sanctuary not only today, but on some other days, about not letting colored folks in to worship. Now I want to tell you that it's an absolute fact that on this very day a member of the Session who was one of the ten that signed the Accord Committee papers . . . was on the front door by appointment [when] a negro came to the front door this day and he sent that negro on his way.[53]

Another speaker lamented that the rotation issue was dividing friends and moved that the matter be tabled. When Russell declared this motion out of order, Milton Knowlton called for the question to be put to the congregation, and ballots were distributed. Forbes Barton requested that the opposition have observers present as the ballots were counted. But the outcome—61% voted in favor of elder rotation—would not be close enough to contest.[54]

The congregational meeting of February 28, 1965, is vividly remembered by many who attended. "There was a lot of shouting, hollering and yelling," recalls William Craddock. "You couldn't believe it was a Presbyterian Church operation." John Adamson remembers it as "an ugly day—really raucous. . . . and there were some really ugly things said." According to Bill Weber, "one of the elders stood up . . . and started yelling at Dr. Russell and accusing him of being dishonest and manipulative . . . it was nasty." Rev. Ed Knox recalls being afraid that "they were going to attack Dr. Russell." Afterward the Russells received anonymous telephone calls, he says, from angry men suggesting they "go back to Alabama or Georgia or wherever."[55]

The congregation reconvened after worship on March 14 to act upon a report from the committee authorized to implement the new "limited active service plan for Ruling Elders." In a last gasp of rebellion, Rives Manker argued that the February 28 congregational meeting had been out of order. But the session hard-liners had been repudiated. A motion to accept the committee's recommendation that the longest-serving session members begin to rotate out of active service passed 932–0.[56]

The Church Splits

The congregational meeting of February 28, 1965, was a milestone in SPC's long and illustrious history, for it signaled the end of twelve solid months of internal turmoil and public notoriety. A *Press-Scimitar* editorial conveyed the sentiments of many when it expressed hope that the church would now resume a beneficial role in the community. But it was far from clear whether SPC's internal rifts could be healed.

Although the results of the congregational vote would not be announced until March 14, by early March the handwriting was on the wall for those who opposed changes in the church's handling of black visitors. On March 8, twelve elders tendered their resignations; meanwhile, some who decided to remain on the session continued to challenge the propriety of the congregational vote. At a meeting March 15 there were attempts to table the plan for elder rotation, to exclude ballot envelopes that lacked proper identification, and to void the results of the vote because, it was claimed, the minimum age for eligible voters should have been set at sixteen (church practice at the time enfranchised all confirmed members). But these efforts failed, as did motions to declare the congregational meeting "void and illegal," plagued by "certain irregularities and errors," and "null, void and of no effect."[57]

When ten new elders were ordained and installed at the end of March, there was widespread hope that the storms of controversy that had buffeted the church during the previous year would dissipate. However, the new session members found themselves at the helm of a vessel that had drifted badly off course; and now that the kneel-in controversy had reached the pages of national publications such as *Christianity Today* and *The Christian Century*, they were forced to navigate under the glare of national scrutiny. With the departure of a dozen "stubborn, unyielding" men whom *The Presbyterian Outlook* had charged with creating "a private club" and failing to "understand the nature of the church of Jesus Christ," the session had avoided the Scylla of denominational intervention. But the Charybdis of church schism continued to loom on the horizon.[58]

Since the middle of 1964 a few dozen SPC members had abandoned ship for other Memphis congregations, but now frustrated parishioners were threatening to construct an entirely new vessel, outfitted to their own specifications. The first wave of departures came in April 1965, when 209 SPC members requested letters of dismissal to the newly formed Independent Presbyterian Church. But the outflow slowed dramatically in the succeeding months, and by the end of 1965 there had been fewer than three hundred defections, hardly a devastating loss for a church of 3,500.[59]

Even though the mother ship had escaped the rough seas of racial controversy, some feared it might be inundated by those who had been excluded from worship during the previous year. Yet the imagined flood of black visitors never arrived. On March 8 the *Press-Scimitar* reported that the same "elderly Negro man" who had been turned away on the morning of the congregational meeting was seated in the church and "listened attentively to the sermon and later remarked on the beautiful singing of the choir." "No one seemed to pay any attention to his presence," one member said. Worship at SPC had been integrated at last, and with a whimper rather than a bang.[60]

Of course, affiliation with SPC had never been a goal of the students or adults whose visits had precipitated the crisis. Once the matter was resolved and publicity waned, it was very unlikely that African Americans in Memphis would leave their own churches to be part of a white congregation, particularly one they had learned to despise. Most of them, in fact, would never set foot in the church.

11

"Not the Church's Advantages, But the City's Disadvantages"

Wrestling with the Past at Second Presbyterian Church

Previous chapters have focused on a brief but pivotal moment in the history of Memphis's Second Presbyterian Church. They offer a thick description of the church in the late 1950s and early 1960s, with focus on its leadership, its factions, its relationships with other institutions and ecclesiastical bodies, and its engagement with the cultural forces of the time. However, a historical snapshot cannot do justice to the dynamic, evolving nature of an institution that continues to thrive nearly fifty years after it relinquished its practice of segregation. This chapter presents a portrait of SPC in the years since the crisis of 1964–65, one that reveals how the church has responded to that trauma and allowed it to shape its identity and mission.

The official history of SPC, written in 1971 by a church elder who was intimately involved in the kneel-in crisis, made no mention of the year-long controversy that had brought the congregation national notoriety and resulted in the departure of several hundred members. The author no doubt wished to project an image of the church's history as a tale of consistent and faithful service to God attended by predictable blessings. For a candid assessment of the kneel-ins' impact on the congregation, we must turn to the annual history for 1965 published by the Women of the Church. By the end of the year, the WOC narrative noted, the church had regained its pride, although now it was

> the pride of accomplishing a difficult task, the pride of overcoming a great sorrow, the quiet pride and dignity of a soldier returning home from battle, bearing the scars of conflict. He will be ever mindful of the conflict, hopefully he will forget the pain, only the scar will remain and it in a sense is a badge of honor to him, in that he was able to survive and do honor to a just cause.[1]

Only decades later would the church publicly acknowledge the "scars of conflict" it sustained during the kneel-in controversy. In the short term, these wounds would quietly heal as SPC worked to restore its reputation.

1968 and Beyond

Memphis's pride in its ability to peacefully negotiate the civil rights revolution was crushed with Martin Luther King, Jr.'s assassination on April 4, 1968. King's murder and the social unrest that followed were a tremendous shock to white Memphians, who, while they could not be considered supporters of Dr. King, realized that he represented a counterweight to more militant elements in the black community. In the aftermath of the tragedy, many frightened whites stayed indoors and armed themselves. Although some believed King "had it coming," most condemned the murder and emphasized the importance of civility; yet nearly all were slow to recognize the depth of black resentment against a power structure that could not shake its plantation mentality.

Jeb Russell was typical of white clergymen in Memphis who sought to guide their congregants in responding to the tragedy of King's assassination. He noted in the *SPC Messenger* that "it is a time to show more courtesy, to perform . . . acts of love." But such calls for compassion were rarely accompanied by a willingness to acknowledge the sort of systemic discrimination that had made the Memphis Sanitation Workers' strike necessary in the first place. How little sensitivity to black suffering was actually present at SPC was indicated by a newspaper article appearing in July 1968, just three months after King's murder. A story in the *Press-Scimitar* featured a fundraising scheme adopted by SPC's Senior High Fellowship, whose members were supporting world missions by hiring themselves out for menial labor during "Slave Month." Obliviousness to slavery's cruel legacy in Memphis was by no means limited to SPC, but auctioning young people as "slaves" to support overseas missions illuminated the very paradox that had been on display during the kneel-in crisis. The church's concern for people of color "overseas" was once again strangely juxtaposed with insensitivity to people of color in neighboring ZIP codes.[2]

SPC's members were likely unconcerned with how African Americans in Memphis viewed their choice of fundraising schemes, but they were quite keen to restore their reputation among Southern Presbyterians. An important step in this direction was taken when SPC finally hosted the PCUS General Assembly in 1970. The first meeting of the General Assembly to be held in Memphis since 1896 was a chance for the congregation to relish the honor it had been denied in 1965, while showing off its better features before the denomination. Fittingly, civil rights and racial reconciliation were central themes at the Assembly. The opening day, for instance, featured a memorial service for Martin Luther King, Jr. keynoted by Morehouse College President-Emeritus Benjamin E. Mays, one of King's mentors and an outspoken advocate of integrated churches. The Assembly also adopted a relatively favorable statement regarding the Black Manifesto and heard a report from the newly formed Black Presbyterian Leadership Council. Titled "Black Expectation: A Challenge by Black Presbyterians to the Presbyterian Church in the United States," the report identified "institutional, white racism" as the denomination's fundamental problem.[3]

Following Jeb Russell's retirement in 1973, SPC called Lane Adams to the church's pulpit. Adams had been a Navy fighter pilot, a big-band singer, and an associate of Billy Graham. But while hiring an evangelical personality of Adams' stature was a coup for SPC, his tenure at the church would be brief and tumultuous. At the congregational meeting where his call to the church was to be confirmed, Adams was opposed by several dozen members who were concerned that he did not meet the academic requirements for ordination in the PCUS. Beset by opposition from those who considered his talents better suited to "show biz," in 1978 Adams announced his resignation. A groundswell of popular support convinced him to stay on, but two years later he resigned amid rumors that he had acted inappropriately with a female teacher at Presbyterian Day School. Elder Zeno Yeates was among those who investigated these rumors on behalf of the SPC session. "The more we dug into this thing the more evidence we found," Yeates recalls. Zeno and Elsie Yeates were among those who left SPC in the midst of the ensuing controversy.[4]

In 1982, SPC called John Richard "Dick" de Witt as pastor. At a time when reunion between the Northern and Southern branches of the Presbyterian Church was imminent, the fact that de Witt hailed from Reformed Theological Seminary in Jackson, Mississippi—an institution founded by conservative Presbyterians, many of whom had left the PCUS—did not bode well for the church's future in the new denomination. PCUS traditionalists had opposed reunion overtures for decades, and from its birth in 1983 the reunified Presbyterian Church (USA) was dogged by concerns that it would be dominated by Northern "liberals." Support for reunion among uneasy PCUS evangelicals was secured with the opening of a seven-year window during which congregations could exit the new denomination while maintaining control of their property.

As the closing of this exit window approached in 1990, SPC had to decide if it would remain part of the PC (USA). A thirty-five-member Unity Committee was charged with studying the question and recommending whether the congregation should make a dignified exit from the denomination before the opportunity to do so with its property expired. Milton Knowlton, who as a young man had kept racially mixed groups from entering the church sanctuary, was in charge of coordinating the vote. Among the minority of members who argued that the church should remain in the PC (USA) was Jeb Russell's daughter, Harriette Coleman. In the end, however, over 85% of the membership voted to leave the denomination and join the Evangelical Presbyterian Church. Most seem to have shared Knowlton's conviction that "Second was totally out of step with where the denomination was going."[5]

The departure further strained SPC's relationship with other Presbyterian churches in the area. While many members believed the PC (USA) had forsaken traditional Presbyterianism, from the outside SPC was viewed more as a magnet for alienated social conservatives than a haven for theological orthodoxy. There was particular resentment toward Rev. de Witt, whom some charged with betraying the denomination to which he had declared loyalty in his ordination vows. It was inevitable, perhaps, that local Presbyterians familiar with the racial controversy at SPC twenty-five years earlier would view the church's departure from the PC (USA) as a delayed reaction to that crisis. While there is no discernible relationship between the two incidents, both reflect the congregation's discomfort with the social and theological ethos of mainline Presbyterianism.[6]

Although SPC lost 230 members in the wake of its exit from the PC (USA) in 1989, half of those had returned within two years. Meanwhile, the presbytery left behind by the church suffered the permanent loss of its largest congregation and a goodly percentage of its operating budget. After the departure, some in the Presbyterian mainline viewed SPC with barely concealed disdain. Bill Weber relates an encounter in which a member of another Presbyterian church told him, "you go to the worse church in town, and my wife won't even drive by it because it makes her physically sick." Undoubtedly, such feelings are rooted in memories of past disputes. But they are nurtured by stereotypes of SPC as a fortress of "old money," a haven for white Memphians unconcerned with the city beyond their church's sprawling plant. If this stereotype was ever accurate, it has become less so in recent years as SPC has become increasingly dedicated to addressing Memphis's legacy of poverty, inequality, and alienation.[7]

Engaging the City

Evidence of this dedication began to emerge in the late 1970s, when SPC helped launch the Neighborhood Christian Center (NCC), a ministry offering tutoring, child care, job assistance, legal help, and free dental and medical care in a depressed North Memphis urban neighborhood. Explaining the church's rationale for supporting the NCC, SPC Pastor Lane Adams noted that "many churches like ours are guilty of going halfway around the world to help people, but won't go halfway around the block to help people." Adams' comments suggested that mission to the world and mission to the city had started to come together in the church's self-understanding.[8]

In the 1980s, SPC embraced a number of urban ministries in Memphis, most of them developed under the aegis of the Memphis Leadership Foundation (MLF), the brainchild of Larry Lloyd, dean of socially conscious white evangelicals in Memphis. As a high-school student in 1968, Lloyd was troubled by the realization that the adults at his church "loved the Bible ... [but] hated Dr. King," and the contradiction haunted him through his college years at Southwestern. Soon after graduating, Lloyd moved into the historic African American neighborhood of Orange Mound and began ministering there. In 1986, he founded the non-denominational MLF to "holistically meet the needs of urban poor men, women, boys and girls who live in under-resourced communities" and to raise awareness of these needs among white evangelicals.[9]

Today SPC continues to support ministries overseen by the NCC at its seven satellite centers across Memphis. In addition, church members are major donors to the Hope Christian Community Foundation, an outgrowth of the MLF founded by Lloyd in 1998 as an endowment for urban ministry in Memphis. SPC's outreach efforts in the city also include the Memphis Center for Urban Theological Studies and several projects in the Berclair community. The church's engagement with this predominantly Hispanic neighborhood began with adoption of Berclair Elementary School through the Memphis City Schools Adopt-a-School program in 2005.[10]

Adopting a public school was not an obvious ministry choice for SPC, as many church families have traditionally sent their children to private schools, including the SPC-affiliated Presbyterian Day School. Nevertheless, hundreds of church volunteers have become engaged at Berclair Elementary, beautifying the school's campus, refurbishing the teachers' lounge, tutoring students, collecting books for summer reading, and providing healthy snacks on state testing days. The SPC–Berclair relationship has not only mobilized church members to invest their time and resources in a Memphis neighborhood with which most of them were unfamiliar; because of significant gains in Berclair students' performance on standardized tests in math and reading/language arts, the collaboration has become a model for other school adopters.[11]

The church's successful partnership with a racially diverse public school where 90% of students qualify for free or reduced lunches convinced church leaders to expand SPC's ministry in the Berclair neighborhood. In 2007, SPC launched Su Casa Family Ministries, an outreach to Hispanic families in the community that offers adult ESL classes and a variety of activities for children. Two years later, Ricardo Green was hired to plant a Hispanic Presbyterian church in the neighborhood. Comunidad Cristiana Esperanza began Sunday-morning worship services at a local Baptist church in 2010.[12]

According to Larry Lloyd, who is uniquely qualified to judge in such matters, today SPC is more generous than any other evangelical church—perhaps any church, period—in ministering to the needs of Memphis's urban poor. How does one explain this development at a wealthy suburban evangelical church with a controversial racial history? In part, the changes at SPC reflect trends in the wider culture of American evangelicalism. Since the 1970s, Ron Sider, Jim Wallis, John Perkins, and other evangelical leaders have tried to convince their co-religionists that social justice is an indispensable dimension of Christian discipleship. Perkins, leader of Voice of Calvary Ministries in nearby Jackson, Mississippi, and advocate of "a radical grassroots social activism," has been particularly influential at SPC, having been invited to speak at the church on numerous occasions. In allowing the social implications of the gospel to inform the church's mission, SPC's leaders have relied on guidance from Perkins, Lloyd, and other advocates of holistic Christianity. Evangelicals who want to discern "what the Bible really says" about poverty and justice, Lloyd observes, are more likely to listen to him than to "liberals" who "don't love the Bible."[13]

But much of the credit for SPC's burgeoning commitment to urban ministry in Memphis must go to Sanders L. "Sandy" Willson, who was called to the church as senior minister in 1995. By the metrics typically used to judge pastors at tall-steeple churches, Willson's first decade at the church was wildly successful: worship attendance doubled, missions giving tripled, and Willson established a reputation as a compelling preacher. At the same time, the pastor helped the church's membership gain a new perspective on the city of Memphis and the church's role in addressing urban problems. What appealed to Willson about SPC, in fact, were "not the church's advantages, but the city's disadvantages." He saw an opportunity to leverage the individual commitments of a few prominent members into a change of direction for the institution.[14]

Under Willson's leadership, SPC has established a clear theological criterion for selecting local ministry partners. "The ministry of Jesus Christ must be exercised holistically," he explains; and an organization that ignores "the ministry of the Word" has not accomplished this holism, no matter how strongly it performs the "ministry of the deed." Willson is reluctant to take credit for SPC's commitment to combining social justice and evangelism. If there hadn't been significant movement in this direction before he arrived, he notes, he would not have had session support when "old timers" in the church challenged his vision. Nevertheless, Willson revels in the fact that a suburban evangelical church with SPC's history is drawing new members who say they are attracted by its involvement in the city.[15]

Two programs are emblematic of the way SPC has begun to leverage its considerable resources to address Memphis's endemic problems of poverty, racial estrangement, and self-segregation. One is the NEXUS mentorship program, launched in 2003, which matches experienced professionals with emerging leaders in an attempt to "duplicate" the mentors' success. A broader aim of the program is improving the local community by fostering interaction across religious, racial, and gender lines. More recently, a group of local business leaders who are also SPC members launched an effort to identify comprehensive solutions to Memphis's perennial urban problems. The Shalom Project, as the initiative is called, received initial funding from the Second Presbyterian Foundation and is headquartered at SPC.[16]

The Shalom Project seeks to positively influence the quality of life in Memphis's urban core by building church partnerships. The first step in this direction was to invite representatives of twenty-two congregations—urban and suburban, black and white—to discuss churches' roles in bringing peace to the city of Memphis. Half of these congregations were in "communities of need"; half were evangelical churches in affluent East Memphis. The next step in the Shalom strategy was to organize information from existing studies and reports for use by research study teams recruited from the participating churches. These teams were then challenged to identify problems in the areas of health care, crime, education, housing, and economic development that could be addressed by vibrant churches. The project's collaborative ethos, says director Fenton Wright, a native Memphian and son of an African American minister, is unprecedented in the city.[17]

World Mission, City Mission

According to long-time SPC member Frances Thompson, part of Sandy Willson's plan for moving church members *into* Memphis was taking them *out of* Memphis. While SPC has a long history of supporting world missions, church members' participation has traditionally consisted of writing checks and attending mission conferences. By developing a program of short-term mission trips, Willson sought to awaken church members to the sorts of problems they could address back home.[18]

On a trip to Vladivostok, Russia, Thompson discovered that it was easier for her to interact with poor people in a Siberian seaport than in her hometown. "I slept in homes . . . I would not dream of entering in Memphis," she says. Why were parts of her hometown, she wondered, as remote to her as Vladivostok when she had spent her entire life in Memphis? For Thompson and many others, the impact of these short-term mission experiences was profound: "When Sandy pushed us out of the little nest of East Memphis into the needy, remote spots of the world, we came back with softened hearts for our city." Realizing she had "never opened up [her] eyes or pushed up [her] sleeves," Thompson decided it was time to "get out there." She now helps fellow church members do the same through CityServe Explorers, a group that organizes monthly site visits to the church's ministry partners in Memphis. "We take people from our church who might be afraid or have never gone to those neighborhoods or want to know what's in their reach to do," Thompson says. "It's an opportunity to hear from God, 'is this where you want me to serve?'"[19]

Like many longtime SPC members, Thompson sees the church's initiatives in the city as a way for SPC to address its past. As she puts it,

> God is in the business of redemption. Since we messed up as a church, how great to get on board with something that is a huge transformation. Why not go where God is working—to the neediest, to the neighborhoods we were once afraid to go to, roll up our sleeves and start working in those places, and start getting away from, not only our reputation, but our own comfort zones and really enter into what God's all about instead of isolating?[20]

Making Amends

As Frances Thompson's reflections suggest, SPC atones for its exclusionary past with an impressive array of outreach activities, many designed to assist the less privileged among Memphis's African American majority. While these ministries do not constitute a specific response to the kneel-in controversy that swirled around the church in the 1960s, congregational leaders have sought to offer such a response through *bona fide* efforts to reconcile with those who were once banned from the church.

The first of these efforts came in the early 1990s, when SPC was part of a ten-day program of Christian outreach aimed at bringing together the city's Christians across racial lines. Life Focus '93 was co-chaired by Dick de Witt of SPC and Alvin Jackson of predominantly black Mississippi Boulevard Christian Church. After the public phase of the program ended, members of the two churches met in small groups designed to facilitate racial reconciliation. Connections forged through Life Focus gave rise to Love Thy Neighbor, an annual biracial Easter worship service that brought together about 45,000 Memphians over several years. One of Life Focus's happy coincidences was an encounter between Rev. de Witt and Lillian Hammond Brown, a member of the Life Focus planning team who had been prohibited from entering SPC in 1964. Over dinner with de Witt and others, Brown mentioned that three decades earlier she had stood in front of his church hoping to be admitted for worship. Embarrassed by this revelation, de Witt offered a public apology for his church's behavior from the pulpit at Mississippi Boulevard.[21]

Upon his arrival at SPC in 1995, Sandy Willson adopted a more systematic approach to addressing the church's racial history. After studying church documents related to the kneel-ins and realizing "what the white community had done here on our campus," he identified and contacted several local African Americans who had been excluded from the church thirty years earlier. Willson invited Brown, Vasco and Maxine Smith, Elaine Lee Turner, and Joan Lee Nelson to a meeting at which church leaders said they were "profoundly sorry and ashamed of what happened . . . [and] intend[ed] to move 180 degrees in the other direction and have been moving there since 1965." When asked to accept a formal apology from the congregation, however, each of the black guests declined.[22]

As Maxine Smith recalls, "we weren't looking for anything. We told [Willson] to do the right thing *now*." Smith believed that current church members could not apologize for the actions of a previous generation and did not want anyone to feel ashamed of something in which they had had no role. Vasco Smith's response was characteristically spirited: "Hell, I was turned away from eating places. I couldn't even drink water. There was a sign saying, 'White Only' on the water fountains. . . . If you wanted to go to the movie you had to go upstairs in the balcony. I couldn't get a sandwich downtown. Couldn't sit down and drink a Coca-Cola. So I promise you I didn't lose any sleep over [what happened at SPC], except to say I just hoped that someday the church would become less prejudiced."[23]

For Brown, simply being sought out for an apology was a sufficient act of penance. In fact, after the meeting she became so fond of Willson and his preaching that she began missing Sunday school at her own church to watch broadcasts of SPC's worship services. "It actually drove a wedge between me and the others in my class," she says. Not everyone at the meeting was ready to forgive and move on, however. Willson vividly recalls the response of Joan Lee Nelson: "With tears she told us how she could not drive down Poplar [Avenue], because she felt a 'demonic presence' when she passed the church. She was a black teenager being shouted at by older white men and she hasn't gotten over it to this day."[24]

According to Susan Nash, who was SPC's Program Executive when Willson made an effort to reach these excluded African Americans, the apology was "the right thing to do . . . the only thing that would help move us forward." But John Adamson, the former junior deacon who refused to guard the doors of the church in 1964, believes the public apology contemplated by Willson may have been problematic for some SPC members. "There are still people in the church whose families would be hurt by [a public apology]," he says. "And I understand that. You have to be sensitive to people's feelings." Willson adds that some feared a public declaration might appear to be moral posturing, while others felt that since de Witt had made a public statement in 1993, further apologies were unnecessary.[25]

With or without a public apology for its history of exclusion, Willson and other church leaders were determined to clarify any lingering misconceptions regarding the church's stand on race relations. In 2001, the SPC session formed a Race Relations Committee whose mission was "gospel-centered racial reconciliation both individually and corporately, in our church and in our city." If the Apostle Paul had written a letter to Memphis Christians, the committee noted,

> it would probably include a strong charge to seek the peace, well-being, and unity of the body of Christ across all racial chasms. It is hard to imagine a more powerful and meaningful demonstration of the reality of the gospel in Memphis than for the members of all the churches to show their love one for another. By this, they, our unbelieving neighbors, will know we are Christians. We dream of a day when people of all races and backgrounds will live, work, worship and serve together arm in arm and heart to heart under the banner of Jesus Christ in the Memphis region. Nothing less is worthy of the gospel of Christ. We believe this is what Jesus would do.[26]

The "Statement of Intention Regarding Race Relations at Second Presbyterian Church" adopted by the church's session in 2002 made no direct reference to the kneel-in controversy of 1964–65. But it did acknowledge "incidences and attitudes of racism, which we deeply regret and firmly renounce." Furthermore, the corresponding ministry plan referred to the document as "a clear rescission of previous race relations statements" (including, presumably, the 1957 "Statement of Policy").[27]

Another sign of the church's commitment to racial reconciliation has been its hiring of African American pastors, a rarity in predominantly white Memphis churches. The first black member of the SPC pastoral staff was Nevlynn Robinson, who served the church during the late 1990s. As Willson notes, Robinson was a true pioneer. "Everyone sees the first African American pastor as the one you're supposed to work out your race issues with," he says. With no other African Americans in the congregation, Robinson's stint at SPC was a lonely one. But the addition of fifteen to twenty active black members has created a different environment for Timothy Russell, who was drawn to Memphis in 2005 to head the SPC-supported Memphis Center for Urban Theological Studies. Now an assistant pastor at SPC, Russell reports that he and his wife have enjoyed "an overwhelmingly gracious reception" at the church.[28]

Fenton Wright, who directs the Shalom Project from his office at the church and spends much of his time working with SPC members and staff, has a similar take on the racial climate there. "It's a place where people are making a genuine effort to live out the gospel in the area of race relations," he says. Wright believes the church has undergone a "true paradigm shift," which he ascribes to Willson's influence, as well as an improving grasp of "what the Scriptures really teach about justice."[29]

A Test Case for Reconciliation: Clayborn Temple

Even when they reflect a sincere desire to improve race relations, the plans of white evangelicals can be frustrated by black resentment and suspicion. SPC's unsuccessful attempt to partner with an African American denomination in planting a congregation in downtown Memphis is an illuminating example of the way good intentions—even when they are well funded—can be hindered by historically conditioned sensitivities. It will be recalled that in 1949, after a century in downtown Memphis, SPC left a deteriorating urban neighborhood, selling its historic building at the corner of Hernando and Pontotoc streets to the African Methodist Episcopal (AME) Church. Eventually renamed Clayborn Temple, the edifice just off Beale Street would become a venue for performers from Mahalia Jackson to Sam Cooke and religious leaders from Martin Luther King, Jr. to Minister Louis Farrakhan.

In 1968, Clayborn Temple was the organizational headquarters for the Memphis sanitation workers whose strike brought King to Memphis. The iconic "I Am A Man" placards that became an international symbol of the strike were printed at the church, which also became a staging point for daily marches to City Hall. When King's last march on March 28, 1968, ended in chaos, many sought sanctuary at Clayborn from rubber bullets and tear gas. It was rumored that the Invaders, a local black militant group, had stashed weapons in the belfry.[30]

Although Clayborn Temple fell into disrepair during the 1970s, the civil rights landmark was added to the National Register of Historic Places in 1979 and, after a half-million-dollar renovation, was rededicated in 1983 as Clayborn-Ball Temple. But the congregation steadily diminished as private residences were lost to downtown building projects. Services were finally suspended in 2001 after a murder in the church's homeless shelter and the conviction of Clayborn's pastor on charges of sexual battery. AME officials gave up on the idea of maintaining a worshipping congregation at the historic site, presiding Elder John Madison telling a reporter that the denomination had entertained giving the church away if it could not be sold for parking at FedEx Forum, which was then under construction.[31]

In July 2002, when four worshippers were killed in the collapse of an 80-year-old Memphis church, the city's older houses of worship came under scrutiny by local government. A nonprofit called Clayborn Temple Restoration Corporation had recently announced plans to convert the church building into a center for literacy training and transitional housing, but these plans had to be shelved when the City of Memphis charged in Environmental Court that Clayborn was under "imminent risk of structural collapse." The building's sagging roof came to the attention of the Memphis City Council, which in June 2003 appropriated $300,000 to stabilize Clayborn and another historic black church that had been declared unsafe. But lawsuits claiming that the appropriations violated church–state separation were filed almost immediately and the money was never disbursed.[32]

As the legality of the City Council's appropriation was debated in the local papers during the summer and fall of 2003, details of the church's dilapidated condition caught the attention of Memphians concerned with the preservation of historic landmarks. Gayle Rose, a local philanthropist with strong connections in the local black community, was asked by Director of Housing and Community Development Robert Lipscomb to help raise $1 million to restore Clayborn. When Rose surveyed the building's condition, she was surprised to see the name "Second Presbyterian Church" engraved over the entrance. As a former SPC member, Rose was aware of the church's racial history and believed SPC's current leadership might see an opportunity for redemption.[33]

With attorney Marty Regan, who as a member of St. Patrick's Catholic Church had been able to negotiate a lease for unused land on the Clayborn property, Rose visited SPC pastor Sandy Willson to ask for the needed $1 million. Willson responded that while he believed many church members could be persuaded to contribute to restoring Clayborn, SPC was not in the museum business. However, Willson said, he had a better idea: SPC and the AME could join forces to renovate the crumbling building, which could become the site of a collaborative ministry led by pastors from both denominations.[34]

Thinking the idea was worth exploring, Rose and Regan brokered a meeting between Willson and AME Bishop Frederick Talbot. "You're probably not interested in cooperating with a bunch of white evangelicals from the suburbs," Willson remembers telling Talbot, "but that building has our name on it, and if in God's providence there's something we should be doing together, we would love to talk to you about it." To Willson's surprise, Talbot was open to considering a joint ministry at Clayborn, and by August 2003 the matter was under discussion by a planning group composed of representatives from SPC and the AME's district council. After reviewing several options for collaboration, members of the group settled upon the most audacious—"a partnership in ministry, mission and community." They began meeting weekly to consider the theological, administrative, missiological, gender, and church–state issues implied in such a partnership.[35]

After months of working to harmonize doctrinal and administrative differences, the planning team reached a formal agreement. SPC would fund renovations at Clayborn up to $5 million (this was an engineering firm's rough estimate of what it would cost to make the church structurally sound) while the AME would provide the land and building and hire a new minister. It was also agreed that the AME could dissolve the partnership at any time, provided it reimburse the Second Presbyterian Church Foundation for the $87,000 it had already spent to stabilize the decaying building. The collaboration was kept out of the news, local papers referring only to "private funds" that had been raised to keep the church from collapsing.[36]

Anyone who remembered the civil rights movement in Memphis could appreciate the significance of a suburban white church that had once turned away black visitors working to restore the spiritual headquarters of Martin Luther King's last civil rights crusade. SPC's leaders were particularly energized by the prospect of the church's former home becoming an outpost of its urban outreach and a symbol of collaboration between black and white Christians. For longtime church members like Justin Towner, who had grown up at SPC downtown and later guarded the East Memphis church from black incursions, the prospect of SPC partnering with the AME in a restored Clayborn Temple had profound personal significance.[37]

It was perhaps a bad omen when in May 2005 the back annex of Clayborn Temple collapsed. Shortly thereafter, with planning for the SPC–AME collaboration nearly complete, Vashti McKenzie replaced the retiring Talbot as bishop of the AME's 13th Episcopal District. At a summer dinner party where the successful alliance was to be celebrated, McKenzie shocked everyone present by handing Willson a check for $87,000 and announcing that the AME wanted out of the deal. "It was sad to me," Willson reflects. "I think we had an opportunity to bring evangelicals and social liberals, black and white, together in a crucial area; if we could have truly done church together and become family, I felt like that would have been one of the biggest lighthouses for the gospel in the center of Memphis."[38]

The AME's first female bishop was apparently troubled by several aspects of the Clayborn plan finalized under her predecessor. In response to Talbot's acquiescence in SPC's insistence that the new church eschew partisan politics and refrain from endorsing candidates, McKenzie declared that she would not have any church in her jurisdiction "muzzled." She also expressed discomfort with the limited leadership role women would have in the new congregation. This is hardly surprising given that McKenzie is the author of two books on developing women leaders. Gender may have figured in the deal's unraveling in another way as well. Susan Nash, a member of the SPC staff who worked closely with the bishop, believes McKenzie concluded that the Clayborn collaboration was too risky a project to be embraced by the AME's first woman prelate.[39]

Following dissolution of the agreement, the AME's 13th Episcopal District launched the Clayborn Temple Restoration Project, with an initial goal of addressing the structural issues cited in Environmental Court. The Project hired an architectural firm and completed court-ordered improvements at the end of 2006. But without SPC's financial resources, the renovation effort languished. Ultimately, AME officials decided to contribute monies raised for the church's restoration to aid victims of natural disasters. In 2009, Clayborn's dilapidated condition once again made news when the church was listed as one of the city's worst "eyesores." In early 2011, as the 25,000-square-foot building continued to molder, it was put up for sale at a price of $1 million. A year later, the transformation of Clayborn into an African American cultural center became part of an urban redevelopment plan being proposed by the city of Memphis.[40]

How the cooperative church venture at Clayborn Temple would have fared is unclear, but it was a remarkable effort in several respects. First, it represented a level of collaboration far exceeding the church pairings and interracial Easter services that for some time have been common in Memphis and other cities. Second, it was extraordinary that representatives of such diverse ecclesiastical bodies were able to reach agreement on a range of theological and practical issues. Each side stood to benefit from the partnership, of course. The AME would resuscitate a dead congregation and preserve a civil rights landmark, and SPC would save a building to which it had strong historical ties while gaining a striking public symbol of its commitment to the city and to racial reconciliation. That the project failed despite all this indicates that, when it comes to bridging the gap between white and black churches, good intentions—and even sound plans—may not be enough.

Assessing the New SPC: External Perspectives

SPC's commitment to addressing its segregated past by embracing urban ministry and pursuing partnerships with black churches can be seen as part of a larger racial reconciliation movement that swept through American evangelicalism in the 1990s. The phenomenon was reflected in Promise Keepers stadium rallies, the Southern Baptist Convention's "Resolution on Racial Reconciliation," and the "Miracle in Memphis"—a dramatic ritual of mutual foot-washing by white and black Pentecostal leaders. But in an extensive study of the reconciliation movement and evangelical attitudes toward race, sociologists Michael O. Emerson and Christian Smith conclude that, despite the explosion of "conferences, books, study guides, videos, speeches, practices by organizations, formal apologies, and even mergers of once racially separate organizations," evangelical efforts at racial healing have been largely ineffective.[41]

According to the analysis conducted by Emerson and Smith, the problem is rooted in a failure of communication. When white evangelicals respond to calls for reconciliation sounded by black leaders such as John Perkins and Tom Skinner, they tend to ignore the systemic features of injustice and racism, emphasizing the "individual-level components [and] leaving the larger racialized social structures, institutions, and culture intact." Perkins, for instance, highlights the connections between reconciliation, "redistribution" (of resources), and "relocation" (challenging patterns of residential segregation). Almost invariably, however, when white evangelicals adopt an agenda for racial healing, the need to work for justice and equality is eclipsed by emphases on forming friendships and cleansing hearts of prejudice.[42]

On the basis of extensive interviews, Emerson and Smith determine that white evangelicals are wont to construe "the race problem" as the result of some combination of individual prejudice, group self-interest, and media fabrication. This construal, they argue, is a product of inherited cultural tools that obscure the impact of historical injustice and the "racialized patterns that transcend and encompass individuals." Even when evangelicals acknowledge racism as a serious societal problem that should be combated by Christians, Emerson and Smith observe, they often see its solution in the "miracle motif"—the conviction that since the cure for social ills is God's spirit convicting individuals of sin, problems like racism will naturally dissipate as people are converted to faith in Christ. Based on these observations, the authors conclude that "white evangelicalism likely does more to perpetuate the racialized society than to reduce it."[43]

In his study of Mission Mississippi—an evangelical racial *rapprochement* initiative launched in Jackson, Mississippi, in 1993—Peter Slade demonstrates how the superficial social analyses favored by white evangelicals are expressed programmatically. According to Slade, Mission Mississippi has managed only a "cheap reconciliation" because securing the support of white evangelicals required movement leaders to decouple reconciliation and justice and eschew anything smacking of the "social gospel." These concessions, Slade argues, created a "deafening silence when it comes to the requirements of justice in the process of racial reconciliation."[44]

Are the reconciliation initiatives in which SPC has participated susceptible to similar criticisms? It is true that evangelical-led reconciliation programs in Memphis such as Life Focus and Love Thy Neighbor have stressed removing racial barriers through church alliances and the cultivation of individual friendships. It is also true that SPC's "Statement of Intention Regarding Race Relations" refers to "build[ing] meaningful relationships" as the most fruitful approach to reconciliation:

> We should be intentional about creating peer-to-peer relationships and fellowship opportunities between congregational communities at Second and African-American churches within the community. We encourage all of our officers and staff to become involved in meaningful, racially-diverse

friendships and associations in our city, especially with like-minded brothers and sisters of differing ethnicity.[45]

However, the SPC statement goes much further, calling on church members to "provide leadership and resources to address social and economic inequities; and . . . consider providing consultation and involvement in emerging African-American businesses." It also encourages members to "demand equal application of law, and to pursue biblical justice." Finally, church leaders are asked to "engage the issues of racial disparity in our economy and educational systems in the Memphis region" and "to develop strategies to use minority vendors." In these ways SPC's "Statement of Intention Regarding Race Relations" transcends the boundaries of evangelical discourse described by Emerson and Smith.[46]

For his part, Willson reiterates this systemic perspective on race relations by preaching that poverty, like wealth, should not be understood simplistically as a result of individual choices. He distinguishes between "neighborhoods of need" and "neighborhoods of choice" and illustrates the concept of "generational poverty" by reminding white Memphians that only 1% of business equity in Memphis is controlled by the African American majority. Willson also employs the term "social justice" (from which many evangelicals demur), although in his view the biblical solution to poverty involves charitable giving, mentoring, and loan forgiveness by individuals rather than government-directed wealth redistribution.[47]

It may be debated whether these are the best strategies for combating structural injustice in an urban setting. But it has to be said that SPC's race relations statement, the social themes in Willson's preaching, and the church's programmatic commitment to establishing "biblical justice" in Memphis indicate a greater awareness of the systemic nature of racial inequality than studies of American evangelicalism would lead us to expect.

Assessing the New SPC: Internal Perspectives

Most SPC leaders recognize that the church has far to go in living out the grand vision to which it has committed itself; nevertheless, the suburban congregation's commitment to addressing urban problems is impressive. What remains elusive is a successful marshalling of its resources to effect concrete change in a specific African American neighborhood of need.

Eddie Foster became involved at SPC in the late 1970s, just as the church was beginning to engage the city through its support of the Neighborhood Christian Center. Regretting that evangelicals had largely forsaken the city after Martin Luther King's death, Foster joined a cadre of young SPC members who were interested in developing a new evangelical mission to urban Memphis. Under

Sandy Willson's influence, Foster's sense of call to serve the poor has deepened considerably. Now the former attorney is full-time director of SPC's Mission Memphis program, which disburses $1.1 million a year in support of about fifty local urban ministries.[48]

Foster is particularly proud of SPC's ministry in the predominantly Hispanic Berclair community. For him, the adoption of Berclair Elementary in 2005 and the neighborhood programs that have evolved from the partnership represent a move away from the "silo" mentality that has often driven church efforts in the inner city. But Foster admits that SPC's endeavors to find traction in African American communities have not been as encouraging. One target for the church's outreach has been Orange Mound, a historic Memphis neighborhood founded in the 1890s, purportedly the first in America to be built by African Americans. But despite the credibility Willson enjoys among local black leaders, the church's efforts to develop a presence in Orange Mound have not produced much fruit. Foster believes the problem is that, despite its new emphasis on outreach to the city, SPC continues to be viewed as a suburban church full of wealthy white people.[49]

Steve Nash is a child of SPC who, like Foster, caught a vision for urban ministry there. He began participating in SPC's programs for youth when his family joined the church in the mid-1970s. After college, Nash volunteered in urban ministry contexts with Young Life and the Neighborhood Christian Center. As he was exposed to a series of SPC-hosted speakers who challenged evangelical Christians to embrace urban problems, Nash's "heart for the city fleshed itself out." He began to envision a full-time ministry that would assist public housing residents trapped in poverty to become "economically self-sufficient through the gospel of Jesus Christ." The result was Advance Memphis, a ministry to Memphians in the Vance Avenue neighborhood (part of the 38126 ZIP code, one of nation's poorest) that offers GED tutoring, dollar-for-dollar matching savings accounts, economic literacy and job readiness training, off-site work experience, and job placement.[50]

After being away from SPC for several years, Nash returned with his family in 2010. As a white man who spends his days with residents of an endemically poor African American neighborhood, he has a unique perspective on SPC's evolving response to Memphis's urban realities. While gratefully acknowledging the church's consistent support for Advance Memphis, Nash is critical of SPC's tendency to approach the city's problems with programs and strategic plans, an approach that has made SPC's work in the city "wider than deep," he says. In Nash's view, "inter-racial ministry has got to be life to life." And it must avoid any hints of paternalism. At Advance Memphis, Nash explains, "we're building relationships and we're learning. Both black and white have things to learn from each other."[51]

Another self-critical observer of SPC's engagement with Memphis is Mitchell Moore, Minister to Young Adults at the church and junior member of the pastoral staff. Raised in an affluent suburb of Chattanooga, Tennessee, Moore recalls with shame his early feelings of superiority and entitlement. This privileged mindset was challenged at Chattanooga's New City Fellowship, an evangelical, interracial congregation affiliated with the Presbyterian Church in America. New City was the only place other than athletic contests Moore recalls seeing blacks and whites mingling, and that left a profound impression on him. Feeling drawn to full-time ministry, following college Moore enrolled at Covenant Seminary in St. Louis in preparation for mission work in Africa. But he ended up accepting a call to SPC instead. "We thought we'd be working with some of the poorest of the poor in East Africa," Moore reflects, "but we're working with some of the richest of the rich in East Memphis."[52]

Moore recognizes great potential at SPC for promoting racial *rapprochement* in Memphis, but remains uncomfortable with some aspects of the church's identity. For one thing, he wishes it better reflected the city's diversity. Can you imagine, he asks, if SPC's membership mirrored the demographics of Memphis? In Moore's view, the church could encourage more diversity through worship that reflected the entire spectrum of Christian experience rather than the exclusivity of one culture. "If someone comes here and doesn't feel comfortable, it's we who have to adjust," he says. Moore is encouraged by the growing number of blacks in the congregation, but he recognizes structural roadblocks to minority participation at SPC. "Just because you have faces at the table," he notes, "doesn't mean the table is level if decisions continue to be made in an old boy network."[53]

Moore is also troubled by the proportion of the church's resources that stay within the church family. Illustrating this point with a reference to SPC-affiliated Presbyterian Day School, Moore notes that "we have built an . . . elite elementary school in a city where the average ACT score is 16." In fact, the artificial-turf athletic field that sits adjacent to the church on the PDS campus was almost enough to keep Moore from accepting a call to the church. SPC could have directed the $1 million used to build the field somewhere it was "really needed," he says. Indeed, in a city where most public high schools do not have their own football stadiums, a state-of-the-art athletic complex reserved for students at a private elementary school is a powerful symbol of disparity.[54]

It would be quite understandable if a thirty-something pastor with a young family refrained from addressing divisive issues out of concern for his job security. To some extent Moore's boldness reflects his identity as part of a younger generation of evangelicals whose commitment to justice and reconciliation is a nonnegotiable aspect of Christian faith. "As long as I'm on the side of Scripture," he says, "I'm ok with whatever happens." But it is also a tribute to the ethos of social consciousness that now reigns at the church.[55]

Finding a Usable Past

Perhaps the best example of how SPC has learned from the "scars of conflict" it sustained in the mid-1960s is the way the church continues to allow past failings to inform its present mission. SPC's willingness to draw lessons from an unpleasant history was on display in 2010, when Memphis's racial fault line was activated by a movement to consolidate city and county schools. In Shelby County, systemic injustice is more evident in public education than in any other area of civic life. The educational equality that was supposed to be achieved by court-ordered bussing has been thwarted in Memphis not only by a mass exodus of families to private schools and white-flight academies, but by the maintenance of separate school districts in the city and suburbs.

In late 2010, the Memphis City School Board, fearing that Shelby County Schools might declare itself a "special school district" and thereby limit its responsibility to fund the education of city students, decided to act preemptively by surrendering its own charter. This move made the suburban school district responsible, in theory at least, for the education of 100,000 students previously served by Memphis City Schools. When the charter surrender was subsequently approved by the Memphis City Council, the matter was in the hands of city residents. If the charter's dissolution was confirmed in a referendum held before state government could intervene, school consolidation in Shelby County would become a reality.

The Memphis school-consolidation debate became national news. To say it was contentious would be akin to pointing out that the Mississippi River floods in the spring. In an already divided city, the consolidation question pitted municipal versus county and state governments, urbanites versus suburbanites, poor versus middle class, and black versus white. As the February 2011 referendum approached, Memphis residents were seeking guidance on how to vote. Should the proposed consolidation be viewed through the lens of institutional efficiency? Of funding equity? Of educational quality? Of social justice? In the early weeks of 2011, religious leaders throughout the area were addressing the controversy. SPC's Sandy Willson gave his take on the issue at a Bible study in January attended by several hundred men.

Willson began by highlighting the obvious disparities between the two school systems. One is 70% white and "made up of families that make more money and [that] has schools whose test scores are higher," he said, while the other is 85% black. The former system, Willson observed, wants to seal itself off in a special school district. In fact, Willson said, in reports of private conversations that had reached him, suburban leaders were framing the question in terms of the need "to preserve our way of life." At this point, Willson became quite animated:

Do you know what that is? That is the 2011 version of 1963. . . . when white churches wouldn't let black people in their churches; this is every bit as bad as that, it's just more subtle. Make no mistake about it. And if you are participating in that, you need to let go of that *real* fast. And if you have any influence on this, you need to address this at the risk of your own popularity—*real* fast.[56]

Willson went on to explain that in the present situation "the heart of a Christian suburbanite in Memphis" should be animated by a desire to help those trapped, through no fault of their own, in substandard public schools. Christians who live in neighborhoods of choice should jump at the chance to assist poorer schools financially, he said. "No matter what your business partner thinks about you and no matter what your customers think about you, no matter what your daddy thinks about you, let's reverse the curse, gentlemen. And let's trust God to bless our city [applause]."[57]

When Mitchell Moore tackled the consolidation issue from the SPC pulpit in February, he too invoked the history of the civil rights movement. Moore told the SPC congregation that affluent Christians should be as concerned with their neighbors' health, employment, and education as with their own. In making his case, Moore mined SPC's history for examples of a countercultural commitment to "others." The church demonstrated its love for the needy, Moore argued, prior to the Civil War when the church educated slaves, and in the 1870s when its pastor remained in the city to minister to victims of a devastating yellow fever epidemic. According to Moore, the church temporarily abandoned its other-centeredness during the kneel-in crisis of 1964–65:

> In the 1960s, a period that was racially charged in this city . . . there were elders in this church who did not want African Americans worshiping in this sanctuary. That's a huge blight on us. We've repented of it privately, we've repented of it publicly, but it doesn't negate that that was a reality. The pastor at the time. . . . preached so faithfully that he had death threats pinned inside his robe before he came into the pulpit.[58]

SPC redeemed itself, Moore claimed, when a majority of the congregation rose up, opposed its renegade elders, and decided it would be guided by the example of Christ rather than by entrenched cultural traditions.

Moore called upon his congregants to adopt a similar attitude with regard to the impending consolidation of Memphis City and Shelby County schools. He reminded them that disparities in educational opportunity would not be remedied by the machinations of politicians or the decisions of courts. But he made clear that SPC's members could not ignore educational inequality, which could be overcome only through a commitment on the part of God's people to love their neighbors as much as they love themselves. "Will we work for others' education? Will we stop the retreat [from the public schools]? Will we go against culture?" Moore asked his congregation. "Will people say of us, `they were a people who operated under the kingdom's standards and not the culture's . . . who, even when the city was fleeing, stayed to serve'?"[59]

Institutional Trauma as a Resource for Mission

Traumas are a part of life—for institutions as well as individuals. Still, SPC has borne more than its share. In the past sixty years the church has endured a pastor's suicide, a racial controversy that drew national attention, a split leading to the establishment of a rival church, a minister who resigned amid charges of sexual misconduct, and a contentious decision to leave the denomination to which it had belonged for over 150 years.

As with individuals, institutions that thrive ultimately turn such traumatic episodes into opportunities for growth. When Senior Minister Anthony Dick took his own life in the church manse in 1958, the official response was silence. "I was around when Dr. Dick shot himself," recalls Charles Murphy, who grew up at SPC and maintains a deep love for the church, "and nobody ever talked about that afterwards. Nobody ever explained, even as we got older, why that happened." When the church's official history was written in 1971, it appeared that the kneel-in controversy would also be buried in an institutional memory hole. But since the 1990s, SPC's leadership has decided to acknowledge the past, make amends, and use the experience to shape a mission informed by a vision of justice and reconciliation.[60]

It is possible to question whether SPC's urban outreach fully gauges the structural dimensions of injustice in Memphis or fully escapes the paternalism that is the bane of affluent whites who want to "help the less fortunate." But one thing is for certain. SPC has done what few other churches in the South—evangelical or otherwise—have been willing to do: directly address its failure to act with Christian charity during the years of the civil rights movement. As the following chapter demonstrates, doing so becomes increasingly difficult with the passage of time.

12

"A Season of Prayer
and Corporate Repentance"

Wrestling with the Past at Independent Presbyterian Church

Perhaps the only church in the South that felt the long-term impact of a kneel-in campaign as deeply as did SPC was Galloway United Methodist Church in Jackson, Mississippi. In addition to being targets of extensive and well-publicized attempts to integrate their worship services, both churches emerged from their kneel-in controversies only after suffering major schisms.

The churches to which these schisms at SPC and Galloway gave rise also had much in common. In both cases, those who founded them maintained that their reasons for doing so were theological rather than racial and lamented that their former churches had exchanged their primary evangelical mission for social and political concerns. Finally, in both cases the new congregations claimed to be preserving the "historic Christianity" that had been relinquished by their mother churches. As a spokesman for those leaving Galloway put it, we "want to sustain John Wesley Methodism in Mississippi without the social gospel, the National Council of Churches, and so forth."[1]

What is more, in both cases disgruntled refugees from these flagship congregations formed churches that retained the denominational name while emphasizing their independence. The three hundred or so members who left SPC in early 1965 founded a congregation calling itself Independent Presbyterian Church (IPC). Similarly, among the five hundred members who departed Galloway the same year were the founders of First Independent Methodist and Riverside Independent Methodist churches. These congregations, established on the same day in August 1965, would be joined in succeeding years by twenty-four other formerly United Methodist congregations in the Association of Independent Methodists (AIM).[2]

It is impossible to identify all the factors that motivated secessionist groups to leave SPC and Galloway in 1965. But it is significant that both these "independent" congregations were determined to uphold segregation, a practice that had been condemned by their former denominations. With regard to the emergence of the AIM, former Galloway pastor W. J. Cunningham does not hesitate to identify the decisive factor. The AIM, he writes, "was founded for reasons of racial segregation. All the dissatisfactions named by the founders were real enough to them; but this is a fact: if Galloway, Capitol Street, and St. Luke's Methodist Churches could have remained permanently segregated as a Methodist principle, the Independent Methodists would have had no reason for being."[3]

As we will see, the same can be said of the establishment of IPC in Memphis. Those who established the church cited many grievances with their former congregation and former denomination. But without the kneel-in crisis at SPC and the awareness that remaining part of the Presbyterian Church (US) would require an increasing tolerance for integration, IPC would not have come into being when it did or attracted those who became its founding members. This is clear not only in the circumstances that precipitated the independents' departure from SPC, but in the character of the church they founded.

The Birth of IPC

On Sunday, March 7, 1965—a week after the fateful congregational meeting at which the SPC membership adopted a rotational plan for service on its session, but before that plan could be implemented—the controversy that had consumed SPC for the previous twelve months came to a symbolic end as a lone black man was seated in the church balcony. This visitor was probably unaware that more than a few of SPC's Sunday-morning regulars were missing. Some two hundred of them, in fact, would be gathering that afternoon at Goldsmith's Civic Center auditorium in Audubon Park to discuss their options. Robert E. Brake, spokesman for the group, admitted that starting a new church might be on the group's agenda, but emphasized that "we are not mad at anybody . . . [or] running from anything."[4]

Those who attended the meeting concluded that Memphis indeed needed a new church, and soon. The following Sunday 340 persons, most of them members or former members of SPC, gathered for worship in the Plaza Theater in East Memphis. Afterward they determined that their upstart congregation—to be known as IPC—would begin regular services the following Sunday under the leadership of Rev. Leonard T. Van Horn of French Camp, Mississippi. Van Horn, a former PCUS pastor who had left the denomination "out of conviction," would become IPC's first permanent minister. Those present at the meeting elected a steering committee that included several of the men who had recently resigned from the SPC session.[5]

One of these SPC refugees, Forbes Barton, articulated the independents' purpose: "We want to have a Bible church, a prayer church and a mission church," he told reporters, "and to worship the Lord, and nothing more." After the rancor and discord Barton and others had experienced at SPC during the previous year, their desire to "worship the Lord and nothing more" was quite understandable. Nevertheless, the prevailing assumption was that the new congregation's founders were primarily motivated by a determination to preserve ecclesiastical segregation. This interpretation of IPC's emergence was taken for granted not only by those who remained at SPC, but by the local press as well. The *Commercial Appeal,* for instance, identified many of IPC's organizers as "persons who had opposed integration at Second Presbyterian Church" and referred to IPC's "segregation policy."[6]

Nevertheless, IPC spokesmen downplayed their desire to preserve ecclesiastical apartheid because they were keen to present themselves not as schismatics creating disunity in the body of Christ, but as godly exiles fleeing from apostasy. For this reason, justifications for IPC's existence focused not on the tumult at SPC during the previous months, but on the perceived devolution of Southern Presbyterianism over several decades. In his first sermon at IPC—titled "Do You Really Want That Old-Time Religion?"—Rev. Van Horn rehearsed some of the ways the PCUS had repudiated its origins. The denomination, he said, had come to dominate individual congregations through "machine government"; it had departed from Scripture by making women eligible for the offices of minister and elder; it had continued to endorse the National Council of Churches and its social programs, despite repeated grassroots efforts to get the denomination to leave the ecumenical organization; it had loosened the standards for divorce; and it had become distracted by "sociological matters" while sinners perished.[7]

A church document published in early 1966 elaborated the notion that IPC's founders had fled the PCUS because it had fatally succumbed to "liberalism." IPC's birth was attributed to "a body of believers [who] . . . were troubled about the liberalism in the churches and were concerned about the power structures, led by liberal men, in the churches from which they came." "They had been praying for years," the document claimed, "for the 'old-time religion' to be preached once again, and they . . . wanted to return to the doctrines held by their forefathers in the Presbyterian church." The independents had forsaken an apostate denomination, in other words, to reclaim a Southern Presbyterian heritage purified of liberal embellishments. Forbes Barton's statement that the independents wanted "a Bible church, a prayer church and a mission church" implied that SPC had ceased being such a church and that by remaining in the PCUS it was rejecting the "old-line Presbyterianism held so dear" by IPC's founders.[8]

This myth of the church's genesis as a recovery of pristine Southern Presbyterian origins continued to inform IPC's self-understanding forty-five years later. In 1965, the church declared in a section of its website removed only in 2010,

> many Memphis families had realized a pressing need to "preserve and perpetuate" the historic Presbyterian profession of faith in our city. Believing that at the time there was no existing Presbyterian denomination in Memphis that was faithful to the historic Reformed Faith and to the great Presbyterian doctrines of grace, these early members chose to remain an independent church, and so named their church. Their desire was to be a church that continued in the faithful tradition of the early Southern Presbyterian Church.[9]

If the independents believed that their mother church had lost its theological way, many at SPC responded in kind, referring facetiously to IPC as "First Segregationist." A more subtle view of SPC's wayward children was expressed in the historical narrative compiled by the Women of the Church in 1965: "It is ironic," the WOC chronicle noted, "that white Christians think the church the last stronghold of segregation when in fact our very own beliefs in the brotherhood and equality of man should make an 'open church door' policy only right in the eyes of God as he has revealed Himself through the Scriptures."[10]

Without doubt, the schism at SPC left hard feelings on both sides. Alienation between the churches was rooted in the facts that most of IPC's charter members had come from SPC, that IPC's first session comprised eleven men who had resigned from the same body at SPC after the fateful congregational meeting there, and that the split severed friendships and strained relations within extended families. Elinor Perkins Daniel is a former SPC member who remembers how the rupture pitted neighbor against neighbor. When Daniel's mother received a phone call inviting her family to join those who were leaving for IPC, she refused. "And that was the end of their relationship," according to Daniel.[11]

Stability, Compatibility, and Spirituality

The independents may have desired "to worship the Lord, and nothing more," as Forbes Barton put it, but they were determined to do so as they saw fit. To ensure that IPC would not have to endure the sort of paralyzing conflict precipitated by the kneel-ins at SPC, they inscribed three principles in the new church's constitution. First, elders would be elected for lifetime service. This would guarantee that older, more conservative men would maintain their influence on the session. Second, church visitors and members would be "compatible" with the congregation.

Third, the church would honor the Southern Presbyterian tradition of the church's "spirituality."[12]

When the concept of compatibility emerged on the day of IPC's first official gathering, its meaning was unclear. The press reported without comment Forbes Barton's claim that the insistence on compatibility "was not a segregation policy," but a way to "avoid anything or anyone who might disturb" the church. But IPC's constitution would leave no doubt as to the sort of compatibility church leaders had in mind. Article III, paragraph 2 stated: "Believing that the scriptures teach that the separation of nations, peoples and groups will preserve the peace, purity and unity of the Church, it is, therefore, the will of this Church that its members and those visiting the Church, its worship services, and all of its activities, shall be compatible with the congregation."[13]

It is not clear what scriptural "teaching" IPC's founders were invoking. The notion that God had allotted distinct regions of the earth to Noah's descendants and reiterated this plan by dispersing the tower builders at Babel were well-developed themes in American biblical exegesis. In the late nineteenth century, Benjamin M. Palmer (1818–1902), a leading Presbyterian divine who spent most of his career in New Orleans, had offered such a reading of Genesis 9–11 as a biblical rationale for separation of the races. More recently, in the 1940s and 1950s, articles in *The Presbyterian Journal* had cited various biblical arguments for segregation, including God's supposed endorsement of demographic division in Genesis.[14]

As pro-segregation arguments went, however, this article of the IPC constitution was unusual, since its focus was segregation *within* the church. Perhaps this reflected a grudging acknowledgement that enforced segregation in the wider culture was rapidly becoming a thing of the past. Or perhaps it revealed a concern that, without a clear policy in place, blacks and their white fellow-travelers would attempt to integrate the church. Whatever the reasons for IPC's explicit policy of excluding visitors and members who were not "compatible" with the congregation, its authors seemed to fear that Sunday morning might well become the last segregated hour.

IPC's founders were well aware that the "compatibility" policy inscribed in their church's constitution would not be acceptable in any of the mainline Protestant denominations. Nevertheless, they articulated this policy with a degree of theological self-assurance that the SPC session had not been able to muster in 1957. In place of vague references to godless communism and race mixing, IPC's constitution declared that the peace and well-being of the church depended on congregational homogeneity. Recalling that in 1957 the SPC session had declined to cite a biblical warrant for its segregation policy, IPC's leaders, some of whom had been members of that body, were determined not to make the same error.

A third aspect of IPC's founding philosophy—the "spirituality of the church"—was only alluded to in the church's constitution, which declared that "the laws and principles of civil and ecclesiastical authority must be kept separated." But IPC's founders knew that the "tradition of the early Southern Presbyterian Church" they sought to restore was virtually synonymous with a "spirituality" doctrine that kept at arm's length all judgments of reigning social patterns. This had been the doctrine's role in the antebellum era, when it was used to deflect criticism of slave culture in the South; and it remained the doctrine's function in the first half of the twentieth century when conservative Presbyterians invoked it to fend off attacks on the Southern way of life.[15]

IPC's founders were not the only Southern Presbyterians convinced that a retrieval of the church's "spirituality" was necessary to save the PCUS from co-optation by advocates of a liberal social agenda. Even as the kneel-in crisis at SPC unfolded, traditionalist Presbyterians in the mid-South were chartering a new seminary (Reformed Theological Institute, later Reformed Theological Seminary) in Jackson, Mississippi, which would be "wholly dedicated to the preservation of, and the propagation of, the original Southern Presbyterian convictions in regard to . . . the concept of the spiritual nature and mission of the church." Less than a decade later, in 1973, zeal to preserve the Church as a "spiritual organism" was a major factor in the exit of 260 PCUS congregations to form the Presbyterian Church in America (PCA).[16]

The Sartelle Years (1977–2005)

The failure of IPC's founders to disclose the church's constitutional stipulation that "nations, peoples and groups" should remain separated and their public descriptions of the new congregation as a "Bible church, a prayer church and a mission church" reveal a conscious decision that their commitment to segregation would be obscured by a myth of origins that portrayed them as zealots for "old-time religion." As the church grew and added younger members, this myth would preclude any serious encounter with the church's past.

A few months after its founding, IPC began holding services at a newly purchased property on Walnut Grove Road two miles from SPC, and by the end of 1965 membership at the church had grown to over four hundred. But in its first decade IPC was regarded as an "older" church with little appeal for youth or young families. That reputation would begin to change in 1977 when IPC hired senior minister John Sartelle, a former PCUS pastor with a deep voice and a deeper Southern drawl. Under Sartelle the church began to attract young couples and families, and hundreds of them came into the church during the 1980s.

Most of these new members knew little or nothing about the circumstances of IPC's founding and Sartelle did not draw undue attention to the church's past. One member recalls him referring obliquely to the church's origins with the explanation that "the men who started IPC were great men; they just had a blind spot. That blind spot was racism." While the church's constitutional commitment to segregation remained in force, it was not an issue during Sartelle's first decade at IPC. In 1985 the congregation voted to rescind the relevant article in its constitution, although this was largely out of concern that, given the Supreme Court's recent decision in *Bob Jones University v. United States* (1983), the church's tax-exempt status might be revoked by the Internal Revenue Service.[17]

Sartelle himself seems to have been less concerned with IPC's policies in the past than with its mission in the present. Under his leadership, the church expanded its ministry in Memphis across racial and socioeconomic lines and became a consistent supporter of urban churches and ministries. Although IPC did not actively pursue racial diversity under Sartelle, it did move steadily away from the attitudes that characterized it at its founding and even gained a few African American members. By the end of Sartelle's tenure in 2005, as the founders' influence waned, the church had attracted a new generation of leaders for whom engagement with the city and racial reconciliation were high priorities.[18]

The New Independents

John Wilfong was drawn to IPC in the early 1980s while a basketball player at Memphis State (as a member of the 1985 Final Four team, he is something of a local celebrity). Wilfong, who had grown up Baptist, began attending a Bible study led by John Sartelle because it was "a place to meet a lot of other college students." Highlighting Reformed themes such as the sovereignty of God, the study began to alter Wilfong's theology. He eventually joined IPC, where today he serves as a deacon.[19]

It is perhaps surprising that someone who spent his early years interacting with African Americans as part of Memphis's basketball culture would end up at IPC. But Wilfong has discovered opportunities at the church to nurture his connection with the black community. One is its support for Streets Ministries, an inner-city outreach organization where Wilfong is a board member. Streets provides underprivileged youth in the 38126 ZIP code with "a safe haven . . . after school, a staff who loves the students unconditionally, and programming to meet the specific needs of each student." Streets offers tutoring, college prep training, recreation, camping, and college tours, along with outreach meetings and Bible studies.[20]

Another medium for ministry to African Americans at IPC is the church's AAU basketball program. "If you spent a week at IPC and you saw the number of people who came through there who use the facilities, you would see a very diverse group of people," Wilfong says. As for the church's unsavory racial past, Wilfong acknowledges that "it's hard to be a church for the city and leave this issue under the rug." But he takes a providential view of the racial controversy that led to IPC's formation. Referring to the story of Joseph in the Bible, Wilfong believes that what human beings intended for evil, God intended for good. "If you think about IPC and the impact this church has had," he says, "an incredible amount of work has been done because God divided a church."[21]

Ken Bennett grew up during the 1960s in one of Memphis's few integrated neighborhoods. As a student at Memphis State, he volunteered with Young Life in a predominantly black high school where, he says, "I gained a heart for African Americans in Memphis." After college, Bennett and his wife became active at St. Patrick's Catholic Church, an urban parish on the edge of the Vance Avenue neighborhood. As Bennett became familiar with the problems of poverty and crime that were endemic to the 38126 ZIP code, "God put the neighborhood on my heart." Since he founded Streets Ministries in 1987, Bennett has ministered full time in this section of urban Memphis where nearly three quarters of residents live below the poverty line and median household income is just above $10,000.[22]

In the early 1990s, the Bennetts were searching for a new church home. Impressed with Streets board members who were active at IPC, they visited the church and were pleasantly surprised by what they found. Although Bennett was aware of the racial controversy that had given birth to the church, he "didn't feel or hear any of that." In fact, he says, "I've never heard racist remarks at IPC, [although] whenever you talk to people who have never had real-life experiences [with blacks] they are prone to make ignorant statements." Bennett stresses that people at IPC have welcomed his message that "the gospel is for everybody and it's okay to feed and clothe people." The church remains supportive of Streets, both financially and with volunteers and other resources.[23]

The Assistant Director of Streets Ministries is Delvin Lane, who grew up in one of the housing projects served by the agency. As a teenager, Lane was an honors student at local Booker T. Washington High School, as well as a drug dealer and gang member "living the street life." In 2000, he "came to know Christ" and shortly afterward joined the staff at Streets. Like Bennett, Lane was impressed by Streets volunteers from IPC and was drawn to the church himself. He knew about its blemished racial history and was aware that the church's only African Americans were in service positions. Nevertheless, he began to develop friendships at IPC and eventually joined with his family.[24]

The Lanes were active at IPC for seven years; in the end, however, the "cultural and economic divide" became too large. It was especially difficult for his kids, Lane says, who were the church's only black youth. But Lane's years at IPC left an impact on him as well as the church. Streets kids now participate in an annual ski trip with IPC's youth group, who in turn visit the Streets facility from time to time. Such small reconciliation projects, Lane says, help allay the fear many whites have in entering black inner-city neighborhoods. It's a fear residents of the Vance Avenue neighborhood witness regularly. "When you got somebody driving from East Memphis to the FedEx Forum for an event, you see 'em at a red light and it's the funniest thing. They are terrified. They think we're like aliens who are gonna jump out and suck their brains out or something. But until you spend some time talking to a person, you're gonna feel like that."[25]

Lane is aware of the disparate ways reconciliation is typically viewed by black and white evangelicals. In his view, many public-housing residents suffer from a generational curse rooted in a system that both aids and enslaves them. When facing such challenges, he says, an exclusive focus on transforming hearts represents a "shallow way of thinking." As he puts it, "there's a much bigger task than soul winning." But Lane believes white evangelicals can understand the systemic nature of black poverty if they make the effort. He likens the experience of some white Streets volunteers he has known to Paul's blinding encounter on the Damascus Road. They come hoping to help kids who are "less fortunate," but leave with an understanding of how these kids' fortunes have been affected by the system in which they've grown up.[26]

Rob Thompson represents the younger professional class that has swelled IPC's membership in recent years. In 2002, after selling an Internet company he started while still in college, Thompson went to work raising money for Streets Ministries at half his previous salary. Despite reservations about the job and a vague commitment to the poor, Thompson says he was profoundly changed while working for Streets. The clarifying moment came as he waited in the drive-through lane of a local fast-food restaurant. Sitting next to him in his car was an HIV-positive prostitute named Doris for whom he was buying a hamburger. Embarrassed by the looks he was getting, Thompson had an epiphany concerning his own unworthiness: "This is what Jesus does for me every day," he realized. In 2009, Thompson left Streets to direct the Memphis Center for Urban Theological Studies.[27]

Unlike many of IPC's younger members, Thompson was quite aware of IPC's racial stigma when he started attending the church in 2003. In fact, he says, in meetings with black community leaders he sometimes hopes he will not be asked where he attends church. But as Thompson's commitment to urban ministry in Memphis has grown, so has his allegiance to IPC and his concern for addressing its past. When Thompson asked an older African American man who had become a mentor whether IPC could be part of the redemptive story in Memphis, he was encouraged to ask himself three questions: "Is it my fight? Can it be won? And can I bear the scars?"[28]

Thompson answered yes to all three questions. But his influence at the church is limited by youth and the fact that he is not a member of the session. So he pursues grass-roots efforts to mobilize IPC members who want to seek the peace and prosperity of the city by "do[ing] something with their faith." For some, this means a Christmastime distribution of food baskets; for others, it involves cooking pre-game meals for the Booker T. Washington High School football team. Indeed, the church offers many avenues of service to the city. IPC has adopted an elementary school through the Memphis City Schools Adopt-a-School Program and supports fifteen local health, education, housing, and youth-training programs, most of which address the needs of the urban poor.[29]

The Past Reasserts Itself

When John Sartelle left IPC in 2005 after twenty-nine years in the pulpit, the church was considerably larger, younger, and more outward-looking than when he arrived in 1977. During Sartelle's tenure, IPC had quietly rescinded its segregation policy, gained its first black members, and become a reliable source of support for Streets and other urban ministry agencies. Most important, it had begun to attract a generation of evangelicals for whom social justice and racial reconciliation were gospel concerns. What the church had not done, however, was honestly confront its segregationist past or challenge the myth that its departure from the PCUS was a purely spiritual quest to recover "old-time religion." Forty years after the church's founding it was widely believed that the ghost of racism had been laid to rest at IPC. This belief would be put to the test by the church's new senior minister.

In 2005 IPC was faced with replacing an iconic figure who had led the congregation for nearly three of its four decades of existence. It turned to John Hardie, a Yale graduate who was pursuing a doctorate at Princeton Theological Seminary. Some IPC members were concerned by Hardie's youth and inexperience, but his academic prowess and his vision for the church were impressive. His Southern background did not hurt either. Within a few months of his arrival at IPC in August 2006, however, Hardie faced growing dissatisfaction within the congregation. Members of the pastoral staff were resistant to being supervised by a younger man, while church officers found Hardie brash and confrontational. These problems might have been dismissed as the sort that accompany any church's adjustment to a new pastor. But then Hardie touched a raw nerve in the congregation.

On November 26, 2006, in the midst of a series of sermons on marriage, Hardie referred to the foreign wives who "turned [Solomon's] heart after other gods" (I Kings 11:4) as a way of underscoring the importance of choosing a spouse "with a heart for the Lord." "Parenthetically," Hardie said, "the Bible does not speak against interracial marriage, despite how Christians have misused [it] in the past." The parenthesis widened as Hardie related an incident from his days as a campus pastor at Auburn University. An African American football player of Hardie's acquaintance shared with another minister that he was dating a white woman. Asked what he thought of the relationship, the minister responded that, while the Bible didn't speak to the matter, he believed the young man would have problems "in this culture." "My dear friend William," Hardie said, "never trusted that man again." Hardie then gave his congregation this solemn charge:

> If there is any lingering vestiges of racism in our hearts regarding inter-
> racial marriage, please, please, I beg of you, repent of that sin. . . .
> Beloved, every person who walks in this church, every person who is
> not Caucasian needs to hear from us that there is no longer any vestiges
> of racism, particularly when it comes to interracial marriage, which, as
> one person challenged me when I was on a college campus back in the
> 1980s, this is the true test of racism.[30]

Hardie's conclusion was unambiguous: "If your son or daughter brings home a person who loves Christ, don't hesitate about the color of their skin."[31]

As a Southerner, a student of Southern Presbyterian history, and the senior minister of a church born in a dispute over segregation, Hardie undoubtedly knew that his words had the potential to offend some older members who strug-gled to accept the multiracial reality of twenty-first-century America. But he could not have known that making attitudes toward intermarriage a litmus test for white racism would shake the church to its core. At a session meeting the day following the offending sermon, IPC's elders relayed "a number of concerns" about comments Hardie had made from the pulpit. Realizing that some mem-bers were not ready for a direct attack on deeply rooted cultural mores, Hardie decided to clarify his views at the church's regular Wednesday-night gathering in what he billed as "a family conversation about race."[32]

Hardie began this "conversation" by conceding that for a young pastor to raise such a difficult issue during his fourth month on the job was "not a particularly wise strategy in a church like this." Then, after quoting from portions of the ser-mon some had found offensive, Hardie restated his argument:

> What I wish I would have said . . . is "You know what? I have three chil-
> dren. When I dream about their marriage, I don't think about them
> marrying a black man or a black woman." In fact, let me be perfectly
> honest with you. If my daughter brought home a black guy. Let me put
> it this way. When I see a black man with a white woman—this is sin, in
> my opinion, I believe I'm in sin when I do this—but I immediately say,

"What's wrong with that woman?" Or if I see a black woman with a
white man, I immediately say "What's wrong with that man?" Now I
think that's sin, beloved, because what I've done is I've made a judgment
based on skin pigmentation.... That is racism, in my view.[33]

Hardie reassured his audience that he was not "pointing the finger" at them; nevertheless, he said, he would not "apologize for God's Word."

Indeed, Hardie would never recant his principled opposition to what he
regarded as unbiblical sentiments. But he would withdraw the implication that
anyone who resisted intermarriage within his or her own family was racist. He
would also try in a number of ways to restore trust with alienated parishioners—
by reiterating his own struggles with racism, by detailing his credentials as a Southerner and a descendant of slaveholders, by decrying the racism of Northerner
"liberals," by acknowledging the "deep wounds" sustained by white Memphians in
the civil rights movement, by pointing out corruption among the city's black
leaders, and by reminding his auditors that Martin Luther King had been attacked
by a deranged black woman. But none of these efforts to identify with church
members' lingering racial resentments diffused the controversy.[34]

What was it in Hardie's homiletic reference to interracial marriage that church
members found distasteful? There is no evidence of direct opposition to Hardie's claim that the Bible does not oppose interracial pairing. In fact, the only
public comments by church members in the wake of the offending sermon concerned its timing. During IPC's "family conversation on race," for instance, an
audience member described the senior minister's decision to broach the issue as
"very, very bad timing." He explained: "If you'd waited till you had been here two
or three years and eased into that, I think it would have been better accepted."
However, the rest of the man's comment indicated that Hardie's timing was not
the only issue. As far as intermarriage goes, the man said,

thank God I don't have that to worry about at this time 'cause all mine are
up and married, but I do have my grandchildren to worry about, and
granddaddy would take a very dim view to that. And granddaddy would
talk to them about it. I've got to say that because I am a Christian . . .
[even though] I'm not a learned Bible man like you are. I've been amazed
at the way you quote the Bible and that's fine. But I did object to that very
much and I just didn't think it was—maybe it wasn't the right time.[35]

It is not immediately apparent what Hardie's timing had to do with this man's
"very dim view" of the prospect of intermarriage within his family. Reading
between the lines, the basic problem appears to have been mistrust. After nearly
thirty years under John Sartelle, IPC members had grown accustomed to a

senior minister who could preach a gospel of reconciliation without drawing unnecessary attention to the racist "blind spot" of some older members. Could
Rev. Hardie treat the church's unique history with equal care? Or would he, in
his youthful zeal to expose sin wherever it might be found, disturb the tacit
agreement the congregation had with its former pastor to focus on the church's
aspirations rather than its origins?

Hardie would have another opportunity to regain members' trust when he
appeared in an adult Sunday School class two weeks following his initial misstep.
But by this time the controversy was burning out of control and one of those adding fuel to the fire was Tom Elkin, adjunct pastor at IPC and regular teacher of the
Primetimers class to which Hardie had been invited. In a lesson the previous week
titled "Is Inter-Racial Marriage Right or Wrong?" Elkin had misleadingly implied
that Hardie was not only defending interracial marriage from those who would
oppose it on grounds of prejudice, but encouraging the practice as well. In Elkin's
view, IPC's senior minister had assessed a practice on which the Bible is silent and
drawn the normative conclusion that Christians were obligated to support it.[36]

Among the problems with this view of racial intermarriage, Elkin argued, was
that it appeared to condemn Southern Presbyterians' spiritual ancestors. For if we
regard one's attitude toward interracial marriage as a way to gauge the soundness of
that person's faith, Elkin reasoned, we implicitly denounce Southern Presbyterian
"worthies" such as Robert L. Dabney and James Henley Thornwell, whose views on
the subject were quite clear. Elkin defended these nineteenth-century divines by
suggesting that their acceptance of slavery was based not so much in personal racism
as in the realization that we are all "slaves to sin." Invoking the sort of commonsense
argument favored by an earlier generation of segregationists, Elkin noted that "all
creatures prefer their own kind . . . even the animals on the Ark entered two by two."[37]

When Hardie addressed the Primetimers class a week later, he seemed to sense
this might be his last opportunity to win over members of the congregation whom
he had alienated. He tried to clarify his position by focusing on the question that
had become the crux of the controversy. "If you're sitting there wondering, 'John,
do you think I'm a racist if I don't want my daughter or granddaughter to get married to a black man?' No, I don't think you're a racist because of that." Opposition
to interracial marriage would not be racist, Hardie emphasized, unless that opposition was based solely on skin color. "I suspect some of you are saying, 'I don't
want this for my son or daughter,'" Hardie said. "I'm saying to you, 'If you're uncomfortable with it, I understand, it does not mean you're a racist. . . . If you can
come up with a way to be opposed in principle to interracial marriage that does
not rest on the color of a person's skin, then have at it."[38]

Desperate to restore credibility with church members who felt that their preference for endogamy was being condemned, Hardie detailed some of his own
negative experiences with African Americans growing up in the integrated

South. He acknowledged harboring prejudice in his own heart, said that he knew from experience how difficult it could be to coexist with blacks, and reiterated that he was not pointing fingers. Yet despite these attempts to convince his auditors that he was one of them, he would not step back from his "settled conviction" that racism is sinful and that for whites the litmus test of racial equality is one's attitude toward interracial marriage.[39]

Hardie's final recorded comments on the matter were, "I really want us to move on from this. How do we move on?" Many church members and officers, however, could not move on. By May 2007 Hardie had resigned as IPC's pastor under pressure from the church's session. Members were divided and confused as a letter purporting to reveal "the truth surrounding Rev. John Hardie's resignation" circulated within the congregation. Acknowledging that Hardie had "unintentionally brought a firestorm of controversy" upon himself by making a "Scriptural stand on the issue of interracial marriage," the letter's author, church member Charles Elliott, alleged that the ensuing criticism by members, deacons, and elders had exposed "the sin of racism in our church."[40]

Elliott conceded that many factors—including an "abrupt and confrontational" style and difficult relations with members of the church staff—had contributed to a rocky start to Hardie's ministry. Yet he tried to separate matters of style from what he regarded as the substantive issue: "While the final reason for John Hardie's resignation was not entirely about the controversy over interracial marriage, one would be naïve or dishonest if he believes that this was not the spark that started the fire. If Independent does not confess and repent of her long-closeted sin of racism, she will never progress in sanctification to become the beautiful bride of Christ she is called to be." As remedies for this situation, Elliott suggested that the entire session and diaconate resign and, in an echo of the crisis at SPC forty years earlier, that IPC adopt a rotating system for elders and deacons.[41]

However one interprets John Hardie's departure from IPC in 2007, there is no question that his decision to invoke interracial marriage as an acid test for white racism was a fateful turn in his brief tenure at the church. It appears that some at the church experienced a powerful emotional reaction to the prospect of interracial dating and marriage, not unlike that felt by members of the SPC session forty years earlier when that body became concerned that the PCUS was promoting "mixed dancing between whites and negroes."

Finally Facing the Past

As younger members swelled the church rolls during the 1970s and 1980s, IPC's leaders had little incentive to revisit the founders' segregationist mindset, which could be dismissed as the sort of blind spot every generation discovers in its ancestors. Particularly after IPC's "compatibility" policy was rescinded in 1985, there was little motivation to make the founders' racial convictions an issue. But the Hardie affair suggested that, even absent a formal endorsement of segregation, the ghost of racism continued to haunt IPC.

However one judged John Hardie's pastoral skills, the controversy that resulted from his decision to defend interracial marriage from the IPC pulpit was a sobering reminder that not all church members shared the moderate racial views taken for granted by white evangelicals of Hardie's generation. For the vast majority of IPC's members, regardless of age, the issue of intermarriage was entirely theoretical. Yet Hardie had insisted on the basis of sound biblical exegesis that categorical opposition to the practice was most likely a sign of sinful prejudice. Many of IPC's lay leaders agreed. For them, it was clear that what Charles Elliott had called the church's "long-closeted sin of racism" had to be brought out into the open. History had to be met head on, perhaps in the spirit of confession and repentance recommended in Elliott's letter.

In replacing Hardie, IPC decided to stay within the church family, promoting Richie Sessions from assistant to senior minister in 2009. But what may have seemed to outsiders like a "safe hire" proved to be the impetus for addressing the issues exposed in John Hardie's brief pastorate. Sessions and a group of respected elders in their forties and fifties concluded that the time had come for church members to engage in serious institutional self-examination. They were motivated not only by evidence that racial prejudice still lurked in the shadows at IPC, but by a recognition that the diminishing clout of the church's founding families created the possibility for meaningful action. And one should not underestimate the impetus provided by awareness that the church's history was going to be the subject of a book.

The self-examination process became official when an ad hoc committee of the IPC session was commissioned to study and make recommendations regarding any actions necessary to address the church's history and to conform to the racial policies of the PCA, which IPC had joined in 2000. The committee met privately for several months before reporting at a regular meeting of the session in October 2010. In preparation for a called session meeting the following week, the committee asked elders to study two documents—a historical presentation dealing with the SPC controversy and the founding of IPC, and excerpts from the PCA's pastoral letter on "The Gospel and Race."[42]

The called session meeting at which these documents were discussed went about as members of the ad hoc committee had expected. Some who were unfamiliar with the controversy from which IPC had been born expressed surprise and shock. Others wondered whether, after forty-five years, it was necessary or even appropriate for the church to make a formal expression of repentance. But the committee had made a case for action based on two indisputable facts. First, the church's founders had misused Scripture to ensure that racial homogeneity would be maintained in the new congregation. Second, the common perception that IPC's founders had fled the PCUS to preserve "old-time religion" masked the unpleasant fact that, whatever their spiritual motivations, their segregationist convictions made it impossible for them to remain within that denomination.

Following its report to the IPC session, the ad hoc committee was directed to bring a proposal to the body's December meeting. The committee did so in a report recommending that the IPC session (1) present the congregation with historical information about IPC's origins and inform it of its endorsement of the PCA's pastoral letter on "The Gospel and Race"; (2) "set aside a season of prayer and study of the Scriptures regarding corporate and individual confession of sin"; (3) "set aside specific time for public confession and repentance regarding the corporate and individual sin of racism"; and (4) "become more intentional and proactive as a church with ministry opportunities for the congregation to serve the city of Memphis as redemptive, Gospel-driven agents seeking the peace and prosperity of *all* of Memphis." These recommendations were unanimously adopted by IPC's session at its meeting on December 14, 2010.

In the fall of 2011, IPC's leadership was busy planning the next step in the church's process of institutional self-examination. Senior Pastor Richie Sessions and Elder Sam Graham wrote a letter to the congregation, informing members that the church's session had been "prayerfully considering how the gospel of Jesus impacts our witness in the city of Memphis." They described what to expect in the coming months:

> First, the gospel is about repentance. IPC has a sinful past in regards to race and if we believe the gospel, we must confess and repent of specific sin if we are to experience true forgiveness. The gospel is also about redemption and we believe that God has redeemed us through Christ. Therefore, we are not to hide any sin, especially our corporate racism. Finally, the gospel is about restoration, and IPC wants to seek the shalom of Memphis and be an agent of restoration and hope to bring glory to Jesus.[43]

Corporate confession and repentance began in earnest at IPC in May 2012 when Sessions began a series of sermons on the sin of racism.

The hope of Sessions and other church leaders is that, as a central element in the church's mission, racial reconciliation will become part of "a continual process of repentance, redemption and restoration that will bring about new relationships between IPC and the increasingly diverse community of Memphis."[44]

An End to Independence

Sessions sums up his vision for IPC's future with a backward glance at the church's founding: "We don't want to be 'independent' anymore," he says. In point of fact, however, IPC officially gave up its independence when it joined the PCA in 2000. Some IPC members have come to regard the Hardie interlude, painful as it was, as a providential opportunity for the church to face its history. It may also have been providential that the controversy over intermarriage at IPC occurred *after* the church had joined the PCA, and *after* the PCA had begun to scrutinize its own history for evidence of racism. This meant, ironically, that IPC's process of corporate self-scrutiny would be guided and measured by just the sort of denominational commitments to racial reconciliation that the church's founders had eschewed in 1965.

The PCA was in many ways a successor to the PCUS faction that had rallied around *The Presbyterian Journal* since the 1940s. Thus it is not surprising that when dissident PCUS groups banded together in 1971 to form the Steering Committee for a Continuing Presbyterian Church, Faithful to the Scriptures and the Reformed Faith, the meeting took place at an annual meeting of *Journal* supporters. Along with opposition to theological liberalism and dissent from "non-biblical" positions on women's ordination, divorce, and abortion, the PCA was heir to the pro-segregation arguments that had routinely appeared in the *Journal* between 1942 and 1966.[45]

The PCA's center of gravity shifted out of the Deep South in 1982 when it merged with the Reformed Presbyterian Church, Evangelical Synod. But the denomination's efforts to address racism in its history did not begin in earnest until two decades later. In 2002, the PCA adopted a controversial overture from Nashville Presbytery that encouraged "racial reconciliation, the establishment of urban and minority congregations, and the enhancement of existing ministries of mercy in our cities, among the poor, and across all social, racial, and economic boundaries." When reaction to this statement exposed "some divisions" within the denomination, the PCA General Assembly commissioned a pastoral letter on race.[46]

The twenty-page pastoral letter titled "The Gospel and Race," adopted by the PCA General Assembly in 2004, identifies racism as a sin requiring "repentance . . . both individually and corporately." The letter represents a significant resource for any church engaged in institutional self-examination. As it relates to IPC's history, two aspects of the "The Gospel and Race" are particularly relevant. First, according to the letter, the "natural affinities" that draw church members together become theologically problematic when "the desire to associate only with like persons becomes justification for the active or passive exclusion or segregation of persons from different backgrounds or for the devaluing of their contribution to the body of Christ." Second, the letter makes clear that God calls Christians to "repent of the sins of [their] history," and finds support for this task in biblical references to "sins of the fathers."[47]

Joining a denomination was not an obvious step for a church as zealously committed to independence as was IPC at its founding. But as it seeks theological leverage for mounting an honest critique of its history, IPC is benefiting from its membership in an ecclesiastical body that has put racism on the theological agenda. With "The Gospel and Race" as background, a new generation of PCA members and pastors, including African Americans who came into the denomination in the 1990s, is beginning to investigate how the condemnation of theological "liberalism" that united the PCA's founders in 1973 often concealed a desire to maintain the South's racial status quo.[48]

Recently, the PCA has gone so far as to identify and purge openly racist churchmen. But there is no known precedent for a PCA congregation engaging in the kind of thoroughgoing self-critique undertaken by IPC in 2010. Thus, its dedication to corporate self-examination can make it a guide for other churches in its denomination and beyond. Particularly as it explores how racist sentiments can be shrouded by a veil of piety, IPC can become a model for congregations that trace their origins to an era when "spirituality," social conservatism, and white racism were intricately linked.[49]

Epilogue

Nearly five decades after the kneel-ins at SPC ended, their complex legacy continues to be felt in Memphis and beyond. Elinor Perkins "Perky" Daniel, the eleven-year-old girl who watched the kneel-ins unfold from the safety of the SPC chapel, is now an ordained minister in the Presbyterian Church (USA). When she assumed the pastorate of Atlanta's Morningside Presbyterian Church during the 1980s, Daniel discovered that no fewer than *five* of her parishioners had been touched by the SPC kneel-ins twenty-five years earlier. Bob Wells and RoseMary Hoye Wells, former Southwestern students, had been among the protesters; John and Pat Clark had been young members at SPC; and Phil Esty had been the church's youth minister.

In 2001, the Wellses followed Daniel to Genesis Community, a new church development meeting temporarily in her home. The three talked often about how their lives had first intersected in 1964 when Bob and RoseMary were young adults expressing their faith through nonviolent protest and Perky was a preteen asking her parents what the protests meant. In 2003, as the three participated with other members of Genesis Community in an integrated worship service at Ebenezer Baptist Church, the home congregation of Martin Luther King, Jr., they could only marvel that their paths had brought them together at the mother church of the civil rights movement.[1]

Pastors, protestors, and church members are not the only ones whose subsequent lives were shaped by the Memphis kneel-ins. Elinor Kelley Grusin, the reporter who covered events at the church for *The Commercial Appeal* in Memphis, is among those who were permanently affected by the controversy. Grusin had grown up on a farm in West Tennessee cotton country before entering Memphis State University in 1958. One of her first big-city lessons about religion and diversity involved a Jewish roommate from the Bronx. Kelley naively invited the girl to join her sorority, only to learn that membership was limited to "Christian girls."[2]

After graduating from Memphis State with a degree in journalism in 1962, Grusin was hired as Religion Editor for *The Commercial Appeal*, where she was the newspaper's only female journalist not assigned to cover society, fashion, or food. "I began interviewing people from all points of view and really getting into the civil rights movement," she says. Grusin's own church background—she grew up attending a Cumberland Presbyterian congregation with fewer than fifty members—hardly prepared her for covering the religious controversies of the early 1960s. Her first big assignment was the 1962 meeting of the Southern Baptist Convention, where debates over integration polarized SBC "messengers." She would later break a national story of ballot-stuffing by supporters of a pro-segregation minister who was elected SBC president. In 1964, as she covered the PCUS General Assembly in Montreat, North Carolina, Kelley would watch as racial controversy convulsed another Protestant denomination.[3]

Because Memphis would become the epicenter of the PCUS segregation crisis of 1964–65, Grusin would experience it at close hand. Her natural sympathies were with the students attempting to worship at SPC. They were there, she observed, "to challenge people to live their religion" while they were received with "just plain meanness," an attitude she encountered personally. "I was met at the door by a burly usher, who blocked my entrance and virtually shoved me out the door," she says. "I know people and institutions change; however, I can never drive by that church without recalling that day to some degree."[4]

The kneel-in controversy at SPC also taught Grusin something about the complexities of human nature. She rode to the 1964 PCUS General Assembly in North Carolina with SPC Elder John Cleghorn, who would spend the meeting defending the church from attacks on its segregation policy. "He was a very likable and highly intelligent individual," she recalls—a fact she found hard to square with his openly segregationist views. Cleghorn taught her that "people are complex and can have what you would consider very hateful views in one area but in other areas they can be good people." As we have seen, Cleghorn turned out to be even more complex than Grusin imagined, as he would dramatically switch sides before the kneel-in controversy at SPC concluded.[5]

In 1966 Kelley asked to be taken off the religion beat. "I was particularly jaded with some of the Christian denominations," she says, having concluded that they were primarily dedicated to sustaining themselves rather than to serving people. The same year Kelley married and converted to Judaism, a decision made easier by her experiences with much of Christendom in Memphis. After moving to five states, first as an Air Force wife and later to earn master and doctorate degrees, Kelley returned to Memphis for good in 1987 with a Ph.D. in journalism. She taught first at Ole Miss and later at the University of Memphis, from which she retired in 2008. In 2007, Elinor Kelley Grusin was honored by the Scripps Howard Foundation as national Journalism Teacher of the Year.[6]

As we have seen, SPC's plan for refurbishing Clayborn Temple as a symbol of interracial and interdenominational cooperation did not materialize. But the church has not abandoned its quest to establish an outpost of racially unified Christianity in downtown Memphis. That quest, in fact, has brought representatives of SPC together with a church planter whose vision for urban ministry was molded by the Memphis kneel-in crisis.

Richard Rieves grew up at Independent Presbyterian Church and, after studying for the ministry with IPC's support, went to work as a church planter for the Presbyterian Church in America. Rieves founded successful churches in Mississippi and Colorado, but his dream was to return to Memphis. Having grown up at a suburban Memphis church founded on racial exclusivity, Rieves felt called to develop an urban interracial congregation in his hometown. While in Memphis for the PCA General Assembly in 2007, he was approached by a group of laymen from SPC who wanted to establish an intentionally multiracial congregation in the downtown area.

When they heard Rieves describe his vision for a "bridge church between the poorest of the poor and the richest of the rich; a church where there truly is no Jew or Greek, no slave or free . . . a group of people 'from the 'hood and from the bluff' really doing life together," the SPC donors knew they had found their man. The following year Rieves returned to Memphis as founding minister of Downtown Presbyterian Church, which held its first worship service in October 2010. As a product of IPC, Rieves views his new venture in ministry as "part of the repentance" for that church's past. "I really feel a burden to see the gospel change Memphis and the church," he says, "because I think the church still is the last institution holding on, willingly or unwillingly, to the past."

Memphis's Downtown Presbyterian Church has brought together a child of IPC, a group of outreach-minded SPC members, and a common quest to establish a beacon of interracial Christianity in downtown Memphis. The warehouse on Tennessee Street that is the church's temporary home lacks the prominence or emblematic power of Clayborn Temple. But given that Downtown Presbyterian owes its existence to suburban Christians who broke fellowship over how racially exclusive the gospel could be, it is a potent symbol of reconciliation. It is fitting that the church's 2012 Easter service was held on the lawn of the National Civil Rights Museum, which occupies the Lorraine Motel, site of Martin Luther King, Jr.'s assassination.[7]

As we have seen, attitudes of regret and repentance are common at the Memphis churches that systematically excluded African Americans nearly fifty years ago. But what of those who were excluded? Some have made their peace, while others continue to struggle with the legacy of the past. Vasco Smith, the black Presbyterian elder who was repeatedly turned away from SPC in 1964, is among those whose wounds were salved by the church's attempts to make amends. After several meetings with Rev. Sandy Willson, in fact, Smith developed a real fondness for SPC's senior minister, whom he came to view as "one of the nicest guys I've ever met." As Smith aged and was able to attend his own church less frequently, he became a fan of SPC's television broadcasts. "Some Sunday mornings when I'm home I listen to Sandy's service. I like him. I like what he has to say in his sermons," Smith said in 2004.[8]

Before he died in 2009, Smith seemed to have made peace with the church that had repeatedly barred him forty-five years earlier. But not all who stood outside SPC hoping to be admitted have been able to do so, and a few cannot pass by the church without feeling physical revulsion. Vivian Carter Dillihunt was not sure what her reaction would be when she entered SPC for the first time in 2010. She had driven past the church "a thousand times" since 1964, but when she attended a banquet there celebrating an urban ministry led by members of her extended family, Dillihunt experienced surprisingly strong feelings.

Realizing that she was seated with one of SPC's pastors, Dillihunt decided to share the details of her kneel-in experience. The pastor listened very attentively, Dillihunt says, and offered her "a very heartfelt apology for what had happened." But when she is asked if the apology brought reconciliation, Dillihunt pauses to reflect. "There's no reconciling what they did," she says finally:

> It's like somebody spitting in your face on purpose and then saying twenty years later, "I'm sorry." You still remember it; it affected you. The Christian thing to do, of course, is to forgive and forget . . . but memories tend to evoke those same feelings later on. We were so young and impressionable, and those were supposed to have been the best years of our lives. Those were not good years for me.[9]

Sadly, students in the "biracial groups" that gathered in front of SPC on Sunday mornings in 1964 made few enduring connections. In this regard, Hortense Spillers' experience was typical. When interviewed forty years after the Memphis kneel-ins, Spillers had difficulty remembering the names of the white students with whom she gathered at the church. She vaguely recalled a young man named Howard. "What did you say his last name was?" she asked the interviewer.

The name, of course, was Romaine. Spillers' path briefly crossed that of Howard Romaine in the spring of 1964—on the sidewalk in front of SPC and in a booth at the Normal Tea Room, where the two were arrested while attempting to integrate the restaurant. A short time after these events, Spillers began graduate school at Memphis State and Romaine left Memphis to study philosophy at the University of Virginia. Spillers eventually became a scholar of African American literature and culture, spending the bulk of her career at Cornell University. Romaine ended up in Atlanta, where he practiced law.

In 2004, at a reunion of Southwestern student activists, Romaine and others searched their memories for the names of those who had stood alongside them outside SPC four decades earlier. The name "Hortense Spillers" rang a bell for him. Romaine found a promising e-mail address and wrote to ask the owner if she were the Hortense Spillers who was protesting segregation at SPC in 1964. She replied that she was, and the two were briefly reacquainted.

A few years later, after moving his law practice to Nashville, Romaine heard that Vanderbilt had hired a group of prominent African American scholars, Spillers among them. The two renewed their acquaintance once again, and this time fell in love. Forty years after their first meeting on the front lines of the non-violent revolution, Spillers and Romaine were together again, bound by affection as well as conviction. A year after their romance began, the two celebrated the anniversary, appropriately, at a Memphis restaurant. Seated with a local scholar who had expressed an interest in their stories, the three made an interesting dinner party: a white lawyer from North Louisiana; a black intellectual from South Memphis; and a curious guest in awe of the way seemingly small decisions shape the trajectories of our lives.

NOTES

Introduction

1. Marshall Frady, "God and Man in the South," *The Atlantic Monthly* (January, 1967): 37–42; 37.

2. After studying the kneel-ins at First Baptist Church in Atlanta during the spring and summer of 1963, Kip Kosek concludes: "That nobody has ever told the story of these events—at the largest Protestant church in the Southeast, in the city that served as the headquarters for the civil rights movement, during the movement's most important year—reveals how little we still know about the role of religion in the struggle for black freedom" (Joseph Kip Kosek, "Civil Rights and Religious Rights in the 1960s," paper delivered at Peace History Society Conference, Winthrop University, Rock Hill, South Carolina, October 30, 2009, 2, in possession of the author).

3. Taylor Branch, *Parting the Waters: America in the King Years, 1954–63* (New York: Simon and Schuster, 1989): 330. While Adam Fairclough's study of the SCLC highlights the role of black churches as sites of mass meetings, strategizing, and occasional violent assaults, the white church as a site of protest is not mentioned and the term "kneel-in" is not listed in the index (Adam Fairclough, *To Redeem the Soul of America: The Southern Christian Leadership Conference and Martin Luther King, Jr.* [Athens: University of Georgia Press, 2001]). The same is true of Clayborne Carson's study of SNCC, *In Struggle: SNCC and the Black Awakening of the 60s* (Harvard University Press, 1981).

4. See S. Jonathan Bass, *Blessed Are the Peacemakers: Martin Luther King Jr., Eight White Religious Leaders, and the "Letter from Birmingham Jail"* (Baton Rouge: Louisiana State University Press, 2001); and Charles Marsh, *God's Long Summer: Stories of Faith and Civil Rights* (Princeton: Princeton University Press, 1997).

5. The fullest description of the Memphis kneel-in campaign of 1964–65 appears in Ernest Trice Thompson, *Presbyterians in the South*, 3 vols. (Richmond: John Knox Press, 1973): 3:549–550, although Thompson implies that the church refused to admit only "Negro worshippers." In Joel L. Alvis, Jr.'s *Race and Religion: Southern Presbyterians, 1946–1983* (Tuscaloosa: University of Alabama Press, 1994), it is called "the most dramatic confrontation by the [PCUS] General Assembly over segregated facilities" (101–102). Alvis, like Thompson, omits the part that students played in the conflict, an aspect of the story that is clarified by Laurie B. Green's *Battling the Plantation Mentality: Memphis and the Black Freedom Struggle* (Chapel Hill: University of North Carolina Press, 2007), which credits "the Intercollegiate NAACP, comprised of students from Southwestern, Memphis State, LeMoyne, and Owen colleges" (255). Taylor Branch refers to the crisis obliquely in *Pillar of Fire: America in the King Years, 1963–65* (New York: Simon and Schuster, 1998): 299–300.

6. Jane Dailey, "Sex, Segregation, and the Sacred after Brown," *Journal of American History* 91:1 (June 2004): 119–144; 144.

7. Jason Sokol, *There Goes My Everything: White Southerners in the Age of Civil Rights, 1945–75* (New York: Knopf, 2006): 309, 328.

8. The observation is often associated with Martin Luther King, Jr. However, in 1962 King credited it to Liston Pope and his 1958 book *The Kingdom beyond Caste.* Since Southern Presbyterian scholar Ben Lacy Rose made the same observation in 1957, placing it in quotation marks to indicate that the notion was already commonplace, it is evident that the saying's origins precede 1958 (Ben Lacy Rose, *Racial Segregation in the Church* [Richmond: Outlook Publishers, 1957]: 3).

9. Rose, *Racial Segregation in the Church*, 3. Cf. Bishop James A. Pike's statement from 1961 that "the church has become the last stronghold of an evil it was supposed to resist" (Bishop James A. Pike, "Bishop Calls Church Bars a 'Stronghold of Evil,'" *Baltimore Afro-American* [October 7, 1961]: 16).

10. Mrs. K. William Chandler, "Church History, 1965," 5 (Presbyterian Heritage Center, Montreat, North Carolina).

Chapter 1

1. See "Little Rock Minister Offers All Races Seats," *Atlanta Daily World* (October 3, 1958): 1; and "Druid Hills Presbyterian Church Opens Its Doors to Negroes Here," *Atlanta Daily World* (March 28, 1959): 4. Black churches sometimes announced that their doors were open to whites as well. (Victor Calverton, "Virginia Church Eyes Integration," *Atlanta Daily World* [June 20, 1956]: 4). Kneel-ins were reported in two Northern cities—Deerfield, Illinois, and Grosse Pointe, Michigan, both in 1960. See "Xmas Kneel-In Held in Ill.," *New York Amsterdam News* (December 31, 1960): 19 and "African Leader Stages Own 'Kneel-In,'" *Baltimore Afro-American* (October 1, 1960): 8. J. H. Jackson, president of the National Baptist Convention, vocally opposed kneel-ins, saying that "when you 'kneel-in' you kneel in judgment of a segregated church" ("Dr. Jackson Talks on Integration Battle," *Chicago Defender* [November 5, 1960]: 1). Another black leader to condemn nonviolent direct action was Rev. W. R. Fairley of Dallas. See "Integration in Reverse: Racial Battle in South Often Gets Confusing," *Norfolk Journal and Guide* (August 27, 1960): 23.

2. In September 1960, John F. Collins, a candidate for the Georgia General Assembly, brought suit in DeKalb County Superior Court against King for "promot[ing] the invasion of a congregation of persons lawfully assembled for divine service and in said invasion the persons so invading at the direction and orders of the defendant demand that they and each of them be seated by persons who have not requested close proximity to said trespassers, all to manifest disturbances of the worshipping of God according to the tenets of the congregation" (John Britton, "Candidate's Suit Aimed at Demonstrations Tossed Out," *Atlanta Daily World* [September 14, 1960]: 1). On NAACP discussions of church visits during the summer of 1960, see Lin Holloway, "Looking On in Norfolk," *Norfolk Journal and Guide* (August 13, 1960): A15. At a March 1960 meeting of the Episcopal Society for Cultural and Racial Unity, a voluntary association headquartered in Atlanta, ESCRU's board of directors adopted a statement predicting that before long, "churchmen will find themselves picketing their own institutions and sitting down in restricted pews." In April, the National Student Christian Federation reported that "in many places students have been refused not only the services of lunch counters but also have been refused admission to the services of the churches" ("The Protests of the Negro Students," *Information Service of the Bureau of Research and Survey of the National Council of Churches of Christ in the United States* 39:13 [June 25, 1960]: 1).

3. http://www.crmvet.org/docs/aa4hr.htm; *The Student Voice* records, in minutes of an August committee meeting, that "the discussion . . . was tabled Saturday in order to plan the initial 'kneel-ins' that Sunday with the Atlanta students. In addition, the committee drafted two press releases and a statement to be distributed at the churches" (*The Student Voice* 1:2 [August, 1960]: 7). Those present included Marion Barry and Bernard Lee. See also "'Kneel-Ins' Protest Atlanta Church Prejudice," *Pittsburgh Courier* (August 20, 1960): B7.

4. "The New Phase: 'Kneel-Ins', 4 Atlanta White Churches Admit Colored Students," *Norfolk Journal and Guide* (August 13, 1960): A1; "Stage 'Kneel-In' at 6 Churches," *Chicago Defender* (August 9, 1960): 1; "'Kneel-In' Project Started in Churches," *New York Amsterdam News* (August 13, 1960): 9.

5. "New Twist: 'Kneel-In' at 6 Ga. Churches," *Chicago Defender* (August 9, 1960): 1.

6. "Let Us Kneel-in Together!" *Christian Century* (August 24, 1960): 963–964; "Provocation, Reprisal Widen the Bitter Gulf," *Life* (May 17, 1963): 29; W. H. Von Dreele, "New England Sea Chanty," *National Review* (September 10, 1960): 177. According to John Algeo, the term "kneel-in" first appeared in the *Tuscaloosa News* on August 8, 1961 (*Fifty Years among the New Words: A Dictionary of Neologisms, 1941–1991* [Cambridge: Cambridge University Press, 1993], 156). In fact, however, the term was being used in black newspapers a year earlier. "Kneel-in" was also employed at times to describe incidents in which protestors knelt or prayed in public spaces such as city halls and courthouses. See, e.g., "Pray for Poor in Kneel-In," *Chicago Daily Defender* (August 7, 1962), 2; *Los Angeles Sentinel* (October 21, 1965): A1; and Frank Hunt, "May Ban Albany, Ga. 'Kneel-in' Protest," *Cleveland Call and Post* (August 4, 1962): 1A.

7. In 1960, King spoke of "courageous student sit-ins, kneel-ins and wade-ins" and promised that "our students will stand-in, sit-in and kneel-in until they awaken the conscience of the white man in the South and around the world." In 1963, he declared that "we will continue to sit in, to stand in, to wade in, and to kneel in." See "'The Negro and the American Dream,' Excerpt from Address at the Annual Freedom Mass Meeting of the North Carolina State Conference of Branches of the NAACP," in Clayborne Carson, ed., *The Papers of Martin Luther King, Jr., Volume V: Threshold of a New Decade, January 1959–December, 1960* [Berkeley: University of California Press, 2005], 510; Dr. Martin Luther King, Jr., "Sit In, Stand In, Wade In, Kneel In," *New York Amsterdam News* [May 25, 1963]: 10). According to *The New York Amsterdam News*, the top story of 1960 was "Sit-ins and Kneel-ins Upset Southern Segregationists" ("Top 10 Stories for 1960," *New York Amsterdam* News [December 31, 1960]:15).

8. "Kneel-Ins," *The Student Voice* 1:2 (August, 1960): 7.

9. James Laue, "Sociology, Sin and Snails," *The Student Voice* 1:2 (August, 1960): 3–4.

10. Cynthia Griggs Fleming, *Soon We Will Not Cry: The Liberation of Ruby Doris Smith Robinson* (Oxford: Rowan and Littlefield, 2000), 56.

11. Harry Brooks, "Presbyterian Assembly Asserts Church's Stand on Integration," *Pittsburgh Courier* (October 8, 1960): 6.

12. Laue, "Sociology, Sin and Snails," 3–4.

13. "Let Us Kneel-in Together!" 963; "Ga. Pastor Asks Open Door Policy," *Baltimore African American* (September 10, 1960): 3; Howard Romaine, "Student States Ideals of Group Making Current National News," *The Sou'wester* (April 24, 1964): 3; Robert J. Norrell, *Reaping the Whirlwind: The Civil Rights Movement in Tuskegee* (New York: Alfred A. Knopf, 1985), 175.

14. "Let Us Kneel-In Together!" 963; Richard B. Martin, "The Guide Post: 'White Only' Worship Place: Church or Club," *Norfolk Journal and Guide* (September 10, 1960): A11A; Norrell, *Reaping the Whirlwind*, 176.

15. "Kneel-Ins," 7. Joseph Kip Kocek, *Acts of Conscience: Christian Nonviolence and Modern American Democracy* (New York: Columbia University Press, 2009), 226, 229, 204.

16. The concepts "spectacle of embrace" and "spectacle of exclusion" have been adapted from Miroslav Wolf, *Exclusion and Embrace: A Theological Exploration of Identity, Otherness, and Reconciliation* (Nashville: Abingdon Press, 1996).

17. "'Kneel-Ins' Protest Atlanta Church Prejudice," B7; "Albany Police Arrest 3 During 'Kneel-In' Try," *Atlanta Daily World* (August 21, 1962): 1; Romaine, "Student States Ideals of Group Making Current National News," 3.

18. Charles Marsh, *God's Long Summer: Stories of Faith and Civil Rights* (Princeton: Princeton University Press, 1997), 129, 134.

19. "FAMU Students In 'Kneel-Ins'," *Chicago Defender* (March 6, 1961): 18.

20. Rodney L. Hurst Sr., *It Was Never about a Hot Dog and Coke: A Personal Account of the 1960 Sit-In Demonstrations in Jacksonville, FL and Ax Handle Saturday* (Livermore, CA: WingSpan Press, 2008), 106–107.

21. "Two Churches Bar Civil Rights Groups in Americus Drive," *New York Times* (August 2, 1965): 1, 15.

22. In Birmingham, kneel-ins originally planned for Palm Sunday were postponed with the thought that they would "be more effective" on Easter ("Alabama Church Kneel-In Protest Called Off," 4); "Easter in Birmingham: Some Church Bias Ends," *Chicago Defender* (April 15, 1963): 3; George Barner, "How Easter Came to Birmingham," *New York Amsterdam News* (April 20, 1963): 42.

23. "'We Have Done Things Which We Ought Not'," *Chicago Defender* (June 22, 1964): 4; "Let Us Kneel-In Together!" 963; "Ga. Pastor Asks Open Door Policy," 3.

24. On July 17, 1964 two Tuskegee Institute professors—one white and one black—entered the church sanctuary at Tuskegee's First Presbyterian Church. When communion was served, the elders passed over the black man and his friend. After Pastor Robert Miller communed the men himself, church members called for his resignation (Norrell, *Reaping the Whirlwind*, 175).

25. Peter C. Murray, *Methodists and the Crucible of Race, 1930–1975* (Columbia: University of Missouri Press, 2004), 147–148; Norrell, *Reaping the Whirlwind*, 176.

26. S. Jonathan Bass, *Blessed Are the Peacemakers: Martin Luther King Jr., Eight White Religious Leaders, and the "Letter from Birmingham Jail"* (Baton Rouge: Louisiana State University Press, 2001), 86; Norrell, *Reaping the Whirlwind*, 157.

27. Harry G. LeFever, *Undaunted by the Fight: Spelman College and the Civil Rights Movement, 1957–1967* (Macon: Mercer University Press, 2005), 57; "Why We Began the 'Kneel-Ins': A Student Symposium," *Atlanta Inquirer* (August 14, 1960): 1.

28. "Why We Began the 'Kneel-Ins'," 1.

29. Joseph Kip Kosek, "Civil Rights and Religious Rights in the 1960s," paper presented at the conference of the Peace History Society, Winthrop University, Rock Hill, South Carolina, October 30, 2009, 5, 6.

30. Writing in 1967, Marshall Frady confirmed that "the rationale most popular throughout the South for all those Sunday morning church-step confrontations was 'Those people didn't come to worship; they came to demonstrate'" ("God and Man in the South," *Atlantic Monthly* [January, 1967], 38).

31. *Holy Week and the Civil Rights Demonstrations at the Churches, A Sermon—Address Delivered April 11, 1965 by Dr. Robert Strong, Minister, Trinity Presbyterian Church, Montgomery Alabama* (n.d.), Civil Rights Collection, Box 130, Salmon Library, University of Alabama Huntsville, 17. In versions of the story appearing in Mark and John, Jesus also overturns the moneychangers' tables, in John with a "whip of cords" (Mk 11:15–17; Jn 2: 14–16). On references to Jesus's "cleansing of the Temple," in addition to the examples in Birmingham and Montgomery cited in Chapter 2 and Memphis in Chapter 10, see "Ga. Church Board Labels Kneel-Iners 'Intruders'," *Chicago Defender* (August 18, 1960): A2. Of course, the story of Jesus's cleansing of the Temple was a double-edged sword, since Jesus's declaration that the Temple was to be a house of prayer "for all the nations" cut in the direction of inclusivity. Occasionally, a white pastor would invoke this aspect of the biblical passage in arguing for church integration, as happened at First Presbyterian Church of Charleston, South Carolina, in 1960 (David L. Chappell, *A Stone of Hope: Prophetic Religion and the Death of Jim Crow* [Chapel Hill: University of North Carolina Press, 2004]: 277n52). In most cases, however, this part of the passage was either ignored or defused exegetically, as in the case of Montgomery's Rev. Robert Strong (see Chapter 2).

32. "Let Us Kneel-In!" 964; "Kneel-Ins," *Information Service of the Bureau of Research and Survey of the National Council of Churches of Christ in the United States* 40:8 (April 15, 1961): 1–2. Actually, the motives argument had been dismissed three years before it was in widespread use. In a 1957 pamphlet by Ben Lacy Rose that denied any scriptural or doctrinal basis for

segregation in the Southern Presbyterian Church, Rose anticipated the objection that "those Negroes who come now to our white churches do not really want to worship, they only want to test us." Rose's response was that white Christians should show the same spirit Christ demonstrated when he used his own testings as "opportunities to witness to the truth" (*Racial Segregation in the Church* [Richmond: Outlook Publishers, 1957]: 20).

33. "Ga. Pastor Asks Open Door Policy," *Baltimore African American* (September 10, 1960): 3. Kenneth J. Foreman, "Motives Committee: News Items with Comments," *Presbyterian Outlook* (September 30, 1963): 9; "Easter in Birmingham," 3; Marsh, *God's Long Summer*, 134; "Two Churches Bar Civil Rights Groups in Americus Drive," 1.

34. Murray, *Methodists and the Crucible of Race*, 148. The one place where it may be said that church visitors intended to create a disturbance was Houston in 1963, where CORE members picketed outside First Baptist Church with signs asking "How Can a Christian Church Be Segregated?" and "Is God Black or White?" The picketing commenced after the church turned down five black candidates for membership ("CORE Pickets Houston Church," *New York Amsterdam News* [October 5, 1963]: 35; "Picket Line On Sundays at Houston Church," *Norfolk Journal and Guide* [October 12, 1963]: A2; "Harassment in the Sanctuary," *Christianity Today* [March 13, 1964]: 40). In June 1962, it was reported that Houston's First Baptist had welcomed blacks to worship, suggesting that white churches viewed black worshippers differently when they were not seen as potential members. See "Houston Church Open to All," *Baltimore Afro-American* (June 2, 1962): 18.

35. "Kneel-Ins," 1.

36. "Negroes Attend 6 Churches," *Atlanta Constitution* (August 8, 1960): 1, 10. There are conflicting versions of how many of the churches refused to seat the students. In addition, while initial reports indicated that the August 7 visitors were "Negro students, mostly members of the Student Nonviolent Coordinating Committee," subsequent accounts made clear that some of the groups were biracial ("Stage 'Kneel-In' at 6 Churches," 1).

37. "Why We Began the 'Kneel-Ins,'" 1.

38. Ibid.

39. "Why We Began the 'Kneel-Ins,'" 1; "Negroes Attend 6 Churches," 10. "Students Visit Seven Churches in Atlanta," *Atlanta Daily World* (August 9, 1960): 1; "'Kneel-In' Project Started in Churches," 9.

40. "Three Atlanta Churches Refuse Negroes Admission," *Presbyterian Outlook* (September 12, 1960): 4. See also "Negroes Continue Kneel-Ins," *Presbyterian Survey* (October, 1960): 51. The five churches accepting visitors on August 14 were First Presbyterian, Central Presbyterian, St. Luke's Episcopal, Lutheran Church of the Redeemer, and Second Ponce de Leon Baptist.

41. "Negroes Attend 6 Churches," 1; "Kneel-Ins Bring Segregated Pew," *Presbyterian Outlook* (September 26, 1960): 1. These varying responses to the kneel-ins led Atlanta Presbytery to adopt a resolution in January 1961 stating that there was "no scriptural warrant to exclude from the fellowship of worship those whom the Gospel includes" ("Local Presbytery to Receive 'All'," *Atlanta Daily World* [January 26, 1961]: 1).

42. "Three Atlanta Churches Refuse Negroes Admission," 4; "3 Atlanta Churches Halt Kneel-In Demonstrations," *Norfolk Journal and Guide* (September 3, 1960): 10.

43. "Negroes Attend 6 Churches," 10; Howard Zinn, "Finishing School for Pickets," *The Nation* (August 6, 1960), http://www.loa.org/images/pdf/Zinn_Finishing_School.pdf; Fleming, *Soon We Will Not Cry*, 56.

44. Angela G. Owen, "Kneel-Ins," *Spelman Spotlight* (December 16, 1960), http://www.gpb.org/georgiastories/docs/the_beat_of_civil_rights-18.

45. http://www.crmvet.org/tim/timhis60.htm#1960savannah; "Kneel-Ins Begin in Savannah with Partial Success," *Atlanta Daily World* (August 23, 1960): 1.

46. "Sav. Methodist Board Official Hits Kneel-Ins," *Atlanta Daily World* (August 19, 1960): 2; "Ga. Church Board Labels Kneel-Iners 'Intruders'," A2.

47. "Kneel-In Begins in Savannah with Partial Success," 1.

48. "Kneel-Ins Here Continue, And Enter 5 Churches," *Atlanta Daily World* (August 30, 1960): 2; "Ga. Pastor Asks Open Door Policy," 3; "Kneel-Ins," *Information Service*, 2; See also, "Sit-in . . . Kneel-in: Demonstrations Spread to White Churches," *Presbyterian Outlook* (August 22, 1960): 4; and Gardiner H. Shattuck, Jr., *Episcopalians and Race: Civil War to Civil Rights* (Lexington: University Press of Kentucky, 2000), 153–154.

49. According to his own recollection, Jim Lawson conducted a nonviolent workshop with LeMoyne students in the summer of 1958 or 1959 (Interview with James M. Lawson, Jr. January 21, 1969, Series VI, 3 [Mississippi Valley Collection, University of Memphis]); "Students Hit Churches and Lunch Counters," *Tri-State Defender* (August 27, 1960): 1; Laurie B. Green, *Battling the Plantation Mentality: Memphis and the Black Freedom Struggle* (Chapel Hill: University of North Carolina Press, 2007), 247; "Negroes Refused at Four Churches: Four Arrests Are Made," *Memphis Press-Scimitar* (August 29, 1960): A15; "3 Churches Reject Negro Worshippers," *Memphis Commercial Appeal* (August 29, 1960): 24.

50. "Negro's Plea: Open Churches to All," *Memphis Press-Scimitar* (August 29, 1960): A15; "Two Negroes, White Arrested at Church," *Tri-State Defender* (September 3, 1960): 2. There is no evidence that state charges were pursued against Exum and Freeman.

51. "Dr. Jones Comments on the Turning Away of Negroes at His Church," *Memphis Press-Scimitar* (September 6, 1960): 6; "Two Negroes, White Arrested at Church," 2. "Negro's Plea: Open Churches to All," A15.

52. "Youth Rally Plans Movie Premiere," *Memphis Commercial Appeal* (August 27, 1960): 8. Student Jevita Edwards related a different version of events to a reporter for the *Tri-State Defender*. According to Edwards, "the contingent was greeted by an usher, who in turn shook the hand of Evander Ford . . . and told [us] that [we] were welcome. The usher asked if we wanted to sit in the back. Evander told the usher 'No, we'd rather sit where we please with the others.' The usher said it was all right with him" ("14 Arrested at 'Public' Meet," *Tri-State Defender* [September 10, 1960]: 1); Interview with Johnnie Rogers Turner, June 21, 2010; Interview with Evander Ford, June 17, 2010.

53. Sherry Lee Hoppe and Bruce W. Speck, *Maxine Smith's Unwilling Pupils: Lessons Learned in Memphis's Civil Rights Classroom* (Knoxville: University of Tennessee Press, 2007), 72; "Judge Terms Negro Action 'A New Low,'" *Memphis Press-Scimitar* (September 1, 1960), 20; "Negroes Arrested at Church Rally," *Memphis Press-Scimitar* (August 31, 1960): 1; "Sit-In Fines are Upheld," *Memphis Press-Scimitar* (April 27, 1961): 2; Interview with Evander Ford, June 17, 2010.

54. Green, *Battling the Plantation Mentality*, 248–249; "Negroes Fined, Held to State: Disturbed Public Worship, Charge," *Memphis Press-Scimitar* (September 1, 1960): 20. "Judge Terms Negro Action 'A New Low,'" 20; "14 Arrested at 'Public' Meet," 1; "Indicted after Shell Incident," *Memphis Press-Scimitar* (September 7, 1960): 21. One of the ten students, Katie Jean Robinson, was found guilty in a separate trial and fined $175 ("$175 Fine in Disturbance," *Memphis Press-Scimitar* [September 26, 1961]): 22).

55. "Sentencing of 8 Students Upheld," *Memphis Press-Scimitar* (March 8, 1962): 18; "Church is Off Limits," *Baltimore Afro-American* (March 17, 1962), 1; "8 Will Appeal to U.S. Court," *Memphis Press-Scimitar* (March 9, 1962): 4; "High Court Denies Negroes Rehearing," *Memphis Press-Scimitar* (May 4, 1962): 7; "Time Given to Appeal," *Memphis Commercial Appeal* (July 3, 1964): 1; "Court Won't Review Overton Sentences," *Memphis Press-Scimitar* (October 10, 1964): 1; "Hearing is Won by 8 Negroes," *Memphis Press-Scimitar* (October 23, 1964): 9; Interview with Evander Ford, June 17, 2010. Charges against Harry James, Jr. and Anita Laverne Stiggers, who had moved out of town and not returned for trial, were dismissed following the commutation of the other students' sentences ("Dismiss Charges Now 5 Years Old," *Memphis Press-Scimitar* [October 7, 1965]): 2).

56. Green, *Battling the Plantation Mentality*, 247–249; Elizabeth Gritter, "Local Leaders and Community Soldiers: The Memphis Desegregation Movement, 1955–1961" (unpublished Senior Honors Thesis, American University, 2001), 87; "Report of Executive Secretary, June 8, 1964–July 7, 1964," Maxine A. Smith—NAACP Collection, Memphis Room,

Memphis Public Library and Information Center; Interview with Evander Ford, June 17, 2010; Interview with Johnnie Rogers Turner, June 21, 2010.

57. "Judge Terms Negro Action 'A New Low'," 20.

Chapter 2

1. On Jacksonville, see Rodney L. Hurst Sr., *It Was Never about a Hot Dog and Coke: A Personal Account of the 1960 Sit-In Demonstrations in Jacksonville, FL and Ax Handle Saturday* (Livermore, CA: WingSpan Press, 2008), Chapter 14. On Alexandria, see "Students Get Welcome at Alexandria Churches," *Baltimore Afro-American* (September 10, 1960): 20 and "'Kneel-Ins' Held at Four Churches," *Washington Post* (August 29, 1960): B1, which also references kneel-ins in Arlington, Virginia, and Montgomery County, Maryland. On Norfolk, see Lin Holloway, "Looking On in Norfolk," *Norfolk Journal and Guide* (August 13, 1960): A15. On New Orleans, see "Kneel-Ins Successful at 2 New Orleans Churches," *Chicago Defender* (September 24, 1960): 3. On Rock Hill, see J. Charles Jones, "Rock Hill and the Charlotte Sit-Ins," http://www.crmvet.org/info/rockhill.htm. On Tallahassee, see "FAMU Students In 'Kneel-Ins,'" *Chicago Defender* (March 6, 1961): 18. On Augusta, see "Two Paine Students Foiled in Kneel-In," *Baltimore African American* (November 18, 1961): 16. On Durham, see "Kneel-ins Cause Little Excitement," *Baltimore Afro-American* (April 21, 1962): 6. On Talladega, see "Students Attempt Church Integration, Arrested," *Chicago Defender* (April 24, 1962): 2. On Raleigh, see "Cities Move to Avoid Becoming 'Birminghams'," *Norfolk Journal and Guide* (May 18, 1963): B2. On Farmville, see "Kneel-in's Lawyer Eyes Church 'Aim'," *Baltimore Afro-American* (May 23, 1964): 3. On Houston, see "CORE Pickets Houston Church," *New York Amsterdam News* (October 5, 1963): 35. On Tuskegee, see Robert J. Norrell, *Reaping the Whirlwind: The Civil Rights Movement in Tuskegee* (New York: Alfred A. Knopf, 1985), 155–159, 174–176. On Lynchburg, see "CORE Workers Stage Lynchburg 'Kneel-in,'" *Baltimore Afro-American* (August 22, 1964): 12. On Wilson, see Charles W. McKinney, Jr., *Greater Freedom: The Evolution of the Civil Rights Movement in Wilson, North Carolina* (Lanham, MD: University Press of America, 2010), 162–163. On Americus, see "Two Churches Bar Civil Rights Groups in Americus Drive," *New York Times* (August 2, 1965): 1, 15; and "Worshippers Barred from Americus Church," *Chicago Defender* (August 2, 1965): 1. Marshall Frady discusses kneel-ins in Tuskegee, Macon, and Americus in "God and Man in the South," *Atlantic Monthly* (January 1967): 37–42. Donald Collins mentions kneel-ins in Marion, Jackson, and Mobile, Alabama (though he does not give dates) in *When the Church Bell Rang Racist: The Methodist Church and the Civil Rights Movement in Alabama* (Macon: Mercer University Press, 1998), 131. Samuel Southard discusses kneel-ins in New Orleans and Alexandria, Virginia, in "Segregation and Southern Churches," *Journal of Religion and Health* 1:3 (April, 1962): 197–221. It is not clear whether kneel-ins took place in Nashville, although one historian claims that in 1962 SCLC leader C. T. Vivian "came up with the idea of 'kneel-ins' that would take the movement to white Christians and compel them to make a moral decision" (Bobby L. Lovett, *The Civil Rights Movement in Tennessee: A Narrative History* [Knoxville: University of Tennessee Press, 2005], 177).

2. This description of the Albany Movement is based on Howard Zinn, *Albany: A Study in National Responsibility* (Atlanta: Southern Regional Council, 1962).

3. "Albany Police Arrest 3 During 'Kneel-In' Try," *Atlanta Daily World* (August 21, 1962): 1; "2 Albany Churches Admit Others Bar Negroes," *Chicago Defender* (August 13, 1962): 2.

4. "Christ Did Not Build Any Racial Walls," *Chicago Defender* (August 22, 1962): 3; Jason Sokol, *There Goes My Everything: White Southerners in the Age of Civil Rights, 1945–1975* (New York: Alfred A. Knopf, 2006), 81; David L. Chappell, *Inside Agitators: White Southerners in the Civil Rights Movement* (Baltimore: Johns Hopkins University Press, 1994), 122–123.

5. "20th-Century Shapers of Baptist Social Ethics: T. B. Maston," http://levellers.wordpress.com/2009/01/11/20th-century-shapers-of-baptist-social-ethics-t-b-maston/;

Paul Harvey, *Freedom's Coming: Religious Culture and the Shaping of the South from the Civil War through the Civil Rights Era* (Chapel Hill: University of North Carolina Press, 2005), 214; Mark Newman, *Getting Right with God: Southern Baptists and Desegregation, 1945–1995* (Tuscaloosa: University of Alabama Press, 2001), 70.

6. Interview with Brooks Ramsey, March 4, 2008.
7. Ibid.
8. Ibid.
9. Ibid.
10. Ibid.
11. Ibid.
12. Rev. and Mrs. Zeb V. Moss, "Open Letter to First Baptist Church Albany, Ga." (October 17, 1962) in the possession of Brooks Ramsey; Sokol, *There Goes My Everything,* 82; Samuel Southard, "Are Southern Churches Silent?" *The Christian Century* (November 20, 1963): 1429–1432; 1432. The danger that racism in the church would undermine Christian missionary efforts was particularly acute for Southern Baptists, whose identity was closely tied to fulfillment of Christ's Great Commission. The link between domestic desegregation and successful foreign missions had been recognized by Southern Baptist Convention boards, newspapers, and clergymen since the mid-1950s (Newman, *Getting Right with God,* 139, 140).
13. Interview with Brooks Ramsey, March 4, 2008.
14. Joseph Kip Kosek, "Civil Rights and Religious Rights in the 1960s," paper presented at the conference of the Peace History Society, Winthrop University, Rock Hill, South Carolina, October 30, 2009, 4, 5; David Andrew Harmon, *Beneath the Image of the Civil Rights Movement and Race Relations: Atlanta, Georgia, 1946–1981,* Studies in African American History and Culture (London: Taylor and Francis, 1996), 150.
15. Kosek, "Civil Rights and Religious Rights in the 1960s," 3, 4, 7, 8.
16. Howard Zinn, *The Southern Mystique* (Cambridge, MA: South End Press, 2002), 81; Charles Brown, "The Epic of Ashton Jones: Dixie-Born White Minister Leads One-Man Crusade for Interracial Brotherhood," *Ebony* (October, 1965): 45–54.
17. "Minister Held as 2 Sit-Ins Fail at First Baptist Church," *Atlanta Constitution* (July 1, 1963): 8; "Court Continues Case of Sit-In Minister," *Atlanta Constitution* (July 2, 1963): 19.
18. Jack Strong, "Sit-In Pastor Gets 18 Months," *Atlanta Constitution* (August 29, 1963): 1.
19. See Ray Perkins, Jr., ed., *Yours Faithfully, Bertrand Russell: Letters to the Editor 1904–1969* (Chicago: Open Court Publishers, 2001), 315.
20. Harmon, *Beneath the Image,* 151; William Worthy, "Aston Jones Case May Stir Scandal," *Washington Afro-American* (December 10, 1963): 15; Kosek, "Civil Rights and Religious Rights in the 1960s," 10; Hal Gulliver, "Sit-In Pastor Freed on $5,000 Bond," *Atlanta Constitution* (March 4, 1964): 9. Other details of the incidents in front of First Baptist—for instance, that church ushers blocked the doors so that the visitors could not enter the sanctuary, that a deacon had tried to kick Jones as he knelt in prayer on the sidewalk, that he had been dragged down two flights of stairs with his head hitting each one, and that he experienced abuse in prison—were reported in black papers. See, e.g., Worthy, "Aston Jones Case May Stir Scandal."
21. "Seek Clemency for Clergyman," *Chicago Defender* (April 24, 1965): 2.
22. "Handclasp of Brotherhood," *Jet* (July 30, 1953): 9. Jones's arrest at First Baptist in Atlanta was reported in the July 18, 1963, issue of the magazine. Jones's long history of arrest and persecution made him one of six "prisoners of conscience" featured in a 1961 *London Observer* article that ultimately gave birth to Amnesty International. At the time, Jones was described by author Peter Benenson as a "sixty-five-year-old minister, who last year was repeatedly beaten-up and three times imprisoned in Louisiana and Texas for doing what the Freedom Riders are now doing in Alabama" (Peter Benenson, "The Forgotten Prisoners," *The London Observer Weekend Review* [May 28, 1961], http://www.hrweb.org/ai/observer.html). Benenson also devoted a chapter to Jones in his book *Persecution* (London: Penguin, 1961).

23. "Alabama Church Kneel-In Called Off," *Chicago Defender* (April 8, 1963): 4; "Easter in Birmingham: Some Church Bias Ends," *Chicago Defender* (April 15, 1963): 3; "Fighting Erupts at Birmingham," *New York Times* (April 15, 1963): 1, 14; Robert Gordon, "Birmingham Churches Split on Kneel-Ins," *Memphis World* (April 20, 1963): 1.

24. "Easter in Birmingham: Some Church Bias Ends," 3; S. Jonathan Bass, *Blessed Are the Peacemakers: Martin Luther King Jr., Eight White Religious Leaders, and the "Letter from Birmingham Jail"* (Baton Rouge: Louisiana State University Press, 2001): 76–79.

25. "Letter from a Birmingham Jail, Martin Luther King, Jr., 1963," http://coursesa.matrix.msu.edu/~hst306/documents/letter.html; "Fighting Erupts in Birmingham," 14; Bass, *Blessed Are the Peacemakers*, 79.

26. "Integrate More Churches in Birmingham Campaign," *Chicago Defender* (April 22, 1963): 1; "Birmingham Churches Split on Kneel-Ins," 1; Robert Gordon, "5 Birmingham Churches Open Doors to Kneel-Ins," *Memphis World* (April 27, 1963): 7; Bass, *Blessed Are the Peacemakers*, 213–215.

27. Bass, *Blessed Are the Peacemakers*, 215–217.

28. Ibid., 84–85.

29. Ibid., 85–86.

30. Charles Marsh, *God's Long Summer: Stories of Faith and Civil Rights* (Princeton: Princeton University Press, 1997), 121, 124.

31. Sokol, *There Goes My Everything*, 104; *The Mississippi Methodist Advocate* (January 2, 1963), http://www.mississippi-umc.org/console/files/oFiles_Library_XZXLCZ/Born_of_Conviction_4QQJSQYW.pdf. On the Jackson kneel-ins, see also Peter C. Murray, *Methodists and the Crucible of Race, 1930–1975* (Columbia: University of Missouri Press, 2004), 148–153.

32. Marsh, *God's Long Summer*, 101.

33. "Jackson Church Admits Negroes, Four Refuse," *Chicago Defender* (June 18, 1963): 4; Anne Moody, *Coming of Age in Mississippi* (New York: Dial Press, 1968): 254; Marsh, *God's Long Summer*, 132; "Miss. Pastor Quits Post over Segregation Issue," *Chicago Defender* (June 24, 1963): 13.

34. "Fail in Efforts to Desegregate Miss. Churches," *Chicago Defender* (July 23, 1963): 5; "U.S. Intervenes in Students Case," *Atlanta Daily World* (October 25, 1963): 1; Marsh, *God's Long Summer*, 135, 138–139. See also "Suit Seeks Halt of Arrests at Miss. Churches," *Atlanta Daily World* (February 14, 1964): 1.

35. "W.J. Cunningham, *Agony at Galloway: One Church's Struggle with Social Change* (Jackson: University Press of Mississippi, 1980): 11–12.

36. Marsh, *God's Long Summer*, 133–134; Cunningham, *Agony at Galloway*, 13.

37. "Fate of Kneel-Ins up to Mississippi," *Baltimore Afro-American* (May 2, 1964): 12; Cunningham, *Agony at Galloway*, 31.

38. Taylor Branch, *Pillar of Fire: America in the King Years, 1963–65* (New York: Simon and Schuster, 1998), 263–264; Cunningham, *Agony at Galloway*, 48, 95; "Barred," *Presbyterian Outlook* (April 6, 1964): 4.

39. "Methodist Bishops Rejected at Jackson Easter Kneel-In," *Baltimore Afro-American* (April 11, 964): 18; Cunningham, *Agony at Galloway*, 59. Visitation sites on Easter Sunday 1964 included Capitol Street Methodist, where two local blacks and seven white seminary professors were met by a line of ushers on the church's front steps.

40. Cunningham, *Agony at Galloway*, 82–84.

41. Cunningham, *Agony at Galloway*, 56, 63. *Association of Independent Methodists: The First Twenty-Five Years 1965–1990* (Jackson, MS: Association of Independent Methodists, 1990): 150–151.

42. David R. Colburn, *Racial Change and Community Crisis: St. Augustine, Florida, 1877–1980* (Columbia University Press, 1985): 66–67; Dan R. Warren, *If It Takes All Summer: Martin Luther King, the KKK, and States' Rights in St. Augustine, 1964* (Tuscaloosa: University of Alabama Press, 2008): 65.

43. Colburn, *Racial Change and Community Crisis*, 65, 165; Branch, *Pillar of Fire*, 279, 285.

44. Colburn, *Racial Change and Community Crisis*, 166–167; Warren, *If It Takes All Summer*, 72. There is a somewhat different description of events in Gardiner H. Shattuck Jr., *Episcopalians and Race: Civil War to Civil Rights* (Lexington: University Press of Kentucky, 2000): 138–139.

45. "'We Have Done Things Which We Ought Not'," *Chicago Defender* (June 22, 1964): 4; Colburn, *Racial Change and Community Crisis*, 169–170.

46. "Bishop Stands by Rector under Fire in Florida," *Baltimore Afro-American* (July 18, 1964): 3; Colburn, *Racial Change and Community Crisis*, 171; Branch, *Pillar of Fire*, 383.

47. "Fla. Church Has Change of Heart: Lifts Bars," *Norfolk Journal and Guide* (April 11, 1964): 1; Warren, *If It Takes All Summer*, 79. There were conflicting reports concerning whether blacks were welcome at Grace Methodist. The *Tri-State Defender* (Memphis) reported in April 1964 that "the previously all-white Grace Methodist Church admitted eight Negroes to its services without incident" ("Negroes Pray in Fla. Church," *Tri-State Defender* [April 11, 1964]: 1).

48. "Fla. Town Churches Stick to Race Bias; Gangs Beat Negroes," *Chicago Defender* (June 3, 1964): 5; Colburn, *Racial Change and Community Crisis*, 163.

49. "Spotlight on St. Augustine," *Christianity Today* (July 17, 1964): 37–38; Colburn, *Racial Change and Community Crisis*, 163, 174; Warren, *If It Takes All Summer*, 140.

50. "Selma Church Admits Negroes for First Time," *Chicago Defender* (March 29, 1965): 10; Bass, *Blessed Are the Peacemakers*, 167; Taylor Branch, *At Canaan's Edge: America in the King Years, 1965–68* (New York: Simon and Schuster, 2006): 184, 189.

51. Shattuck, *Episcopalians and Race*, 154–157; Branch, *At Canaan's Edge*, 209–210; 273; 352.

52. Bruce Ashcroft, Mark Anderson III, and Mrs. Allen L. Knox, *In Remembrance: The Centennial History of Trinity Presbyterian Church* (n.p., n.d.): 51. There was an incident in August 1960 in which three white worshippers attended Montgomery's Dexter Avenue Baptist Church, from whose pulpit Martin Luther King, Jr. had recently departed, but they appear to have been "curiosity seekers" ("Integration in Reverse: Racial Battle in South Often Gets Confusing," *Norfolk Journal and Guide* [August 27, 1960]: 23).

53. *In Remembrance*, 56, 62, 64; "Letter to the PCUS Board of Christian Education from the Elders of Trinity Presbyterian Church, Montgomery, Alabama, June 3, 1957," *Presbyterian Journal* (June 19, 1957): 6–8; 7.

54. *In Remembrance*, 65.

55. *Holy Week and the Civil Rights Demonstrations at the Churches, A Sermon—Address Delivered April 11, 1965 by Dr. Robert Strong, Minister, Trinity Presbyterian Church, Montgomery Alabama* (n.d.), Civil Rights Collection, Box 130, Salmon Library, University of Alabama Huntsville. Winton Blount had been appointed in 1964 by President Lyndon Johnson to the National Citizens Committee for Community Relations, whose job it was to advise the White House on the enforcement of the Civil Rights Act of 1964. In 1969, President Richard Nixon appointed Blount to the post of United States Postmaster General.

56. *In Remembrance*, 65. Apparently, there were no incidents at any of the churches.

57. *Holy Week and the Civil Rights*, 2, 3, 5. Significantly, Strong's first southern pastorate was at First Church, Augusta, Georgia, where the Presbyterian Church in the Confederate States of America was founded in 1861.

58. Ibid., 8–9, 11, 14. Strong was quick to add that "nothing like the significance that is attached to a southern incident follows upon such events as the dreadful riots in the northern cities during the summer of 1964" (11).

59. Ibid., 12, 15–16.

60. Ibid., 17. Strong added that "there is evidence that in some instances these sorts of groups have been paid to do this kind of work, so that not only is there an obvious insincerity but on occasion an element of commercialism appears" (17).

61. Ibid., 16–17.

62. Ibid., 19, 21, 23.

63. Ibid., 17; "Progress in Alabama," *Presbyterian Outlook* (July 12, 1965): 5–6.

64. "Progress in Alabama," 6, 7.

65. "Montgomery Church Has Negro Worshippers," *Presbyterian Outlook* (April 19, 1965): 3.

66. Collins, *When the Church Bell Rang Racist*, 128–130.

67. "'Action of Session, Not of Minister' Refuses Two Blacks Admittance at Sumter Presbyterian Church," *Presbyterian Survey* (February 9, 1970): 4; "Segregation Abolished at First Church, Sumter," *Presbyterian Survey* (February 23, 1970): 4.

Chapter 3

1. "Report of Executive Secretary, February 6–March 5, 1963" (Maxine A. Smith—NAACP Collection, Memphis Room, Memphis Public Library and Information Center). Noting that "the majority in attendance at the recent meetings of the Intercollegiate Chapter have been white students," Smith met with a group of LeMoyne undergraduates in an effort to involve more of them.

2. Interview with Lewis Donelson, June 29, 2004; Interview with Harry Wellford, October 1, 2009. The vote at Idlewild Presbyterian was not unanimous and the church did lose members over this and other stands taken under its racially moderate pastor Paul Tudor Jones. In addition to Idlewild, the students were welcomed at Evergreen Presbyterian, First Baptist, Bellevue Baptist (at which visitors had been arrested in 1960), Calvary Episcopal, St. Mary's Episcopal, and Centenary Methodist (Carl R. Pritchett, "What Happened at Memphis, May 10, 1964," 2, in possession of Bethesda Presbyterian Church).

3. Interview with Jim Bullock, March 17, 2009; Mrs. K. William Chandler, "Church History: the Year of Our Lord, Nineteen Hundred and Sixty-Four," 1, 3 (Presbyterian Heritage Center, Montreat, North Carolina). "Memphis, 1965?," *Presbyterian Outlook* (April 27th, 1964): 3. Some church members claim that SPC was warned of an impending visit. It may be that news of visits to other Memphis churches convinced some at SPC that they would be targeted as well. It is also possible that the church expected to be visited because there was a precedent for testing churches that were scheduled to host meetings of the PCUS General Assembly. See "Druid Hills Presbyterian Church Opens Its Doors to Negroes Here," *Atlanta Daily World* (March 28, 1959): 4.

4. "Biracial Group Plans 2nd Presbyterian Visit," *Memphis Press-Scimitar* (April 4, 1964): 13; "Mixed Group Again Tried to Enter Church," *Memphis Press-Scimitar* (April 20, 1964): 7.

5. "2nd Presbyterian Bars Students 6th Sunday in Row," *Memphis World* (April 25, 1964): 1. The weekly paper included Sunday's news, despite a Saturday publication date.

6. "Private Police Block 'Kneel-Ins' from Presbyterian Church: Church's Men Guard Doors in Person," *Tri-State Defender* (April 25, 1964): 1.

7. "2nd Presbyterian Says 'No' for 7th Sunday," *Memphis World* (May 2, 1964): 1, 4; "Second Presbyterian Church is Unyielding," *Tri-State Defender* (May 2, 1964): 1; "7th Attempt to Enter Second Presbyterian," *Memphis Press-Scimitar* (April 27, 1964): 8. The *Defender* reported that "when Howard Romaine, a Southwestern senior from New Iberia, La., attempted to talk to one woman who upbraided the elders for their policy of strict segregation, he was escorted off the church property and not allowed to return though he attempted to do so several times" (Ibid.).

8. "Private Police Block 'Kneel-Ins' from Presbyterian Church," 1.

9. Interview with Robert G. Patterson, July 2, 2004; Kay Pittman "Surprise March by Students Greets Clements, Walters," *Memphis Press-Scimitar* (January 18, 1964): 1, 2; "Report of Executive Secretary, April 8, 1964–May 5, 1964" (Maxine A. Smith—NAACP Collection, Memphis Room, Memphis Public Library and Information Center).

10. Elinor Kelley, "Presbyterians Face Busy Session," *Memphis Commercial Appeal* (April 11, 1964): 8; "Big Decisions Facing Church," *Memphis Commercial Appeal* (April 23, 1964): 29; "Memphis Probable Site of Church Assembly," *Memphis Commercial Appeal* (April 24, 1964): 7; "Hopes Dimmed for Assembly: Memphis' Presbyterian Bid for 1965 Is Shaken by Race Resolution," *Memphis Commercial Appeal* (April 25, 1964): 8; "Memphis Gets

1965 Assembly: Heated Presbyterian Debate about Segregation is Resolved," *Memphis Commercial Appeal* (April 26, 1964): section 2, 8; "Church Extends Stand on Race: Presbyterian Assembly Says None Can be Barred from Worship," *Memphis Commercial Appeal* (April 28, 1964): 7; "Ministers' Reaction Varied on Church's Race Progress," *Memphis Commercial Appeal* (May 2, 1964): 14.

11. A special meeting of the SPC session was called for March 23, the day following the first visits, "due to efforts of newspapers to secure information on having negroes come into the Church." It is not known whether the papers referred to were local (Minutes of the Session of Second Presbyterian Church, Memphis, Tennessee, March 23, 1964, 3). Carl R. Pritchett, "What Happened at Memphis," 2; Benjamin Muse, *Memphis* (Atlanta: Southern Regional Council, 1964): 45; Michael K. Honey, *Going Down Jericho Road: The Memphis Strike, Martin Luther King's Last Campaign* (New York: W. W. Norton, 2007): 129; Laurie B. Green, *Battling the Plantation Mentality: Memphis and the Black Freedom Struggle* (Chapel Hill: University of North Carolina Press, 2007): 254. As Muse described the policy of Memphis's daily papers, "articles are published from time to time giving summaries of desegregation, and these are presented in language tending to make the public proud of the progress Memphis is making" (*Memphis*, 27).

12. Elinor Kelley, "Second Presbyterian Resists Attempts to Force Change," *Memphis Commercial Appeal* (May 4, 1964): 4.

13. Drawn by *The Commercial Appeal's* own J. P. Alley when he worked for the paper between 1916 and 1934, Hambone was literally the remnant of a bygone era. Until discontinued in 1968, "Hambone's Meditations" often ran adjacent to stories of progress in civil rights (Honey, *Going Down Jericho Road*, 128, 225). The single-panel cartoon depicted "a caricature of a Negro, balding, wearing baggy pants, and sometimes a defeated-looking hat. Hambone is always engaged in some menial activity, such as bringing in an armload of wood or sweeping and dusting. He utters pithy sayings." See http://www.afscme.org/union/history/mlk/in-memphis-a-special-report-from-the-southern-regional-council/in-memphis-more-than-a-garbage-strike/the-february-23-march.

14. Carl Pritchett, "To the Ushers and Other Representatives of the Second Presbyterian Church of Memphis, Tenn.," (May 3, 1964), in the possession of Charles Murphy. Pritchett suggests that Kelley was invited to the church that morning by the students ("What Happened at Memphis, May 10, 1964," 3); Elinor Kelley, "Second Presbyterian Resists Attempts to Force Change," *Memphis Commercial Appeal* (May 4, 1964): 4. That afternoon the *Press-Scimitar* carried an article containing much the same information. It spoke of "visiting students, some 15 or 20, mostly negro with four or five whites" (Thomas M. Pappas, "Second Presbyterian Prayer: 'Guide Us in Race Issue," *Memphis Press Scimitar* [May 4, 1964]: 13). Kelley recalls that the Sunday following publication of her article she returned to the church with her notebook but was met at the door by two ushers who "turned [her] around at the door by the shoulders and sent [her] out" (Interview with Elinor Kelley Grusin, August 6, 2004).

15. "The Second Presbyterian Situation," *Memphis Press-Scimitar* (May 7, 1964): 6; "Presbyterian Stand is Hit," *Memphis Commercial Appeal* (May 3, 1964): section 5, 3. A letter from a resident of Washington, D.C. pointed out that churches in Carl Pritchett's part of the country had their own problems with integration (Paul Boone, "Northern View on 'Barring," *Memphis Commercial Appeal* [May 10, 1964]): section 5, 3.

16. Francis Butler Simkins and Charles Pierce Roland, *A History of the South*, 4th ed. (New York: Knopf, 1972), 635.

17. Letter from Robert J. Hussey to Mr. Hayden J. Kaden, Sr., April 7, 1964 (in the possession of Hayden Kaden).

18. Letter from Rev. C. Rodney Sunday to Mr. Robert J. Hussey, April 9, 1964 (in the possession of Hayden Kaden).

19. Ibid.

20. Ibid.

21. Letter from Robert J. Hussey to Dr. C. Rodney Sunday, April 13, 1964 (in the possession of Hayden Kaden).

22. Stephen M. Findlay, "The Role of Bi-Racial Organizations in the Integration of Public Facilities in Memphis, Tennessee, 1954–1964" (unpublished paper, Memphis and Shelby County Collection, Memphis Public Library and Information Center): 19; George Lewis, *Massive Resistance: The White Response to the Civil Rights Movement* (London: Hodder Arnold, 2006): 92.

23. Letter from Willis E. Ayers, Jr. to Mrs. C. Rodney Sunday, May 2, 1964 (in the possession of Hayden Kaden); Letter from Mrs. C. Rodney Sunday to Willis E. Ayers, Jr., May 6, 1964 (in the possession of Hayden Kaden). Ayers's name does not appear in the 1964–65 *Year Book of Second Presbyterian Church*, but a Mrs. Willis E. Ayers is listed as a church member;

24. "Second Presbyterian Church is Unyielding," 1.

25. "Second Presbyterian Church is Unyielding," 1; Pritchett, "What Happened at Memphis," 2.

26. Pritchett, "What Happened at Memphis, 2; Thomas N. Pappas, "Presbytery Stand on Race Expected," *Memphis Press-Scimitar* (January 25, 1965): 1; "Church Refuses NAACP Couples," *Memphis Press-Scimitar* (April 6, 1964): 1. In late April, the *Tri-State Defender* reported that a white youth from Illinois who was touring the South on a bicycle asked to join the group but "was turned away because of his casual attire" ("Private Police Block 'Kneel-Ins,'" 1). As W. J. Cunningham notes of students from other parts of the country who visited Galloway Methodist in Jackson, Mississippi, it did not help their cause that they were characterized by "bizarre personal dress . . . slovenly, unkempt, 'the great unwashed'" (Cunningham, *Agony at Galloway*, 52).

27. Howard Romaine confirmed that college officials had communicated the church's threat to students, warning them that "Second Presbyterian church officials are threatening to withdraw support from the university if its students continue to make integration demands on them" ("Second Presbyterian Church is Unyielding," 1).

28. Jameson Jones, "The Power of Knowledge," talk delivered at Phi Beta Kappa induction ceremony, Rhodes College, May 15, 1998, in the possession of Michael Cody.

29. "Second Presbyterian Church is Unyielding," 1; Charles E. Diehl, "Moving a College (Read at a Meeting of 'The Egyptians,' October 25, 1956)," 13 (College Archives, Barret Library, Rhodes College); Alfred O. Canon, "From the Ivy-Covered Tower," n.d. (College Archives, Barret Library, Rhodes College).

30. Alfred O. Canon, "From the Ivy-Covered Tower."

31. Interview with Winton Smith, November 19, 2010.

32. Interview with Catherine Freeberg, September 23, 2009.

33. "Students Halt Church Try," *Memphis Press-Scimitar* (May 24, 1964): 1.

34. *Minutes of the Synod of Tennessee of the Presbyterian Church in the United States, One Hundred Forty-Ninth Annual Session, June 15–17, 1964* (Presbyterian Heritage Center, Montreat, North Carolina): 17.

35. Paul Tudor Jones, "The College Related Church," address to the Synod of Tennessee, June 15, 1964, 3 (College Archives, Barret Library, Rhodes College).

36. "Statement by Robert M. Hasselle, Jr. Pertaining to Rejection by Officers of Second Presbyterian Church," n.d., document in the possession of Henry Hasselle.

37. *Second Presbyterian Church Messenger* (June 7, 1964).

38. "Statement by Robert M. Hasselle, Jr." Hasselle and Ringold had, in fact, tried on at least one occasion to enter the church with black students. Thus it is possible that on May 24 Hasselle was recognized as having been among the student protestors in previous weeks (Interview with Robert Hasselle, October 23, 2009).

39. Letter from Robert M. Hasselle, Sr. to Dr. Granville Sherman, June 3, 1964, in possession of Henry Hasselle; Letter from Robert J. Hussey to Robert M. Hasselle, June 30, 1964, in the possession of Henry Hasselle; Letter of Robert J. Hussey to Robert M. Hasselle, Jr, July 6, 1964, in possession of Henry Hasselle. Bob Hasselle explains that as an active churchman his father "had to deal with these Second Presbyterian elders on many occasions . . . and they had been uncooperative on a number of issues." "I wouldn't call him a real advocate of integration," Hasselle says.

40. "Memphis Vote," *Presbyterian Outlook* (November 9, 1964): 1.

41. Minutes of Memphis Presbytery, Stated Meeting, July 21, 1964 (Presbyterian Heritage Center, Montreat, North Carolina): 13; Interview with Lewis Donelson, June 29, 2004; Susan Carter, "Desegregation Plea is Heard," *Memphis Press-Scimitar* (July 21, 1964): 1.

42. Roger Hart, "FOCUS: Second Presbyterian Church," *Sou'wester* (January 8, 1965): 2.

43. "Mixed Group Barred at Memphis Church," *Memphis Commercial Appeal* (January 25, 1965): 17; Pappas, "Presbytery Stand on Race Expected," 1; "Church Elders Defy Ministers, Bar Negroes: Group Plays Hide and Peek with Camera," *Tri-State Defender* (January 30, 1965): 1; "Second Church's Problem," *Memphis Press-Scimitar* (January 26, 1965): 6. Letters to the editor by William G. Finger and Warren S. Webb originally appeared in the *Memphis Press-Scimitar* and were reprinted in the February 22, 1965, issue of *The Presbyterian Outlook*. It is not clear what role, if any, Southwestern students played in the winter kneel-ins. According to Maxine Smith's monthly report of NAACP activity, those seeking to worship at SPC were "representatives of the Intercollegiate Chapter along with the Branch's First Vice President and Executive Secretary [Maxine and Vasco Smith]" ("Report of the Executive Secretary, January 5–February 2, 1965" [Maxine A. Smith—NAACP Collection, Memphis Room, Memphis Public Library and Information Center]).

44. Minutes of Memphis Presbytery, Stated Meeting, January 26, 1965 (Presbyterian Heritage Center, Montreat, North Carolina): 13, 16, 17, 18.

45. In 1963 SPC's annual contribution to Memphis Presbytery was nearly $133,000, compared to less than $80,000 each from Idlewild and Evergreen, the second and third largest churches in the presbytery, and less than $10,000 from historic First Church. The average contribution of the presbytery's churches was less than $8,000 (Minutes of Memphis Presbytery, Stated Meeting, July 21, 1964, 24).

Chapter 4

1. On the paradoxes of Memphis, see Wanda Rushing, *Memphis and the Paradox of Place: Globalization and the American South* (Chapel Hill: University of North Carolina Press, 2009).

2. Benjamin Muse, *Memphis* (Atlanta: Southern Regional Council, 1964): 1, 2, 48; John Herbers, "Integration Gains in Memphis; Biracial Leadership Takes Hold," *New York Times* (April 5, 1964): 45.

3. "Presbyterians Mothered New Congregations: Second Church, Organized in Warehouse, Sponsored Three Others," *Memphis Press-Scimitar* (February 21, 1927): 12; Aubrey Ballard, "Second Presbyterian to Mark Centennial," *Memphis Commercial Appeal* (December 24, 1944): section 1, 5; George M. Apperson, "Lincoln, the Churches, and Memphis Presbyterians," *American Presbyterians* (summer, 1994): 97–107; Perre Magness, "Second Presbyterian Celebrates 150 Years," *Memphis Commercial Appeal* (November 3, 1994): E2.

4. George M. Apperson, "Heroism in a Lost Cause," *Presbyterian Voice* 15:2 (April 2004), http://www.synodoflivingwaters.org/the_voice/0404/06heroism.html.

5. Apperson, "Lincoln, the Churches, and Memphis Presbyterians," 102, 97. A facsimile of the document appears in Charles C. Gillespie, *A History of the Second Presbyterian Church of Memphis, Tennessee, 1844–1971* (Memphis: Second Presbyterian Church, 1971): 13. The signed, handwritten presidential order was donated by SPC to Southwestern in 1970 by William W. Goodman (Jerry Robbins, "Order Signed by Lincoln Donated to Southwestern," *Memphis Press-Scimitar* [February 4, 1970]: 37).

6. Sherita Johnson-Burgess, "Story Corps" Interview with Justin Towner, November 17, 2007 (in the possession of Justin Towner); Gillespie, *A History of the Second Presbyterian Church*, 27, 28, 38, 45, 52; "The Second Presbyterian Church of Memphis" (Box 66747, Mississippi Valley Collection, University of Memphis).

7. Mervin Rosenbush, "Downtown's Second Presbyterian Church Is Proud of Its Social Service Program," *Memphis Press-Scimitar* (April 5, 1941): 3. Such articles were often based on church publications like "The Second Presbyterian Church of Memphis (On the Corner of

Hernando and Pontotoc Streets)," printed by direction of the church session in 1934 (archives of Second Presbyterian Church, Memphis, Tennessee).

8. "Nine Pastors Have Served Church Here in 88 Years: Second Presbyterian Church, Organized in 1884, Has Had Interesting History, Being Parent Organization of Five Daughter Churches," *Memphis Commercial Appeal* (September 3, 1932): 12; "The Second Presbyterian Church of Memphis (On the Corner of Hernando and Pontotoc Streets)."

9. "Story Corps" Interview with Justin Towner.

10. Gillespie, *A History of the Second Presbyterian Church*, 60; David M. Reimers, *White Protestantism and the Negro* (New York: Oxford University Press, 1965): 159.

11. Gillespie, *A History of the Second Presbyterian Church*, 70–71; John Driscoll, "Second Presbyterian Buys Big Church Site: Seven and a Half Acre Tract Will Cost $25,000," *Memphis Commercial Appeal* (February 12, 1945): 9; "Second Presbyterian's Past Recalled by Modern Plant: First Meeting Was in Cotton Warehouse in 1844, But New Million Dollar Addition Will Give Church 'Most Complete Facilities' in City," *Memphis Commercial Appeal* (July 27, 1957): 20.

12. Interview with Harold Jackson, September 22, 2009; Interview with Mac and Muriel Hart, November 27, 2009.

13. http://en.wikipedia.org/wiki/Frank_Minis_Johnson; Interview with William O'Neal, March 8, 2011; Taylor Branch, *Parting the Waters: America during the King Years, 1954–63* (New York: Simon and Schuster, 1988): 147; Martin Luther King, Jr., *Stride Toward Freedom: The Montgomery Story* (New York: Harper & Brothers, 1958): 114–115.

14. "Church to Wrestle Angel of Crisis," *Memphis Commercial Appeal* (January 30, 1965): 8.

15. The connection between Presbyterians and the College actually reaches back to 1837 (see W. Raymond Cooper, *Southwestern at Memphis 1848–1948* [Richmond: John Knox Press, 1948], Chapter 1).

16. John N. Waddel, *Memorials of Academic Life: Being An Historical Sketch of the Waddel Family, Identified Through Three Generations with the History of the Higher Education in the South and Southwest* (Richmond: Presbyterian Committee of Publication, 1891): 511.

17. Cooper, *Southwestern at Memphis*, 104–105, 110.

18. "Victory for Dr. Diehl," *Memphis Commercial Appeal* (October 6, 1933): 8. The volume of pamphlets produced by the Diehl Affair apparently gave rise to an overture to the 1933 PCUS General Assembly against "circularizing."

19. *The Official Report of the Hearing of the Charges Preferred By Eleven Presbyterian Ministers Against President Charles E. Diehl Held On Tuesday, February 3rd, 1931 by the Board of Directors of Southwestern* (Memphis: Committee on Publication of Southwestern at Memphis, 1931): 26. Diehl's own view was that the biblical authors were inspired to create an "authoritative and trustworthy and progressive revelation of God's will and nature."

20. *The Official Report of the Hearing*, 33, 29, 36.

21. Letter from A. P. Moore to Rev. David Park, May 12, 1932 (College Archives, Barret Library, Rhodes College).

22. "Diehl Conciliates Southwestern Foes," *Memphis Commercial Appeal* (October 6, 1933): 6; J. P. Robertson, *Needed Changes in Southwestern College: An Address to the Ministers, Elders and Others of the Synods of Alabama, Louisiana, Mississippi and Tennessee* (n.p., 1931): 3; W. S. Lacy, *An Answer to the Charges Made by the President, His Associates and the Board of Southwestern against the Eleven Ministers of Memphis and W. S. Lacy* (Memphis: n.p., 1931): 4; W. S. Lacy, *Southwestern at the Cross-Roads: Some of the Evidence Supporting the Petition of the Eleven Presbyterian Ministers of Memphis* (Memphis: n.p., 1931): 11; Letter from A. P. Kelso to Charles E. Diehl, May 11, 1931 (College Archives, Barret Library, Rhodes College); Letter from A. P. Moore to Rev. David Park, May 12, 1932.

23. Charles E. Diehl, "Memoranda Concerning Petition Recently Filed By Certain Presbyterian Ministers of Memphis," 3 (College Archives, Barret Library, Rhodes College); *Give the Truth and Southwestern a Chance* (n.p., 1931?): 2–3; Charles E. Diehl, Sermon upon Retirement as PCUS Moderator (May 1942) (College Archives, Barret Library, Rhodes College). On

one occasion, preaching on Micah 6:8 and the prophet's charge "to do justice, and to love kindness, and to walk humbly with your God," Diehl concluded that "here we have the essentials of a universal religion" (Felix Gear, "Dr Diehl: His Service in the Church," 13 [Felix Gear Papers, Presbyterian Heritage Center, Montreat, North Carolina]).

24. *The Official Report of the Hearing*, 39; "Statements Made at the Meeting of the Synod of Tennessee, October 5, 1938" (College Archives, Barret Library, Rhodes College). One local minister proclaimed that while his own daughter was a student at Southwestern he had never found "anything to indicate that the institution is not absolutely sound, through and through." "If I had a hundred children," he continued, "I would be glad for all of them to go to Southwestern."

25. *Southwestern Catalog* (1946–47): 19; "The Classic of Classics," n.d. (College Archives, Barret Library, Rhodes College).

26. Annual Report of the Dean, October 1950 (College Archives, Barret Library, Rhodes College); advertisement appearing in *The Presbyterian Survey* in 1964.

27. *Southwestern Presbyterian University Catalog* (1878–79): 81.

28. Waddel, *Memorials of Academic Life*, 528, 529.

29. Norman White, "Non-Religious Student Speaks," *Sou'wester* (November 1, 1963): 3; Grace A. Fitzgerald, "'Chapel is What Students Make It'," *Sou'wester* (November 1, 1963): 2; "Hack," "Chapel Revisited," *Sou'wester* (October 9, 1964): 2. In the 1960s, chapel services at Southwestern were held four times per week. Monday, Tuesday, and Wednesday meetings were "convocations" consisting of varied programs, with a corporate worship service on Thursday. Attendance at these four weekly meetings was "compulsory" with two caveats: Students in their first three years were allowed ten "cuts" per year, while seniors were allotted an unlimited number of absences. These concessions had been made as the student body outgrew the capacity of a single meeting space on campus. Although two-thirds of students voted to discontinue required chapel in the fall of 1966, it was not abolished until 1968.

30. Bert Ringold and Horace Hull, "Socialistic Fate?" *The Sou'wester* (October 12, 1962): 2; "President Urges Mature Reactions," *The Sou'wester* (October 5, 1962): 1; Roger Hart, "Letter to the Editor: A Call for Courage," *The Sou'wester* (September 21, 1962): 2.

31. "Freshman Vespers: Campbell is Coming," *The Sou'wester* (May 10, 1963): 1; "'Right to Examine Ideas is Main Issue in Election,'" *The Sou'wester* (November 22, 1963): 1; "Seminar Shows Student Concern for Civil Rights Bill Implications," *The Sou'wester* (October 4, 1963): 1. On white Mississippians' views of Campbell and Silver, see Peter Slade, *Open Friendship in a Closed Society: Mission Mississippi and a Theology of Friendship* (New York: Oxford University Press, 2009): 24–38.

32. Kay Pittman, "Surprise March by Students Greets Clements, Walters," *Memphis Press-Scimitar* (January 18, 1964): 1, 2; Laurie B. Green, *Battling the Plantation Mentality: Memphis and the Black Freedom Struggle* (Chapel Hill: University of North Carolina Press, 2007): 255.

33. Ernest Trice Thompson, *Presbyterians in the South*, 3 vols. (Richmond: John Knox Press, 1963–1973): 3:539; "Presbyterians Seek Bias End in Institutions," *Atlanta Daily World* (May 3, 1960): 1; "Southern Presbyterians Asked to Drop Race Bias," *Atlanta Daily World* (April 17, 1963): 1. In a memorandum to the Southwestern board in 1962, Rhodes placed "its long tradition of no Negroes in the student body" at the top of a list of reasons Southwestern had not been among the colleges benefiting from a $100 million Ford Foundation matching grant program aimed at strengthening liberal education ("Memorandum to the Members of the Board of Directors of Southwestern at Memphis," July 20, 1962). In another memorandum two years later Rhodes indicated that the college's acceptance of blacks only as "day students" was going to make it difficult to attract foundation support in the upcoming capital funds drive ("Memorandum to Members of the Board of Directors of Southwestern at Memphis," July 3, 1964). The decision to accept blacks as "residential applicants" was made in October 1964 (all documents in College Archives, Barret Library, Rhodes College).

34. Albert Bruce Curry, *History of the Second Presbyterian Church of Memphis, Tennessee* (Memphis: Adams Printing and Stationery, 1936): 75, 52; Minutes of Congregational Meeting, Second Presbyterian Church, June 29, 1930 (Archives of Second Presbyterian Church, Memphis, Tennessee).

35. Walker L. Wellford, *Facts about the Southwestern Controversy* (Memphis: n.p., 1931): 7; Letter from J. P. Robertson "To the Ministers of the Four Synods," April 6, 1931 (College Archives, Barret Library, Rhodes College); Lacy, *Southwestern at the Cross-Roads*, 5–6; *The Official Report of the Hearing*, 31.

36. "Statements Made at the Meeting of the Synod of Tennessee, October 5, 1938."

37. Interview with John and Pat Clark, July 10, 2004.

38. KBG, "A Southwestern Student Prays," *The Sou'wester* (September 28, 1962): 2.

39. "The Seeker," *The Sou'wester* (October 19, 1962): 2.

40. Letter from Henry Edward Russell to Dr. Peyton N. Rhodes, November 13, 1962 (College Archives, Barret Library, Rhodes College).

41. Letter from Peyton N. Rhodes to Dr. Henry E. Russell, November 2, 1962 (College Archives, Barret Library, Rhodes College).

42. "Fund Drive to Start: $175,000 to be Sought for Southwestern," *Memphis Commercial Appeal* (March 2, 1964): A19.

Chapter 5

1. "Memphis, 1965?" *Presbyterian Outlook* (April 27, 1964): 3. In its April 20 issue, the *Outlook* had published an article by Lawrence F. Haygood, pastor at Parkway Gardens Presbyterian Church in Memphis, who wrote that "churches which, through their Sessions, turn Negroes away from their worship have usurped a power which does not belong to them. To turn a worshipper away from the services of the church is the same thing as turning God away." Although Haygood did not mention SPC, he certainly knew that kneel-ins were under way there, since students would attend his church after being repelled from SPC (Lawrence F. Haygood, "For an Inclusive Church," *Presbyterian Outlook* [April 20, 1964]: 5).

2. Donald W. Shriver, ed., *The Unsilent South: Prophetic Preaching in Racial Crisis* (Atlanta: John Knox Press, 1965): 14.

3. Dwyn M. Mounger, "Racial Attitudes in the Presbyterian Church in the United States, 1944–1954," *Journal of Presbyterian History* 48 (winter, 1970): 38–68; 38. Joel L. Alvis, Jr., *Religion and Race: Southern Presbyterians 1946–1983* (Tuscaloosa: University of Alabama Press, 1994): 6. In 1898, many black Presbyterian congregations formed an Afro-American Presbyterian Church, but later rejoined the PCUS in a segregated Snedecor Memorial Synod.

4. Alvis, *Religion and Race*, 99; "Church Sends Help across Race Line," *Presbyterian Survey* (February 1964): 52; Margaret Dysart, "What Christian Can Deny a Child?" *Presbyterian Survey* (January 1964): 55.

5. Shriver, *The Unsilent South*, 15; Mounger, "Racial Attitudes," 61, 63. "Southern Presbyterians Vote to Open Church Rolls," *Atlanta Daily World* (June 1, 1954): 1; "Presbyterians Renew Blast on Segregation," *Atlanta Daily World* (June 8, 1955): 1.

6. Mounger, "Racial Attitudes," 48; "Letter to the PCUS Board of Christian Education from the Elders of Trinity Presbyterian Church, Montgomery, Alabama, June 3, 1957," *Presbyterian Journal* (June 19, 1957): 6–8; 7; Morton H. Smith, *How is the Gold Become Dim: the Decline of the Presbyterian Church, U.S., As Reflected in Its Assembly Actions* (Jackson, MS: Committee for a Continuing Presbyterian Church, Faithful to the Scriptures and the Reformed Faith, 1973): 154.

7. Mounger, "Racial Attitudes," 55, 58; "'Young Turks' in Action," *Presbyterian Journal* (June 24, 1964): 12; "The Humor Was Lost," *Presbyterian Survey* (January, 1965): 8; "An Assembly of Action," *Presbyterian Survey* (June, 1964): 4.

8. Mounger, *Racial Attitudes*, 40. Overture from the Presbytery of East Alabama, *Minutes of the One-Hundred-Fourth General Assembly of the Presbyterian Church in the United States* (Atlanta: Office of the General Assembly, 1964): 43–44.

9. Mounger, "Racial Attitudes," 42–44; "S. C. Criticizes Assembly, Asks Reconsideration," *Presbyterian Journal* (June 10, 1964): 6; Alvis, *Religion and Race*, 51–53; Frank Joseph Smith, *The History of the Presbyterian Church in America*, Silver Anniversary Edition (Lawrenceville, GA: Presbyterian Scholars Press, 1999): 46; Kenneth Taylor, "The Spirituality of the Church: Segregation, *The Presbyterian Journal*, and the Origins of the Presbyterian Church in America," *Reformed Perspectives Magazine* 9:34 (August 19–August 25, 2007), http://thirdmill.org/the-spirituality-of-the-church.

10. Julia Kirk Blackwelder, "Southern White Fundamentalists and the Civil Rights Movement," *Phylon* 40:4 (1979): 334–341; 334–336; L. Nelson Bell, "A Layman and His Faith: Relevance," *Christianity Today* (May 10, 1963): 26–27; "The Race Revolution," *Christianity Today* (December 6, 1963): 18–19; "The Church and Political Pronouncements," *Christianity Today* (August 28, 1964): 29–31; David L. Chappell, *A Stone of Hope: Prophetic Religion and the Death of Jim Crow* (Chapel Hill: University of North Carolina Press, 2004): 277n52.

11. "Leave It to Nature," *Presbyterian Survey* (July, 1964): 8; "'Concerns' Statement Adopted," *Presbyterian Journal* (October 14, 1964): 4; "The Church and Political Pronouncements," 29–31; "Presbyterians: Concern vs. Concerned." *Time* (October 13, 1967), http://www.time.com/time/magazine/article/0,9171,837385,00.html.

12. Peter Slade, *Open Friendship in a Closed Society: Mission Mississippi and a Theology of Friendship* (New York: Oxford University Press, 2009): 100; Ernest Trice Thompson, *The Spirituality of the Church: A Distinctive Doctrine of the Presbyterian Church in the United States* (Richmond: John Knox Press, 1961): 24–25.

13. R. A. Lapsley, in *How is the Gold Become Dim*, 17.

14. Thompson, *Presbyterians in the South*, 3:509–510.

15. "States' Rights and Human Rights," *Minutes of the Eighty-Ninth General Assembly of the Presbyterian Church in the United States* (Atlanta: Office of the General Assembly, 1949): 177–193; "The Theological Basis for Christian Social Action," *Minutes of the One-Hundred-Sixth General Assembly of the Presbyterian Church in the United States* (Richmond: Office of the General Assembly, 1966): 160–165; 160, 161.

16. "The Assembly in Detail," *Presbyterian Journal* (May 13, 1964): 7–11, 19; 9, 10; Hartley, "The 104th General Assembly," 10; "Race, NCC Seen as Big Issues in General Assembly April 23–29," *Presbyterian Survey* (April, 1964): 45; "A Voice of Protest," *Presbyterian Survey* (July, 1964): 6.

17. Alvis, *Religion and Race*, 100; "S. C. Criticizes Assembly," 6.

18. Thompson, *Presbyterians in the South*, 3:539, 547; "The Relationship between the Races in the Area Served by the Presbyterian Church U.S.," *Minutes of the One-Hundred-Third General Assembly of the Presbyterian Church in the United States* (Atlanta: Office of the General Assembly, 1963): 154–155.

19. *The Book of Church Order of the Presbyterian Church in the United States* (Atlanta: Stated Clerk of the General Assembly of the Presbyterian Church in the United States, 1965): 130.

20. Ben Lacy Rose, *Racial Segregation in the Church* (Richmond: Outlook Publishers, 1957): 25.

21. Ben Lacy Rose, "Should Deacons Vote to Seat Worshippers?" *Presbyterian Survey* (January 1964): 28; "Overture to the General Assembly from the Presbytery of Montgomery (Virginia)," *Minutes of the One-Hundred-Fourth General Assembly*, 26.

22. Shriver, *The Unsilent South*, 100; Alvis, *Religion and Race*, 85, 105, 111; "Southern Presbyterians Decry Washington March," *Atlanta Daily World* (August 23, 1963): 2; "A Brief History of Bethesda Presbyterian Church, 'The Church That Named Bethesda,'" http://bethesdapresbyterian.org/notes/Our_History.

23. "Overture from the Presbytery of Potomac," *Minutes of the One-Hundred-Fourth General Assembly*, 39; "Supplemental Report of the Standing Committee on Assembly Operation," *Minutes of the One-Hundred-Fourth General Assembly*, 76. Writing to his congregation, Pritchett confessed that the resolution "was drawn up by some of the informed officials of the Assembly and our church" ("A Pastoral Letter, Sunday, May 3, 1964," 1 [in the possession of Bethesda Presbyterian Church]). According to *The Presbyterian Journal*, a group fasted

over the weekend in preparation for forcing a reconsideration of this action on Monday ("The Assembly in Detail" [May 13, 1964]: 11).

24. Hartley, "The 104th General Assembly," 11. *Minutes of the One-Hundred-Fourth General Assembly*, 76, 77.

25. "Bars Are Up at Memphis Second," *Presbyterian Outlook* (May 11, 1964): 8; "Memphis, Second," *Presbyterian Outlook* (May 18, 1964): 8.

26. Letter from Malcolm P. Calhoun to Hayden J. Kaden, April 30, 1964 (in the possession of Hayden Kaden).

27. Carl R. Pritchett, "No Moment of Greatness" (April 29, 1964), 1, 2 (in the possession of Bethesda Presbyterian Church).

28. Pritchett, "No Moment of Greatness," 1, 2, 3.

29. Carl Pritchett, "A Pastoral Letter, Sunday, May 3, 1964": 1.

30. Carl R. Pritchett, "What Happened at Memphis, May 10, 1964" (in the possession of Bethesda Presbyterian Church): 2, 4.

31. Pritchett, "What Happened at Memphis," 2.

32. Pritchett, "What Happened at Memphis," 3.

33. Pritchett, "What Happened at Memphis," 4.

34. Pritchett, "What Happened at Memphis," 5, 6, 7. Lawrence F. Haygood, "The Triumphant Life of the Poor in Spirit," in Shriver, *The Unsilent South*, 152–165; 156–157. See also "White Maryland Minister Refused Admittance to Second Presbyterian," *Tri-State Defender* (May 9, 1964): 1–2.

35. Pritchett, "What Happened at Memphis," 7.

36. Smith, *History of the Presbyterian Church in America*, 192. Hartley, "The 104th General Assembly," 10; "The General Assembly of 1964 Addressed Its Concern to Local Sessions of the Presbyterian Church US in A Pastoral Letter on Race," *Presbyterian Survey* (July, 1964): 12–13; "Christianity Is a Demonstration," *Presbyterian Survey* (July, 1964): 4–5.

37. "Bars Are Up at Memphis Second," 8; "Memphis, Second," 8.

38. "Message to Memphis," *Presbyterian Outlook* (June 1, 1964): 4; "Texas Presbyterians Attack Plans to Meet in Memphis," *Memphis Commercial Appeal* (May 21, 1964): 1; "Protest Church Assembly Here," *Memphis Press-Scimitar* (May 21, 1964): 36.

39. "Memphis Second and the 1965 Assembly," *Presbyterian Outlook* (June 29, 1964): 3–4; "Ministers Protest Church Segregation," *Baltimore Afro-American* (June 20, 1964): 5; Letter from Westminster Fellowship Council to the General Assembly in care of Stated Clerk James Millard, August 18, 1964 (in the possession of Hayden Kaden).

40. "202 Missionaries Appeal to Their Home Church," *Presbyterian Outlook* (April 27, 1964): 5–6; 5. It is not clear whether the April appeal was composed or signed with knowledge of what was happening in Memphis, although it did bear the signatures of Donald and Mary Bobb, missionaries in the Congo who were supported directly by SPC. In September, thirty-two newly commissioned missionaries (thirteen of them bound for Congo) added their names to the letter ("Outgoing Missionaries Sign Plea to the Church," *Presbyterian Outlook* [September 7, 1964]: 2).

41. "Open Letter to the Presbyterian Church, U.S. From the Congo Mission," *Presbyterian Outlook* (October 19, 1964): 2. See also *"To: The Presbyterian Church US; From: the American Presbyterian Congo Mission; Regarding: racial discrimination,"* *Presbyterian Survey* (November, 1964): 43.

42. Minutes of the Session of Second Presbyterian Church, Memphis, Tennessee, June 28, 1964, 1; Interview with Hugh Farrior, November 27, 2009. Farrior reports that several months later he received a courteous but evasive reply from Rev. Jeb Russell.

43. "Christian Solution of Race Problem Urged by Leader," *Atlanta Daily World* (November 10, 1957): 1; "Presbyterians Seek Bias End in Institutions," *Atlanta Daily World* (May 3, 1960), 1. Samuel Southard commented on this phenomenon in 1963: "Missionaries on furlough have often spoken against segregation to southern white audiences that have

never before heard a white man condemn it. They have been listened to because they present racial prejudice as a stumbling block to evangelization of the heathen and a scandal to whites who call themselves Christian. It is hard to silence missionaries from one's home state" ("Are Southern Churches Silent?" *Christian Century* [November 20, 1963]: 1429–32; 1432).

44. Ben Lacy Rose, "When Negroes Are Barred from Worship, What Can Be Done about It?" *Presbyterian Survey* (July, 1964): 18; See also "Controversy on Open-Door Race Policy Involves '65 Assembly Host Church," *Presbyterian Survey* (July, 1964): 36.

45. "Memphis, 1965?" 8; John H. Leith, "The Bible and Race," *Presbyterian Outlook* (July 27, 1964): 6.

46. "Memphis Church Regrets Site Change," *Presbyterian Journal* (February 10, 1965): 5–6; "An Emergency?" *Presbyterian Journal* (February 10, 1965): 12. In a letter to the *Journal's* editor, Harry E. Atkinson wrote that "the circumstances as they exist today at the Second Church are no different from the circumstances that existed at the time of the 104th Assembly . . . and no amount of postulating by the Moderator that an emergency exists can create an emergency out of the situation. . . ." (*Journal* [March 3, 1965]: 1).

47. Letter from Felix Gear to John Randolph Taylor, May 14, 1964 (Felix Gear Papers, Presbyterian Heritage Center, Montreat, North Carolina).

48. In early December 1965, Rev. Don M. Wardlaw of Shady Grove Presbyterian Church in Memphis informed Moderator Gear that "a number of us ministers here are discussing what would be the most appropriate action for Memphis Presbytery to take should the Session of Second Presbyterian Church maintain its present policy regarding the seating of those who present themselves for worship." Wardlaw believed that a decision regarding a change of venue for the 1965 General Assembly would have to be made no later than the presbytery's January meeting. "We would like to know your opinion," he wrote, "about how long we of Memphis Presbytery should and can wait for a change of policy at Second before we take some action as a Presbytery" (Letter from Don M. Wardlaw to Felix Gear, December 3, 1964 [Felix Gear Papers, Presbyterian Heritage Center, Montreat, North Carolina]); Letter from Charles C. Gillespie to Felix Gear, December 19, 1964 (Felix Gear Papers, Presbyterian Heritage Center, Montreat, North Carolina).

49. Felix Gear, "Dr Diehl: His Service in the Church," undated typewritten document (Felix Gear Papers, Presbyterian Heritage Center, Montreat, North Carolina).

50. Felix B. Gear, "Every Christian In South Must Have Felt a Real Sense of Shame." The undated article appeared in a Memphis newspaper in December 1946 (press clipping in the possession of Elizabeth Caldwell).

Chapter 6

1. Minutes of the Session of Second Presbyterian Church, Memphis, Tennessee, August 19, 1957, 2. Apparently there was a precedent for all women of Memphis Presbytery to be welcomed at meetings held at SPC. See "Presbyterian Women Will Meet Thursday: 60 Churches to be Represented at Two-Day Session," *Memphis Commercial Appeal* (February 16, 1954): 17.

2. Minutes of the Session of Second Presbyterian Church, Memphis, Tennessee, October 7, 1957, 3.

3. Minutes of the Session of Second Presbyterian Church, Memphis, Tennessee, October 7, 1957, 4; "Segregation Backed by Church Leaders, Second Presbyterian Session to Propose Policy, Opposes Mixed Meets," *Memphis Commercial Appeal* (October 10, 1957): 5. The *Commercial Appeal* reported that while SPC was the first Presbyterian church in Memphis to move toward adoption of such a policy, Idlewild Church had discussed a similar policy some time earlier and First Presbyterian had a policy of segregation "within the church itself" ("2nd Presbyterian Takes Action on Segregation, Will Avoid Integrated Conferences But Plan with Negro Adults," *Memphis Press-Scimitar* [October 9, 1957]: 14).

4. Interestingly, many Presbyterians in Little Rock supported desegregation of public schools, earning the ire of Governor Faubus, who called them "Communists." Marion Boggs, pastor

of the Second Presbyterian Church in the city, was a particularly outspoken advocate of moderation and cooperation during the crisis (Joel L. Alvis, Jr., *Religion and Race: Southern Presbyterians 1946–1983* [Tuscaloosa: University of Alabama Press, 1994]: 69, 108).

5. Alvis, *Religion and Race*, 30–31.

6. Ibid., 85, 87; Minutes of the Session of Second Presbyterian Church, Memphis, Tennessee, October 7, 1957, 3.

7. Around the same time that SPC adopted its "Statement of Policy," *Presbyterian Journal* co-founder L. Nelson Bell warned that integrated youth conferences could have "tragic and disastrous results" (Alvis, *Religion and Race*, 52); Dwyn M. Mounger, "Racial Attitudes in the Presbyterian Church in the United States, 1944–1954," *Journal of Presbyterian History* 48 (winter, 1970): 38–68; 45; Ernest Trice Thompson, *Presbyterians in the South*, 3 vols. (Richmond: John Knox Press, 1963–1973): 3:540. Even religious moderates were careful to avoid the impression that they endorsed interracial coupling. When an interdenominational group of Atlanta clergymen published a statement in 1957 urging Christians to obey the laws of the land, they disavowed any support for racial amalgamation (*Presbyterians in the South*, 3:546).

8. Minutes of the Session of Second Presbyterian Church, Memphis, Tennessee, October 7, 1957, 3.

9. Mrs. K. William Chandler, "Church History: the Year of Our Lord, Nineteen Hundred and Sixty-Four," 2 (Presbyterian Heritage Center, Montreat, North Carolina).

10. Alvis, *Religion and Race*, 55, 97–98; Peter Slade, *Open Friendship in a Closed Society: Mission Mississippi and a Theology of Friendship* (New York: Oxford University Press, 2009): 108. The same year L. Nelson Bell, leader of Southern Presbyterian traditionalists, declared in *Life* magazine that "Christians should recognize that there is no biblical or legal justification for segregation" (Chappell, *A Stone of Hope*, 117).

11. George Lewis, *Massive Resistance: The White Response to the Civil Rights Movement* (New York: Hodder Education, 2006): 73, 96. The SPC session's Cold War mentality was evident in May 1961, when Elder Alonzo Carroll announced that after the meeting he would distribute information on "the movement of Communism requested by the Session," and in January 1963, when the "Fallout Shelter Committee" reported that the church could be used "for supplies consisting of medical radiological, water, and minimum feed requirements to sustain 943 people for a period of seven days" (Minutes of the Session of Second Presbyterian Church, Memphis, Tennessee, May 15, 1961, 5; January 21, 1963, 2).

12. Minutes of the Session of Second Presbyterian Church, Memphis, Tennessee, May 14, 1962, 3. The motion was tabled, but in June 1963 Rev. Russell did inform the congregation that "the policy of each camp [at Nacome] is to notify the parents of those children who may be assigned to a cabin with a negro camper, giving them the opportunity to change the cabin assignment if there are objections" (Minutes of the Session of Second Presbyterian Church, Memphis, Tennessee, June 17, 1963, 2).

13. Minutes of the Session of Second Presbyterian Church, Memphis, Tennessee, June 17, 1963, 1.

14. Minutes of the Session of Second Presbyterian Church, Memphis, Tennessee, June 16, 1963, 1.

15. Minutes of the Session of Second Presbyterian Church, Memphis, Tennessee, January 20, 1964, 2.

16. Interview with John Adamson, November 19, 2009.

17. Interview with John Adamson, July 7, 2003.

18. Interview with Bill Weber, November 19, 2009.

19. Interview with John and Pat Clark, July 10, 2004.

20. Interview with Don McClure, Sr., December 2, 2009.

21. Interview with Milton Knowlton, November 23, 2009.

22. Ibid.

23. Ibid.

24. Interview with Justin Towner, October 7, 2010.

25. Interviews with Justin Towner, August 6, 2004; October 7, 2010.
26. Interview with Hortense Spillers, August 16, 2004.
27. Interview with Zeno and Elsie Yeates, August 24, 2004.
28. Interview with Millen Darnell, March 7, 2008.
29. Ibid.
30. Interview with William Craddock, Jr., June 16, 2010.
31. Ibid.
32. *The Book of Church Order of the Presbyterian Church in the United States*, 81.
33. Interview with William Craddock, Jr., June 16, 2010.
34. Interview with Phil Esty, July 10, 2004.
35. Ibid.
36. Ibid.
37. Interview with Ed Knox, August 25, 2004. Minutes of the Session of Second Presbyterian Church, Memphis, Tennessee, July 20, 1964, 2.
38. Interview with Ed Knox, August 25, 2004.
39. Interview with Ed Knox, August 25, 2004; Letter from H. E. Russell, C. Phil Esty, James Hazelwood, and Edward J. Knox to "Friends in Christ," January 21, 1965 (Box 66747, Mississippi Valley Collection, University of Memphis). The letter also called attention to the constitutional amendment approved by the 1964 General Assembly and subsequently ratified by a majority of presbyteries.
40. Interview with Ed Knox, August 25, 2004.
41. Interview with Millen Darnell, March 7, 2008; Interview with Wilson and Jane Northcross, July 14, 2004; Letter from Mrs. Jane C. Nall to Rev. W. Walter Johnson, June 26, 1964 (in the possession of Hayden Kaden); "Notes on Jane Patterson's Conversation with Ladye Margaret Arnold, October 22, 1995" (in the possession of Jane Patterson); Interview with John and Pat Clark, July 10, 2004.
42. Interview with William Craddock, Jr., June 16, 2010; Interview with Martha McKee, August 27, 2010; Interview with Wilson and Jane Northcross, July 14, 2004; Interview with Zeno and Elsie Yeates, August 24, 2004.
43. Interview with William Craddock, Jr., June 16, 2010. A document from the Accord Committee mentions Margaret C. Askew, Luzanne W. Tayloe, Martha L. Roark, and Anne R. Seay as among those who had assisted in confirming signatures (Minutes of the Session of Second Presbyterian Church, Memphis, TN, February 15, 1965, 1, 2).
44. *1964–65 Year Book, Second Presbyterian Church, Poplar at Goodlett, Memphis, Tennessee* (n.p, n.d.): 23–42; Thomas N. Pappas, "Second Presbyterian Vote Keeps Segregation Policy," *Memphis Press-Scimitar* (February 10, 1965): 17. A few months later, in October 1964, Southwestern Professor of Bible Julius Melton told another presbytery-wide gathering of women at SPC that "white man cannot meet black man as brother in Christ in church on Sunday without meeting him as brother on Monday as well" ("Presbyterian Pastor Flays Disunity," *Memphis Commercial Appeal* [October 10, 1964]: 10).
45. Chandler, "Church History: the Year of Our Lord, Nineteen Hundred and Sixty-Four," 1, 3.
46. Ibid., 2.
47. Ibid., 3.
48. Ibid., 2, 3. David L. Chappell notes that during the Little Rock crisis of 1957 the Council of Church Women of Little Rock and North Little Rock went on record condemning forced segregation and criticizing Governor Orval Faubus's actions (David L. Chappell, "Diversity within a Racial Group: White People in Little Rock 1957–1959," *Arkansas Historical Quarterly* 54:4 [winter, 1995]: 444–456; 444). Samuel Southard relates that in the 1940s when deacons at First Baptist Church in Vicksburg, Mississippi, declared that blacks could not visit the church without their permission, members of the woman's missionary society defied them by declaring they would invite anyone they pleased to speak at their meetings ("Are Southern Churches Silent?" *Christian Century* [November 20, 1963]: 1429–1432; 1431).

49. Mrs. K. William Chandler, "Church History: the Year of Our Lord, Nineteen Hundred and Sixty-Five," 3 (Presbyterian Heritage Center, Montreat, North Carolina).

50. Presbyteries could, with or without a congregation's request, dissolve the relationship between a church and one of its ruling elders or deacons following a hearing to determine whether such an action was necessary "for the Church's welfare." Although a congregational majority could request dissolution of the active relationship between the church and an officer without censure, it remained the session's decision whether or not to take this action (*The Book of Church Order of the Presbyterian Church in the United States* [Atlanta: Stated Clerk of the General Assembly of the Presbyterian Church in the United States, 1965]: 82).

51. Minutes of the Session of Second Presbyterian Church, Memphis, Tennessee, April 29, 1964, 2–3.

52. The quotations are from Elder Charles C. Gillespie. See "Church to Wrestle Angel of Crisis," *Memphis Commercial Appeal* (January 30, 1965): 8; and Susan Carter, "2nd Church Race Ruling Postponed," *Memphis Press-Scimitar* (July 22, 1964): 33.

53. Interview with Jack Connors, July 7, 2003; Carl R. Pritchett, "What Happened in Memphis, May 10, 1964," 4 (in the possession of Bethesda Presbyterian Church).

54. Minutes of the Session of Second Presbyterian Church, Memphis, Tennessee, April 29, 1964, 3; Interview with Herbert Rhea, August 17, 2004.

55. Interview with Herbert Rhea, August 17, 2004.

56. Interview with Jack Connors, July 7, 2003.

Chapter 7

1. Kay Pittman, "Surprise March by Students Greets Clement, Walters," *Memphis Press-Scimitar* (January 18, 1964): 1–2.

2. Interview with Jim Bullock, March 17, 2009.

3. Davis W. Houck and David D. Dixon, eds., *Rhetoric, Religion and the Civil Rights Movement, 1954–1965* (Waco: Baylor University Press, 2006): 295; Interview with Jim Bullock, August 21, 2003.

4. Interview with Jim Bullock, August 21, 2003.

5. Ibid.

6. Interview with Michael Braswell, August 1, 2011; Interview with Jim Bullock, August 21, 2003.

7. Interview with Jim Bullock, August 21, 2003.

8. Interview with Jim Bullock, March 17, 2009.

9. Interview with Jim Bullock, August 21, 2003.

10. Ibid.

11. Interview with Jim Bullock, March 17, 2009.

12. Interview with Jim Bullock, April 15, 2004.

13. Interview with Jim Bullock, March 17, 2009.

14. E-mail from Howard Romaine, March 12, 2010.

15. E-mail from Howard Romaine, March 7, 2010; E-mail from Howard Romaine June 24, 2003.

16. Gregg L. Michel, *Struggle for a Better South: The Southern Student Organizing Committee, 1964–69* (New York: Palgrave Macmillan, 2004): 60.

17. "Student States Ideals of Group Making Current National News," *The Sou'wester* (April 24, 1964): 3. In an earlier press release, Romaine had written that the NAACP Intercollegiate Chapter's Non-Violent Committee was "very much interested in promoting the real meaning of Brotherhood in our community. Members of this group feel a deep moral obligation to help make more meaningful the principles of Christianity" (Press Release dated April 12, 1964, Maxine A. Smith—NAACP Collection, Memphis Room, Memphis Public Library and Information Center).

18. Interview with Howard Romaine, July 6, 2003.

19. Ibid.
20. "Church Statement Brings Rebuttal," *Memphis Press-Scimitar* (May 5, 1964): 1.
21. Interview with Howard Romaine, July 6, 2003.
22. Quoted in *Newsletter of the Southern Student Organizing Committee* (May, 1965): 1; http://mdah.state.ms.us/arrec/digital_archives/sovcom/index.php.
23. Interview with Robert Morris, February 24, 2011.
24. Ibid; E-mail message from Robert Morris (January 5, 2012).
25. Ibid.
26. Morris's journey is described in his self-published *The Faith of a Seeker*, http://www.seeker-faith.com/.
27. Interview with Bob Hall, August 8, 2004.
28. Bob Hall, "Non-Violent Group Gains National TV Recognition," *The Sou'wester* (May 8, 1964): 3.
29. Roger Hart, "Letter to the Editor: A Call for Courage," *The Sou'wester* (September 21, 1962): 2.
30. Pittman, "Surprise March by Students Greets Clement, Walters," 1; Interview with Roger Hart, August 8, 2004.
31. Roger Hart, "Campus Ministers Association Plans Three Social Projects," *The Sou'wester* (January 10, 1964): 2.
32. Interview with Roger Hart, August 8, 2004.
33. Ibid.
34. Ibid.
35. Interview with Rocky Ward, November 27, 2009.
36. Ibid.
37. Letter from Rev. C. Rodney Sunday to Mr. Robert J. Hussey, April 9, 1964, in the possession of Hayden Kaden.
38. E-mail from Hayden Kaden, June 20, 2011.
39. Interview with Hayden Kaden, November 22, 2004.
40. Interview with Elizabeth Currie Williams, July 31, 2004.
41. Ibid.
42. Ibid.
43. Interview with Dossett Foster, September 21, 2010.
44. Interview with K. C. Ptomey, March 21, 2008.
45. Ibid.
46. Ibid.
47. Ibid.
48. "The Other Side of Discipleship," Senior Sermon preached by K. C. Ptomey, Jr., Caldwell Chapel, Louisville Presbyterian Seminary, Louisville, Kentucky, November 8, 1966.
49. Interview with K. C. Ptomey, March 21, 2008.
50. D. Cameron Murchison, "Easter Vigil: Mark 16:1–8," in David Bartlett and Barbara Brown Taylor, eds., *Feasting on the Word: Preaching the Revised Common Lectionary, Year B, Volume 2* (Louisville, KY: Westminster/John Knox, 2008): 356.
51. Ibid.
52. Interview with Cam Murchison, April 27, 2010.
53. Interview with Winton Smith, November 19, 2011.
54. Ibid.
55. Interview with Robert Wells, June 23, 2003.
56. Ibid.
57. Ibid.
58. Interview with Ervin Haas Bullock, April 15, 2004.
59. Ibid.
60. Ibid.
61. Ibid.
62. Ibid.

63. Ibid.
64. Interview with Jacquelyn Dowd Hall, August 8, 2004.
65. Ibid.
66. Ibid.
67. E-mail from Martha Overholser Whitney, April 27, 2010; Interview with Martha Overholser Whitney, May 4, 2010.
68. Interview with Rose Mary Hoye Wells, September 23, 2010.
69. Ibid.
70. Ibid.
71. Ibid.
72. Ibid.

Chapter 8

1. David Halberstam, *The Children* (New York: Fawcett, 1998): 49, 217.
2. James M. Lawson, Jr. "From a Lunch-Counter Stool," in Francis L. Broderick and August Meier, eds., *Negro Protest Thought in the Twentieth Century* (Indianapolis: Bobbs-Merrill, 1965): 274–281; 280; Michael K. Honey, *Going Down Jericho Road: The Memphis Strike, Martin Luther King's Last Campaign* (New York: W. W. Norton, 2007): 80. Looking back in 1969, Lawson referred to the Memphis "Freedom Movement," which lasted eighteen months and led to five hundred arrests, as "abortive." In his view, the "scattered picketing" that occurred in downtown Memphis between March 1960 and November 1961 did not qualify as the sort of consistent direct action that was essential to "real confrontation." Interviews with James M. Lawson, Jr. July 21, 1969 (Series VI): 14; August 21, 1969 (Series VII): 15, 16, 17 (Mississippi Valley Connection, University of Memphis).
3. Interview with Maxine Smith, June 14, 2010; Interview with James M. Lawson, Jr. August 12, 2010.
4. Interview with James M. Lawson, Jr., August 12, 2010; Interview with James M. Lawson, Jr. January 21, 1969 (Series IV): 6–7, (Series V): 10–11 (Mississippi Valley Collection, University of Memphis).
5. Interview with James M. Lawson, Jr., August 12, 2010; Lawson, "From a Lunch-Counter Stool," 278.
6. Interview with James M. Lawson, Jr. August 12, 2010; Interview with James M. Lawson, Jr. July 21, 1969 (Series VI): 18; August 21, 1969 (Series VII): 43.
7. Flyer in possession of Hayden Kaden. Lawson led workshops from March 14 to April 4, 1964, while the SPC kneel-ins were under way ("Four Non-Violent Workshops Set for Saturdays," *Tri-State Defender* [March 7, 1964]: 1). Lawson's ten commandments of nonviolent protest appeared in the Birmingham campaign a year earlier in the form of a "commitment card" each would-be protestor was asked to sign (Martin Luther King, Jr., *Why We Can't Wait* [New York: Penguin, 2000]: 51).
8. Lawson, "From a Lunch-Counter Stool," 275. As Southern Secretary for the Fellowship of Reconciliation beginning in 1957, and later as Director of Non-Violent Education for the SCLC, Lawson led multi-day workshops in cities across the South—including Little Rock; Jackson, Mississippi; Columbia, South Carolina; Charlottesville, Virginia; Savannah, Georgia; Memphis; Nashville; Albany; and Birmingham. Among veterans of these workshops were John Lewis, Stokely Carmichael, Marion Barry, and Charles Sherrod (Interview with James M. Lawson, Jr., August 12, 2010; Interview with James M. Lawson, Jr. January 21, 1969 [Series V]: 2–4, [Series VI]: 3 [Mississippi Valley Collection, University of Memphis]).
9. Interview with Vasco Smith, June 24, 2004.
10. Ibid.
11. Ibid.
12. Maxine Smith had been raised Baptist and Vasco African Methodist Episcopal. Upon returning to Memphis in 1955, they joined the newly established Parkway Gardens Presbyterian Church, which was attracting members of the black middle class, including top

officers of the local NAACP (Lawrence F. Haygood, "The Triumphant Life of the Poor in Spirit," in Donald W. Shriver, Jr., ed., *The Unsilent South: Prophetic Preaching in Racial Crisis* [Richmond: John Knox Press, 1965]: 152–65; 152, 157).

13. Another of the kneel-in participants who died relatively young is Armstead Robinson, who in 1964 was a junior at Hamilton High School. After graduating from Yale University (his honors thesis dealt with blacks and Reconstruction in Memphis), Robinson pursued graduate work in history and eventually became an influential scholar of the Civil War.

14. "Negro Student Addresses WF," *The Sou'wester* (January 10, 1964): 3. The article described Purdy as chairman of a group called "Students for Equal Treatment."

15. "Sit-In Students Held to Jury," *Memphis Press-Scimitar* (April 17, 1964): 5; "Student Jailed on Extortion Letter Charge," *Memphis Press-Scimitar* (May 5, 1964): 2; Letter from Joe Purdy to Nicholas H. Karris (Box 10386, Mississippi Valley Collection, University of Memphis).

16. "Brief Disturbance at Normal Café," *Memphis Press-Scimitar* (May 7, 1964): 8; "Trying for Truce in Café Picketing," *Memphis Press-Scimitar* (May 8, 1964): 2; "Negroes Served by Tea Room," *Memphis Press-Scimitar* (July 6, 1964): 1.

17. Interview with Maxine Smith, June 14, 2010; Interview with Vivian Carter Dillihunt, August 17, 2004; Interview with Hortense Spillers, August 16, 2004.

18. Interview with Hortense Spillers, August 16, 2004.

19. Interview with George Purdy, Carolyn Purdy McGhee, Delores Purdy McDowell, and Donna Purdy Fitchpatric, November 21, 2010.

20. "Tha Artivist Presents," W.E. A.L.L. B.E. News Radio (July 6, 2008), http://www.blog-talkradio.com/weallbe/2008/07/06/tha-artivist-presentswe-all-be-news-radio; "Negro Only Memphis Cadet to Win Valor Award," *Jet* (December 5, 1963): 22; Interview with Coby Smith, July 29, 2003.

21. Interview with Coby Smith, July 29, 2003.

22. Ibid.

23. Ibid.

24. Honey, *Going Down Jericho Road*, 85–7; 230–7; *At the River I Stand*. Dir. David Appelby, Allison Graham, and Steven John Ross. California Newsreel, 1993. Film.

25. Interview with Coby Smith, July 29, 2003.

26. Interview with Hortense Spillers, August 16, 2004.

27. Ibid.

28. Ibid.

29. Ibid.

30. Ibid.

31. Ibid.

32. Interview with Harold Taylor, June 26, 2003.

33. Ibid.

34. Ibid.

35. Ibid.

36. Ibid.

37. Interview with Earl Stanback, July 9, 2003.

38. Ibid.

39. Ibid.

40. Ibid.

41. Ibid.

42. Interview with Elaine Lee Turner, August 14, 2003.

43. Ibid.

44. Ibid.

45. Ibid.

46. Ibid.

47. Ibid; http://www.heritagetoursmemphis.com/burkle.html.

48. Interview with Vivian Carter Dillihunt, August 17, 2004.

49. Interview with Elaine Lee Turner, August 14, 2003.

50. http://dillihunt.com/bio.htm.

51. Interviews with Lillian Hammond Brown, June 30, 2003; July 8, 2010.

52. Ibid.

53. Ibid.

54. Interview with Coby Smith, July 29, 2003; Interview with Elaine Lee Turner, August 14, 2003.

55. Interview with Robert Wells, June 27, 2003; Interview with Elizabeth Currie Williams, July 30, 2004; Interview with Elaine Lee Turner, August 14, 2003; Interview with Hortense Spillers, August 16, 2004; Interview with Vivian Carter Dillihunt, August 17, 2004.

56. Kenneth J. Foreman, "Motives Committee: News Items with Comments," *Presbyterian Outlook* (September 30, 1963): 9 (mimeographed copy of leaflet in the possession of Charles Murphy).

57. Ibid.

58. On the connection of Henry Russell with Sen. Richard Russell, see "Private Police Block 'Kneel-Ins' from Presbyterian Church: Church's Men Guard Doors in Person," *Tri-State Defender* (April 25, 1964): 1; "Presbyterians U.S. Nail the Door Open," *Christianity Today* (May 22, 1964), 809; "Church Race Row Moves Meeting," *Atlanta Journal* (January 27, 1965): 33; and "'Young Turks' in Action," *Presbyterian Journal* (June 24, 1964): 12. Carl Pritchett had heard this explanation for the kneel-ins before visiting Memphis and confidently debunked it upon returning to Maryland: "The fact that the senior minister of this church is a brother to a United States Senator has absolutely nothing to do with their 'vigils' at this church. There is no doubt in my mind about this. It is a pure coincidence" (Carl R. Pritchett, "What Happened at Memphis, May 10, 1964," 3 [in the possession of Bethesda Presbyterian Church]).

59. Interview with Hortense Spillers, August 16, 2004.

60. Minutes of the Session of Second Presbyterian Church, Memphis, Tennessee, April 29, 1964, 3. In June 1964, SPC member Mrs. Jane C. Nall wrote to a Presbyterian leader in Texas claiming that "it is a well-known fact that two of the white students are avowed atheists, and these students were from Southwestern College, a Presbyterian college. Every authority at Southwestern from the President on down is aware of this fact. Indeed, the authorities at the college made the statement that they would be glad when the leader of the group of students, an atheist, graduated from Southwestern this June. How can you and the General Assembly condemn Dr. Russell and our elders and give solace to atheists?" (Letter from Mrs. Jane C. Nall to The Rev. Mr. Walter Johnson, June 26, 1964, in the possession of Hayden Kaden).

61. Jason Sokol, *There Goes My Everything: White Southerners in the Age of Civil Rights, 1945–1975* (New York: Alfred A. Knopf, 2006): 56–7.

62. Carl R. Pritchett, "What Happened at Memphis, May 10, 1964," 3, 7 (in the possession of Bethesda Presbyterian Church).

63. Ibid., 3. Interview with Jacqueline Dowd Hall, August 8, 2004.

Chapter 9

1. W. J. Cunningham, *Agony at Galloway: One Church's Struggle with Social Change* (Jackson: University Press of Mississippi, 1980): 50.

2. "Private Police Block 'Kneel-Ins' from Presbyterian Church: Church's Men Guard Doors in Person," *Tri-State Defender* (April 25, 1964): 1. Interview with Jim Bullock, March 7, 2010.

3. Interview with Joanna Russell Hogan, March 22, 2008; Interview with Harriette Russell Coleman, March 14, 2008.

4. Interview with Cay Russell Davis, April 19, 2009; Interview with Jeb Russell, Jr., November 4, 2010.

5. Interview with Howard Hazelwood, August 17, 2010.

6. Ibid.

7. Ibid.

8. Interview with Horace Houston, September 30, 2009.

9. Ibid.

10. Ibid.

11. Interview with Clifton Kirkpatrick, June 29, 2004.

12. Ibid.

13. Ibid.

14. Jerry Van Marter, "PCUSA Is At 'Tipping Point' of Renewal, Kirkpatrick Says," *Presbyterian Layman* (February 28, 2007), http://www.layman.org/News.aspx?article=20334.

15. Rev. Dr. Larry Brown, "Church in Memphis Was Committed to Historic Presbyterianism," *Presbyterian Layman* (March 2, 2007), http://www.layman.org/LettersToTheEditor.aspx?article=203582007.

16. Interviews with Perky Daniel, July 10, 2004, and April 7, 2010.

17. Ibid.

18. Interview with Lib Caldwell, February 28, 2009.

19. Ibid.

20. Ibid.

21. Ibid.

22. Ibid.

23. Ruth Duck, "Second Presbyterian Church Experiences," (April 28, 2010), document in the possession of Ruth Duck.

24. Interview with Ruth Duck, April 28, 2010.

25. Ibid.

26. Ibid. Jeanne Stevenson-Moessner is another child of SPC who went on to serve the Presbyterian Church as an ordained minister, teacher, and scholar. She has no direct memories of the SPC kneel-ins (she was in tenth grade at the time) but remembers being told that the church "resisted their presence in the sanctuary because their desire to gain entrance to the church was for political gain, not personal spiritual renewal." After studying at Princeton Theological Seminary and the University of Basel, Stevenson-Moessner became an ordained minister in the PCUSA, a women's advocate, and an author and editor of books on the pastoral care of women. (Interview with Jeanne Stevenson-Moessner, September 7, 2004; E-mail message, June 11, 2008; E-mail message May 16, 2010.)

27. Interview with John Slater, December 2, 2009.

28. Ibid.

29. Ibid.

30. Interview with Frank Jemison, November 30, 2009.

31. Ibid.

32. Interview with Ed Beasley, September 25, 2009.

33. Ibid.

34. Ibid.

35. Ibid.

36. Interview with Carole Branyan, September 28, 2009.

37. Interview with Dale Seay Kasab, May 4, 2010.

38. Ibid.

39. Ibid.

40. Interview with Charles Murphy, October 9, 2009.

41. Charles M. Murphy, "Reflections from Second Presbyterian's Period of Racial Challenge during 1963–65" (November 2, 2009) (in the possession of Charles Murphy).

42. Ibid.

43. Charles Murphy, "Second Presbyterian Controversy," *Sou'wester* (April 1, 1964): 5.

44. Charles M. Murphy, "Reflections from Second Presbyterian's Period of Racial Challenge during 1963–65" (November 2, 2009).

45. Interview with Jim Williamson, April 3, 2012.

46. Ibid.

47. James Williamson, *The Ravine* (Santa Fe: Sunstone Press, 2012).

48. E-mail message from Minna Thompson Glenn, April 14, 2010.

49. E-mail message from Alex Thompson, September 30, 2009.

50. E-mail message from Minna Thompson Glenn, April 14, 2010.

51. Interview with John McKee, August 27, 2010.

52. Ibid.

53. Interview with Elizabeth Wall, October 6, 2010.

54. Ibid.

55. Ibid.

56. Interview with Fred Flinn, August 26, 2010.

57. Ibid.

58. Interview with Jon Housholder, August 6, 2010.

59. Ibid.

60. Ibid.

Chapter 10

1. Minutes of the Session of Second Presbyterian Church, Memphis, Tennessee, October 7, 1957, 3; March 23, 1964, 3. Members of the expanded Policy Committee were Robert Hussey, Rives Maker, John Cleghorn, Maurice Miller, and C. D. Askew.

2. Minutes of the Session of Second Presbyterian Church, Memphis, Tennessee, April 29, 1964, 2–3.

3. Ibid.

4. Ibid.

5. Ibid.

6. Minutes of the Session of Second Presbyterian Church, Memphis, Tennessee, April 29, 1964, 1.

7. Minutes of the Session of Second Presbyterian Church, Memphis, Tennessee, May 6, 1964, 2. The session responded to the board that it was "now giving prayerful consideration to the communication from the General Assembly" and would consider a meeting with representatives of the Board at a later date (Ibid.).

8. Minutes of the Session of Second Presbyterian Church, Memphis, Tennessee, August 20, 1962, 2; January 21, 1963, 4; May 18, 1964, 2.

9. Minutes of the Session of Second Presbyterian Church, Memphis, Tennessee, June 22, 1964, 1; June 28, 1964, 1; July 20, 1964, 1–2. In October, Bell wrote to Felix Gear in order to communicate the SPC session's position as related to him by Elder Horace Hull (Letter from L. Nelson Bell to Felix Gear, October 10, 1964 [Felix Gear Papers, Presbyterian Heritage Center, Montreat, North Carolina]).

10. Minutes of the Session of Second Presbyterian Church, Memphis, Tennessee, September 21, 1964, 2.

11. Minutes of the Session of Second Presbyterian Church, Memphis, Tennessee, October 21, 1964, 2; October 25, 1964, 1, 2.

12. Minutes of the Session of Second Presbyterian Church, Memphis, Tennessee, November 23, 1964, 2, 3. The fifty votes counted at the November 23 meeting were more than twice the number cast in October when the invitation was temporarily rescinded. The SPC *Year Book* for 1964–65 lists seven elders emeritus.

13. Minutes of the Session of Second Presbyterian Church, Memphis, Tennessee, November 30, 1964, 2.

14. Minutes of the Session of Second Presbyterian Church, Memphis, Tennessee, January 18, 1965, 3–4.

15. E-mail from Harriette Russell Coleman, June 13, 2010.

16. http://en.wikipedia.org/wiki/Southern_Manifesto; http://en.wikipedia.org/wiki/ Civil_Rights_Act_of_1964; Jason Sokol, *There Goes My Everything: White Southerners in*

the Age of Civil Rights, 1945–1975 (New York: Alfred A. Knopf, 2006): 202. Jeb Russell seems to have taken a rather benign view of his brother's political outlook, which he characterized as the view that "any man in business ought to be able to employ anybody he wants to . . . [he'd] rather have freedom on everybody's part. And he would say if a man wanted everybody [he employed] to be red-headed and freckled face, that was his right if it was his business and that was just the general philosophy on which he predicated his stand" ("The Reverend 'Jeb' Edward Russell," 45–46, [Oral History #27, Richard B. Russell, Jr. Oral History Project, Richard B. Russell Library for Political Research and Studies, University of Georgia Libraries, Athens, Georgia]).

17. Interview with James Aydelotte, March 15, 2011; Interview with Mac and Muriel Hart, November 27, 2009; Interview with William O'Neal, March 8, 2011.

18. Ernest Trice Thompson, "Foreword," in Donald W. Shriver, Jr., ed., *The Unsilent South: Prophetic Preaching in Racial Crisis* (Richmond: John Knox Press, 1965): 9–10. Four of the nineteen pastors whose sermons are included in the book had lost their pulpits at the time of publication; Interview with William O'Neal, March 8, 2011.

19. Interview with William Russell, March 20, 2011.

20. Ibid.

21. E-mail from Harriette Russell Coleman, June 13, 2010; Interview with Harold Jackson, September 22, 2009; Interview with K. C. Ptomey, March 21, 2008; Interview with Denby Brandon, Jr., July 8, 2004; Interview with Fred Flinn, August 26, 2010; "Notes on Jane Patterson's Conversation with Ladye Margaret Arnold, October 22, 1995" (document in the possession of Jane Patterson).

22. "Church to Wrestle Angel of Crisis," *The Commercial Appeal* (January 30, 1965): 8; Letters from Felix Gear to H. E. Russell, December 26 and December 28, 1964 (Felix Gear Papers, Presbyterian Heritage Center, Montreat, North Carolina).

23. This reconstruction of the sermon is based on a document titled "Statement by Dr. Jeb E. Russell to Second Presbyterian Church 1/24/65" (Box 66947, Mississippi Valley Collection, University of Memphis) and Russell's own sermon notes in the possession of Harriette Russell Coleman.

24. Ibid.

25. Ibid.

26. Ibid. It is significant that the Isaiah passage Russell invokes in this sermon is the very one cited by Jesus in the story of his "cleansing of the Temple," which the SPC session had cited in its letter to the congregation the previous April.

27. Ibid.

28. According to PCUS polity, as few as twenty-seven presbytery-elected commissioners could request a special meeting of the General Assembly, assuming at least eighteen of these commissioners were ministers and seven were ruling elders, and at least twelve presbyteries and five synods were represented (*The Book of Church Order of the Presbyterian Church in the United States* [Atlanta: Stated Clerk of the General Assembly of the Presbyterian Church in the United States, 1965]: 50). SPC's position had been communicated to Gear by the session's Stated Clerk in a letter reassuring him that "Second Church is prepared and looking forward to giving the General Assembly and its commissioners a cordial reception" (Letter from Granville Sherman to Felix Gear, January 19, 1965 [Felix Gear Papers, Presbyterian Heritage Center, Montreat, North Carolina]).

29. "Church Race Row Moves Meeting," *Atlanta Journal* (January 27, 1965): 33. See also "Red Hats in Profusion," *Christianity Today* (February 12, 1965): 60, and "Moderator Changes Assembly Meeting Place," *Presbyterian Survey* (March 1965): 50.

30. Letter from Felix Gear to Dr. Granville Sherman, January 23, 1965 (Felix Gear Papers, Presbyterian Heritage Center, Montreat, North Carolina); "Minister Deplores Convention Shift," *Memphis Press-Scimitar* (January 27, 1965): 2; Felix B. Gear, "The 1965 General Assembly," *Presbyterian Outlook* (February 8, 1965): 4; Felix B. Gear, "Progress in a Time of Tension," *Presbyterian Outlook* (April 26, 1965): 5, 6.

31. "John Calvin's Doctrine Equated with Dictum," *Presbyterian Journal* (September 30, 1964): 6; Letter from Louise R. Goddard to Felix Gear, July 1, 1964, and anonymous undated letter addressed to Gear (Felix Gear Papers, Presbyterian Heritage Center, Montreat, North Carolina).

32. Letter in Felix Gear Papers, Presbyterian Heritage Center, Montreat, North Carolina.

33. "Meet the Moderator: A Man of Stability, Sensitivity," *Presbyterian Survey* (June 1964): 14; Joel L. Alvis, Jr., *Religion and Race: Southern Presbyterians 1946–1983* (Tuscaloosa: University of Alabama Press, 1994): 66–67. Another aspect of Gear's experience that may have influenced his decision in the SPC matter is the three-week visit he made to the Church's mission in Congo in December 1964. It is difficult to imagine that his interactions with Presbyterian missionaries and Congolese Christians did not influence his response to the racial controversy he would face on his return.

34. "'Door' Left Open by Presbyterians," *Memphis Press-Scimitar* (January 27, 1965): 4. Russell and others apparently learned of the change while attending the winter meeting of Memphis Presbytery on January 26 (see "Minister Deplores Convention Shift," *Memphis Press-Scimitar* [January 27, 1965]: 2); "2nd Presbyterian Will Reconsider," *Memphis Press-Scimitar* (January 28, 1965): 24. The following Sunday, February 6, a "biracial group of four students" was turned away from the church.

35. "2nd Presbyterian Race Resolution," *Memphis Press-Scimitar* (February 1, 1965): 5; Thomas N. Pappas, "Second Presbyterian Vote Keeps Segregation Policy," *Memphis Press-Scimitar* (February 10, 1965): 17; "Second Church's Session Reply," *Memphis Press-Scimitar* (February 10, 1965): 8; "Two Meetings at Second Church," *Memphis Press-Scimitar* (January 30, 1965): 4.

36. Fourteen letters to the session (representing 18 votes) were opposed to changing church policy, while 111 letters (representing 192 votes) favored change (Minutes of the Session of Second Presbyterian Church, Memphis, Tennessee, January, 30, 1965, 5). At a session meeting following worship on January 31, Elder Horace Hull asked if there were elders who "under any circumstances were opposed to admitting negro visitors" and requested that they communicate this fact to him (Minutes of the Session of Second Presbyterian Church, Memphis, Tennessee, January, 31, 1965, 1).

37. Minutes of the Session of Second Presbyterian Church, Memphis, Tennessee, January 30, 1965, 3–4.

38. Ibid.

39. Minutes of the Session of Second Presbyterian Church, Memphis, Tennessee, February 8, 1965, 4; January 30, 1965, 4. Thomas BeVier, "Presbyterians 'Study' Racial Policy," *Memphis Commercial Appeal* (January 31, 1965): 1; "Seating Policy Adopted by Second Church Elders," *Presbyterian Journal* (February 24, 1965): 6; Pappas, "Second Presbyterian Vote Keeps Segregation Policy," 17. See also "Second Church Position Stated," *Memphis Press-Scimitar* (February 9, 1965): 14.

40. Private Police Block 'Kneel-Ins' from Presbyterian Church: Church's Men Guard Doors in Person," *Tri-State Defender* (April 25, 1964): 1; "Second Presbyterian Church is Unyielding," *Tri-State Defender* (May 2, 1964): 1.

41. Thomas C. Farnsworth, William S. Craddock, Jr., Alvin Wunderlich, Jr., James H. Wetter, Richard E. Shubert, W. S. Craddock, Sr., Harry Baird, Jr., Rodney Baber, Robert M. Metcalf, Jr., John C. Patton, Irby Seay, and [indecipherable], "To the Clerk of Our Session," November 19, 1964 (document in the possession of Harriette Russell Coleman).

42. Ibid.

43. Minutes of the Session of Second Presbyterian Church, Memphis, Tennessee, February 8, 1965, 3–4. According to session minutes, rotation of elders on the basis of the denomination's "limited service plan" had been under advisement by the Policy Committee four years earlier (Minutes of Second Presbyterian Church, Memphis, Tennessee, May 15, 1961, 5).

44. *Book of Church Order*, paragraphs 5:2, 29:11; Mrs. K. William Chandler, "Church History, 1965," 3, 4 (Presbyterian Heritage Center, Montreat, North Carolina); Thomas N. Pappas,

"2nd Presbyterian Gets Petition to Rotate Elders," *Memphis Press-Scimitar* (February 13, 1965): 3. According to the WOC history by Mrs. K. William Chandler, two groups— Elders for the Preservation of Second Presbyterian Church and Group for the Preservation of Second Presbyterian Church—emerged in response to the Accord Committee's challenge. The first favored change, the latter continuation of the current policy.

45. "Crisis in Church: Threat of Charges, Dr. Russell Says," *Memphis Press-Scimitar* (February 15, 1965): 12. In handwritten notes for another address around this time, Russell called the interpretation given the church's "policy of racial segregation" by elders who were "watching the doors" an "evil thing that cannot be justified before God or man." "The most farfetched or ridiculous use of the Bible," Russell charged, "cannot sustain the elders on this act of exclusion." He called upon the elders "to rectify this unseemly situation which is injurious to the spiritual welfare of this congregation and community and which hinders the work on every mission field" (undated handwritten document in the possession of Harriette Russell Coleman).

46. Minutes of the Session of Second Presbyterian Church, Memphis, Tennessee, February 15, 1965, 6; "A Petition to Call a Congregational Meeting of All Members of Second Presbyterian Church" (document in possession of Charles Murphy). The petition also called for the establishment of an advisory board "to be composed of those elders desiring emeritus status, rather than being placed in line for rotation back on the Session. Said advisory board to replace and perform the duties now given to the Session's standing policy committee."

47. Minutes of the Session of Second Presbyterian Church, Memphis, Tennessee, February 15, 1965, 1, 2; "Petition Circulated in Memphis 2d Church," *Presbyterian Outlook* (March 1, 1965): 3. On February 17, the *Press-Scimitar* reported that some 1,300 signatures in support of the congregational meeting had been collected. The communication from the Accord Committee, signed by Zeno Yeates, noted that Margaret C. Askew, Luzanne W. Tayloe, Martha L. Roark, Anne R. Seay, Theron M. Lemly, and J. Irby Seay, Jr. had assisted in the count (Minutes of the Session of Second Presbyterian Church, Memphis, Tennessee, February 15, 1965, 5).

48. Minutes of the Session of Second Presbyterian Church, Memphis, Tennessee, February 15, 1965, 2, 3. According to a document in the possession of Charles Murphy, a copy of Manker's plan was made available to church members at or before the congregational meeting. The Accord Committee reported to the session that 1,012 signatures had been checked and found in order (Minutes of the Session of Second Presbyterian Church, Memphis, Tennessee, February 15, 1965, 5).

49. Minutes of the Session of Second Presbyterian Church, Memphis, Tennessee, February 15, 1965, 6. Thomas N. Pappas, "Second Church to Admit Negroes," *Memphis Press-Scimitar* (February 17, 1965): 1; "Second Church Changes Policy," *Memphis Press-Scimitar* (February 18, 1965): 4; "2nd Presbyterian Letters 'Mystery,'" *Memphis Press-Scimitar* (February 20, 1965): 5; "2nd Presbyterian To Vote Sunday," *Memphis Press-Scimitar* (February 22, 1965): 11. See also "Church Drops Color Bar after Threat," *Baltimore African American* (February 6, 1965): 19.

50. The description of the congregational meeting in the paragraphs that follow is based on minutes, brief press reports, an annual "history" of SPC produced by the Women of the Church, and the recollections of some of those who attended, including Charles Murphy, who took detailed notes of the discussion (Charles Murphy, "Personal Notes from Second Presbyterian Congregational Meeting, February 28, 1965," transcribed and edited, November 7, 2009).

51. "Second Presbyterian Meeting Tomorrow; Statement Issued," *Memphis Press-Scimitar* (February 27, 1965): 6. For an example of a press report that cast elder rotation in terms of "retirement," see "Church Approves Elders' Retirement: Nine Will be Relieved of Duties on March 28," *Memphis Commercial Appeal* (March 15, 1965): 13.

52. Minutes of Congregational Meeting, Second Presbyterian Church, Memphis, Tennessee, February 28, 1965.

53. Ibid.
54. According to a letter received by Charles Murphy some twenty years later, John Cleghorn acknowledged that motions to table were one of the delaying tactics used by racial hard-liners on the SPC session (Interview with Charles Murphy, October 9, 2009).
55. "Elders' Terms Limited by Memphis, Second," *Presbyterian Outlook* (March 8, 1965): 3; Interview with William Craddock, Jr. June 16, 2010; Interview with John Adamson, July 7, 2003; Interview with Bill Weber, November 19, 2009; Interview with Ed Knox, August 25, 2004.
56. "Rotate Plan Voted by Second Church," *Memphis Press-Scimitar* (March 1, 1965): 4; "Second Church Takes its Stand," *Memphis Press-Scimitar* (March 2, 1965): 6; Thomas N. Pappas, "Split Is Talked at 2nd Church," *Memphis Press-Scimitar* (March 8, 1965): 1; "New Church Being Planned in Memphis," *Presbyterian Outlook* (March 22, 1965): 14.
57. Minutes of the Session of Second Presbyterian Church, Memphis, Tennessee, April 19, 1965, 2, 3; March 15, 1965, 3. At its meeting April 19, the session accepted the resignations of Marvin S. Ellis, Jr., L. U. Pitts, D. E. Wagner, Walter M. Napier, Marshall D. Kelly, Leland Stanford, W. Likely Simpson, Robert E. Brake, T. Payne Flinn, Jr., Forbes M. Barton, Robert J. Hussey, and Max E. Houser. At the same meeting, the resignations of Robert Ruffin, Stuart McCloy, and Russell Kirn were announced.
58. "Relocated Assembly," *Presbyterian Outlook* (February 8, 1965): 8.
59. *The Christian Century* reported that "during the months-long debate over the issue, no policy was ever adopted that excluded Negroes as such" ("Race and Rotation," *The Christian Century* [March 26, 1965]: 693). See also "Protestant Panorama," *Christianity Today* (February 12, 1965): 536; Minutes of the Session of Second Presbyterian Church, Memphis, Tennessee, March 15, 1965, 2; June 8, 1964, 2–4.
60. "Church Lowers Racial Barrier," *Memphis Press-Scimitar* (March 8, 1965): 1.

Chapter 11

1. Mrs. K. William Chandler, "Church History, 1965," 1 (Presbyterian Heritage Center, Montreat, North Carolina).
2. *Second Presbyterian Church Messenger* (April 12, 1968): 1; "'Slaves on Call' In Good Cause," *Memphis Press-Scimitar* (July 4, 1968): 5. According to the congregational history compiled by the Women of the Church, "Slave Days" had been a fundraising scheme for the church's youth since at least 1964.
3. Barbara Dianne Savage, *Your Spirits Walk Beside Us: The Politics of Black Religion* (Cambridge: Harvard University Press, 2008): 218; *Minutes of the One-Hundred-Tenth General Assembly of the Presbyterian Church in the United States* (Atlanta: Office of the General Assembly, 1970): 283. Some of the more conservative commissioners to the 1969 General Assembly were displeased that a memorial service for Dr. King had been approved for 1970 and filed a resolution declaring that the decision to hold the service "did not express the views of the members of the Church-at-large." The dissenters accused King of having communist connections, of supporting "violence, murder, [and] lying," and of publicly denying the Virgin Birth and the Resurrection (Frank Joseph Smith, *The History of the Presbyterian Church in America*, Silver Anniversary Edition [Lawrenceville, GA: Presbyterian Scholars Press, 1999]: 101).
4. Philip Maclin, "Congregation Tries to Dissuade Adams," *Memphis Press-Scimitar* (October 2, 1978): 12; Interview with Elsie and Zeno Yeates, August 24, 2004.
5. Interview with Milton Knowlton, November 23, 2009; Interview with Harriette Russell Coleman, March 14, 2008.
6. Presbyterian historian Joel L. Alvis, Jr. writes of SPC's decision to leave the Presbyterian Church (USA): "Though there is no documentable relationship with these later events and though they can never be held to be the exclusive cause of later action, it is reasonable here to hold that 'the past is prologue'" (Alvis, *Religion and Race*, 103).

7. Interview with Bill Weber, November 19, 2009.

8. Tim Stafford, "Memphis's Other Graceland," *Christianity Today* (January 13, 2009), http://www.ctlibrary.com/ct/2009/january/35.42.html; Shirley Downing, "Church's Volunteer Mission Extends Helping Hands to Poor," *Memphis Commercial Appeal* (July 7, 1980): 9; Interview with Larry Lloyd, August 2, 2010; http://www.ncclife.org/index2.html.

9. http://www.mlfonline.org/about.php.

10. http://hopememphis.com/about/history/; http://www.mcuts.org/; http://www.ncclife.org/.

11. The Staff and Volunteers of Second Presbyterian Church, Memphis, Tennessee, "A Blueprint for Adopting a School," 11, http://www.2pc.org/media/blueprint-for-adopting-schools.pdf; "MissionUSA Takes on New Organizational Structure," http://www.2pc.org/article/missionusa-takes-on-new-organizational-structure/.

12. Interview with Eddie Foster, March 9, 2011.

13. Interview with Fred Flinn, August 26, 2010; Interview with Larry Lloyd, August 2, 2010.

14. http://www.2pc.org/about-us/our-staff/sandy-willson/; Interview with Sandy Willson, August 18, 2010.

15. Interview with Sandy Willson, August 18, 2010.

16. http://www.nexusleaders.org/.

17. Interview with Fenton Wright, August 10, 2010; http://www.theshalomproject.org/.

18. Interview with Frances Thompson, September 9, 2010.

19. Ibid.

20. Ibid.

21. Interview with Lillian Hammond Brown, July 10, 2004.

22. Interview with John Adamson, July 6, 2004; Interview with Sandy Willson, August 18, 2010.

23. Interview with Vasco Smith, June 24, 2003; Interview with Maxine Smith, August 9, 2005.

24. Interview with Lillian Hammond Brown, July 10, 2004; Interview with Sandy Willson, August 18, 2010.

25. Interview with Susan Nash, May 18, 2011; Interview with John Adamson, July 6, 2003.

26. "Statement of Intention Regarding Race Relations at Second Presbyterian Church" (2002), http://www.2pc.org/media/race-relations-at-second.pdf.

27. Ibid.

28. Interview with Lillian Hammond Brown, June 30, 2003; Interview with Sandy Willson, August 18, 2010; Interview with Timothy Russell, August 9, 2010.

29. Interview with Fenton Wright, August 10, 2010.

30. Michael K. Honey, *Going Down Jericho Road: The Memphis Strike, Martin Luther King's Last Campaign* (New York: W. W. Norton, 2007): 44, 395; Michael Lollar, "Iconic 'I Am A Man' Poster on Auction," *Memphis Commercial Appeal* (February 22, 2010), http://www.commercialappeal.com/news/2010/feb/22/iconic-poster-on-auction/; http://storycorps.org/blog/griot-booth/memphis-tn/a-community-sanctuary/; http://trianglenoirmemphis.org/library/Triangle%20Noir%20Charrette%20013012.pdf.

31. Jacintha Jones, "Future Unclear As Now-Empty Historic Church Clayborn-Ball, Physically and Spiritually, Falls On Hard Times," *Memphis Commercial Appeal* (August 13, 2001): B1.

32. Jacinthia Jones and Lela Garlington, "Church's Collapse Points up Others in Decline," *Memphis Commercial Appeal* (July 26, 2002): A1; Blake Fontenay, "Arena Work Rattles Old Church Restorers But Experts Say Vibration is Not a Threat," *Memphis Commercial Appeal* (November 8, 2002): B1; Pamela Perkins, "Clayborn Temple Has to be Braced: $150,000— Renovators Cite 'Immediate Risk of Collapse'," *Memphis Commercial Appeal* (February 15, 2003): B1; Thomas Jordan, "Council Approves $300,000 to Restore 2 Churches—'These are Our History'," *Memphis Commercial Appeal* (June 13, 2003): B1; Blake Fontenay, "City to Aid 2 Historic Churches—Council Approves $150,000 Each," *Memphis Commercial Appeal* (November 19, 2003): B1; Pamela Perkins, "Foes Will Press Fight on City's Funds for Church Renovations," *Memphis Commercial Appeal* (November 20, 2003): B6.

33. Interview with Gayle Rose, May 6, 2011.

34. Interview with Gayle Rose, May 6, 2011; Interview with Sandy Willson, August 18, 2010.

35. Interview with Sandy Willson, August 18, 2010; Interview with Marty Regan, May 6, 2011; "Notes of Meeting at Second Presbyterian Church, August 12, 2003" (document in the possession of Marty Regan).

36. Interview with Sandy Willson, August 18, 2010; Pamela Perkins, "Churches Proceed with Stabilization," *Memphis Commercial Appeal* (March 4, 2004): B2.

37. Interview with Justin Towner, August 6, 2004; Sherita Johnson-Burgess, Story Corps Interview with Justin Towner, November 17, 2007.

38. Interview with Gayle Rose, May 6, 2011; Interview with Sandy Willson, August 18, 2010.

39. Interview with Susan Nash, May 18, 2011.

40. Scott Shepard, "Restoration of Historic Clayborn Temple May Soon Be Under Way," *Memphis Business Journal* (April 16, 2006), http://www.bizjournals.com/memphis/stories/2006/04/17/tidbits1.html; Michael Finger, "Eyesores: The Flyer's Guide to the Ugliest Places in Town," *Memphis Flyer* (April 2, 2009), http://www.memphisflyer.com/memphis/eyesores/Content?oid=1442896; Melissa Scheffler, "Clayborn Temple in Desperate Shape," *MyFox Memphis* (July 27, 2009), http://www.myfoxmemphis.com/dpp/news/tennessee/072909_Civil_Rights_History_Forgotten_at_Clayborn_Temple, accessed August, 2010; Melissa Scheffler, "Millions of Dollars and Inspiration Needed for Clayborn Temple," *MyFox Memphis* (November 12, 2009), http://www.myfoxmemphis.com/dpp/news/local/111209_millions+of+dollars+and+inspiration+needed+for+clayborn+temple, accessed August, 2010; http://www.loopnet.com/Listing/16980549/280-Hernando-Street-Memphis-TN/; Linda A. Moore, "Prospective Buyer Makes Offer for Clayborn Temple," *Memphis Commercial Appeal* (July 22, 2011), http://www.commercialappeal.com/news/2011/jul/22/prospective-buyer-makes-church-offer/.

41. Michael O. Emerson and Christian Smith, *Divided by Faith: Evangelical Religion and the Problem of Race in America* (New York: Oxford University Press, 2000); Douglas A. Blackmon, "For Heaven's Sake: Racial Reconciliation becomes a Priority for the Religious Right," *The Wall Street Journal* [June 23, 1997], http://www.slaverybyanothername.com/other-writings/for-heavens-sake-racial-reconciliation-becomes-a-priority-for-the-religious-right/.

42. Emerson and Smith, *Divided by Faith*, 52, 63, 54.

43. Ibid., 76, 90, 117, 130, 170.

44. Peter Slade, *Open Friendship in a Closed Society: Mission Mississippi and a Theology of Friendship* (New York: Oxford University Press, 2009): 75, 126, 123.

45. "Statement of Intention Regarding Race Relations at Second Presbyterian Church" (2002), http://www.2pc.org/media/race-relations-at-second.pdf.

46. Ibid.

47. Sandy Willson, "Let Go of Stuff," Amen Bible Study (January 27, 2011), http://www.2pc.org/resources/audio-library/let-go-of-stuff/.

48. Interview with Eddie Foster, March 9, 2011.

49. Ibid.

50. Interview with Steve Nash, July 1, 2010; http://www.advancememphis.org/index.php?page=history.

51. Interview with Steve Nash, July 1, 2010.

52. Interview with Mitchell Moore, October 7, 2010.

53. Ibid.

54. Ibid.

55. Interview with Mitchell Moore, October 7, 2010.

56. Willson, "Let Go of Stuff."

57. Ibid.

58. Mitchell Moore, "The Jesus Mission: Loving Your Neighbor" (February 13, 2011), http://www.2pc.org/resources/audio-library/the-jesus-mission-loving-your-neigbor/.

59. Ibid.
60. Interview with Charles Murphy, October 9, 2009.

Chapter 12

1. W. J. Cunningham, *Agony at Galloway: One Church's Struggle with Social Change* (Jackson: University of Mississippi Press, 1980): 63.
2. According to the official history of AIM, the organization was formed on June 20, 1965, from the "desire to organize a Methodist Church in Mississippi built on the heritage of the past." The history of the organization refers only once to "forced integration," but repeatedly to "excessive involvement in various aspects of American's social, economic and political history," "the left-leaning stance of the [Methodist] hierarchy," "the prospect of forced, sudden and radical changes in society," and "the blatant and racial socialism advocated by the National Council of Churches" (*Association of Independent Methodists: The First Twenty-Five Years, 1965–1990* [Jackson, MS: Association of Independent Methodists, 1990]: 150–151, 11, 10, 6, 7, 8, 9–10).
3. Cunningham, *Agony at Galloway*, 63–64.
4. Thomas N. Pappas, "Split Is Talked at 2nd Church," *Memphis Press-Scimitar* (March 8, 1965): 1; "Not All at Meeting Favor New Church," *Memphis Press-Scimitar* (March 9, 1965): 1; "2nd Church Splinter Group Will Meet," *Memphis Press-Scimitar* (March 11, 1965): 24.
5. Untitled document celebrating IPC's first year of existence (Archives of IPC, Memphis, Tennessee); "Presbyterians to Form New Church," *Memphis Commercial Appeal* (March 15, 1965): 20; "New Church Group Meets at Theater," *Memphis Press-Scimitar* (March 15, 1965): 18. According to the *Commercial Appeal*, the oxymoronic concept of an independent Presbyterian church was introduced by Rev. Van Horn, who told the congregation that "unless you use the word 'Independent' in your name, the machine boys will come after you in court for using the word 'Presbyterian'" ("Presbyterians to Form New Church," 20).
6. "'Independent' Church is Forming in Memphis," *Presbyterian Outlook* (March 29, 1965): 14; "Presbyterians to Form New Church," 20; SPC's Women of the Church, in their narrative history of the congregation for 1965, noted that the new church had "adopted a segregation policy" (Mrs. K. William Chandler, "Church History, 1965," 5 [Presbyterian Heritage Center, Montreat, North Carolina]).
7. "Presbyterians to Form New Church," 20.
8. Untitled document celebrating IPC's first year of existence (Archives of IPC, Memphis, Tennessee); "'Independent Church is Forming in Memphis," 14.
9. http://www.indepres.org/templates/cusindpres/details.asp?id=30618&;PID=244346, accessed August 2010. The second and third sentences of this paragraph were removed from the church's website sometime in 2011.
10. Mrs. K. William Chandler, "Church History, 1965," 5 (Presbyterian Heritage Center, Montreat, North Carolina).
11. Interview with Elinor Perkins Daniel, July 10, 2004.
12. Another aspect of the IPC constitution that reflected the founders' desire to avoid a repeat of their experience at SPC appears in the section on congregational meetings: "No one under sixteen years of age shall be entitled to a vote in the affairs of this Church at any time," Article 5, Paragraph D (Archives of IPC, Memphis, Tennessee).
13. Thomas N. Pappas, "New Church Organized on 'Compatible' Basis," *Memphis Press-Scimitar* (March 15, 1965): 18; "Constitution of Independent Presbyterian Church of Memphis, Tennessee, Inc.," Article 3, Paragraph 2 (Archives of IPC, Memphis, Tennessee).
14. On Palmer, see Stephen R. Haynes, *Noah's Curse: The Biblical Justification of American Slavery* (New York: Oxford University Press, 2002). Of *The Presbyterian Journal*, Kenneth Taylor writes: "The *Journal*'s 1942–1966 theological case for segregation had four overlapping legs: the curse of Noah, divine approval of geographical segregation and disapproval of

miscegenation, biblically-mandated cultural segregation, and Jesus's implicit support for segregation" ("The Spirituality of the Church: Segregation, *The Presbyterian Journal*, and the Origins of the Presbyterian Church in America," *Reformed Perspectives Magazine* 9:34 [August 19–August 25, 2007]: 4, http://thirdmill.org/the-spirituality-of-the-church).

15. "Constitution of Independent Presbyterian Church of Memphis, Tennessee, Inc," Preamble (Archives of IPC, Memphis, Tennessee).

16. "New Seminary Started by Miss.-Memphis Group," *Presbyterian Outlook* (May 25, 1964): 3–4. On efforts to recover the church's "spirituality" by the *Southern Presbyterian Journal*, and later by the Presbyterian Church in America, see Frank Joseph Smith, *The History of the Presbyterian Church in America*, Silver Anniversary Edition (Lawrenceville, GA: Presbyterian Scholars Press, 1999): 6, 8, 17.

17. Interview with Ken Bennett, July 14, 2010; Interview with Sam Graham, April 15, 2010; Interview with Richard Pratt, December 20, 2010.

18. Interview with Ken Bennett, July 14, 2010.

19. Interview with John Wilfong, July 27, 2010.

20. http://www.streetsministries.org/aboutus.

21. Interview with John Wilfong, July 27, 2010.

22. Interview with Ken Bennett, July 14, 2010; "Vance Avenue Collaborative Preliminary Planning Framework" (June 2010), http://www.memphis.edu/planning/pdfs/Planning_Framework.pdf.

23. Interview with Ken Bennett, July 14, 2010.

24. Interview with Delvin Lane, August 12, 2010.

25. Ibid.

26. Ibid.

27. Interview with Rob Thompson, October 28, 2010. According to its website, the mission of the Memphis Center for Urban Theological Studies is "to provide affordable, accessible, and accredited theological education and training for those serving in the urban context in order to transform Memphis and the Mid-South for the Kingdom of Christ" (http://www.mcuts.org/about/history-and-mission/).

28. Interview with Rob Thompson, October 28, 2010.

29. http://www.indepres.org/templates/cusindpres/details.asp?id=30618&;PID=539868, accessed August 2010.

30. "Undivided Devotion," November 26, 2006, http://media.indepres.org/sermoncatalog/?recordnumber=281&smonth=&syear=&title=&sermonid=&stype=&speaker=&scripture=&;keywords=.

31. Ibid.

32. John Hardie, "A Family Conversation on the Gospel and Race," November 29, 2006, http://www.indepres.org/templates/cusindpres/details.asp?id=30618&;PID=646103, accessed August 2010.

33. Ibid.

34. Hardie, "A Family Conversation on the Gospel and Race"; John Hardie, "Why the Gospel Overcomes Racial Barriers" (Ephesians 2:16), December 10, 2006, http://www.indepres.org/templates/cusindpres/details.asp?id=30618&;PID=646103, accessed August 2010.

35. Hardie, "A Family Conversation on the Gospel and Race." In another comment, a man who identified himself as part of the church's only interracial couple responded that he didn't have "three to five years to get to know Hardie before [he preaches] the gospel to us."

36. Audio of Tom Elkin's Sunday School lesson in IPC's Primetimer Class on December 3, 2006, was accessed from the church's website in late 2010. It has since been removed.

37. Ibid.

38. Hardie, "Why the Gospel Overcomes Racial Barriers."

39. Ibid.

40. Ibid.

41. Letter from Charles Blake Elliott to Friends and Fellow Members of Independent Presbyterian Church, May 5, 2007.

42. E-mail message from Sam Graham, October 27, 2010; "The Gospel and Race," document of an Ad Hoc Committee of the Session of Independent Presbyterian Church (November 2010); "Report by the Session's Ad Hoc Committee—11/22/2010: Response to PCA Pastoral Letter on The Gospel and Race" (November, 2010).

43. E-mail from Richie Sessions, August 18, 2011.

44. Ibid.

45. Taylor, "The Spirituality of the Church." In his history of the PCA, Frank Joseph Smith downplays the role of racism in the organizations and publications that contributed to the denomination's founding. Smith seems to underestimate how adept Southern whites could be during the 1960s and 1970s at dressing reactionary social positions in theological garb.

46. Taylor, "The Spirituality of the Church."; "PCA Position Paper on Racial Reconciliation" (2002), http://www.pcahistory.org/pca/race.html.

47. "The Gospel and Race: A Pastoral Letter," 1, 10, 12, 13, 14–15, http://pcamna.org/churchplanting/PDFs/RacismPaperFinal%20Version%2004-09-04.pdf.

48. See, e.g., Anthony Bradley, "Why didn't they tell us?: the racist & pro-segregation roots of the formation of RTS, the PCA, and the role of First Prez in Jackson, Miss in all of it," *The Institute* (July 2, 2010), http://bradley.chattablogs.com/archives/2010/07/why-didnt-they.html. Peter Slade describes how the doctrine of the church's spirituality continues to be embraced in prominent PCA churches and how it is used to eschew issues of race and justice. Slade argues that in Jackson's First Presbyterian Church (PCA), for instance, a retrieval of the distinctive Southern Presbyterian doctrine is linked with opposition to addressing systemic racism (*Open Friendship in a Closed Society: Mission Mississippi and a Theology of Friendship* [New York: Oxford University Press, 2009]: 115).

49. Sonia Scherr, "Church Denomination Roots out Racism," *Southern Poverty Law Center Intelligence Report* (summer 2010), http://www.splcenter.org/get-informed/intelligence-report/browse-all-issues/2010/summer/rooting-out-racism.

Epilogue

1. E-mail from Perky Daniel, July 3, 2004.

2. Interview with Elinor Kelley Grusin, August 2, 2004; E-mail from Elinor Kelley Grusin, August 28, 2011.

3. Ibid.

4. Ibid.

5. Ibid.

6. Interview with Elinor Kelley Grusin, August 2, 2004; http://www.memphis.edu/releases/mar08/grusin.htm.

7. Interview with Richard Rieves, May 18, 2011; http://www.downtownpres.com/.

8. Interview with Vasco Smith, June 24, 2003.

9. Interview with Vivian Carter Dillihunt, July 18, 2011.

BIBLIOGRAPHY

"$175 Fine in Disturbance." *Memphis Press-Scimitar* (September 26, 1961): 22.

"'Action of Session, Not of Minister' Refuses Two Blacks Admittance at Sumter Presbyterian Church." *Presbyterian Survey* (February 9, 1970): 4.

"'Concerned Presbyterians'!" *Presbyterian Journal* (July 1, 1964): 12.

"'Concerns' Statement Adopted." *Presbyterian Journal* (October 14, 1964): 4.

"'Independent' Church is Forming in Memphis." *Presbyterian Outlook* (March 29, 1965): 14.

"'Kneel-In' Project Started in Churches." *New York Amsterdam News* (August 13, 1960): 9.

"'Kneel-Ins' Held at Four Churches." *Washington Post* (August 29, 1960): B1.

"'Kneel-Ins' Protest Atlanta Church Prejudice." *Pittsburgh Courier* (August 20, 1960): B7.

"'Right to Examine Ideas is Main Issue in Election.'" *The Sou'wester* (November 22, 1963): 1.

"'Slaves on Call' In Good Cause." *Memphis Press-Scimitar* (July 4, 1968): 5.

"'We Have Done Things Which We Ought Not.'" *Chicago Defender* (June 22, 1964): 4.

"'Young Turks' in Action." *Presbyterian Journal* (June 24, 1964): 12.

"14 Arrested at 'Public' Meet." *Tri-State Defender* (September 10, 1960): 1.

"2 Albany Churches Admit Others Bar Negroes." *Chicago Defender* (August 13, 1962): 2.

"202 Missionaries Appeal to Their Home Church." *Presbyterian Outlook* (April 27, 1964): 5–6.

"20th-Century Shapers of Baptist Social Ethics: T. B. Maston." http://levellers.wordpress. com/2009/01/11/20th-century-shapers-of-baptist-social-ethics-t-b-maston/.

"2nd Church Splinter Group Will Meet." *Memphis Press-Scimitar* (March 11, 1965): 24.

"2nd Presbyterian Bars Students 6th Sunday in Row." *Memphis World* (April 25, 1964): 1.

"2nd Presbyterian Says 'No' for 7th Sunday." *Memphis World* (May 2, 1964): 1, 4.

"2nd Presbyterian Takes Action on Segregation, Will Avoid Integrated Conferences But Plan with Negro Adults." *Memphis Press-Scimitar* (October 9, 1957): 14.

"3 Atlanta Churches Halt Kneel-In Demonstrations." *Norfolk Journal and Guide* (September 3, 1960): 10.

"3 Churches Reject Negro Worshippers." *Memphis Commercial Appeal* (August 29, 1960): 24.

"7th Attempt to Enter Second Presbyterian." *Memphis Press-Scimitar* (April 27, 1964): 8.

"8 Will Appeal to U.S. Court." *Memphis Press-Scimitar* (March 9, 1962): 4.

"A Brief History of Bethesda Presbyterian Church, 'The Church That Named Bethesda.'" http:// bethesdapresbyterian.org/notes/Our_History.

"A Fellowship of Concern." *Presbyterian Outlook* (January 1, 1964): 1.

"A Voice of Protest." *Presbyterian Survey* (July, 1964): 6.

"African Leader Stages Own 'Kneel-In.'" *Baltimore Afro-American* (October 1, 1960): 8.

"Alabama Church Kneel-In Protest Called Off." *Chicago Defender* (April 8, 1963): 4.

"Albany Police Arrest 3 During 'Kneel-In' Try." *Atlanta Daily World* (August 21, 1962): 1.

"An Assembly of Action." *Presbyterian Survey* (June 1964): 4.

"An Emergency?" *Presbyterian Journal* (February 10, 1965): 12.

"Anti-Demonstrations." *Presbyterian Survey* (July 1965): 6.

"Barred." *Presbyterian Outlook* (April 6, 1964): 4.

"Bars Are Up at Memphis Second." *Presbyterian Outlook* (May 11, 1964): 8.

"Big Decisions Facing Church." *Memphis Commercial Appeal* (April 23, 1964): 29.

"Biracial Group Plans 2nd Presbyterian Visit." *Memphis Press-Scimitar* (April 4, 1964): 13.

"Bishop Stands by Rector under Fire in Florida." *Baltimore Afro-American* (July 18, 1964): 3.

"Born of Conviction." *The Mississippi Methodist Advocate* (January 2, 1963), http://www.mississippi-
    umc.org/console/files/oFiles_Library_XZXLCZ/Born_of_Conviction_4QQJSQYW.pdf.

"Brief Disturbance at Normal Café." *Memphis Press-Scimitar* (May 7, 1964): 8.

"Christ Did Not Build Any Racial Walls." *Chicago Defender* (August 22, 1962): 3.

"Christian Solution of Race Problem Urged by Leader." *Atlanta Daily World* (November 10, 1957): 1.

"Christianity Is a Demonstration." *Presbyterian Survey* (July 1964): 4–5.

"Church Elders Defy Ministers, Bar Negroes: Group Plays Hide and Peek with Camera." *Tri-State
    Defender* (January 30, 1965): 1.

"Church Extends Stand on Race: Presbyterian Assembly Says None Can be Barred from Worship."
    Memphis Commercial Appeal (April 28, 1964): 7.

"Church is Off Limits." *Baltimore Afro-American* (March 17, 1962): 1.

"Church Race Row Moves Meeting." *Atlanta Journal* (January 27, 1965): 33.

"Church Refuses NAACP Couples." *Memphis Press-Scimitar* (April 6, 1964): 1.

"Church Sends Help across Race Line." *Presbyterian Survey* (February 1964): 52.

"Church Statement Brings Rebuttal." *Memphis Press-Scimitar* (May 5, 1964): 1.

"Church to Wrestle Angel of Crisis." *Memphis Commercial Appeal* (January 30, 1965): 8.

"Cities Move to Avoid Becoming 'Birminghams.'" *Norfolk Journal and Guide* (May 18, 1963): B2.

"Constitution of Independent Presbyterian Church of Memphis, Tennessee, Inc." Archives of
    Independent Presbyterian Church, Memphis, Tennessee.

"Controversy on Open-Door Race Policy Involves '65 Assembly Host Church." *Presbyterian
    Survey* (July, 1964): 36.

"CORE Pickets Houston Church." *New York Amsterdam News* (October 5, 1963): 35.

"CORE Workers Stage Lynchburg 'Kneel-in.'" *Baltimore Afro-American* (August 22, 1964): 12.

"Court Continues Case of Sit-In Minister." *Atlanta Constitution* (July 2, 1963): 19.

"Court Won't Review Overton Sentences." *Memphis Press-Scimitar* (October 10, 1964): 1.

"Diehl Conciliates Southwestern Foes." *Memphis Commercial Appeal* (October 6, 1933): 6.

"Dismiss Charges Now 5 Years Old." *Memphis Press-Scimitar* (October 7, 1965): 2.

"Dr. Jackson Talks on Integration Battle." *Chicago Defender* (November 5, 1960): 1.

"Dr. Jones Comments on the Turning Away of Negroes at His Church." *Memphis Press-Scimitar*
    (September 6, 1960): 6.

"Druid Hills Presbyterian Church Opens Its Doors to Negroes Here." *Atlanta Daily World* (March
    28, 1959): 4.

"Easter in Birmingham: Some Church Bias Ends." *Chicago Defender* (April 15, 1963): 3.

"Fail in Efforts to Desegregate Miss. Churches." *Chicago Defender* (July 23, 1963): 5.

"FAMU Students In 'Kneel-Ins.'" *Chicago Defender* (March 6, 1961): 18.

"Fate of Kneel-Ins up to Mississippi." *Baltimore Afro-American* (May 2, 1964): 12.

"Fighting Erupts at Birmingham." *New York Times* (April 15, 1963): 1, 14.

"Fla. Church Has Change of Heart: Lifts Bars." *Norfolk Journal and Guide* (April 11, 1964): 1.

"Fla. Town Churches Stick to Race Bias; Gangs Beat Negroes." *Chicago Defender* (June 3, 1964): 5.

"Four Non-Violent Workshops Set for Saturdays." *Tri-State Defender* (March 7, 1964): 1.

"Freshman Vespers: Campbell is Coming." *The Sou'wester* (May 10, 1963): 1.

"Fund Drive to Start: $175,000 to be Sought for Southwestern." *Memphis Commercial Appeal*
    (March 2, 1964): A19.

"Ga. Church Board Labels Kneel-Iners 'Intruders.'" *Chicago Defender* (August 18, 1960): A2.

"Ga. Pastor Asks Open Door Policy." *Baltimore African American* (September 10, 1960): 3.

"Hack." "Chapel Revisited." *Sou'wester* (October 9, 1964): 2.

"Handclasp of Brotherhood." *Jet* (July 30, 1953): 9.

"Harassment in the Sanctuary." *Christianity Today* (March 13, 1964): 40.

"Hearing is Won by 8 Negroes." *Memphis Press-Scimitar* (October 23, 1964): 9.

"High Court Denies Negroes Rehearing." *Memphis Press-Scimitar* (May 4, 1962): 7.

"Hopes Dimmed for Assembly: Memphis' Presbyterian Bid for 1965 Is Shaken by Race Resolution." *Memphis Commercial Appeal* (April 25, 1964): 8.

"Houston Church Open to All." *Baltimore Afro-American* (June 2, 1962): 18.

"How Can A Sinner Be 'A Man after God's Own Heart'?" *Presbyterian Survey* (June 1965): 33.

"Indicted after Shell Incident." *Memphis Press-Scimitar* (September 7, 1960): 21.

"Integrate More Churches in Birmingham Campaign." *Chicago Defender* (April 22, 1963): 1.

"Integration in Reverse: Racial Battle in South Often Gets Confusing." *Norfolk Journal and Guide* (August 27, 1960): 23.

"Involvement Deplored." *Presbyterian Survey* (January, 1964): 9.

"Jackson Church Admits Negroes, Four Refuse." *Chicago Defender* (June 18, 1963): 4.

"Judge Terms Negro Action 'A New Low'." *Memphis Press-Scimitar* (September 1, 1960): 20.

"Kneel-in's Lawyer Eyes Church 'Aim'." *Baltimore Afro-American* (May 23, 1964): 3.

"Kneel-Ins Begin in Savannah with Partial Success." *Atlanta Daily World* (August 23, 1960): 1.

"Kneel-Ins Bring Segregated Pew." *Presbyterian Outlook* (September 26, 1960): 1.

"Kneel-ins Cause Little Excitement." *Baltimore Afro-American* (April 21, 1962): 6.

"Kneel-Ins Here Continue, and Enter 5 Churches." *Atlanta Daily World* (August 30, 1960): 2.

"Kneel-Ins Successful at 2 New Orleans Churches." *Chicago Defender* (September 24, 1960): 3.

"Kneel-Ins." *Information Service of the Bureau of Research and Survey of the National Council of Churches of Christ in the United States* 40:8 (April 15, 1961): 1–2.

"Kneel-Ins." *The Student Voice* 1:2 (August 1960): 7.

"Leave It to Nature." *Presbyterian Survey* (July, 1964): 8.

"Let Us Kneel-in Together!" *Christian Century* (August 24, 1960): 963–964.

"Letter to the PCUS Board of Christian Education from the Elders of Trinity Presbyterian Church, Montgomery, Alabama, June 3, 1957." *Presbyterian Journal* (June 19, 1957): 6–8.

"Little Rock Minister Offers All Races Seats." *Atlanta Daily World* (October 3, 1958): 1.

"Local Presbytery to Receive 'All'." *Atlanta Daily World* (January 26, 1961): 1.

"Memorandum to Members of the Board of Directors of Southwestern at Memphis" (July 3, 1964). College Archives, Barret Library, Rhodes College.

"Memorandum to the Members of the Board of Directors of Southwestern at Memphis" (July 20, 1962). College Archives, Barret Library, Rhodes College.

"Memphis Church Regrets Site Change." *Presbyterian Journal* (February 10, 1965): 5–6.

"Memphis Gets 1965 Assembly: Heated Presbyterian Debate about Segregation is Resolved." *Memphis Commercial Appeal* (April 26, 1964): section 2, 8.

"Memphis Probable Site of Church Assembly." *Memphis Commercial Appeal* (April 24, 1964): 7.

"Memphis Second and the 1965 Assembly." *Presbyterian Outlook* (June 29, 1964): 3–4.

"Memphis Vote." *Presbyterian Outlook* (November 9, 1964): 1.

"Memphis, 1965?" *Presbyterian Outlook* (April 27, 1964): 3.

"Memphis, Second." *Presbyterian Outlook* (May 18, 1964): 8.

"Message to Memphis." *Presbyterian Outlook* (June 1, 1964): 4.

"Methodist Bishops Rejected at Jackson Easter Kneel-In." *Baltimore Afro-American* (April 11, 1964): 18.

"Minister Held as 2 Sit-Ins Fail at First Baptist Church." *Atlanta Constitution* (July 1, 1963): 8.

"Ministers Protest Church Segregation." *Baltimore Afro-American* (June 20, 1964): 5.

"Ministers' Reaction Varied on Church's Race Progress." *Memphis Commercial Appeal* (May 2, 1964): 14.

"Miss. Pastor Quits Post over Segregation Issue." *Chicago Defender* (June 24, 1963): 13.

"MissionUSA Takes on New Organizational Structure." http://www.2pc.org/article/missionusa-takes-on-new-organizational-structure/.

"Mississippi Group Threatens Church Split." *Atlanta Daily World* (November 5, 1959): 8.

"Mixed Group Again Tried to Enter Church." *Memphis Press-Scimitar* (April 20, 1964): 7.

"Mixed Group Barred at Memphis Church." *Memphis Commercial Appeal* (January 25, 1965): 17.

"Montgomery Church Has Negro Worshippers." *Presbyterian Outlook* (April 19, 1965): 3.

"NCC Denies Recruitment of Volunteers." *Presbyterian Journal* (July 22, 1964): 4.

"Negro Only Memphis Cadet to Win Valor Award." *Jet* (December 5, 1963): 22.

"Negro Student Addresses WF." *The Sou'wester* (January 10, 1964): 3.

"Negro's Plea: Open Churches to All." *Memphis Press-Scimitar* (August 29, 1960): A15.

"Negroes Arrested at Church Rally." *Memphis Press-Scimitar* (August 31, 1960): 1.

"Negroes Attend 6 Churches." *Atlanta Constitution* (August 8, 1960): 1, 10.

"Negroes Continue Kneel-Ins." *Presbyterian Survey* (October, 1960): 51.

"Negroes Fined, Held to State: Disturbed Public Worship, Charge." *Memphis Press-Scimitar* (September 1, 1960): 20.

"Negroes Pray in Fla. Church." *Tri-State Defender* (April 11, 1964), 1.

"Negroes Refused at Four Churches: Four Arrests Are Made." *Memphis Press-Scimitar* (August 29, 1960): A15.

"Negroes Served by Tea Room." *Memphis Press-Scimitar* (July 6, 1964): 1.

"New Church Group Meets at Theater." *Memphis Press-Scimitar* (March 15, 1965): 18.

"New Seminary Started by Miss.-Memphis Group." *Presbyterian Outlook* (May 25, 1964): 3–4.

"New Twist: 'Kneel-In' at 6 Ga. Churches." *Chicago Defender* (August 9, 1960): 1.

"Nine Pastors Have Served Church Here in 88 Years: Second Presbyterian Church, Organized in 1884 [*sic*], Has Had Interesting History, Being Parent Organization of Five Daughter Churches." *Memphis Commercial Appeal* (September 3, 1932): 12.

"Not All at Meeting Favor New Church." *Memphis Press-Scimitar* (March 9, 1965): 1.

"Notes of Meeting at Second Presbyterian Church, August 12, 2003." In the possession of Marty Regan.

"Notes on Jane Patterson's Conversation with Ladye Margaret Arnold, October 22, 1995." In the possession of Jane Patterson.

"Open Letter to the Presbyterian Church, U.S. From the Congo Mission." *Presbyterian Outlook* (October 19, 1964): 2.

"Outgoing Missionaries Sign Plea to the Church." *Presbyterian Outlook* (September 7, 1964): 2.

"PCA Position Paper on Racial Reconciliation" (2002). http://www.pcahistory.org/pca/race. html.

"Picket Line on Sundays at Houston Church." *Norfolk Journal and Guide* (October 12, 1963): A2.

"Pray for Poor in Kneel-In." *Chicago Daily Defender* (August 7, 1962), 2.

"Presbyterian Pastor Flays Disunity." *Memphis Commercial Appeal* (October 10, 1964): 10.

"Presbyterian Stand is Hit." *Memphis Commercial Appeal* (May 3, 1964): section 5, 3.

"Presbyterian Women Will Meet Thursday: 60 Churches to be Represented at Two-Day Session." *Memphis Commercial Appeal* (February 16, 1954): 17.

"Presbyterians Mothered New Congregations: Second Church, Organized in Warehouse, Sponsored Three Others." *Memphis Press-Scimitar* (February 21, 1927): 12.

"Presbyterians Renew Blast on Segregation." *Atlanta Daily World* (June 8, 1955): 1.

"Presbyterians Seek Bias End in Institutions." *Atlanta Daily World* (May 3, 1960): 1.

"Presbyterians to Form New Church." *Memphis Commercial Appeal* (March 15, 1965): 20.

"Presbyterians U.S. Nail the Door Open." *Christianity Today* (May 22, 1964): 809.

"Presbyterians US Take Part in Selma Negro Voter Rights Demonstrations." *Presbyterian Survey* (May 1965): 40.

"Presbyterians: Concern vs. Concerned." *Time* (October 13, 1967). http://www.time.com/time/ magazine/article/0,9171,837385,00.html

"President Urges Mature Reactions." *The Sou'wester* (October 5, 1962): 1.

"Private Police Block 'Kneel-Ins' from Presbyterian Church: Church's Men Guard Doors in Person." *Tri-State Defender* (April 25, 1964): 1.

"Progress in Alabama." *Presbyterian Outlook* (July 12, 1965): 5–6.

"Protest Church Assembly Here." *Memphis Press-Scimitar* (May 21, 1964): 36.

"Provocation, Reprisal Widen the Bitter Gulf." *Life* (May 17, 1963): 29.

"Race, NCC Seen as Big Issues in General Assembly April 23–29." *Presbyterian Survey* (April, 1964): 45.

"Report by the Independent Presbyterian Church Session's Ad Hoc Committee—11/22/2010: Response to PCA Pastoral Letter on The Gospel and Race" (November 2010).

"S.C. Criticizes Assembly, Asks Reconsideration." *Presbyterian Journal* (June 10, 1964): 6.

"Sav. Methodist Board Official Hits Kneel-Ins." *Atlanta Daily World* (August 19, 1960): 2.

"Second Church's Problem." *Memphis Press-Scimitar* (January 26, 1965): 6.

"Second Presbyterian Church is Unyielding." *Tri-State Defender* (May 2, 1964): 1.

"Second Presbyterian's Past Recalled by Modern Plant: First Meeting Was in Cotton Warehouse in 1844, But New Million Dollar Addition Will Give Church 'Most Complete Facilities' in City." *Memphis Commercial Appeal* (July 27, 1957): 20.

"Seek Clemency for Clergyman." *Chicago Defender* (April 24, 1965): 2.

"Segregation Abolished at First Church, Sumter." *Presbyterian Survey* (February 23, 1970): 4.

"Segregation Backed by Church Leaders, Second Presbyterian Session to Propose Policy, Opposes Mixed Meets." *Memphis Commercial Appeal* (October 10, 1957): 5.

"Selma Church Admits Negroes for First Time." *Chicago Defender* (March 29, 1965): 10.

"Seminar Shows Student Concern for Civil Rights Bill Implications." *The Sou'wester* (October 4, 1963): 1.

"Sentencing of 8 Students Upheld." *Memphis Press-Scimitar* (March 8, 1962): 18.

"Sit-In Fines are Upheld." *Memphis Press-Scimitar* (April 27, 1961): 2.

"Sit-In Students Held to Jury." *Memphis Press-Scimitar* (April 17, 1964): 5.

"Sit-in . . . Kneel-in: Demonstrations Spread to White Churches." *Presbyterian Outlook* (August 22, 1960): 4.

"Southern Presbyterians Asked to Drop Race Bias." *Atlanta Daily World* (April 17, 1963): 1.

"Southern Presbyterians Decry Washington March." *Atlanta Daily World* (August 23, 1963): 2.

"Southern Presbyterians Set Laudable Example." *Atlanta Daily World* (May 3, 1958): 6.

"Southern Presbyterians Vote to Open Church Rolls." *Atlanta Daily World* (June 1, 1954): 1.

"Spotlight on St. Augustine." *Christianity Today* (July 17, 1964): 37–38.

"Stage 'Kneel-In' at 6 Churches." *Chicago Defender* (August 9, 1960): 1.

"Statement Adopted by the Session of the First Presbyterian Church of Jackson, Mississippi." *Southern Presbyterian Journal* (June 19, 1957): 8.

"Statement by Robert M. Hasselle, Jr. Pertaining to Rejection by Officers of Second Presbyterian Church." n.d. In the possession of Henry Hasselle.

"Statement of Intention Regarding Race Relations at Second Presbyterian Church" (2002). http://www.2pc.org/media/race-relations-at-second.pdf.

"Statements Made at the Meeting of the Synod of Tennessee, October 5, 1938." College Archives, Barret Library, Rhodes College.

"Student Jailed on Extortion Letter Charge." *Memphis Press-Scimitar* (May 5, 1964): 2.

"Student States Ideals of Group Making Current National News." *The Sou'wester* (April 24, 1964): 3.

"Students Attempt Church Integration, Arrested." *Chicago Defender* (April 24, 1962): 2.

"Students Get Welcome at Alexandria Churches." *Baltimore Afro-American* (September 10, 1960): 20.

"Students Halt Church Try." *Memphis Press-Scimitar* (May 24, 1964): 1.

"Students Hit Churches and Lunch Counters." *Tri-State Defender* (August 27, 1960): 1.

"Students Visit Seven Churches in Atlanta." *Atlanta Daily World* (August 9, 1960): 1.

"Suit Seeks Halt of Arrests at Miss. Churches." *Atlanta Daily World* (February 14, 1964): 1.

"Summons to a Vital Witness: Forty Presbyterian, U.S., Churchmen Make a Joint Appeal." *Presbyterian Outlook* (December 21, 1964): 5–6.

"Synods Vote Variety of Vexing Issues." *Presbyterian Survey* (August 1964): 37.

"Texas Presbyterians Attack Plans to Meet in Memphis." *Memphis Commercial Appeal* (May 21, 1964): 1.

"Tha Artivist Presents." W.E.A.L.L.B.E. News Radio (July 6, 2008). http://www.blogtalkradio.com/weallbe/2008/07/06/tha-artivist-presentswe-all-be-news-radio.

"The Assembly in Detail." *Presbyterian Journal* (May 13, 1964): 7–11, 19.

"The Church and Political Pronouncements." *Christianity Today* (August 28, 1964): 29–31.

"The Classic of Classics." n.p., n.d. College Archives, Barret Library, Rhodes College.

"The General Assembly of 1964 Addressed Its Concern to Local Sessions of the Presbyterian Church US in A Pastoral Letter on Race." *Presbyterian Survey* (July 1964): 12–13.

"The Gospel and Race." Document of an Ad Hoc Committee of the Session of Independent Presbyterian Church (November 2010).

"The Gospel and Race: A Pastoral Letter." http://pcamna.org/churchplanting/PDFs/Racism-PaperFinal%20Version%2004-09-04.pdf.

"The Humor Was Lost." *Presbyterian Survey* (January, 1965): 8.

"The New Phase: 'Kneel-Ins,' 4 Atlanta White Churches Admit Colored Students." *Norfolk Journal and Guide* (August 13, 1960): A1.

"The Other Side of Discipleship." Senior Sermon preached by K. C. Ptomey, Jr., Caldwell Chapel, Louisville Presbyterian Seminary, Louisville, Kentucky, November 8, 1966.

"The Protests of the Negro Students." *Information Service of the Bureau of Research and Survey of the National Council of Churches of Christ in the United States* 39:13 (June 25, 1960): 1.

"The Race Revolution." *Christianity Today* (December 6, 1963): 18–19.

"The Second Presbyterian Church of Memphis (On the Corner of Hernando and Pontotoc Streets)." Archives of Second Presbyterian Church, Memphis, Tennessee.

"The Second Presbyterian Church of Memphis." Box 66747, Mississippi Valley Collection, University of Memphis.

"The Second Presbyterian Situation." *Memphis Press-Scimitar* (May 7, 1964): 6.

"The Seeker." *The Sou'wester* (October 19, 1962): 2.

"Three Atlanta Churches Refuse Negroes Admission." *Presbyterian Outlook* (September 12, 1960): 4.

"Time Given to Appeal." *Memphis Commercial Appeal* (July 3, 1964): 1.

"To: The Presbyterian Church US; From: the American Presbyterian Congo Mission; Regarding: Racial Discrimination." *Presbyterian Survey* (November 1964): 43.

"Trying for Truce in Café Picketing." *Memphis Press-Scimitar* (May 8, 1964): 2.

"Two Churches Bar Civil Rights Groups in Americus Drive." *New York Times* (August 2, 1965): 1, 15.

"Two Negroes, White Arrested at Church." *Tri-State Defender* (September 3, 1960): 2.

"Two Paine Students Foiled in Kneel-In." *Baltimore African American* (November 18, 1961): 16.

"U.S. Intervenes in Students Case." *Atlanta Daily World* (October 25, 1963): 1.

"Vance Avenue Collaborative Preliminary Planning Framework" (June 2010). http://www.memphis.edu/planning/pdfs/Planning_Framework.pdf.

"Victory for Dr. Diehl." *Memphis Commercial Appeal* (October 6, 1933): 8.

"White Maryland Minister Refused Admittance to Second Presbyterian." *Tri-State Defender* (May 9, 1964): 1–2.

"Why We Began the 'Kneel-Ins': A Student Symposium." *Atlanta Inquirer* (August 14, 1960): 1.

"Worshippers Barred from Americus Church." *Chicago Defender* (August 2, 1965): 1.

"Xmas Kneel-In Held in Ill." *New York Amsterdam News* (December 31, 1960): 19.

"Youth Rally Plans Movie Premiere." *Memphis Commercial Appeal* (August 27, 1960): 8.

1964–65 Year Book, Second Presbyterian Church, Poplar at Goodlett, Memphis, Tennessee (n.p, n.d.).

Algeo, John, ed. *Fifty Years among the New Words: A Dictionary of Neologisms, 1941–1991.* Cambridge: Cambridge University Press, 1993.

Alvis, Joel L. Jr. *Race and Religion: Southern Presbyterians, 1946–1983.* Tuscaloosa: University of Alabama Press, 1994.

Annual Report of the Dean (October 1950). College Archives, Barret Library, Rhodes College.

Apperson, George M. "Heroism in a Lost Cause." *Presbyterian Voice* 15:2 (April, 2004). http://www.synodoflivingwaters.org/the_voice/0404/06heroism.html.

Apperson, George M. "Lincoln, the Churches, and Memphis Presbyterians." *American Presbyterians* (summer 1994): 97–107.

Ashcroft, Bruce, Mark Anderson III, and Mrs. Allen L. Knox. *In Remembrance: The Centennial History of Trinity Presbyterian Church*, n.p., n.d.

Association of Independent Methodists: The First Twenty-Five Years 1965–1990. Jackson, MS: Association of Independent Methodists, 1990.

At the River I Stand. Dir. David Appelby, Allison Graham, and Steven John Ross. California Newsreel, 1993. Film.

Atkinson, Harry E. Letter to the Editor, *Presbyterian Journal* (March 3, 1965): 1.

Ballard, Aubrey. "Second Presbyterian to Mark Centennial." *Memphis Commercial Appeal* (December 24, 1944): section 1, 5.

Barner, George. "How Easter Came to Birmingham." *New York Amsterdam News* (April 20, 1963): 42.

Bass, S. Jonathan. *Blessed Are the Peacemakers: Martin Luther King Jr., Eight White Religious Leaders, and the "Letter from Birmingham Jail."* Baton Rouge: Louisiana State University Press, 2001.

Bell, L. Nelson. "A Layman and His Faith: Lost Perspective." *Christianity Today* (July 31, 1964): 23.

Bell, L. Nelson. "A Layman and His Faith: Relevance." *Christianity Today* (May 10, 1963): 26–27.

Benenson, Peter. "The Forgotten Prisoners." *The London Observer Weekend Review* (May 28, 1961). http://www.hrweb.org/ai/observer.html.

Benenson, Peter. *Persecution*. London: Penguin, 1961.

Blackmon, Douglas A. "For Heaven's Sake: Racial Reconciliation becomes a Priority for the Religious Right." *The Wall Street Journal* (June 23, 1997). http://www.slaverybyanothername.com/other-writings/for-heavens-sake-racial-reconciliation-becomes-a-priority-for-the-religious-right/.

Blackwelder, Julia Kirk. "Southern White Fundamentalists and the Civil Rights Movement." *Phylon* 40:4 (1979): 334–341.

Bradley, Anthony. "Why didn't they tell us?: the racist & pro-segregation roots of the formation of RTS, the PCA, and the role of First Prez in Jackson, Miss in all of it." *The Institute* (July 2, 2010). http://bradley.chattablogs.com/archives/2010/07/why-didnt-they.html.

Branch, Taylor. *At Canaan's Edge: America in the King Years, 1965–68*. New York: Simon and Schuster, 2006.

Branch, Taylor. *Parting the Waters: America in the King Years, 1954–63*. New York: Simon and Schuster, 1989.

Branch, Taylor. *Pillar of Fire: America in the King Years, 1963–65*. New York: Simon and Schuster, 1998.

Britton, John. "Candidate's Suit Aimed at Demonstrations Tossed Out." *Atlanta Daily World* (September 14, 1960): 1).

Brooks, Harry. "Presbyterian Assembly Asserts Church's Stand on Integration." *Pittsburgh Courier* (October 8, 1960): 6.

Brown, Charles. "The Epic of Ashton Jones: Dixie-Born White Minister Leads One-Man Crusade for Interracial Brotherhood." *Ebony* (October 1965): 45–54.

Calverton, Victor. "Virginia Church Eyes Integration." *Atlanta Daily World* (June 20, 1956): 4.

Canon, Alfred O. "From the Ivy-Covered Tower." n.p., n.d. College Archives, Barret Library, Rhodes College.

Carson, Clayborne. *In Struggle: SNCC and the Black Awakening of the 60s*. Harvard University Press, 1981.

Carter, Susan. "2nd Church Race Ruling Postponed." *Memphis Press-Scimitar* (July 22, 1964): 33.

Carter, Susan. "Desegregation Plea is Heard." *Memphis Press-Scimitar* (July 21, 1964): 1.

Chandler, Mrs. K. William. "Church History, 1965." Presbyterian Heritage Center, Montreat, North Carolina.

Chandler, Mrs. K. William. "Church History: the Year of Our Lord, Nineteen Hundred and Sixty-Four." Presbyterian Heritage Center, Montreat, North Carolina.

Chappell, David L. "Diversity within a Racial Group: White People in Little Rock 1957–1959." *Arkansas Historical Quarterly* 54:4 (winter 1995): 444–456.

Chappell, David L. *Inside Agitators: White Southerners in the Civil Rights Movement.* Baltimore: Johns Hopkins University Press, 1994.

Chappell, David L. *A Stone of Hope: Prophetic Religion and the Death of Jim Crow.* Chapel Hill: University of North Carolina Press, 2004.

Colburn, David R. *Racial Change and Community Crisis: St. Augustine, Florida, 1877–1980.* Columbia University Press, 1985.

Collins, Donald. *When the Church Bell Rang Racist: The Methodist Church and the Civil Rights Movement in Alabama.* Macon: Mercer University Press, 1998.

Cooper, W. Raymond. *Southwestern at Memphis 1848–1948.* Richmond: John Knox Press, 1948.

Cunningham, W. J. *Agony at Galloway: One Church's Struggle with Social Change.* Jackson: University of Mississippi Press, 1980.

Curry, Albert Bruce. *History of the Second Presbyterian Church of Memphis, Tennessee.* Memphis: Adams Printing and Stationery, 1936.

Dailey, Jane. "Sex, Segregation, and the Sacred after Brown." *Journal of American History* 91:1 (June, 2004): 119–144.

Diehl, Charles E. "Memoranda Concerning Petition Recently Filed By Certain Presbyterian Ministers of Memphis." College Archives, Barret Library, Rhodes College.

Diehl, Charles E. "Moving a College (Read at a Meeting of 'The Egyptians,' October 25, 1956). College Archives, Barret Library, Rhodes College.

Diehl, Charles E. Sermon upon Retirement as PCUS Moderator (May 1942). College Archives, Barret Library, Rhodes College.

Downing, Shirley. "Church's Volunteer Mission Extends Helping Hands to Poor." *Memphis Commercial Appeal* (July 7, 1980): 9.

Driscoll, John. "Second Presbyterian Buys Big Church Site: Seven and a Half Acre Tract Will Cost $25,000." *Memphis Commercial Appeal* (February 12, 1945): 9.

Dysart, Margaret. "What Christian Can Deny a Child?" *Presbyterian Survey* (January 1964): 55.

Emerson, Michael O., and Christian Smith. *Divided by Faith: Evangelical Religion and the Problem of Race in America.* New York: Oxford University Press, 2000.

Fairclough, Adam. *To Redeem the Soul of America: The Southern Christian Leadership Conference and Martin Luther King, Jr.* Athens: University of Georgia Press, 2001.

Findlay, Stephen M. "The Role of Bi-Racial Organizations in the Integration of Public Facilities in Memphis, Tennessee, 1954–1964." Unpublished Paper. Memphis and Shelby County Collection, Memphis Public Library and Information Center.

Finger, Michael. "Eyesores: The Flyer's Guide to the Ugliest Places in Town." *Memphis Flyer* (April 2, 2009). http://www.memphisflyer.com/memphis/eyesores/Content?oid=1442896.

Fitzgerald, Grace A. "'Chapel is What Students Make It.'" *Sou'wester* (November 1, 1963): 2.

Fleming, Cynthia Griggs. *Soon We Will Not Cry: The Liberation of Ruby Doris Smith Robinson.* Oxford: Rowan and Littlefield, 2000.

Fontenay, Blake. "Arena Work Rattles Old Church Restorers But Experts Say Vibration is Not a Threat." *Memphis Commercial Appeal* (November 8, 200): B1.

Fontenay, Blake. "City to Aid 2 Historic Churches—Council Approves $150,000 Each." *Memphis Commercial Appeal* (November 19, 2003): B1.

Foreman, Kenneth J. "Motives Committee: News Items with Comments." *Presbyterian Outlook* (September 30, 1963): 9.

Frady, Marshall. "God and Man in the South." *The Atlantic Monthly* (January 1967): 37–42.

Gear, Felix. "Dr Diehl: His Service in the Church." Undated typewritten document. Felix Gear Papers, Presbyterian Heritage Center, Montreat, North Carolina.

Gillespie, Charles C. *A History of the Second Presbyterian Church of Memphis, Tennessee, 1844–1971.* Memphis: Second Presbyterian Church, 1971.

Gordon, Robert. "5 Birmingham Churches Open Doors to Kneel-Ins." *Memphis World* (April 27, 1963): 7.

Gordon, Robert. "Birmingham Churches Split on Kneel-Ins." *Memphis World* (April 20, 1963): 1.

Green, Laurie B. *Battling the Plantation Mentality: Memphis and the Black Freedom Struggle.* Chapel Hill: University of North Carolina Press, 2007.

Gritter, Elizabeth. "Local Leaders and Community Soldiers: The Memphis Desegregation Movement, 1955–1961." Unpublished Senior Honors Thesis, American University, 2001.

Gulliver, Hal. "Sit-In Pastor Freed on $5,000 Bond." *Atlanta Constitution* (March 4, 1964): 9.

Halberstam, David. *The Children*. New York: Fawcett, 1998.

Hall, Bob. "Non-Violent Group Gains National TV Recognition." *The Sou'wester* (May 8, 1964): 3.

Hardie, John. "A Family Conversation on the Gospel and Race." November 29, 2006. http://www.indepres.org/templates/cusindpres/details.asp?id=30618&PID=646103, accessed August 2010.

Hardie, John. "Undivided Devotion" November 26, 2006. http://media.indepres.org/sermon catalog/?recordnumber=281&smonth=&syear=&title=&sermonid=&stype=&speaker=& scripture=&;keywords=.

Hardie. John. "Why the Gospel Overcomes Racial Barriers" (Ephesians 2:16), December 10, 2006. http://www.indepres.org/templates/cusindpres/details.asp?id=30618&PID=646103, accessed August 2010.

Harmon, David Andrew. *Beneath the Image of the Civil Rights Movement and Race Relations: Atlanta, Georgia, 1946–1981*. Studies in African American History and Culture. London: Taylor and Francis, 1996.

Hart, Roger. "Campus Ministers Association Plans Three Social Projects." *The Sou'wester* (January 10, 1964): 2.

Hart, Roger. "FOCUS: Second Presbyterian Church." *Sou'wester* (January 8, 1965): 2.

Hart, Roger. "Letter to the Editor: A Call for Courage." *The Sou'wester* (September 21, 1962): 2.

Hartley, Ben H. "The 104th General Assembly." *Presbyterian Survey* (June 1964): 10.

Harvey, Paul. *Freedom's Coming: Religious Culture and the Shaping of the South from the Civil War through the Civil Rights Era*. Chapel Hill: University of North Carolina Press, 2005.

Haygood, Lawrence F. "For an Inclusive Church." *Presbyterian Outlook* (April 20, 1964): 5.

Haygood, Lawrence F. "The Triumphant Life of the Poor in Spirit." In *The Unsilent South: Prophetic Preaching in Racial Crisis*, ed. Donald W. Shriver, 152–165. Atlanta: John Knox Press, 1965.

Haynes, Stephen R. *Noah's Curse: The Biblical Justification of American Slavery*. New York: Oxford University Press, 2002.

Helms, Jesse. "Mob Rule." *Presbyterian Journal* (July 8, 1964): 14.

Herbers, John. "Integration Gains in Memphis; Biracial Leadership Takes Hold." *New York Times* (April 5, 1964): 45.

Holloway, Lin. "Looking On in Norfolk." *Norfolk Journal and Guide* (August 13, 1960): A15.

"Holy Week and the Civil Rights Demonstrations at the Churches, A Sermon"—Address delivered April 11, 1965, by Dr. Robert Strong, Minister, Trinity Presbyterian Church, Montgomery, Alabama. Civil Rights Collection, Box 130, Salmon Library, University of Alabama Huntsville.

Honey, Michael K. *Going Down Jericho Road: The Memphis Strike, Martin Luther King's Last Campaign*. New York: W. W. Norton, 2007.

Hoppe, Sherry Lee, and Bruce W. Speck. *Maxine Smith's Unwilling Pupils: Lessons Learned in Memphis's Civil Rights Classroom*. Knoxville: University of Tennessee Press, 2007.

Houck, Davis W., and David D. Dixon, eds. *Rhetoric, Religion and the Civil Rights Movement, 1954–1965*. Waco: Baylor University Press, 2006.

http://dillihunt.com/bio.htm.

http://en.wikipedia.org/wiki/Frank_Minis_Johnson.

http://hopememphis.com/about/history/.

http://www.2pc.org/about-us/our-staff/sandy-willson/.

http://www.advancememphis.org/index.php?page=history.

http://www.crmvet.org/tim/timhis60.htm#1960savannah.

http://www.downtownpres.com/.

http://www.heritagetoursmemphis.com/burkle.html.

http://www.mcuts.org/.

http://www.mcuts.org/about/history-and-mission/.

http://www.memphis.edu/releases/mar08/grusin.htm.

http://www.mlfonline.org/about.php.

http://www.ncclife.org/index2.html.

http://www.nexusleaders.org/.

http://storycorps.org/blog/griot-booth/memphis-tn/a-community-sanctuary/.

http://www.streetsministries.org/aboutus.

http://www.theshalomproject.org/.

http://trianglenoirmemphis.org/library/Triangle%20Noir%20Charrette%20013012.pdf.

Hunt, Frank. "May Ban Albany, Ga. 'Kneel-in' Protest." *Cleveland Call and Post* (August 4, 1962): 1A.

Hurst, Rodney L. Sr. *It Was Never about a Hot Dog and Coke: A Personal Account of the 1960 Sit-In Demonstrations in Jacksonville, FL and Ax Handle Saturday.* Livermore, CA: WingSpan Press, 2008.

Interview with Bill Weber, November 19, 2009.

Interview with Bob Hall, August 8, 2004.

Interview with Brooks Ramsey, March 4, 2008.

Interview with Cam Murchison, April 27, 2010.

Interview with Catherine Freeberg, September 23, 2009.

Interview with Coby Smith, July 29, 2003.

Interview with Delvin Lane, August 12, 2010.

Interview with Don McClure, Sr., December 2, 2009.

Interview with Dossett Foster, September 21, 2010.

Interview with Doy Daniels, Memphis, February 19, 2010.

Interview with Earl Stanback, July 9, 2003.

Interview with Ed Knox, August 25, 2004.

Interview with Eddie Foster, March 9, 2011.

Interview with Elaine Lee Turner, August 14, 2003.

Interview with Elinor Kelley Grusin, August 6, 2004.

Interview with Ervin Haas Bullock, April 15, 2004.

Interview with Evander Ford, June 17, 2010.

Interview with Fenton Wright, August 10, 2010.

Interview with Frances Thompson, September 9, 2010.

Interview with Gayle Rose, May 6, 2011.

Interview with George Purdy, Carolyn Purdy McGhee, Delores Purdy McDowell, and Donna Purdy Fitchpatric, November 21, 2010.

Interview with Harold Jackson, September 22, 2009.

Interview with Harold Taylor, June 26, 2003.

Interview with Harry Wellford, October 1, 2009.

Interview with Hayden Kaden, November 22, 2004.

Interview with Herbert Rhea, August 17, 2004.

Interview with Hortense Spillers, August 16, 2004.

Interview with Howard Romaine, July 6, 2003.

Interview with Hugh Farrior, November 27, 2009.

Interview with Jack Connors, July 7, 2003.

Interview with Jacquelyn Dowd Hall, August 8, 2004.

Interview with Jim Bullock, March 17, 2009.

Interview with James M. Lawson, Jr. August 12, 2010.

Interview with James M. Lawson, Jr. August 21, 1969. Series VII. Mississippi Valley Connection, University of Memphis.

Interview with James M. Lawson, Jr. January 21, 1969. Series IV. Mississippi Valley Collection, University of Memphis.

Interview with James M. Lawson, Jr. January 21, 1969. Series V. Mississippi Valley Collection, University of Memphis.

Interview with James M. Lawson, Jr. January 21, 1969. Series VI. Mississippi Valley Collection, University of Memphis.

Interview with James Williamson, April 3, 2012.

Interviews with Jim Bullock, August 21, 2003; April 15, 2004; March 17, 2009.

Interviews with John Adamson, July 7, 2003; July 6, 2004; November 19, 2009.

Interview with John and Pat Clark, July 10, 2004.

Interview with John Wilfong, July 27, 2010.

Interview with Johnnie Rogers Turner, June 21, 2010.

Interviews with Justin Towner, August 6, 2004; October 7, 2010.

Interview with K. C. Ptomey, March 21, 2008.

Interview with Ken Bennett, July 14, 2010.

Interview with Larry Lloyd, August 2, 2010.

Interview with Lewis Donelson, June 29, 2004.

Interviews with Lillian Hammond Brown, June 30, 2003; July 8, 2010.

Interview with Elizabeth Currie Williams, July 31, 2004.

Interview with Mac and Muriel Hart, November 27, 2009.

Interview with Martha McKee, August 27, 2010.

Interview with Martha Overholser Whitney, May 4, 2010.

Interview with Marty Regan, May 6, 2011.

Interview with Maxine Smith, June 14, 2010.

Interview with Michael Braswell, August 1, 2011.

Interview with Millen Darnell, March 7, 2008.

Interview with Milton Knowlton, November 23, 2009.

Interview with Mitchell Moore, October 7, 2010.

Interview with Phil Esty, July 10, 2004.

Interview with Richard Pratt, December 20, 2010.

Interview with Richard Rieves, May 18, 2011.

Interview with Rob Thompson, October 28, 2010.

Interview with Robert G. Patterson, July 2, 2004.

Interview with Robert Hasselle, October 23, 2009.

Interview with Robert Morris, February 24, 2011.

Interview with Robert Wells, June 23, 2003.

Interview with Rocky Ward, November 27, 2009.

Interview with Roger Hart, August 8, 2004.

Interview with RoseMary Hoye Wells, September 23, 2010.

Interview with Sam Graham, April 15, 2010.

Interview with Sandy Willson, August 18, 2010.

Interview with Steve Nash, July 1, 2010.

Interview with Susan Nash, May 18, 2011.

Interview with Timothy Russell, August 9, 2010.

Interview with Vasco Smith, June 24, 2004.

Interview with Vivian Carter Dillihunt, August 17, 2004.

Interview with William Craddock, Jr., June 16, 2010.

Interview with William O'Neal, March 8, 2011.

Interview with Wilson and Jane Northcross, July 14, 2004.

Interview with Winton Smith, November 19, 2010.

Interview with Zeno and Elsie Yeates, August 24, 2004.

Johnson-Burgess, Sherita. "Story Corps" Interview with Justin Towner, November 17, 2007. In the possession of Justin Towner.

Jones, J. Charles. "Rock Hill and the Charlotte Sit-Ins." http://www.crmvet.org/info/rockhill.htm.

Jones, Jacintha. "Future Unclear As Now-Empty Historic Church Clayborn-Ball, Physically and Spiritually, Falls On Hard Times." *Memphis Commercial Appeal* (August 13, 2001): B1.

Jones, Jacinthia and Lela Garlington. "Church's Collapse Points up Others in Decline." *Memphis Commercial Appeal* (July 26, 2002): A1.

Jones, Jameson. "The Power of Knowledge." Talk delivered at Phi Beta Kappa induction ceremony, Rhodes College, May 15, 1998. In the possession of Michael Cody.

Bibliography

Jones, Paul Tudor. "The College Related Church." Address to the Synod of Tennessee, June 15, 1964. College Archives, Barret Library, Rhodes College.

Jordan, Thomas. "Council Approves $300,000 to Restore 2 Churches—'These are Our History.'" *Memphis Commercial Appeal* (June 13, 2003): B1.

KBG. "A Southwestern Student Prays." *The Sou'wester* (September 28, 1962): 2.

Kelley, Elinor. "Presbyterians Face Busy Session." *Memphis Commercial Appeal* (April 11, 1964): 8.

Kelley, Elinor. "Second Presbyterian Resists Attempts to Force Change." *Memphis Commercial Appeal* (May 4, 1964): 4.

King, Martin Luther, Jr. "Letter from a Birmingham Jail, Martin Luther King, Jr., 1963." http://coursesa.matrix.msu.edu/~hst306/documents/letter.html.

King, Martin Luther, Jr. "'The Negro and the American Dream.' Excerpt from Address at the Annual Freedom Mass Meeting of the North Carolina State Conference of Branches of the NAACP." In *The Papers of Martin Luther King, Jr., Volume V: Threshold of a New Decade, January 1959–December 1960*, ed. Clayborne Carson. Berkeley: University of California Press, 2005.

King, Martin Luther, Jr. "Sit In, Stand In, Wade In, Kneel In." *New York Amsterdam News* (May 25, 1963): 10.

King, Martin Luther, Jr. *Stride Toward Freedom: The Montgomery Story*. New York: Harper & Brothers, 1958.

King, Martin Luther, Jr. *Why We Can't Wait*. New York: Penguin, 2000.

Kocek, Joseph Kip. *Acts of Conscience: Christian Nonviolence and Modern American Democracy*. New York: Columbia University Press, 2009.

Kosek, Joseph Kip. "Civil Rights and Religious Rights in the 1960s." Paper delivered at Peace History Society Conference, Winthrop University, Rock Hill, South Carolina, October 30, 2009.

Lacy, W. S. *An Answer to the Charges Made by the President, His Associates and the Board of Southwestern against the Eleven Ministers of Memphis and W. S. Lacy*. Memphis: n.p., 1931.

Lacy, W. S. *Southwestern at the Cross-Roads: Some of the Evidence Supporting the Petition of the Eleven Presbyterian Ministers of Memphis*. Memphis: n.p., 1931.

Laue, James. "Sociology, Sin and Snails." *The Student Voice* 1:2 (August 1960): 3–4.

Lawson, James M., Jr. "From a Lunch-Counter Stool." In *Negro Protest Thought in the Twentieth Century*, ed. Francis L. Broderick and August Meier, pp. 274–281. Indianapolis: Bobbs-Merrill, 1965.

LeFever, Harry G. *Undaunted by the Fight: Spelman College and the Civil Rights Movement, 1957–1967*. Macon: Mercer University Press, 2005.

Leith, John H. "The Bible and Race." *Presbyterian Outlook* (July 27, 1964): 6.

Letter from A. P. Kelso to Charles E. Diehl, May 11, 1931. College Archives, Barret Library, Rhodes College.

Letter from A. P. Moore to Rev. David Park, May 12, 1932. College Archives, Barret Library, Rhodes College.

Letter from Charles Blake Elliott to Friends and Fellow Members of Independent Presbyterian Church, May 5, 2007.

Letter from Charles C. Gillespie to Felix Gear, December 19, 1964. Felix Gear Papers, Presbyterian Heritage Center, Montreat, North Carolina.

Letter from Don M. Wardlaw to Felix Gear, December 3, 1964. Felix Gear Papers, Presbyterian Heritage Center, Montreat, North Carolina.

Letter from Felix Gear to John Randolph Taylor, May 14, 1964. Felix Gear Papers, Presbyterian Heritage Center, Montreat, North Carolina.

Letter from Granville Sherman to Felix Gear, January 19, 1965. Felix Gear Papers, Presbyterian Heritage Center, Montreat, North Carolina.

Letter from H. E. Russell, C. Phil Esty, James Hazelwood, and Edward J. Knox to "Friends in Christ." January 21, 1965. Box 66747, Mississippi Valley Collection, University of Memphis.

Letter from Henry Edward Russell to Dr. Peyton N. Rhodes, November 13, 1962. College Archives, Barret Library, Rhodes College.

Letter from J. P. Robertson "To the Ministers of the Four Synods." April 6, 1931. College Archives, Barret Library, Rhodes College.

Letter from Joe Purdy to Nicholas H. Karris. Box 10386, Mississippi Valley Collection, University of Memphis.

Letter from Malcolm P. Calhoun to Hayden J. Kaden, April 30, 1964. In the possession of Hayden Kaden.

Letter from Mrs. C. Rodney Sunday to Willis E. Ayers, Jr., May 6, 1964. In the possession of Hayden Kaden.

Letter from Mrs. Jane C. Nall to Rev. W. Walter Johnson, June 26, 1964. In the possession of Hayden Kaden.

Letter from Peyton N. Rhodes to Dr. Henry E. Russell, November 2, 1962. College Archives, Barret Library, Rhodes College.

Letter from Rev. C. Rodney Sunday to Mr. Robert J. Hussey, April 9, 1964. In the possession of Hayden Kaden.

Letter from Robert J. Hussey to Dr. C. Rodney, Sunday, April 13, 1964. In the possession of Hayden Kaden.

Letter from Robert J. Hussey to Mr. Hayden J. Kaden, Sr., April 7, 1964. In the possession of Hayden Kaden.

Letter from Robert J. Hussey to Robert M. Hasselle, June 30, 1964. In the possession of Henry Hasselle.

Letter from Robert M. Hasselle, Sr. to Dr. Granville Sherman, June 3, 1964. In the possession of Henry Hasselle.

Letter from Westminster Fellowship Council to the General Assembly in care of Stated Clerk James Millard, August 18, 1964. In the possession of Hayden Kaden.

Letter from Willis E. Ayers, Jr. to Mrs. C. Rodney Sunday, May 2, 1964. In the possession of Hayden Kaden.

Letter of Robert J. Hussey to Robert M. Hasselle, Jr., July 6, 1964. In the possession of Henry Hasselle.

Lewis, George. *Massive Resistance: The White Response to the Civil Rights Movement.* New York: Hodder Education, 2006.

Lollar, Michael. "Iconic 'I Am A Man' Poster on Auction." *Memphis Commercial Appeal* (February 22, 2010). http://www.commercialappeal.com/news/2010/feb/22/iconic-poster-on-auction/.

Los Angeles Sentinel (October 21, 1965): A1.

Lovett, Bobby L. *The Civil Rights Movement in Tennessee: A Narrative History* Knoxville: University of Tennessee Press, 2005.

Maclin, Philip. "Congregation Tries to Dissuade Adams." *Memphis Press-Scimitar* (October 2, 1978): 12.

Magness, Perre. "Second Presbyterian Celebrates 150 Years." *Memphis Commercial Appeal* (November 3, 1994): E2.

Marsh, Charles. *God's Long Summer: Stories of Faith and Civil Rights.* Princeton: Princeton University Press, 1997.

Martin, Richard B. "The Guide Post: 'White Only' Worship Place: Church or Club." *Norfolk Journal and Guide* (September 10, 1960): A11A

Maxine A. Smith—NAACP Collection. Memphis Room, Memphis Public Library and Information Center.

McKinney, Charles W. Jr. *Greater Freedom: The Evolution of the Civil Rights Movement in Wilson, North Carolina.* Lanham, MD: University Press of America, 2010.

Michel, Gregg L. *Struggle for a Better South: The Southern Student Organizing Committee, 1964–69.* New York: Palgrave Macmillan, 2004.

Minutes of Congregational Meeting, Second Presbyterian Church, June 29, 1930. Archives of Second Presbyterian Church, Memphis, Tennessee.

Minutes of Memphis Presbytery, Stated Meeting, January 26, 1965. Presbyterian Heritage Center, Montreat, North Carolina.

Minutes of Memphis Presbytery, Stated Meeting, July 21, 1964. Presbyterian Heritage Center, Montreat, North Carolina.

Minutes of the Eighty-Ninth General Assembly of the Presbyterian Church in the United States. Atlanta: Office of the General Assembly, 1949.

Minutes of the Ninety-Fourth General Assembly of the Presbyterian Church in the United States. Atlanta: Office of the General Assembly, 1954.

Minutes of the One-Hundred-Fourth General Assembly of the Presbyterian Church in the United States. Atlanta: Office of the General Assembly, 1964.

Minutes of the One-Hundred-Sixth General Assembly of the Presbyterian Church in the United States. Richmond: Office of the General Assembly, 1966.

Minutes of the One-Hundred-Tenth General Assembly of the Presbyterian Church in the United States. Atlanta: Office of the General Assembly, 1970.

Minutes of the One-Hundred-Third General Assembly of the Presbyterian Church in the United States. Atlanta: Office of the General Assembly, 1963.

Minutes of the Session of Second Presbyterian Church, Memphis, Tennessee. Archives of Second Presbyterian Church, Memphis, Tennessee.

Minutes of the Synod of Tennessee of the Presbyterian Church in the United States, One Hundred Forty-Ninth Annual Session, June 15–17, 1964. Presbyterian Heritage Center, Montreat, North Carolina.

Moody, Anne. *Coming of Age in Mississippi.* New York: Dial Press, 1968.

Moore, Linda A. "Prospective Buyer Makes Offer for Clayborn Temple." *Memphis Commercial Appeal* (July 22, 2011). http://www.commercialappeal.com/news/2011/jul/22/prospective-buyer-makes-church-offer/.

Moore, Mitchell. "The Jesus Mission: Loving Your Neighbor" (February 13, 2011). http://www.2pc.org/resources/audio-library/the-jesus-mission-loving-your-neigbor/.

Moss, Rev. Zeb V. and Mrs. "Open Letter to First Baptist Church Albany, Ga." (October 17, 1962). In the possession of Brooks Ramsey.

Mounger, Dwyn M. "Racial Attitudes in the Presbyterian Church in the United States, 1944–1954." *Journal of Presbyterian History* 48 (winter 1970): 38–68.

Murchison, D. Cameron. "Easter Vigil: Mark 16:1–8." In *Feasting on the Word: Preaching the Revised Common Lectionary, Year B, Volume 2,* eds. David Bartlett and Barbara Brown Taylor. Louisville: Westminster/John Knox, 2008.

Murray, Peter C. *Methodists and the Crucible of Race, 1930–1975.* Columbia: University of Missouri Press, 2004.

Muse, Benjamin. *Memphis.* Atlanta: Southern Regional Council, 1964.

Newman, Mark. *Getting Right with God: Southern Baptists and Desegregation, 1945–1995.* Tuscaloosa: University of Alabama Press, 2001.

Newsletter of the Southern Student Organizing Committee (May 1965): 1. http://mdah.state.ms.us/arrec/digital_archives/sovcom/imagelisting.php.

Norrell, Robert J. *Reaping the Whirlwind: The Civil Rights Movement in Tuskegee.* New York: Alfred A. Knopf, 1985.

Owen, Angela G. "Kneel-Ins." *Spelman Spotlight* (December 16, 1960). http://www.gpb.org/georgiastories/docs/the_beat_of_civil_rights-18.

Pappas, Thomas N. "New Church Organized on 'Compatible' Basis." *Memphis Press-Scimitar* (March 15, 1965): 18.

Pappas, Thomas N. "Presbytery Stand on Race Expected." *Memphis Press-Scimitar* (January 25, 1965): 1.

Pappas, Thomas M. "Second Presbyterian Prayer: 'Guide Us in Race Issue." *Memphis Press Scimitar* (May 4, 1964): 13.

Pappas, Thomas N. "Second Presbyterian Vote Keeps Segregation Policy." *Memphis Press-Scimitar* (February 10, 1965): 17.

Pappas, Thomas N. "Split Is Talked at 2nd Church." *Memphis Press-Scimitar* (March 8, 1965): 1.

Paul Boone, "Northern View on 'Barring'." *Memphis Commercial Appeal* (May 10, 1964): section 5, 3.

Perkins, Pamela. "Churches Proceed with Stabilization." *Memphis Commercial Appeal* (March 4, 2004): B2.

Perkins, Pamela. "Clayborn Temple Has to be Braced: $150,000—Renovators Cite 'Immediate Risk of Collapse.'" *Memphis Commercial Appeal* (February 15, 2003): B1.

Perkins, Pamela. "Foes Will Press Fight on City's Funds for Church Renovations." *Memphis Commercial Appeal* (November 20, 2003): B6.

Perkins, Ray, Jr., ed. *Yours Faithfully, Bertrand Russell: Letters to the Editor 1904–1969.* Chicago: Open Court Publishers, 2001.

Pike, James A. "Bishop Calls Church Bars a 'Stronghold of Evil.'" *Baltimore Afro-American* (October 7, 1961): 16.

Pittman, Kay. "Surprise March by Students Greets Clements, Walters." *Memphis Press-Scimitar* (January 18, 1964): 1, 2.

Pritchett, Carl. "A Pastoral Letter, Sunday, May 3, 1964." In the possession of Bethesda Presbyterian Church.

Pritchett, Carl. "To the Ushers and Other Representatives of the Second Presbyterian Church of Memphis, Tenn." (May 3, 1964). In the possession of Charles Murphy.

Pritchett, Carl R. "No Moment of Greatness" (April 29, 1964). In the possession of Bethesda Presbyterian Church.

Pritchett, Carl R. "The March on Washington." In *The Unsilent South: Prophetic Preaching in Racial Crisis,* ed. Donald W. Shriver, 99–108. Atlanta: John Knox Press, 1965.

Pritchett, Carl R. "What Happened at Memphis, May 10, 1964." In the possession of Bethesda Presbyterian Church.

Reimers, David M. *White Protestantism and the Negro.* New York: Oxford University Press, 1965.

Ringold, Bert, and Horace Hull. "Socialistic Fate?" *The Sou'wester* (October 12, 1962): 2.

Robbins, Jerry. "Order Signed by Lincoln Donated to Southwestern." *Memphis Press-Scimitar* (February 4, 1970): 37.

Robertson, J. P. *Needed Changes in Southwestern College: An Address to the Ministers, Elders and Others of the Synods of Alabama, Louisiana, Mississippi and Tennessee* (n.p., 1931).

Rose, Ben Lacy. *Racial Segregation in the Church.* Richmond: Outlook Publishers, 1957.

Rose, Ben Lacy. "When Negroes Are Barred from Worship, What Can Be Done about It?" *Presbyterian Survey* (July 1964): 18.

Rose, Ben Lacy. "Should Deacons Vote to Seat Worshippers?" *Presbyterian Survey* (January 1964): 28.

Rosenbush, Mervin. "Downtown's Second Presbyterian Church Is Proud of Its Social Service Program." *Memphis Press-Scimitar* (April 5, 1941): 3.

Rushing, Wanda. *Memphis and the Paradox of Place: Globalization and the American South.* Chapel Hill: University of North Carolina Press, 2009.

Savage, Barbara Dianne. *Your Spirits Walk Beside Us: The Politics of Black Religion.* Cambridge: Harvard University Press, 2008.

Scheffler, Melissa. "Clayborn Temple in Desperate Shape." *MyFox Memphis* (July 27, 2009). http://www.myfoxmemphis.com/dpp/news/tennessee/072909_Civil_Rights_History_Forgotten_at_Clayborn_Temple, accessed August, 2010.

Scheffler, Melissa. "Millions of Dollars and Inspiration Needed for Clayborn Temple." *MyFox Memphis* (November 12, 2009). http://www.myfoxmemphis.com/dpp/news/local/111209_million s+of+dollars+and+inspiration+needed+for+clayborn+temple, accessed August, 2010. http://www.loopnet.com/Listing/16980549/280-Hernando-Street-Memphis-TN/.

Scherr, Sonia. "Church Denomination Roots out Racism." *Southern Poverty Law Center Intelligence Report* (summer 2010). http://www.splcenter.org/get-informed/intelligence-report/browse-all-issues/2010/summer/rooting-out-racism.

Second Presbyterian Church Messenger (April 12, 1968).

Second Presbyterian Church Messenger (June 7, 1964).

Shattuck, Gardiner H. Jr. *Episcopalians and Race: Civil War to Civil Rights.* Lexington: University Press of Kentucky, 2000.

Shepard, Scott. "Restoration of Historic Clayborn Temple May Soon Be Under Way." *Memphis Business Journal* (April 16, 2006). http://www.bizjournals.com/memphis/stories/2006/04/17/tidbits1.html.

Shriver, Donald W. ed., *The Unsilent South: Prophetic Preaching in Racial Crisis.* Atlanta: John Knox Press, 1965.

Simkins, Francis Butler, and Charles Pierce Roland. *A History of the South*, 4th ed. New York: Knopf, 1972.

Siracusa, Anthony C. "Understanding Militant Non-violence within Memphis' Modern Civil Rights Movement: The Leadership and Witness of the Rev. James M Lawson, Jr." Unpublished paper written for 2007 Rhodes Institute for Regional Studies.

Slade, Peter. *Open Friendship in a Closed Society: Mission Mississippi and a Theology of Friendship.* New York: Oxford University Press, 2009.

Smith, Frank Joseph. *The History of the Presbyterian Church in America.* Silver Anniversary Edition. Lawrenceville, GA: Presbyterian Scholars Press, 1999.

Smith, Morton H. *How is the Gold Become Dim: the Decline of the Presbyterian Church, U.S., As Reflected in Its Assembly Actions.* Jackson, MS: Committee for a Continuing Presbyterian Church, Faithful to the Scriptures and the Reformed Faith, 1973.

Sokol, Jason. *There Goes My Everything: White Southerners in the Age of Civil Rights, 1945–75.* New York: Knopf, 2006.

Southard, Samuel. "Are Southern Churches Silent?" *The Christian Century* (November 20, 1963): 1429–1432.

Southard, Samuel. "Segregation and Southern Churches." *Journal of Religion and Health* 1:3 (April 1962): 197–221.

Southwestern Catalog (1946–47).

Southwestern Presbyterian University Catalog (1878–79).

Stafford, Tim. "Memphis's Other Graceland." *Christianity Today* (January 13, 2009). http://www.ctlibrary.com/ct/2009/january/35.42.html.

Strong, Jack. "Sit-In Pastor Gets 18 Months." *Atlanta Constitution* (August 29, 1963): 1.

Taylor, Kenneth. "The Spirituality of the Church: Segregation, *The Presbyterian Journal*, and the Origins of the Presbyterian Church in America." *Reformed Perspectives Magazine* 9:34 (August 19–August 25, 2007). http://thirdmill.org/the-spirituality-of-the-church).

The Book of Church Order of the Presbyterian Church in the United States. Atlanta: Stated Clerk of the General Assembly of the Presbyterian Church in the United States, 1965.

The Official Report of the Hearing of the Charges Preferred By Eleven Presbyterian Ministers Against President Charles E. Diehl Held On Tuesday, February 3rd, 1931 by the Board of Directors of Southwestern. Memphis: Committee on Publication of Southwestern at Memphis, 1931.

The Staff and Volunteers of Second Presbyterian Church, Memphis, Tennessee. "A Blueprint for Adopting a School." http://www.2pc.org/media/blueprint-for-adopting-schools.pdf.

Thompson, Ernest Trice. *Presbyterians in the South*, 3 vols. Richmond: John Knox Press, 1963–1973.

Thompson, Ernest Trice. *The Spirituality of the Church: A Distinctive Doctrine of the Presbyterian Church in the United States.* Richmond: John Knox Press, 1961.

Von Dreele, W. H. "New England Sea Chanty." *National Review* (September 10, 1960): 177.

Waddel, John N. *Memorials of Academic Life: Being An Historical Sketch of the Waddel Family, Identified Through Three Generations with the History of the Higher Education in the South and Southwest.* Richmond: Presbyterian Committee of Publication, 1891.

Warren, Dan R. *If It Takes All Summer: Martin Luther King, the KKK, and States' Rights in St. Augustine, 1964.* Tuscaloosa: University of Alabama Press, 2008.

Watson v. City of Memphis, 373 U.S. 526 [1963]. http://supreme.justia.com/us/373/526/case.html.

Wellford, Walker L. *Facts about the Southwestern Controversy.* Memphis: n.p., 1931.

White, Norman. "Non-Religious Student Speaks." *Sou'wester* (November 1, 1963): 3.

Willson, Sandy. "Let Go of Stuff." *Amen Bible Study* (January 27, 2011). http://www.2pc.org/resources/audio-library/let-go-of-stuff/.

Wingfield, Marie Gregson. "The Memphis Interracial Commission." *West Tennessee Historical Society Papers* 21 (1967): 93–107.

Wolf, Miroslav. *Exclusion and Embrace: A Theological Exploration of Identity, Otherness, and Reconciliation*. Nashville: Abingdon Press, 1996.

Worthy, William. "Aston Jones Case May Stir Scandal." *Washington Afro-American* (December 10, 1963): 15.

Zinn, Howard. *Albany: A Study in National Responsibility*. Atlanta: Southern Regional Council, 1962.

Zinn, Howard. "Finishing School for Pickets." *The Nation* (August 6, 1960). http://www.loa.org/images/pdf/Zinn_Finishing_School.pdf.

Zinn, Howard. *The Southern Mystique*. Cambridge, MA: South End Press, 2002.

INDEX